EXPERT SYSTEMS IN LIBRARIES

edited by

Rao Aluri

Burr-Brown Corporation Library

and

Donald E. Riggs

Arizona State University

ABLEX PUBLISHING CORPORATION
NORWOOD, NEW JERSEY

Printed in the United States of America

Library of Congress Cataloging-in-Publication Data

Expert systems in libraries / edited by Rao Aluri and Donald E. Riggs.
p. cm.
Includes bibliographical references.
ISBN 0-89391-589-0
1. Expert systems (Computer science)—Library applications.
2. Libraries—Automation. I. Aluri, Rao. II. Riggs, Donald E.
Z678.93.E93E94 1990
025'.00285416—dc20 90-263
CIP

Ablex Publishing Corporation
355 Chestnut Street
Norwood, New Jersey 07648

CONTENTS

PREFACE

A new phenomenon known as "expert systems" is rapidly becoming part of the librarian's vocabulary. Expert systems offer a level of technology sophistication that has never been experienced in the library world. For the very first time, we now have machines that can "talk" intelligently with humans. Expert systems run on personal computers and are commonly carried on skeletal systems known as "shells." A shell is a software package designed for the creation of specific expert systems.

An expert system is a subset of artificial intelligence which is a subfield of computer science concerned with designing systems that perform human-like, intelligent functions. In order to meet the requirements of a genuine expert system, the intelligent capabilities of humans must be rivaled; in essence, the human's thinking/reasoning processes are cloned. For example, the expert system must: ask intelligent questions, solve problems, explain reasoning, and justify conclusions. An expert system is basically an intelligent computer program that uses knowledge and inference procedures to solve problems that are difficult enough to require significant human expertise for their solutions.

Expert systems are being used in a variety of fields. More than $25 million per year is being spent by U.S. industries on expert systems research. The application of expert systems in libraries has only occurred within the past few years. One of the primary drawbacks to using expert systems in libraries is that of defining a workable domain. Using an expert system to teach and monitor the implementation of the second edition of the Anglo-American Cataloging Rules is doable. However, believing an expert system can perform all duties of a reference librarian is foolish. The interaction between the reference librarian and the user is a complex endeavor encompassing many unanticipated challenges and other human anomalies. Nevertheless, an expert system can improve the effectiveness of a reference librarian in many ways. Other library areas that can reap benefits from expert systems include: bibliographic instruction, indexing, and management. We will witness other uses of expert systems in libraries in the near future.

This volume provides a background on expert systems, gives examples of their applications in libraries, and outlines future library implications. The editors genuinely thank all those who contributed to this work.

Rao Aluri
Technical Librarian
Burr-Brown Corporation
Tucson, AZ

Donald E. Riggs
Dean of University Libraries
Arizona State University, Tempe

INTRODUCTION

Twenty-five persons contributed to *Expert Systems in Libraries*. The chapters represent various library areas and are presented in a systematic manner (e.g., beginning with an overview of expert systems and ending with a futuristic viewpoint).

Richard G. Vedder, in the first chapter, discusses the broad aspects of expert systems. He describes what is involved with building expert systems and their essential components.

In Chapter 2, Kenneth R. Harmon defines and describes the software necessary for expert systems. Examples of software are presented.

Samuel T. Waters, associate director of the National Agricultural Library, explains the role of expert systems and artificial intelligence in Chapter 3. Special emphasis is given to the application of expert systems in reference at the National Agricultural Library.

POINTER, a microcomputer program that simulates a government documents librarian, is detailed by Karen F. Smith in Chapter 4. The rationale and the limitations of this system are described.

Refsearch is a system that can simultaneously characterize a question and the source(s) which may give the desired answer(s). Much research has been done on the refinement of this system by Howard D. White and Diana Woodward which is discussed in Chapter 5.

James R. Parrott discusses the implementation of reference models in expert systems in Chapter 6. He also explains and provides an example of how an expert system can assist online reference in Chapter 9.

Intelligent computer-assisted instruction in an expert systems environment is discussed by Connie V. Dowell and Phillip Crews in Chapter 7. They trace the history of computer-assisted instruction and give their viewpoints on the present and future "intelligent" components of CAI.

Donald Nute explains how an expert system can assist with identifying available scholarships in Chapter 8. A logical explanation is given for choosing PROLOG as the programming language for SCHOLAR.

The "whys" and "hows" of using components of expert systems in automating descriptive cataloging is provided in Chapter 10 by Diane Vizine-Goetz, Stuart Weibel, and William Oskins. Their methodology will be helpful to others interested in developing an automated descriptive cataloging system.

Ann M. Sandberg-Fox provides an overview of what is required in using the intellectual aspects of expert systems in the selection of the main entry. Catalogers will find Chapter 11 useful.

Chapter 12 explains the role of expert systems in the selection of search keys. Online searchers will better understand the significance of search keys after reading Raya Fidel's piece.

Online retrieval's use of search intermediaries is well defined by Mark Chignell, Lee Jaffe, Philip J. Smith, Deborah Krawczk, and Stephen J. Shute. Knowledge-based search intermediaries is the central theme of Chapter 13.

Susanne M. Humphrey provides a thorough description of the Medical Indexing Expert System (MedIndEx) in Chapter 14. Background information and examples of this National Library of Medicine expert system are delineated.

Chapter 15 contains a lengthy discussion on the applications of knowledge-based systems to libraries. Irene L. Travis underscores the urgency of using expert systems' techniques in classification.

E. Dale Cluff focuses on the management and budgetary aspects of expert systems in Chapter 16. Planning for expert systems and their impact library personnel are crucial concerns that must be addressed by library administrators.

Co-editor Donald E. Riggs provides his futuristic views on library experts systems in Chapter 17.

Co-editor Rao Aluri prepared an extensive bibliography which will be useful for those persons wanting to learn more about expert systems.

1

An Overview of Expert Systems

Richard G. Vedder
Business Computing Information Systems Department
University of North Texas

INTRODUCTION

This chapter presents a brief overview to the subject of expert systems. "Brief" needs emphasizing as there are entire books devoted to each of the major topics covered. The author urges the reader to explore the list of references at the end of this chapter to learn more. Please note, by the way, that there is considerable debate about "proper" definitions for artificial intelligence, expert systems, and other related terms.

Artificial intelligence (AI) is an interdisciplinary branch of computer science. The word "interdisciplinary" is most appropriate, as many different fields of study contribute to AI. Cognitive psychology, for instance, provides AI with models for learning and memory retention. Philosophy shares methodologies for logical reasoning. Linguistics contributes frameworks for machine understanding of oral and written communication. Electrical engineering provides mechanisms for vision, touch, and the other human senses. At the same time, AI systems provide opportunities for testing the theories of psychologists, philosophers, linguists, and others.

Artificial intelligence is concerned with developing computer systems which reason and behave in ways a neutral observer would consider "human." Alan Turing (1950), one of the founders of computer science and AI, suggested that a computer would be truly intelligent if in a blind test it could persuade a human (located in another room) at least half the time that it also was human. On the other hand, Hubert Dreyfus (1972) has vigorously argued the absolute impossibility of any computer system ever behaving in a truly human fashion. He believes that the emotional, spiritual, and creative essence of humanity can never develop in a computer, and that without these qualities no entity can be "human." Needless to say, artificial intelligence is a controversial topic.

Just as AI is a subdivision of computer science, so too the quest for developing humanlike qualities in computers has led to many branches within AI (Figure 1.1). Some of these branches are very research-oriented; for instance game-playing systems try to play games like chess or poker with the skill of a master

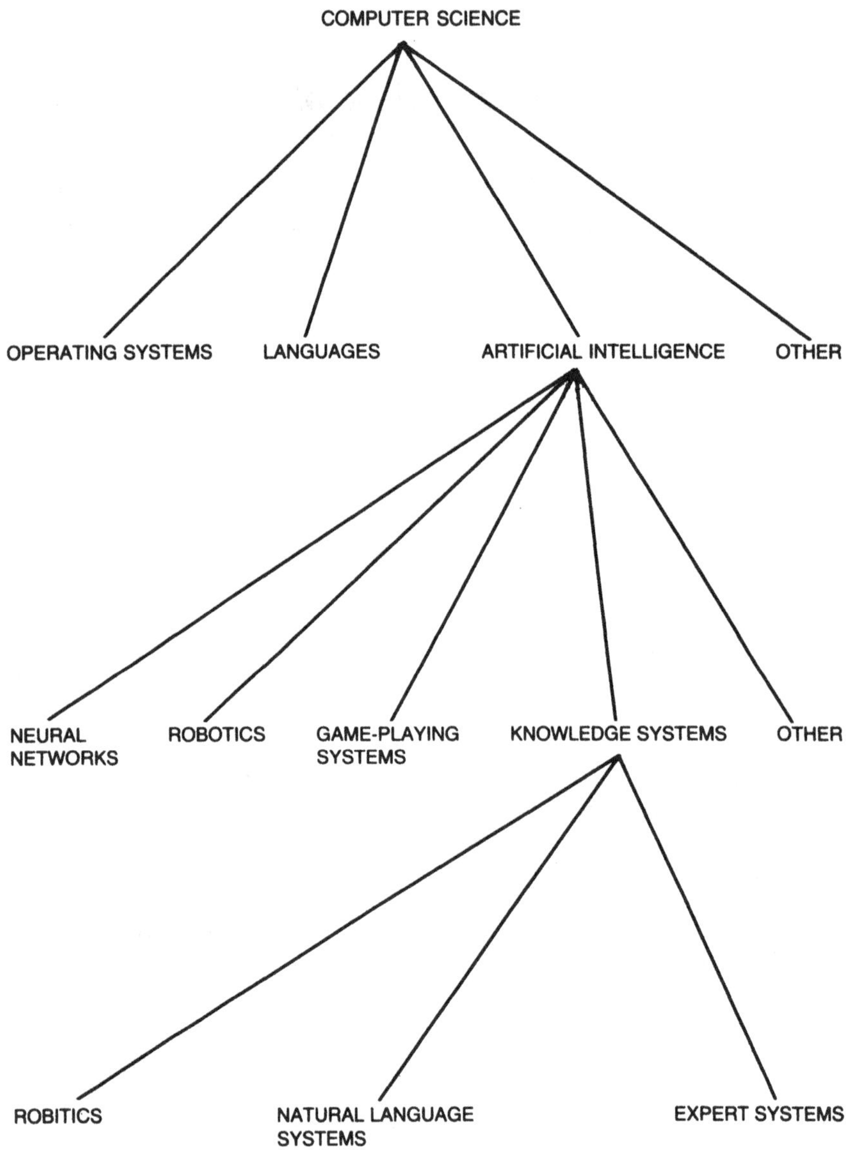

Figure 1.1 A Conceptual Framework for Artificial Intelligence

expert. Game-playing systems are one way AI researchers can study how humans select an appropriate solution for a problem having a myriad of possible answers.

KNOWLEDGE SYSTEMS

Other branches of AI have moved beyond pure research. They seek to apply what is known of AI science; they produce marketable AI technologies. One such branch is robotics, which seeks to give computers human mobility and sensory capabilities. Another is knowledge, or knowledge-based, systems. These systems use stored knowledge and inference reasoning (deriving new facts from known facts) to solve problems in a specific area, called a domain.

Data are items or elements which describe persons, places, ideas, events, or other things. By themselves data are meaningless; they are just fragments which might eventually prove meaningful. When humans give data relationships which explain their importance or significance, data become meaningful; they become information. Knowledge is an integrated collection of information which, when used, produces a competent level of performance.

An example will help clarify this hierarchy of knowledge. A student hearing a lecture receives a stream of constant audiovisual data from the speaker. The student amalgamates pieces of data until they have meaning, and usually stores the resulting information in a notebook. By the end of the term the student will have mentally assembled and integrated enough information to become knowledgeable in the subject. Examinations test for this knowledgeability or competency.

Knowledge systems are based on the idea that humans commonly use many types of knowledge when solving problems. Two of the most important forms of knowledge are factual knowledge and heuristic knowledge. Factual knowledge is the type of learning a person usually gains from reading books and attending school. It is material commonly agreed with and shared; it is public knowledge. Factual knowledge provides a set of general theories. It can suggest highly structured solution processes, called algorithms, for solving problems in a finite number of steps.

Heuristic knowledge is the type of learning a person gains from experience. Heuristics are rules of thumb or situation-specific theories. Since each person's experiences are unique, heuristic knowledge is personal and private. People use heuristic knowledge every day to solve problems. On the other hand, the value of heuristic knowledge is tempered by the fact that it deals with probabilities. That is, the solutions it offers do not always work.

Consider the following heuristic suggested by a police officer (Parker, 1987):

> Suspects fleeing the scene of a crime in a car will make right turns more often than left—a normal reaction, as they do not want to waste valuable time waiting for cross-traffic to clear. If you didn't see which way they went, try turning right.

This is a valuable heuristic, but a place where this rule of thumb would not work is in England, where people normally drive on the left side of the street. One-way streets are another exception. This illustrates both the power and the limitation of heuristics. Nevertheless, it is the capacity for using heuristic knowledge which distinguishes artificial intelligence systems, and especially knowledge systems, from regular computer programs.

Knowledge systems include robotics (those aspects requiring knowledge to interpret visual evidence), natural language systems (which use syntactical, grammatical, and linguistic knowledge to interpret written or spoken human language), and expert systems.

EXPERT SYSTEMS

Expert systems are computer programs which inform, make recommendations, or solve problems in a manner and at a level of performance comparable to that displayed by a human expert in the field. The name leaves something to be desired, for to date most expert system applications are decidedly not expert. The analogy of the medieval European guild system is instructive here. A man became an acknowledged expert in his craft (e.g., shoemaking) only after spending many years learning first as an apprentice and then as a journeyman. Likewise, one should think of expert systems in the same vein: Most display only an apprentice level of ability, while very few are truly expert. Consequently, expert systems store, use, and display expertise to varying degrees.

Expertise is aggregated knowledge. It is a collection of skills and abilities which allows some humans to analyze and solve problems far more efficiently than others. Experts are competent because of their expertise.

Expertise includes many traits relevant for expert systems. For instance, experts possess extensive factual and heuristic knowledge about their specialty. During the learning process, an expert can efficiently reorganize or restructure this body of knowledge as needed. Another trait of expertise is the use of efficient problem-solving skills. It is probably this aspect of an expert's behavior that most impresses other people.

Expertise involves knowing when to break the rules. The famous Macedonian ruler and general Alexander the Great confronted the problem of the Gordion Knot. It was said that whoever loosened the Knot would become ruler of all Asia (i.e., the Persian Empire). Many had tried to untie it with no success. Alexander's solution was to cut the Knot in two with his sword. He knew when to break the rules.

One of the most important facets of expertise is the ability to justify decisions and explain results. It is this quality of an expert which helps instill confidence, trust, and acceptance of that person's judgments. Without this trait people will ignore even the best expert in the world.

There are other qualities which distinguish expert systems from traditional data processing systems. Expert systems favor heuristic, not algorithmic, solutions to problems. Most computer systems use algorithms to solve highly structured problems, such as generating a monthly payroll. However, many real-world problems have unique or uncertain aspects for which traditional algorithmic solutions are impractical or unworkable. Expert systems employing heuristics can often suggest better solutions.

Another important contrast is that expert systems use inference reasoning. Traditional computer systems solve problems by employing algorithmic solutions in a repetitive fashion. Some expert systems use still other forms of logic, such as causal reasoning.

EXPERT SYSTEM ARCHITECTURE

In designing expert systems, AI researchers have tried to imitate the workings of the human mind as well as the behavior of human experts. Consequently most expert system applications incorporate a number of components (Table 1.1). Foremost among these is the knowledge base, analogous to long-term memory in humans. The knowledge base stores facts, rules of thumb (i.e., heuristics), and opinions or beliefs using one or more schemes for representing this knowledge.

Perhaps the simplest (and certainly the most common) knowledge representation scheme is IF-THEN rules. This structure has at least two parts, but it may have more. The IF part contains a set of one or more conditions which must be met before the rule can be used. The THEN part is a set of one or more actions or consequences which occur when a rule does fire. A sample rule is:

IF
  The car will not start, and
  The fuel gauge works, and
  The fuel gauge reads "Empty"
THEN
  The car is out of fuel.

If an expert system's knowledge base uses rules, it may be called a rule-based expert system or, more simply, a rule-based system.

Rules are excellent for representing some types of knowledge, like procedural ("how to do it") knowledge. However, other types (e.g., declarative or temporal knowledge) require different representation structures, such as frames.

Just as the knowledge base is analogous to long-term memory in humans, so too the expert system's working memory is analogous to human short-term memory. This is the place where the computer stores a description of the problem and tracks its solution effort. It is also the place where the expert system keeps a

Table 1.1 Components of an Expert System

- Knowledge Base
- Working Memory
- Inference Engine
- Explanation Facility
- Appropriate User Interface
- Knowledge Acquisition Subsystem

record of data gained from external sources like measuring instruments or questions posed to the user.

The inference engine is a program which manipulates or processes the contents of the knowledge base and of working memory to solve problems. The inference engine tries to pattern-match the set of known facts with what is needed to fire as many rules as possible. If no rules fire, the expert system seeks more data from external sources.

Various control methods guide the reasoning process. Frequently an expert system will start with a possible solution (goal) and try to associate it with what is known about the problem. This method is called backward chaining or goal-driven reasoning. Alternatively, the expert system begins without any goal in mind and lets the data point the way. This is called forward chaining or data-driven reasoning. Sometimes both methods are used on the same problem. Humans do this when playing guessing games (or solving murder mysteries). One begins with little to go on and thus asks very general questions to elicit more facts (data-driven). When suspicions at last form, the questioning becomes much more pointed to confirm or refute the hypothetical solution (goal-driven). Sometimes a problem domain is so complex that a group of expert systems must attack different parts of the task. This is called blackboarding, after the name given to the common workspace shared by all expert systems of this type.

Because very little in this world is absolutely true or false all the time, inference engines deal with the problem of uncertainty. AI scientists have offered several ways of meeting this challenge, none of which are entirely satisfactory. One common technique is to attach a numerical measure of belief, called a certainty factor (CF), to each rule. The CFs of all fired rules are combined using mathematical techniques to produce an overall CF attached to the expert system's conclusion. This sounds fine until one realizes that the subjective judgment of a human expert derived each rule's CF in the first place. And human experts love to differ with each other, as any sampling of economists or political commentators will frequently show.

Expert systems require other components to maximize their effectiveness. Just as human experts must defend their judgments to inspire confidence, expert systems need an explanation facility to display and justify their reasoning. Any computer system used by humans must have a user interface appropriate to the task at hand and the skill level of the user group. Finally, there must be a way for adding new knowledge to the knowledge base. Some day this knowledge acquisition subsystem will be totally automated and the expert system will truly "learn." Currently humans usually must feed new knowledge into expert systems (e.g., by adding new rules). Moreover, humans must integrate the new knowledge with the old, and restructure the knowledge base as needed.

TOOLS FOR BUILDING EXPERT SYSTEMS

Just as carpenters use tools to build houses, so also do engineers use tools to build software applications. Instead of hammers and saws, they use computer hardware (e.g., personal computers, printers, plug-in boards). Instead of nails and screws, they use programming languages and software packages (e.g., BASIC, Lotus' 1-2-3).

Hardware tools for expert systems range in complexity (and cost) from personal computers to mainframes to specialized AI machines for applications written in LISP or PROLOG. With respect to IBM-type personal computers (the only hardware tool mentioned here), these machines should have at least 512K of main memory and two 360K floppy drives. Because expert system applications consume great quantities of memory, many software tools now require (or at least strongly prefer) a 80286 or 80386 machine with 1M or more of main memory and a hard disk. The type of monitor is unimportant; let the needs of the application make this choice.

There are many classes of software tools for building expert systems. This section examines three of the most common. Note that these tools, like all software development tools, differ in flexibility, power, and ease of use. Generally speaking, the easier a tool is to use the less flexible (and powerful) it is. The developers of these "easier" tools have made a number of design decisions for you. While more convenient, these decisions also act as constraints on what you can do with the tool.

One class is made up of general programming languages, such as C, Pascal, BASIC, and COBOL. A number of people already know how to use these languages, and the resulting applications are easily portable (transportable) from machine to machine. On the other hand, all of these languages are designed for numeric processing, not for the processing of ideas and concepts (symbolic processing) required by AI. This flaw can hurt overall efficiency of the software product as well as increase the difficulty of the actual construction process.

A second class of tool is the symbolic programming languages (e.g., LISP and PROLOG). These tools have the significant advantage of being designed for symbolic processing (as opposed to numeric). On the other hand, they can be somewhat difficult to learn. They may require special hardware to handle the extra demands on computer memory which they can make. Applications built with these languages are not as readily portable as with conventional programming languages (although this constraint is easing). Nevertheless, symbolic programming languages are powerful tools for developing AI applications. They are especially useful for experimental work and for building customized applications.

A third class is expert system shells. In its simplest form, a shell is an expert system without a knowledge base. All one has to do is add a knowledge base customized for the problem at hand. Usually the more expensive the shell, the greater the ability to change any or all of the other components to suit a given need.

Most shells run on personal computers. Shells are relatively easy to learn. They greatly speed prototyping and experimentation because it is so easy to experiment. And shells can generate powerful expert system applications. On the other hand, convenience of use sacrifices flexibility, and this can be an important tradeoff to consider for some applications. Shells are also generally incompatible with one other. If for some reason it becomes necessary to change shells during the development process, this incompatibility will force much reworking.

Obviously it is very important to choose the right tools for any job. Try not to let available hardware force the choice of a software tool. It is far better to let the requirements of the application (such as the type of knowledge representation scheme required) drive the selection process.

BUILDING EXPERT SYSTEMS

The process of planning, building, installing, and maintaining an expert system application is called knowledge engineering. The technologists who engage in this activity are called knowledge engineers. They serve as intermediaries between the AI world and the user community. Although prototype development may proceed rather quickly, most expert system development projects take months or years to complete. Some are never finished; the problem under consideration alters characteristics so rapidly that the knowledge engineers are aiming at an ever-moving target.

At the top-most level, the knowledge engineering process starts with one or more knowledge engineers eliciting fragments of expertise from a volunteer human expert. The engineer uses an expert system building tool to incorporate the knowledge, gathered mainly from interviews, into a prototype application. The relationship between the human expert and the knowledge engineer is a highly iterative one: elicitation, construct and evaluate, more elicitation, more construction, and so on. If all goes well, eventually the expert system application is ready for use. Trained staff are responsible for updates and other maintenance, unless the problem is so dynamic as to require the continuing services of a knowledge engineer.

Moving to a lower level of detail, building an expert system application involves seven development phases (Waterman, 1986; Harmon and King, 1985). Phase one is *identification*. Project management chooses a suitable problem domain (not an easy task), one or more knowledge engineers, and a willing, articulate, available human expert. Phase two is *conceptualization*, the extraction from the expert by the knowledge engineer of fragments of expertise. Phase three is *formalization*. Studying the results of conceptualization, the engineer decides what type of knowledge representation best suits the expertise under consideration. The representation scheme determines the nature of the hardware and software tools the knowledge engineer will use to build the application. Phase four is *implementation*, the actual construction phase. Phase five is *testing*. The purpose of this phase is to examine how well the prototype solves sample problems using the contents of its knowledge base. Depending on the outcome, earlier phases may need repeating.

Many expert system applications move no farther than phase five. Sometimes an expert systems approach is an inappropriate solution for the problem at hand. More often progress is delayed because expert systems technology is still evolving. For those applications which finally pass testing, two more phases await. Phase six is *integration*. As with any computer application, expert systems cannot operate in a vacuum. There must be a measure of integration, of blending with other computer systems online, or with relevant practices current within the user organization. Phase seven is *maintenance*. This phase covers all activities required to keep the expert system application online and productive for the intended user group. At this time, evaluation or review processes might uncover new problems suitable for an expert systems approach, thus starting the development process all over again.

Waterman (1986) and Harmon and King (1985) contain excellent discussions of the many issues associated with building expert system applications. Read their comments before striking out on your own.

SOME DRAWBACKS WITH USING EXPERT SYSTEMS

Expert system applications realize significant benefits. However, current expert systems technology has important limitations. Anyone contemplating construction of an expert system must bear these constraints in mind.

As mentioned earlier, expert systems (as with all computer systems) hate uncertainty and vagueness. The present array of solutions for this problem, such as certainty factors, have flaws. This is an important constraint for some potential applications.

Another limitation is that most expert systems require a narrowly defined problem domain. Unlike that of a human expert, the performance of an expert system does not degrade gracefully—it crashes (i.e., provides no answer, or gives a wrong answer). Humans possess metaknowledge: They have knowledge about what they know. They know what kinds of problems they are qualified to handle and which they must pass on to someone else. Humans realize that there are limits to their expertise. Most expert systems are very stupid in this respect. They only have "shallow" knowledge of their problem domain and they do not know their limits. Moreover, the contents of their knowledge bases depend on what domain problems or situations the human expert could think of. So when presented with an unanticipated or novel problem, most expert systems will fail (crash) miserably.

Most expert systems are terrible learners. This difficulty has two important consequences. First, knowledge engineers must serve as conduits between the minds of human experts and the expert system applications under development. This knowledge acquisition process is the most critical bottleneck in building expert systems. Second, human intervention is necessary to enlarge the knowledge bases and reorganize them when needed. If the chosen problem domain is a dynamic one requiring many changes and updates to the knowledge base over time, the extra staff needed may be an unacceptable continuing cost.

BENEFITS OF USING EXPERT SYSTEMS TECHNOLOGY

Why should one consider an expert systems approach when developing a computer application? Certainly expert systems can help lesser-skilled people solve problems by delivering automated expertise gathered from highly skilled people. However, this technology can offer many more benefits. Some are immediately recognizable, while others are less so. The following discussion samples both types.

As with any well-designed and well-maintained computer system, expert systems can provide their users with constant, uniform, and timely assistance. These benefits are traits which even the most talented of humans cannot always achieve. These abilities improve reliability and confidence in the expert system. They also make it possible for an expert system to supply help in the absence of human experts, such as at the library reference desk at 1 a.m.

A less obvious benefit concerns intangible assets. An intangible asset is something which has real or potential benefit, yet is not physical like a piece of property or office equipment. Although their exact monetary value is difficult to assess, intangible assets can have great benefit. The reputation of an organization is an example.

The expertise, skills, and general experience of each employee is an intangible asset. When an employee leaves the library (e.g., retires) that intangible asset leaves too. This can represent a substantial loss to the library. Consequently each organization struggles with the problem of dealing with these sometimes invaluable losses. Expert systems, containing a portion of one or more person's expertise, can help solve this problem. They can make this form of intangible asset more tangible and enduring. They have the potential for serving organizations as a form of collective memory.

A third benefit concerns the knowledge and expertise stored within an expert system. Being computerized, a knowledge base is easily duplicated. It may be as easy as placing a formatted blank diskette in drive B and entering the DOS command COPY A:*.* B:. In other words, expert systems can distribute—and democratize—knowledge and expertise. The potential impact of this attribute (for good or ill) may someday rival the effects of the printing press. It certainly suggests new possible information resources for the libraries of tomorrow.

A fourth benefit of expert systems directly affects human experts. Most people do not use their work time efficiently or effectively. Among the myriad of reasons for this is the distraction of performing mundane tasks. These activities are especially costly for human experts, who find themselves "wasting" their time and expertise.

A common solution is to shift, or off-load, such responsibilities to others. The medical profession provides a good example. Not all that long ago, if you visited a doctor's office the doctor was your sole examiner. Today nurses or other medical technicians conduct the initial interview and examination of patients. Only afterward does the doctor see you. In other words, to make better use of their time (expertise), human experts often give necessary but less demanding tasks to subordinates.

Finally, a most significant benefit of expert systems is their ability to serve humans as intelligent assistants. Just as the machines of industrial revolution support manual work, expert systems (and other AI-based systems) can support mental work. They can help explore alternatives, track the correctness of a decision-making process, or provide cool thinking in times of organizational crisis. The potential for improving the quality and effectiveness of human endeavors is considerable.

REFERENCES

Dreyfus, H. (1972). *What computers can't do: A critique of artificial reason*. New York: Harper & Row.

Harmon, P., & King, D. (1985). *Expert systems: Artificial intelligence in business*. New York: John Wiley & Sons.

Parker, T. (Ed.). (1987). *Rules of thumb* (Vol. 2). Boston: Houghton-Mifflin.

Turing, A. (1950). Computing machinery and intelligence. *Mind, 59*(236), 433–460.

Waterman, D. A. (1986). *A guide to expert systems*. Reading, MA: Addison-Wesley.

2

Software for Expert Systems

Kenneth R. Harmon
The KRH Group
Loveland, CO

INTRODUCTION

Expert systems offer the professional librarian a new way to use the computers which are becoming increasingly common in library environments. Whether the computers are being used in procedural tasks, planning tasks, or service tasks, expert systems can improve productivity and service, and change the way library staff and patrons think about computers and their use. Expert systems are tools to aid in decision making, communications, database searching, and monitoring large information networks. Eventually, the use of expert systems will be as common as the use of personal computers.

Expert systems combine knowledge and a knowledge control process, called an inference engine, to analyze and solve problems. To fully realize the potential of expert systems for librarianship, it is necessary to understand the characteristics of expert systems, how they are developed and how they are distinguished from conventional computer systems. In this chapter, expert system software is defined and described. First, conventional software programming and expert system software programming are compared. Second, expert system programming languages are described and compared. Third, expert system tools and environments are identified and distinguished according to mainframe or PC[1] environments. Fourth, "near" expert systems are described and their differences from expert systems identified. Finally, some thoughts on the application of expert systems in librarianship are included.

CONVENTIONAL AND EXPERT SYSTEM PROGRAMMING

Expert systems are not a special type of computer system. Rather they are special ways of organizing knowledge and employing knowledge manipulation schemes to allow greater flexibility in handling certain types of knowledge. Conventional

[1] The designation PC is intended to refer to the generic "personal computer" and is not limited to a specific vendor or product.

programs attempt to reduce problem situations to mathematical concepts which can be manipulated according to carefully designed algorithms. The process is linear and is dependent on complete and accurate information and procedures. Expert systems, on the other hand, manipulate logical constructs, sentences, and objects in relational matrices. The information may be incomplete, uncertain, and speculative.

Both conventional and expert system programs require a user/operator to enter information into a database and to activate manipulation of the database to produce an output. Expert systems, however, add components to enhance the process and alter procedures to permit manipulation of the knowledge base which contains nonnumeric data.

Knowledge Base

Expert systems employ a knowledge base consisting of facts and rules. The knowledge base is similar, but not analogous, to the conventional computer program or database. All contain rules of action; however, the knowledge base is dynamic, in that the facts and rules can be made to act upon each other using a reasoning process based on facts and relations among facts to answer queries and form new facts. A program or database can only be revised and queried by direct operator intervention.

Inference Engine

Expert systems substitute an inference engine for the interpreter/compiler of conventional programming. The inference engine is a reasoning mechanism which incorporates a search strategy and which acts upon the knowledge base. The most common reasoning system is the IF-THEN simple logic rule. IF a certain condition exists, THEN a certain conclusion results. The search strategy directs the system to identify the optimum starting point at which to employ the reasoning mechanism.

Reasoning mechanisms. The two most common reasoning mechanisms in use are forward chaining and backward chaining. Forward chaining is the easiest method to understand. If the premise clause of a rule (the IF part) matches the reality of the situation presented, then the conclusion part of the rule (the THEN part) is asserted as a fact in the knowledge base. For example, if the rule states: "*If it is raining, I will need an umbrella*" then, if in fact it is raining, I will add that fact to the knowledge base and the expert system will conclude that I need an umbrella. This new fact (*I need an umbrella*) is added to the knowledge base.

Backward chaining attempts to prove the hypothesis from facts and rules already present in the knowledge base or from information derived from querying the system user. For example, the rules in the knowledge base may include: *If it is raining and I am outside, I will need an umbrella* and *If I need an umbrella and I do not have an umbrella, I will get wet.* If my objective is to establish whether I will get wet, the system will first locate the rule which, if triggered, would result in that conclusion. If *I do not have an umbrella* is already in the knowledge base, the system will seek to establish whether I need an umbrella. To do so, the system must know if I am outside and if it is raining. If it already has one of these facts (*I am outside*), the system will ask me "*Is it raining?*". If I answer yes, the system will conclude that I will get wet. If I answer no, the system will either conclude that I will not get wet or that it has insufficient information to absolutely confirm that I will not get wet.

Search strategies. There are also several search strategies employed in expert systems operations. The most common are depth first, breadth first and a hybrid of the two called best first (Hu, 1987). Since most rule structures are of a hierarchical form, we can visualize the rule structure as a tree with several nodes and branches. We may or may not begin the search at the very highest node, but wherever we begin is called the root node. In depth first searching, the strategy selects a node (*Node 1*) at the level below the root node if the root node is not the desired, or target, node. If *Node 1* is not the target node, the search strategy selects a node (*Node 2*) below *Node 1* which is related to *Node 1*. This process will proceed until a node at the lowest level of the hierarchy, called a termination node, is reached. If the target node has still not been found, the search strategy will back up to the last level at which a decision point was encountered, and select a node (*Node 3*) with the same parent (*Node 1*) as the node previously tested at this level. The search strategy will proceed from this point down through the hierarchy again. This process will continue as the nodes are examined top to bottom across the tree.

Breadth-first searching examines all the nodes at a specific level in the hierarchy before moving to the next level down. The efficiency of using either approach depends, of course, on the location of the target node. At the initiation of the search process, however, the location of the target node is usually unknown. If the location of the target node can be estimated, then a combination of approaches can be employed. For example, if the system I am using performs electronic diagnosis, I may know that certain components related to the one in which I am interested are six levels down in the hierarchy. I can select my root node at level six, and initiate a depth-first approach at that point. Developing a hybrid search strategy is more difficult than either of the other two approaches, but usually it increases the efficiency of the process.

Probability

Sophisticated expert systems may provide a probability factor regarding the "chance" that I will get wet without an umbrella. For example, if I need an umbrella and I do not have an umbrella, I still may *not* get wet. I may have a newspaper which I can hold over my head, or I may be able to run from storefront to storefront under awnings. Therefore, I may want to establish my chances of getting wet without an umbrella as only 90 percent. Using a probability factor, I can do this.

The incorporation of probability recognizes the fact that human experts, on whom expert systems are based, often use incomplete or uncertain information in making decisions. Use of such information is based on experience or heuristic knowledge, also called "rules of thumb." While decisions made using such information may be in error, the use of uncertainty allows action to be taken when additional information is unavailable or too expensive to obtain.

Explanation Facility

An expert system differs from a conventional programming environment in that it frequently offers a review capability regarding its decision-making process. Anyone using the system can ask for a summary of the rules and facts used by the system to arrive at its conclusions. In this way, whether the user agrees or disagrees with the conclusion, the context in which the conclusion was drawn can be examined. Conventional programming environments do not provide such explanation without querying the programming code, a laborious task requiring knowledge of the programming language and its capabilities.

User Interface

The expert system places more emphasis on the user interface than the conventional program because the system accepts statements and questions which contain non-numeric and incomplete data. Because the expert system is query/response oriented, it provides friendly interfaces using menu selection or short answer responses. The system may use natural language formats, accepting answers which are close to if not precisely identical to those in the knowledge base. The system may permit multiple points of entry into the knowledge base, allowing the problem-solving process to focus on those portions of the knowledge base most relevant to the specific problem without the tedium of reviewing irrelevant portions of the knowledge base. Finally, since the system interface acts as the entry point for development of the knowledge base (through the addition of new rules, new facts, and case studies), it may also provide several features to aid knowledge base developers. Such features may include explanations of terms used in the knowledge base, audit trails of rules fired and facts asserted, how and why explanations of the reasoning behind a specific conclusion, and basic knowledge base editing functions.

EXPERT SYSTEM LANGUAGES

The ability of expert systems to manipulate facts and rules in nonlinear ways is a result of the nature of the languages developed for expert system programming.

While many of the expert system tools which will be described later in this chapter are being developed in conventional programming languages, the sophisticated expert systems first developed for mainframe computer applications were done so in special artificial intelligence languages. This section of the chapter will review the programming languages associated with expert systems.

Computer languages with which most programmers are familiar are called programming, or higher-level, languages. Below the higher-level languages are machine language and assembly language, highly complex languages directly related to how the computer manipulates binary code and symbols to process data. FORTRAN, COBOL, BASIC, C, and PASCAL are common programming languages. Expert system programming languages are also higher-level languages, but are designed for a specific purpose. Just as FORTRAN is a mathematics and science language while COBOL is a business language, LISP, PROLOG, and Smalltalk have been developed for the specific purpose of manipulating objects, sentences, and relations among concepts for the development of expert systems.

LISP

The LISt Processing language was developed by John McCarthy in 1958, about the same time as the development of FORTRAN, the oldest higher-level programming language still in regular use (Fields, 1987). The intent of LISP was to manipulate words, called atoms, and sentences, called lists, rather than numbers. LISP was the first of the symbolic languages, developed to manipulate symbols using logic rather than numbers using numeric operations. Symbolic languages recognize relations and patterns among objects, making it possible to manipulate knowledge bases of facts and rules rather than numbers and equations.

LISP connects words, sentences, and other LISP programs according to relations among these elements. Related elements do not need to be adjacent in the knowledge base, since each list contains pointers to other lists, atoms, or programs to which it is related. One of the strengths of LISP is its modularity. There are two basic operators in LISP (forms and functions) which allow an almost infinite number of relations among elements in the knowledge base. This substantial flexibility resulted in the development of multiple versions of LISP between the 1960s and the 1980s. LISP was standardized in 1985 with the introduction of Common LISP.

One of the drawbacks to using LISP has been the slowness of its execution and the large amount of memory required to store the program. Another drawback has been the necessity of using LISP-oriented hardware, or LISP machines. These are computers whose basic operating system is written in LISP to speed the manipulation of the data by avoiding interpretation or compiling of LISP programs into a more common operating system. LISP machines are expensive and prevent easy exchange of LISP programs among computing environments. Recently, some LISP programs have begun to be available on PC-based machines, and the development of more powerful PCs (such as 80386 processor PC-ATs) should speed the availability of LISP programming on affordable computers.

PROLOG

The PROLOG (PROgramming in LOGic) language was developed in 1970 at the University of Marseilles (Harmon, Maus, & Morrissey, 1988). The basis of PROLOG is not lists, but a simplified version of predicate calculus. In other words, PROLOG is a true logic programming language based on logical relations among elements. To develop a PROLOG program, the operator asserts facts about specified objects and rules about their relationships, and then queries the program as to the truthfulness of other assertions about the objects or their relationships. The basic statement which defines the relationship between objects is called a clause. As an example, the phrase *John loves Mary* would take the form *loves(john, mary)* as a PROLOG clause. PROLOG provides conclusions to inquiries based on the relationships and characteristics of the objects.

The strength of PROLOG is that it can infer facts from other facts, based on its use of conclusions and clauses. PROLOG can be run on personal computers as well as mainframe computers. There are several versions of PROLOG, including the recent addition of TurboPROLOG from Borland International. While PROLOG has not enjoyed the same popularity as LISP in the United States, it has been very well received in European countries and in Japan.

Smalltalk

Smalltalk is the most commonly known member of the object-oriented languages; it was developed by scientists at Xerox PARC (Palo Alto Research Center) in the early 1970s (Fields, 1987). Its original intent was to provide a more user-friendly conventional programming environment through a windowing format and use of icons to represent commands. Smalltalk has been successfully applied to development of expert systems. Object-oriented languages combine data and data manipulation procedures into objects. An object may be an integer, a character string, or an array, a combination of integers and strings. The objects communicate with each other using messages composed of commands as to what is to be done to solve problems. The objects then are left to complete the required task in whatever manner is most appropriate or fitting. For example, in the problem 1 + 4 =, the 1 and 4 are objects and the + and = are messages. The result, 5, is another object.

The manner most appropriate or fitting for a particular object to solve a problem is based on the private data contained within the object and the data and data manipulation procedures inherited from its parent object. For example, the new object 5 inherits the fact that it is the result of the object/message operation 1 + 4 = while also being able to function as the independent object 5.

Each object contains a pointer to its parent object, except the original object, referred to as the class of all classes. An object is an instance of a class of objects which share certain characteristics. A class can share a particular structure, respond to similar messages, and respond to those messages in similar ways. This ultimate parent object, the class of all classes, contains the minimum data and data manipulation procedures common to all objects. Smalltalk contains over 100 classes, although fewer than 10 classes are fundamental to building Smalltalk programs.

New objects are created when the system solves a problem or when the system operator defines a new way for an existing object to respond to a situation. This process of creating new objects is referred to as instantiation, because the new object is an instance of an older object.

A simplified example of an object-oriented system is windowing as used in conventional databases. Each Smalltalk object is like a window created from a previous window, with a separate set of data and data manipulation procedures, and which can be used to create new windows, resulting in a complex structure several levels deep. The strength of this process is in the fact that each object can represent a new program, carrying with it all of the programming code of the previous program and containing new elements. Smalltalk-80 is a PC environment version of Smalltalk.

Conventional Programming Languages

Although special expert system languages have been developed, conventional programming languages can also be used to develop expert systems. BASIC, PASCAL, C, and even FORTRAN and COBOL have been used to develop expert systems. Some programs written in LISP and PROLOG are being converted to C to make them more acceptable to the growing expert systems market. Most expert system tools are written in conventional programming languages.

The development of TurboPROLOG, C+ + (an object-oriented version of C) and Flavors (an object-oriented version of LISP), the conversion of LISP and PROLOG based systems to C and the existence of expert system shells indicate that the development of expert systems is possible for end users and programmers with a wide range of programming experience. In fact, one of the key objectives of the development of expert systems is to allow nonprogrammers to be able to employ sophisticated decision-making tools without the necessity of advanced computer system education.

ENVIRONMENTS AND TOOLS

Three ways to develop expert systems are: (a) To hire a programming staff familiar with expert system programming languages and inductive/deductive concepts to develop a customized expert system to meet your needs; (b) To contract with a company which provides expert system development services to build a customized system; or (c) To obtain one of the expert system environments or tools offered by commercial vendors. Environments and tools (distinguished later in this section) provide a programming structure which simplifies the process of building an expert system. The environments and tools include a generic inference engine and a method for translating facts and relationships into rules. The user simply supplies the domain-specific facts and information. The fact that the inference engine and rule development procedures are separate from the knowledge base allows the user to apply the same tool to several different knowledge bases.

As an analogy, financial records and mailing lists represent special problem domains. Like expert system tools, spreadsheet and database management programs require the user to enter these data into an existing framework or structure, defining the relationships among the financial records or list elements. Unlike the expert system tools, however, the extent to which these programs can act upon the data elements to create new relationships or to yield new knowledge is limited. The recent development of intelligent advisors and decision support systems, as aids for spreadsheet and database management programs, is a step in this direction. However, these "near" expert systems are not true expert systems since their *what if?* capabilities are very limited.

Environments

An expert system environment offers a separate knowledge-base and inference engine, separate reasoning mechanism and search strategy, and the ability to enter facts and rules into the knowledge base. Expert system programming languages do not offer these capabilities. However, environments do not offer the editing features to facilitate knowledge-base development available with most expert system tools. Environments are usually more robust than tools, in that they can build more complex expert systems. They are often written in expert system programming languages rather than conventional languages. Recently, however, some of the expert system environments have been offered in conventional as well as expert system languages. This trend reflects the desire of expert system product developers to increase the use of expert systems by end users who do not possess extensive computer programming skills.

Expert system environments are sometimes referred to as large expert system tools, where rule bases may exceed 1500 rules. Environments would include KEE (Intellicorp), ART (Inference Corp.), OPS5 (Verac, Inc.), Knowledge Craft (Carnegie Group) and LOOPS (Xerox Corp.).

Tools

Expert system tools range from friendly interfaces to allow nonprogrammers to develop expert systems for specific applications to elaborate shells almost identical to full environments (Citrenbaum, Geissman, & Schultz, 1987). The interface may include simple menu-driven commands, the ability to list all rules and facts and show their relationships in tree structures, editing capabilities similar to basic word processing features, how and why explanations, and vocabulary libraries to define words used in the knowledge base. Expert system tools can be classified according to type, with the categories based on the level of sophistication of the tool and on the method for acquiring and representing knowledge (Hu, 1987; Harmon, Maus, & Morrissey, 1988).

Inductive tools build knowledge bases established on examples. Whether the knowledge base is large or small, the rules are derived by the system from the examples entered by the user. Because the rules derived and the procedures for manipulating the rules once they have been derived are weak, these systems are generally used for monitoring a knowledge engineering development task or for instructional purposes. Since there is very little use of human experts with inductive tools, they are often referred to as knowledge-based tools. The systems developed from their use are called knowledge-based systems. Examples of inductive systems of this type are Expert-Ease (Softsync, Inc.), Personal Consultant Easy (Texas Instruments), EXSYS (EXSYS, Inc.), and TIMM (General Research).

Simple rule-based tools are often characterized by small (10–500) rule bases and PC-environment compatibility. The rules are developed by the operator using rule development guidelines appropriate to the tool. These tools do not contain methods to group rules into context trees, and their application is limited to basic instructional purposes. Examples include Insight-2+ (Level Five Research), KES (Software Architecture and Engineering), and M.1 (Teknowledge, Inc.).

Structured rule-based tools do offer context trees, allowing subsets of the rule base to be reviewed without the necessity of reviewing the entire rule base. They also offer probability factors and sophisticated editing capabilities. Two examples are VP-Expert (Paperback Software) and Personal Consultant Plus (Texas Instruments).

Hybrid tools are very complex tools which may be logic-, frame-, or object-based. They are generally run on large mainframe computers, although some hybrid tools are being developed for the PC environment. Their application is frequently for development of other tools rather than for development of expert systems directly. ESP Advisor (Expert Systems International) is an example of a rule-based hybrid tool.

Domain-specific tools have not been commercially developed at this time. However, as expert systems become more widely used, this category can be expected to expand (Harmon, Maus, & Morrissey, 1988). These tools are intended to develop expert systems in narrowly defined areas. Thus, their structure will permit rapid knowledge base development.

NEAR EXPERT SYSTEMS

Some applications programs for computer systems, especially in the PC environment, are beginning to add "intelligent" components. These components, referred to as intelligent advisors or decision support systems, are called near-expert systems because they are tools which aid the user in manipulating the data in spreadsheets, database management systems, database search systems, and other relatively complex applications programs. The Q&A (Symantec Corp.) Intelligent Assistant (IA) module is one example. This module acts as a natural language processor to aid in searching and manipulating the file. Through the use of a built-in vocabulary and additional words entered by the user, the IA can perform searching and manipulation actions using fewer keyboard commands. Lotus HAL (Lotus Development Corporation), used with the Lotus 1-2-3 program, is another example of a tool which assists the user in interpreting the data entered into the spreadsheet program. It allows the user to type English-like phrases instead of commands to query the spreadsheet. Guru (Micro Data Base Systems, Inc.) acts in a manner similar to HAL, but offers more complex interpretation features. For example, GURU offers morphological, lexical, parser, semantic, and pragmatic analyses of English sentence equivalents of commands (Anacker, 1987). This allows the command language of GURU to be a very powerful tool for interfacing with business software.

Decision support systems or decision analysis systems assist decision makers in weighing options and planning strategies. They review goals and objectives input by users for inconsistencies and missing information. It is important to remember that these systems do not make decisions based on input, but only review decisions suggested by the user based on the data previously entered and on probabilities assigned to alternatives and outcomes. One example is Judgment Software (Cogensys Corp.) which creates a judgment model analogous to human decision making. The model is developed through an induction approach based on scenarios entered by an operator. The system, once developed, can review other case studies and simulate the human decision making process.

IDENTIFYING APPLICATIONS

The choices among large, mid-sized and small expert systems, mainframe or PC environments and conventional or expert system programming languages are driven by several factors. The computing environment in which the task is to be undertaken will influence the scope of the task. If skilled programming personnel and adequate computing facilities are available, the custom-designed expert system approach may be a viable option. If cost constraints are emphasized, one of the expert system tools in a PC environment will be preferable.

One of the key factors will be the scope of the problem and the choice of the problem domain. Some problems in particular domains may require several thousand rules. Systems of this size would necessitate large computing systems and processing capabilities beyond the scope of most of the tools described. It is very important, therefore, to develop a plan prior to beginning the design and development of an expert system. A plan would include several factors on which decisions would need to be made before selection of a computing environment or an expert system tool could occur.

The type of problem and problem domain are important factors. Expert systems have been developed to address decision-making, procedural, database manipulation, diagnostic, planning, monitoring, and management problems. Some of these areas, especially those with more easily identifiable rules and more clearly defined procedures, lend themselves to expert system applications more readily than others. Two important issues in selecting an appropriate problem are: Is the project technically feasible and does the project address a real need?

One way to answer these questions is to begin by developing a prototype system to address a small part of the overall target problem. In these cases, a tool may be adequate to build a sufficient rule base to estimate the size of the total project rule base. The rules should be derived from a codified set of procedures or some other clearly stated structure. Use of human experts should be minimized at this point, due to the high personnel costs and time involved, and the introduction of uncertainty.

If experts are used, the extent of their knowledge and the type of knowledge they possess will influence the decision to use expert system tools or programming languages. While the tools will facilitate knowledge base and rule development, the languages will allow the capture of the nuances of experiential knowledge. The presence of heuristics, or "rules of thumb," within an expert's knowledge can provide uniqueness to an expert system and permit incorporation of this individual experience and common sense. Unfortunately, "rules of thumb" are difficult elements to encode into an expert system rule base, since they usually introduce a degree of uncertainty into the knowledge base which must be addressed.

The existence of staff who can allocate time to the project is another consideration. Development of the knowledge base, familiarization with the computing system and programming languages or expert system tools, knowledge of the domain in which the expert system is to be employed, and translation of the expertise into usable rules are all time-consuming tasks. Relegating the tasks among members of a project team is possible; however, some degree of cross-training among team members must be present to insure consistency of the final product.

Within the library community, the use of PC-based expert system tools is probably the most practical approach. Due to cost constraints, limitations on personnel time and lack of a large number of domain experts with advanced computer skills, the use of prepackaged tools provides an easy, user-friendly introduction to the field of expert systems. The fact that many areas of librarianship are characterized by clearly defined procedural steps and existing knowledge bases also suggests use of commercially available tools.

In the future, however, familiarity with expert system languages, tools, and environments will serve professional librarians very well. The areas of knowledge acquisition, generation, storage and retrieval, manipulation, and dissemination will become increasingly important to all segments of society. Expert systems will provide the common interface to those areas.

REFERENCES

Anacker, P. (1987). Intelligent interfaces. *PC AI*, *1*(3), 49–53.

Citrenbaum, R., Geissman, J. R., & Schultz, R. (1987). Selecting a shell. *AI Expert*, *2*(9), 30–39.

Fields, S. (1987). Surveying AI languages. *PC AI*, *1*(1), 28-35.

Harmon, P., Maus, R., & Morrissey, W. (1988). *Expert systems: Tools and applications*. New York: John Wiley and Sons, Inc.

Hu, D. (1987). *Programmer's reference guide to expert systems*. Indianapolis: Howard W. Sams & Company.

3

Expert Systems and Artificial Intelligence in Reference*

Samuel T. Waters
National Agricultural Library
Beltsville, MD

WHAT REFERENCE LIBRARIANS DO

From one point of view, reference work may be thought of as what reference librarians and information service personnel do. These activities run the gamut from sitting at a desk in a library and serving as a receptionist, to working independently of any institution while soliciting clients, and providing or re-working and repackaging information perceived to be of potential use to one or more clients. Between these extremes lies a broad spectrum of activities, creating information products as well as providing information services. Answering directional questions blends into referral and ready reference—providing guidance to information sources likely to contain the answers to specific questions, or even providing the answers themselves. Beyond ready reference lies the misty domain of the complex query, requiring in-depth exploration and extensive search, and often the use of online databases.

Prerequisite to all this is the organization of the reference infrastructure: developing the reference collection, even selecting the online databases most likely to be used; developing the vertical files; and consulting with technical services staff on materials to be acquired for the general collections. And then there is the systematic work of creating information products likely to be of use to the clientele: brochures, bibliographies, pathfinders, collected tables of contents of selected journals, and other current awareness products.

Reference work is not just answering questions and creating pre-packaged information products. Frequently, reference librarians find that instructing users in the arcana of bibliographic work is desirable and even necessary. This spans the spectrum from simple guidance in use of the card catalog to extensive bibliographic instruction in topics such as accessing the literature in a specific field or the use of online databases. In some libraries, reference librarians even instruct in the use of microcomputers and their software.

EXPERT SYSTEMS OR ADVISORS

Expert systems and their sibling advisory systems can be of use in many if not all aspects of reference work. Expert systems are computer-based systems which can function at the level of human experts in carrying out such complex and vital tasks as medical diagnosis. Advisory systems function at a lower level of expertise, giving the kind of advice that a knowledgeable worker might in such mundane tasks as troubleshooting a microcomputer problem, or deciding the best mode for shipping a parcel of a given size and weight. Certainly the systems developed to date to assist in reference work have been more closely akin to advisory systems than to true expert systems. This distinction is an important one to make in the real world, since the word "expert" can generate unrealistic expectations that may result in the "Is that all there is to it?" reaction which can kill a proposal in the blink of an eye. Perhaps the best solution is to refer to them as knowledge-based systems, since "in the knowledge is the power."

Why Expert Systems?

Why should reference librarians be interested in creating expert systems? Wouldn't such systems simply be likely to put the reference librarian out of work? One answer is that advisory systems would simply free the expert librarian from the drudgery of answering directional questions and doing simple ready reference, allowing the librarian to spend more time on truly professional aspects of the job.

Library administrators, on the other hand, should need little persuasion. Imagine a reference librarian who can be cloned and placed wherever needed; who receives no salary; never sleeps, gets sick or takes coffee breaks or vacations; never resigns, retires, or dies; never gets tired, forgetful, or irritable; and never bluffs about what one knows. Talk about productivity improvement!

And why should *you* want to know more about expert systems in reference? An Australian author suggests that you may wish to be "the tall, confident one standing near the centre of the bar and holding forth to a crowd of admirers" (Naylor, 1983). Or you may simply wish to share in the excitement of participating in the early stages of the application of a new technology to your own work in your own library. Somewhat more altruistically, you might wish to be part of a process that may result in the development of a total information system with the potential for radically increasing the accessibility of all knowledge. More about that later!

READY REFERENCE

Among the early successful working applications of expert systems to libraries was a microcomputer-based ready reference program for Federal documents. Created in 1984 by SUNY Buffalo and supported by a grant from the Council on Library Resources, it was "born of desperation" due to understaffing of the documents department in the Lockwood Library (Smith, Shapiro, & Peters, 1984). The system contains a set of menus leading to a description of a reference tool likely to meet the information need of a requestor. Approximately 50 reference works are listed in the system (Smith, 1986a). The development program was written in LISP, the favorite artificial intelligence programming language in the United States, and later converted to BASIC to run on an IBM PC. According to a handout distributed at the ACRL Conference in 1986, "POINTER" could be used by other libraries which would alter the BASIC code to fit their own particular situation (Smith, 1986b).

Expert System for Records Retrieval at the National Archives

At the National Archives and Records Administration, archivists used their expertise to guide them in retrieving appropriate records to satisfy the requests of their users, a process that has much in common with library reference work. In 1986 they received reports from the American Management Systems, Inc. (AMS), a firm they had contracted to develop an expert system, designed "to emulate the methods by which archivists 'navigate' through the Archives' very large complex holdings as they search for records" (American Management Systems, Inc., 1986).

The contractor chose to use an expert system "shell" to build the system. A shell is a software package written to facilitate the creation of specific expert systems. Shells enable "knowledge engineers" to develop expert systems with relative ease, rather than building them from scratch using an artificial intelligence (AI) programming language such as LISP, as was done for POINTER. AMS selected the M.1 shell, which ran on an IBM PC and was marketed at that time by Teknowledge, Inc. M.1 built systems that are primarily rule-driven (i.e., they use rules in an IF THEN format to provide advice to the user). This shell used certainty factors to delineate the expert's confidence in a given conclusion. The shell also had interfaces to the assembly programming language and to dBaseII data files. In response to selections from a series of menus concerning the search topics and the time period of interest, the system provided guidance on where to look: specific indices or other finding aids, or the title of a particular set of records in the Archives.

Advisory Systems at the National Agricultural Library

The National Agricultural Library (NAL) began development of an advisory system for ready reference in 1985. The short-term objective was to create a system for use in a relatively narrow field of agriculture, that "could aid end users themselves in locating either appropriate information sources or the specific answers to their questions without professional assistance" (Waters, 1986). The long-range goal, however, was to create a system that could be used by librarians to develop advisory systems for different fields of knowledge, and would permit those knowledge bases to be linked together in a single, growing system covering much broader subject areas.

NAL staff located an expert system shell that seemed to meet all their requirements. "1st-CLASS" permitted development on an IBM PC; it was relatively inexpensive and very easy to learn, and allowed linkage of multiple knowledge bases. A license for unlimited dissemination of expert systems developed using the software was included in the purchase price of $495.

Proof of concept. The first task was to develop a "proof of concept." The software uses a spreadsheet-like format to carry abbreviations of the menu questions and the responses to the different items selected. It is quite simple to attach extensive text to any or all of these abbreviations: Information that will show up on the screen instead of the abbreviations when the system is in use. But before entering any data, it is necessary to determine factors that bear on the use of different types of reference books, such as topic and kind of question. Then one sets up examples, each occupying a row on the spreadsheet format, with a specific value under each factor, leading to a specific reference work likely to answer that type of question. To illustrate, one entry might have a value of "statistics" under the factor "type of information;" the value "agriculture" under the factor "topic;" and under the factor "response," a reference tool such as "Agricultural Statistics" might be suggested when someone selected these values from consecutive menus on the screen. For each such suggestion, a percentage was entered, reflecting the librarian's degree of confidence that the reference book cited would be likely to answer any reasonable question relating to the values selected from the menu.

A number of examples were loaded into the knowledge base, with some brief text attached. However, a single knowledge base could contain only 31 different responses (reference sources). Therefore, a simple procedure was used to link several separate knowledge bases together, providing access to a larger number of reference sources. Contrary to comments in a recent comparative review of expert system software (Vedder et al., 1989), NAL staff found this technique easy to implement.

Since the shell contained means for linking to external databases and systems, it was decided to test these capabilities in the "proof of concept." A short program was written in BASIC, asking the user to furnish feedback as to what the specific question was; whether the answer was found in the reference source recommended; and what suggestions the user had for improving the system. This program was linked to specific responses in the advisory system.

At the same time, another staff member wrote script files for Crosstalk telecommunications software. These were linked to advisory system responses to requests for citations on various agricultural topics. Users were offered the opportunity to look for additional citations in an online database. When they chose this option, the script files instructed the telecommunications program to dial up a specified commercial online system automatically and log on to a selected database. The AGRICOLA database prepared by NAL was one of those connected to the system. Because it seemed unlikely that any library would want end users not trained in DIALOG or BRS to do their own online searching at the library's expense, we also successfully tested connection of the advisor to a CD-ROM player with a bibliographic file searchable by a DOS-based program. Now that many databases have become available on CD-ROM, there will be no connect charges to deter use once such links are made.

Prototype development. Once the "proof of concept" phase was successfully completed, the coordinators of the NAL Aquaculture Information Center decided to build a prototype ready reference advisor in the field of aquaculture (Hanfman, 1989). Their first step, as in the case of POINTER, was to determine the types of aquaculture questions most frequently asked by their patrons. (There seems to be little point in providing answers to questions not likely to be asked.) As they gained a clearer idea of the query types, they began experimenting with ways of structuring the knowledge base. After one false start, they settled on a hierarchical chain of files that began by asking whether the user wanted information about the field in general or about a specific commercial species. If a given species is of interest, the user is asked whether it is a plant or animal. This is done to limit the number of choices presented in a single menu, since too many tend to discourage a user. At the present time, the aquaculture information advisor, christened AQUAREF, contains information on seven animal and two plant species. After selecting a species, one is given a choice of a number of different types of information, leading to suggestions of one or more appropriate reference sources. In cases where there is no reference tool that contains material on a very narrow topic, or where an existing source may not be completely up-to-date, our aquaculture coordinators have furnished actual data (e.g., names and addresses of trade associations) to answer the question. One option now available in AQUAREF is that of choosing an automatic connection to the Aquatic Sciences and Fisheries Abstract (ASFA) database on CD-ROM in order to locate additional citations on a specific topic.

Dissemination. Although the AQUAREF advisor is still far from completely covering all commercially important species, it certainly contains enough data to be useful, especially for a reference librarian not very knowledgeable in the field of aquaculture. It can serve not merely as a prototype, but as a pilot, or early production system as well. Using the "1st-CLASS" shell, a "run-time" version of the software together with the knowledge base has been generated for distribution. This version permits users to consult the knowledge base, but not to modify it or to create a new one. NAL is now distributing this advisor, together with six others in various fields related to agriculture, through its electronic bulletin board (Waters & Schneider, 1989). Three of the advisors were prepared by university librarians trained in expert systems development at NAL; the others were done by different NAL staff members.

Bulletin board distribution can diffuse information about expert system use in libraries, demystifying it, and may perhaps encourage other libraries to build their own advisors. It is possible that some libraries will use software that will permit eventual linking of their files with those built at NAL, and perhaps even in a larger system not necessarily confined to the field of agriculture.

While the development of autonomous, isolated expert systems is useful, something even more significant is now possible: A process for the cooperative building of a new knowledge medium, more powerful by far than books, since the latter can only store knowledge and not apply it (Stefik, 1986). NAL has now begun this process, linking compatible knowledge bases on a number of agricultural topics.

Transition. New "shells" are already appearing that have most of the advantages of 1st-CLASS plus many new ones. NAL has begun exploring the transition. The changes required in switching knowledge bases from an earlier version of that software to a newer, more powerful software sibling called "Fusion" were quite simple. It is not unreasonable to expect that one will be able to import the old knowledge bases into many new systems without undue difficulty. Even if this is not the case, we will have begun the important task of knowledge codification, and in the process, may have taken some small steps toward the development of metaknowledge—knowledge about knowledge—essential in structuring knowledge bases of the future.

Other Reference Advisors

A number of other reference advisors are now under development. One example, using 1st-CLASS, is the Goucher College Biographical Reference Advisor (Bielawski & Lewand, 1988). Among subject-oriented advisors also using 1st-CLASS, the National Library of Medicine has just released for evaluation the first part of a very extensive system on medical statistics, called MEDSTAT. Earlier, Nell Carter of Austin College in Sherman, Texas, used 1st-CLASS to develop a reference advisor on American literature (Alberico, 1987). Kenneth Quinn, California State College at Pomona, used 1st-CLASS to build an advisor on engineering. A number of other ready reference advisors have recently been reported in meetings on expert systems, including an interesting advisor on business information sources done by Ralph Alberico of James Madison University, using the VP-Expert shell.

SOME PRACTICAL HINTS AND THEORETICAL CONSIDERATIONS

Reference librarians interested in developing a ready reference advisor might wonder how large a knowledge base to build. To maximize the likelihood of finishing what you start, it is wise to plan a small system on a relatively narrow topic. To increase the potential significance of your work, plan so that your small knowledge base can be made part of a larger advisor later on!

A reasonable size for an advisor might be 50 to 100 responses, each occupying one or two microcomputer screens at most. The fact that POINTER's coverage was at the lower bounds of this range, with the coverage of AQUAREF slightly larger, tends to reinforce this judgment. Furthermore, several leading guides to reference sources seem to divide their coverage into classes of items of about this size. Both the "Guide to Reference Sources" (Sheehy, 1976) and the "Guide to the Agricultural Literature" (Blanchard & Farrell, 1981) break their topical categories into such groups. It seems that these earlier projects, engaged in a similar task of organizing reference sources, may provide useful clues to the structuring of knowledge in the new medium.

Some idea of the size of the job of developing ready reference advisors covering the universe of knowledge can be obtained by assuming the existence of some 50 major fields of knowledge, as in Sheehy's Guide. Each of those broad fields such as agriculture might have some 50 to 100 important subdivisions, for a maximum of 5,000 subclasses, each one to be covered by an expert system. In each subclass, 50 to 100 reference sources might be useful, for a total of 250,000 to 500,000 ready reference sources cited overall. Looking at these figures another way, each of the 50 major categories might cite up to 10,000 reference sources. In partial confirmation, the standard published guide to reference sources in the field of agriculture noted above (Blanchard & Farrell, 1981) contains about 6,000 items. If one were to limit sources to standard reference tools, as Richardson does in a recent review, the magnitude of the project would be much less (Richardson, 1989). However, reference work in specialized fields draws on specialized sources in addition to those included in the general reference corpus. In any case, the project goal does not seem impossible, or even totally overwhelming, if a lot of librarians will join in its pursuit.

Experience at NAL indicates that building a knowledge base of some 50 to 100 items can be accomplished within a reasonable period of time (e.g., several months of part-time effort by two reference librarians). The DuPont Corporation probably has developed more (over 300) operational expert systems to date than any other organization. It has used two microcomputer-based shells, Insight 2+ and 1st-CLASS. DuPont provides 2-day courses in expert system building skills. According to DuPont's Ed Mahler, "Of 20 people who take our course, normally five will have a system in field test within 2 weeks. Another 10 will have a system in the field within 2 months" (Williamson, 1987). Accomplishment of usable results within such a time frame seems to be good for the morale of both the system builders and the administrator who has allowed this diversion of effort from the demanding daily routine.

One other practical hint, referred to earlier, is that presenting overlong lists of items on a menu may only serve to baffle or discourage the end user. Offering a choice from more than five to seven items on a screen can be avoided by making a further breakdown into several subcategories. Dealing with an additional menu may be less distasteful than dealing with too many items on a single menu.

Another point, illustrated by POINTER, is that the type of literature, such as patents, government documents, or statistics, can be just as useful as subject matter as an organizing focus. Either can serve as a primary or secondary approach to the literature.

Natural Language Front Ends

Development and extension of information advisor systems whets the appetite for further improvements. Expert systems form only one branch of artificial intelligence. Natural language understanding is another important branch. Wedding a pseudonatural language front end to an advisor would reduce the need for use of an elaborate set of menus (e.g., allowing a question about catfish culture to bypass earlier menus in the aquaculture hierarchy). Fusion, a "big brother" of 1st-CLASS, does offer users the option of filling in blanks on a microcomputer screen rather than selecting terms from consecutive menus. Of course, each word filled in must correspond to one of the permissible values previously selected by the developer, or the user will be referred to the menu of terms related to the "blank."

Several microcomputer software packages that link natural language words and phrases to an expert system now exist. GURU, an expert system shell that currently costs $6,000, combines those capabilities with spreadsheet, database management, word processing, graphics, and telecommunications software in a single package (Helliwell, 1986). English Knowledge Systems, Inc., currently advertises a product called "JAKE: Natural Language Processing Using C," for $495. According to the ad, JAKE is being used for expert systems as well as database queries.

OTHER REFERENCE FUNCTIONS

Directional Questions

Expert system shells offer opportunities for the development of systems aimed at automatically answering the most frequently asked directional questions. Using a computer to describe the location of often-sought tools such as unabridged dictionaries, atlases, encyclopedias, and so on, could be a boon to the overworked librarian. And asking a courteous computer for the location of facilities such as restrooms, cloakrooms, water fountains, photocopy machines, and reference desks may be easier for the bashful customer than dealing with a harried librarian. If the computer uses graphic symbols, including floor diagrams, as well as words, results might be even better. A number of shells now offer the ability to create site-specific directional systems using computer graphics. For example, 1st-CLASS Fusion offers the ability to capture graphics screens generated by other programs and to display them during a consultation session.

Bibliographic Instruction

Another type of expert system, IMSATT, derives its strength more from pictures than words. IMSATT is both a course-authoring system and an expert system operating on a microcomputer attached to an interactive videodisc ("Intelligent disc application ready," 1987). It is being used by the USDA Extension Service to demonstrate plant disease diagnosis and pest identification activities. IMSATT was also used by the University of Maryland, along with its own "TIES" hypertext software, in a cooperative project with NAL to develop an interactive videodisk system for instructing users in online searching. Called AGRICO-Learn, since its major focus is on AGRICOLA, NAL's comprehensive bibliographic database for agriculture, the system uses a touch screen and records a user's progress through the course (Butler, 1987).

A similar system, combining an expert system and an optical disc-based system to train Medline end users, is being designed at the University of Texas Health Science Center in Houston. It is planned to utilize Assistant, Tutorial, and Thesaurus modes (Nelson, 1987).

It is clear that course-authoring systems and expert system shells using decision trees have much in common. In fact, an expert system for reference work developed at the University of Waterloo was built using Digital Equipment Corporation's "Courseware Authoring System" software on a VAX minicomputer (Parrott, 1986). Bibliographic instruction is only one of a number of functions, including pointing to appropriate ready reference sources, within the scope of that project.

Of course, it is quite possible for someone to use an expert system as a learning tool, simply by following each branch of the decision tree incorporated in the system (Harmon & King, 1985). Unfortunately, except when expert systems are designed primarily for training, they seldom embody accepted instructional design principles. NAL, for example, is using advice from instructional designers in developing a cataloging tutor using HyperCard, but has not done so in developing other expert systems.

Instructional videodiscs are often developed using course-authoring languages or systems. In contrast to expert systems, they tend to focus on the trainee, determining the user's initial knowledge level, assessing progress periodically, detecting typical errors and implementing appropriate strategies to assist the user in overcoming them. Interestingly, many aspects of instructional design are paralleled in the reference interview, a critical part of the reference process.

The Reference Interview

Determining what a user really wants may be the single most crucial operation in complex reference work. The biggest problem encountered may lie in helping a user find an answer when the user is not certain what he or she is looking for—and may experience a change of mind as the search progresses.

User profile. In order to offer appropriate assistance, it is necessary to have some information about the user. A project at the Mellon Library of Chatham College in Pittsburgh will attempt to include such questions in an expert system, seeking to define the user's reading level, the stage in the research process where the user finds her or himself, and the user's knowledge of the topic to be searched, in the range from novice to expert. The NAL advisor on food and nutrition reference sources does something similar to the last item mentioned: It asks whether the user is approaching the system as a consumer, educator, or researcher, and varies the question menus and the responses accordingly.

The Mellon Library project also will try to learn the user's degree of familiarity with the search system (Nelson, 1987). Our perception of the capabilities of a system may affect the way we phrase our questions and thus determine the "answer" we obtain. Searching a fully indexed online database as if it were subject to the limitations of a card catalog, for example, would unnecessarily limit system output. And awareness of the availability of knowledge organization aids such as classification schemes, thesauri and authority files can make a significant difference. Thus, query negotiation must often be a two way street, with the librarian or the expert system itself offering relevant information about the system as needed. Context-dependent help screens are a common software tool sometimes used in expert system packages to provide assistance to the user.

Other aspects of knowledge about the user could also be helpful. Information about the user's learning style might be valuable in expert system work, since it could determine the most appropriate knowledge representation and inference modes for communicating with the user. In addition, the query negotiation process should elicit information about the nature of the user's knowledge need. Is it for the location of a known item, or a subject search; a few good recent citations, a comprehensive bibliography, or a state of the art summary? The amount of information desired and its recency are important, as are the purposes for which it is sought and how soon it is needed.

In principle, it should be possible to use an expert system shell to build a free-standing knowledge acquisition tool that reminds a reference librarian of appropriate questions, structuring reference interviews to insure that most relevant issues are considered. The task awaits your expertise!

Complex Reference Work

Much of the preceding discussion has been concerned with advisory systems as pointers to reference source books, and as limited providers of factual data. But ready reference work is very different in some respects from in-depth reference work. Ready reference is relatively simple, and largely concerned with factual data, while professional reference often deals with complex concepts in depth. Sometimes complex reference searches are confined exclusively to non-electronic sources, but as more and more sources become available in electronic form, searching of electronic files becomes essential.

Citation retrieval. Expert systems that advise on the selection of databases relevant to an online search query can readily be incorporated in software that facilitates dial-up, log-on, query translation into the language of the online system, searching, and post-processing of an online search. For example, the commercial EasyNet system incorporates a database advisor in its semi-intelligent gateway to online databases. Unfortunately, since most of the online databases use Boolean search, relying on exact matching of terms, the process omits the use of artificial intelligence at a crucial point: in the search itself.

Full text retrieval. Several trends now exist that will lead within the next five years to the availability of huge amounts of textual data in electronic form, ready for searching. First, standards are being developed for author or editor tagging of key parts of manuscripts written on word processors. Uniform field identification will not only facilitate editing and photo-composition, but the indexing and searching of the complete text of publications as well. Furthermore, intelligent optical text recognition techniques are now offering the possibility of converting massive amounts of text from hard copy to searchable electronic form at reasonable costs in the relatively near future. And of course, dense electronic storage media such as CD-ROM are permitting low-cost storage of and access to full text.

Searching collections of full text raises to a new level the problems encountered in citation retrieval. Techniques for searching bibliographic files are likely to require alteration to enable searchers to refine and limit the output of searches through huge volumes of text—to avoid being buried under the haystack while searching for the needle. Boolean matching of terms is being supplemented in some new software by probabilistic systems with relevance feedback. Such a system "infers the probability of relevance of documents in a specific collection to a specific query and ranks them accordingly" (Hildreth, 1989). Personal Librarian, the search software successor to SIRE, does this and more: It permits the user to select a highly relevant target document, and see terms associated with it in similar documents in the collection. The user can then construct his own cluster of terms associated with the topic or concept on which he is seeking information.

Concept searching. Boolean searching requires users to know all the relevant terms describing a subject. In concept searching, related terms are linked together, so that documents relevant to a search can be located, even if they contain none of the terms used in the original query. One new concept search package, TOPIC, uses object-oriented programming, which originated in artificial intelligence research. TOPIC treats a hierarchical outline describing the concept as a search object (Freedman, 1989). All this seems a good deal more intelligent than straight Boolean matching. Still another package, Tome Searcher, permits free text query input, and maps query terms to a thesaurus, permitting the user to broaden or narrow the search by using the syndetic structure of the thesaurus. The National Agricultural Library is using Tome Associates to develop an experimental package in the field of animal welfare, expanding the overall Tome thesaurus to enable it to deal with the special terminology of this relatively narrow field.

Creating "Smart" Reference Books

Libraries will shortly be able to purchase a "smart" multi-media encyclopedia using concept searching, on a CD-ROM (Helgerson, 1989). A number of organizations not in the commercial sector are also engaged in projects to facilitate access to the full text of reference books. The National Library of Medicine has undertaken an Online Reference Works in Medicine program, featuring electronic access to a medical reference book, "Mendelian Inheritance in Man" by Dr. Victor McKusick (Goldstein, 1989). Dr. Goldstein is investigating the use of an object-oriented approach to retrieval from this work. Object-oriented programming has already begun to infiltrate conventional programming techniques, and this AI-based technique may well have an important impact on information retrieval.

Hypermedia. It has been suggested that "the user, rather than being possessed of a simple straightforward need requiring an equally straightforward match with documents in the system, may instead be a wonderfully complicated creature with associations firing in all directions and information interests to match" (Bates, 1986). Bates proposes online systems that will help the users define their needs, learn about the system and its capabilities, explore the different knowledge tracks available, and select those items most relevant to their need as refined through the search process. Such a system requires the display of related terms, topics, and publications, and would use graphic displays of classification trees and hedges in its "front end system mind," which is described as a dense semantic network. The commercial encyclopedia noted above uses a somewhat similar approach.

Hypermedia software aims more at information exploration than at information retrieval. It has not been until recently a notable focus of artificial intelligence research. Nevertheless, hypertext software can be used to create expert systems directly, although they may better be used to complement the strengths of expert system software. A number of expert system building tools now offer hypertext capability as well, including 1st-CLASS HT and KnowledgePro. At the request of FAO, the Food and Agriculture Organization of the UN, NAL recently contracted with a knowledge engineering group that used KnowledgePro (an object-oriented tool) to assist NAL in creating an intelligent reference work covering African aquaculture. Called REGIS, the document also includes a small expert system (Mace, 1989).

In seeking continued development of this product, FAO is asking NAL for addition of a Boolean search capability together with an expert system front end. This serves to confirm the intuitive belief that intelligent software ought to allow individuals to approach a document or collection of documents using any or all of a number of different modalities for search and browsing.

Adding knowledge value to documents by selecting and adding internal links is an extremely labor-intensive activity. Would the value of the products be great enough to warrant the investment of time and effort? Fortunately, computer software is becoming available to assist in this procedure. Texas Instruments has just announced a "software process" called HyperTRANS, which at least partially automates the development of hypermedia systems. There is also a very inexpensive set of microcomputer software packages, called MINDS, that apparently assists the developer in defining the structure of indices to a text file, and then creates the indexes, permitting a user to explore the file. According to one reviewer, the query facility "let me track, quickly and smoothly, where chunks of information were in the chapters and view their relationship" (Shepard, 1989). Automated assistance in creating hypertext files may soon alter the cost-benefit ratio of this type of work very favorably—but there still will be more than enough for reference librarians to do.

COMPUTER ARCHITECTURES IN FUTURE REFERENCE WORK

Parallel Processing

A fundamental change in computer architecture has already started to have application in subject searching. Early in the history of computing, the decision was made to build machines that would carry out procedures sequentially, working from a central processing unit to memory and back. Many procedures however, do not require a large number of computations that must be carried out serially. If transactions in some procedures were carried out in parallel, the final results could be obtained much more quickly. Computers have been built with multiple processors to do just that. High-speed text array processors have been used specifically for subject searching. Files of computerized bibliographic records are automatically split into smaller groups and matched against the same query stored in several processors set up side by side, reducing batch processing time to levels not too far from online searching.

Massively Parallel Computers

Massively parallel computers are now being used for searching full text. The Connection Machine can be configured with over 65,000 processing elements, each with connections to all its physically neighboring elements and each able to store 4,096 bits of memory (Stanfill & Kahle, 1986). Storing about a page of text in each processor, this machine can rapidly check terms initially supplied by the searcher against each document to identify apparently relevant ones. The searcher selects the most relevant items and the machine searches significant words in those documents against all the other documents in the file, ranking the closest matches to the selected document as the most relevant.

This user feedback results in high relevance and recall simultaneously, while in Boolean searching these factors vary oppositely. Earlier, we noted a somewhat similar search capability being offered in a microcomputer package called Personal Librarian, reflecting the fact that programming can sometimes be used to make serial machines act as if they were parallel. Nevertheless, the brute force power of the Connection Machine presages impressive possibilities for electronic searching.

Parallel architectures enable investigation of reasoning "from memories of specific episodes" rather than by the induction of rules based on regularities in the data, as a primary mode for machine reasoning (Stanfill & Waltz, 1986). The storage and search capacity of massively parallel machines permit the search of every item in memory for the "best match" to a request. Knowledge acquisition is the major limiting factor in the development of expert systems, based as it often is on the extraction of rules from human experts. Systems that require only the acquisition of cases, rather than rules, may be simpler to build. And in the real world, where exact matches are infrequent, decisions based on "remembering" similar cases rather than only those that are exactly identical may be more useful, as we see sometimes in medical diagnosis. In the future, expert systems for locating information relevant to user needs and consonant with a user profile might benefit from memory of similar searches for similar users in the past, without absolute dependence on the creation of rule-based systems: One more reason for keeping records of reference requests and answers!

Neural Networks

Neural networks may utilize massively parallel computers, but take a giant step beyond them, since they model their activity to a certain extent on the way that some believe the human brain operates. Just emerging from the experimental realm into commercial use, neurocomputers emphasize the multiplicity of connections between their processors, standing in for neurons. Software acts either to stimulate or inhibit messages among the processors, and through "weighting" enables them to communicate the level of stimulus, rather than being limited to the off/on mode of response typical of most digital computing.

The numerous communication links in a neurocomputer permit a single input to stimulate many processors, which in turn stimulate many others and restimulate the originals, rapidly involving whole regions of processors. Fortunately, the system does not remain in a continuous wild oscillation, but settles into a steady state. This process resembles human associative memory in the fact that what can be recalled is a function of the strengths of the connections among all the processors involved, not just the changed status of data resident in each processor.

Neurocomputers can be trained by inputting target values for a process, continuously strengthening connections that move the system responses closer to the target and weakening those that do not, as the system generates and tests responses. In this learning process, the neurocomputer is building associative memories, electronic patterns it derives that may not be identical to those that humans have discovered in the past in carrying out a similar task. The implications of machines that can learn are awesome, even as applied to the process of locating information relevant to a user request.

Neural network software that runs on microcomputers is also available, though a math co-processor in the machine is usually required for best response times. Some of this software has been used as rule-building front ends for expert systems, as well as to construct systems that solve the same kinds of problems as expert systems. In reference-related work, it seems possible that neural nets could be helpful in refining current awareness profiles, improving their search algorithms based on user feedback about the relevance of documents selected. But even from such an application it is still a giant step to the intelligent agent, or "knowledge navigator," "an intelligent librarian" as the president of Apple Computer calls it (Sculley, 1989).

CONCLUSION

Our profession is about to witness a fundamental paradigm shift. Many have already noted a movement from book and document-oriented library work to an increasing emphasis on information service. Now we are on the eve of a landmark change, to dealing with knowledge as our basic professional concern. We will be building knowledge bases to assist in knowledge location and utilization, and we may find ourselves acting as "knowledge engineers" in the development of user-oriented knowledge access systems in specialized fields, precursors of the knowledge navigator.

The multiplicity of knowledge needs that must be addressed in complex reference work will require powerful hybrid systems for knowledge representation and interference. The options in building reference knowledge bases are almost overwhelming in their variety and complexity, and in the rate at which new choices are presenting themselves. Nevertheless, we must not let ourselves be deterred from beginning now to carry out the simple basic groundwork for the expert reference system of the future. As Candide advised, "Let us work in our gardens!"

REFERENCES

Alberico, R. (1987). Knowledge representation: The realm of the possible. *Small computers in libraries, 7*(10), 8.

American Management Systems, Inc. (1986). *Methodology for developing an expert system for information retrieval at the National Archives and Records Administration.* Arlington, VA, MS-1.

Bates, M. (1986). Subject access in online catalogs: A design model. *Journal of the American Society for Information Science, 37*, 357–376.

Bielawski, L., & Lewand, R. (1988). *Expert systems development: Building PC-based applications.* Wellesley, MA: QED Information Sciences, 63.

Blanchard, J., & Farrell, L. (1981). *Guide to sources for agricultural and biological research.* Berkeley: University of California Press.

Butler, R. (1987). New technologies: Computerizing the future. In *Research for tomorrow, 1986 Yearbook of Agriculture* (pp. 297–298). Washington, DC: U.S. Department of Agriculture.

Freedman, B. (1989). Verity upgrades Topic text manager. *PC Week, 6*(23), 10.

Goldstein, C. M. (1989). Full text retrieval from structured text. *Bulletin of the American Society for Information Science, 15*(6), 11. Washington, DC: American Society for Information Science.

Hanfman, D. (1989). AquaRef: An expert advisory system for reference support. *The Reference Librarian, 23*, 113–133.

Harmon, P., & King, D. (1985). *Expert systems: Artificial intelligence in business.* New York: Wiley.

Helgerson, L. (1989). Individualized education in the 1990s with CD-ROM. *CD-ROM enduser, 1*(1), 6–9.

Helliwell, J. (1986). Guru: brave new expert system? *PC magazine, 5*(10), 151–163.

Hildreth, C. (1989). *Intelligent interfaces and retrieval methods.* Washington, DC: Library of Congress.

Intelligent disc application ready. (1987). *Instruction delivery systems, 1*(2), 12.

Mace, S. (1989). Regis merges two technologies. *InfoWorld, 11*(12), 15–18.

Naylor, C. (1983). *Build your own expert system.* New York: Halstead Press.

Nelson, N. (1987). The archaeopteryx at year's end. *Information today, 4*(1), 20.

Parrott, J. R. (1986). Expert systems for reference work. *Microcomputers for information management, 3*, 155–171.

Richardson, J. (1989). Toward an expert system for reference service: A research agenda for the 1990s. *College and research libraries, 50*, 231–248.

Sculley, J. (1989). The knowledge navigator: A look at tomorrow. *PC AI, 3*(1), 31.

Sheehy, E. P. (1976). *Guide to reference books* (9th ed.). Chicago: American Library Association.

Shepard, S. J. (1989). A new approach to hypertext: MINDS. *AI expert, 4*(9), 69.

Smith, K. F. (1986a). Robot at the reference desk? In D. A. Nitecki (Ed.), *Energies for transition, proceedings of the fourth national conference of the Association of College and Research Libraries* (pp. 198–201). Chicago: Association of College and Research Libraries.

Smith, K. F. (1986b). *POINTER, the microcomputer reference program for federal documents.* Buffalo, NY: SUNY at Buffalo.

Smith, K. F., Shapiro, S., & Peters, S. (1984). *Final report on the development of a computer assisted government documents reference capability: First phase.* Buffalo, NY: SUNY at Buffalo.

Stanfill, C., & Kahle, B. (1986). Parallel free-text search on the Connection Machine System. *Communications of the ACM, 29,* 1229–1239.

Stanfill, C., & Waltz, D. (1986). Toward memory-based reasoning. *Communications of the ACM, 29,* 1213–1228.

Stefik, M. (1986). The next knowledge medium. *AI magazine, 7*(1), 42–43.

Vedder, R. G., Fortin, M. G., Lemmerman, S. A., & Johnson R. N. (1989). Five PC-based expert systems for business reference: An evaluation. *Information technology and libraries, 8,* 48.

Waters, S. T. (1986). Answerman, the expert information specialist: An expert system for retrieval of information from library reference books. *Information technology and libraries, 5,* 204–212.

Waters, S., & Schneider, K. (1989). Expert advisory systems loaded on ALF. *Agricultural Libraries Information Notes, 15*(1), 2–3.

Williamson, M. (1987). At DuPont, expert systems are key to AI implementation. *PC Week, 4*(2), 35.

4

POINTER: The Microcomputer Reference Program for Federal Documents

Karen F. Smith
Lockwood Library
State University of New York at Buffalo

INTRODUCTION

POINTER is a microcomputer program that simulates what a government documents librarian does when fielding queries from potential users of the federal documents collection. It is called POINTER because all it does is direct users to reference sources; it does not tell them how to use the sources, what access terminology to use, nor how to interpret the citations found there. POINTER is designed to get people started, on their own, with no help from library staff. After responding to a series of yes/no questions and menu choices on the CRT screen, the user receives a short list of likely reference tools to consult.

The expertise of POINTER lies in the questions it asks the user in order to adequately define the information need and in the linkages which connect those defined needs to the reference books which are best for satisfying them. The computer program utilized by POINTER to simulate the outcome of this type of librarian/user interaction is written in BASIC and provides predictable responses. In other words, the logic is "hard-wired." POINTER is not a system designed to reason independently nor does it have knowledge of the special features and possible uses of the reference books built into it. Thus, POINTER is not an expert system. POINTER is a computer-assisted reference program—inspired by expert systems developments of the recent past, and aspiring to be upgraded to a real expert system in the future. The basis for POINTER was work done in the summer of 1984, supported by a grant from the Council on Library Resources under the Faculty/Librarian Cooperative Research Program.

WHAT IS POINTER SUPPOSED TO DO?

POINTER was designed to be a stand-in for the librarian at the documents reference desk. It is supposed to provide minimal service to patrons during weekend and evening hours and when the librarian is busy with other patrons or occupied with other duties. The key word here is minimal. Decisions were made at the beginning to limit the scope of the project to keep it manageable. At the present time POINTER is limited to the federal documents collection. The outcome of a search is limited to a list of relevant reference books. The choices provided are limited to those deemed most likely to be needed, and the knowledge base is limited to the experience of just one librarian.

In order to provide a substitute for the librarian, one needs to know what it is that the librarian does. Turning to the library literature, we find that the reference process has been studied and reported on extensively. Some of the models have been developed in greater detail than others, but all involve the following steps:

1. A person has an information need.
2. The person verbalizes that need.
3. The reference librarian interviews the person in order to rephrase, refine, or augment the query statement.
4. The reference librarian considers the type of access points to be searched.
5. The reference librarian selects specific reference books to search.

IDENTIFYING THE INFORMATION NEEDS OF DOCUMENT USERS

We were able to determine what the information needs of the document patrons might be by analyzing a collection of reference queries gathered over an 18-month period (January 1983 through June 1984) as an administrative by-product of the normal operation of the documents department, where a reference transaction form is filled out for every query that is not a directional question. As a means of categorizing the queries, we considered a model developed by Gerald Jahoda and Judith Braunagel (1980). Every reference query consists of two components: the subject (or "given") of the query and the information needed about the subject (the "wanted"). There are between 48 and 96 combinations of givens and wanteds (depending upon how you count the wanteds), but some combinations are more likely to occur than others. For instance, you would probably never get a patron asking for the location of an abbreviation. Our final report to the funding agency outlines the 20 combinations of givens and wanteds for which there were examples in the collection of document reference queries, lists some actual questions, and relates them to possible answer providing sources (Smith, Shapiro, & Peters, 1984).

After coding 1,071 queries, we found that the frequency with which people start with the various givens is: specific publication, 55.6 percent; term or subject, 25.6 percent; place, 13.4 percent; organization, 4.6 percent; and person, 0.8 percent. The most frequently needed types of information are: document location, 49.7 percent; numeric information, 25.8 percent; and general or background information, 17.8 percent. The primary inference to be made from this data is that a very large number of people in this particular documents department are seeking the location of a specific known item.

SELECTING SPECIFIC REFERENCE BOOKS

The librarian's ability to translate a patron's query into a request for a particular reference tool is a fundamental but still mysterious form of expertise—librarianship's equivalent of the gardener's "green thumb." In theory, the above-mentioned groups of similar reference queries should suggest separate search strategies based on the different types of reference tools appropriate for each group. For example, if the meaning of an abbreviation can be found using a dictionary, handbook, or manual, then by extracting a short list of the dictionaries, handbooks, and manuals from our overall list of government document reference tools, we should be well on our way to narrowing the search for the meaning of the acronym, FTC. In reality, a grouping such as dictionaries, handbooks, and manuals is too general to be completely useful.

Because of the above reasons, we abandoned the systematic approach to reference queries and began to look more closely at the individual reference tools, trying to figure out what the special features of each title were and under what circumstances we would be apt to recommend the use of it. Most of the reference tools fall into the broad category of Indexes, Bibliographies, and Abstracts, although there is another large category of primary publications such as the *Code of Federal Regulations* and the *Congressional Record*. Indexing and abstracting tools are differentiated by the material covered such as "hearings" or "statistics," or by type of access points such as "title" or "subject" or "number." Many of the tools cover all three branches of government but some are limited to just one. There are many examples of special purpose finding lists such as the *List of CFR Parts Affected* or *Treaties In Force*. Even if only one question in a thousand requires knowledge of executive orders, no self-respecting documents reference system could ignore the methods of locating them. Drawing on our sense of what should be in the system, what users would be asking for, and what features of the reference tools were particularly distinctive, we put together the following system, which is now called POINTER. It includes approximately 80 reference sources.

WHAT DOES POINTER LOOK LIKE?

POINTER is meant to be out in the public area on a dedicated microcomputer. The user does not have to sign on, load the program, or do anything but follow the directions on the screen. The first screen welcomes the person to the department and explains that the system covers federal documents only. At the end of each path, if the person indicates he or she has no other questions, the system recycles back to this welcoming screen. There is no RESET option, but if someone abandons the search in midstream the next user can quickly get back to the beginning by answering the questions posed on the computer screen to finish the previous transaction.

The screen after the welcoming screen explains the importance of SuDoc numbers, the system of classification used for the separate documents collection at Lockwood Library. If the person has such a number, he or she is directed to go to the shelves. If unsure whether the number in question actually is a SuDoc number, he or she is shown some examples of typical configurations and told to look for a colon which is a distinctive feature of SuDoc numbers.

The user is then presented with the main menu (although it is not labeled as such). From our analysis of the questions, we saw that we could divide patrons into two roughly equal groups: those with some sort of bibliographic citation, and those without. Applying our "rule of thumb" that titles are easier to work with than agency names, the first choice on this menu is: looking for a particular document/know the title. However, a peculiarity of documents reference work is the fact that many items people are looking for, such as bills or executive orders, do not have prominent titles but are readily retrieved by their numbers. So the second choice on the menu is: looking for a particular document/know the number. The third choice is: looking for information or publications on some subject. POINTER presents these as menu choices rather than as single questions to be responded to serially. Titles are further categorized into:

1. One time publications
2. Periodicals
3. Semi-annual, annual, or less frequent but regular publications
4. One of a numbered series
5. Public laws.

Numbers are categorized as numbers of:

1. Bills
2. Public laws
3. House or Senate reports or documents
4. Technical reports
5. Presidential executive orders.

Sources of information on a subject are categorized as:

1. Biographic information
2. Numeric data, such as census data or statistical information
3. Laws concerning some subject
4. Regulations concerning some subject
5. Court cases concerning some subject

6. Executive orders or Presidential statements concerning some subject
7. Information contained in legislative histories, hearings, reports, debates, or other legislative publications
8. Directory information: names, addresses, phone numbers of people or organizations
9. Information contained in bills or proposed legislation
10. Information contained in treaties
11. Information contained in scientific or technical reports
12. Information about grants, fellowships, or employment opportunities
13. Information contained in periodical articles
14. Information contained in pamphlets or books.

Some of the categories are subdivided further. If the subdivision is by date, the user may be asked to specify (type in) a year or to choose a time range from the menu. Finally, at the end of a path, the system suggests some reference books to try. The output typically looks like the example shown in Figure 4.1. If a printer is attached, the person can use the "Print Screen" function to get a paper copy of the list of reference books, their call numbers, and locations. The program could be modified to automatically send the output to a printer.

It is a generally accepted truism in the library world that patrons don't always ask their real question. However, we had to assume that people really do know what they want and can focus on that need while using an impersonal system such as POINTER.

HOW DOES POINTER WORK?

POINTER is written in BASIC in a very straightforward manner. Dialog with the user is primarily through menu choices as described above. Input from the user is tested against IF-THEN condition statements (which is as close as this system gets to "rules"). The reference book titles are stored as subroutines which are called up and PRINTED as required. The entire program runs from memory so the diskette can be removed for safekeeping after the program is loaded. Figure 4.2 shows selected lines from the program which convey the style of programming and the manner in which various tasks are accomplished.

RATIONALE

It was of overriding concern to come out at the end of this project with a system that:

1. Could actually be used
2. Could be used on library equipment
3. Could be maintained by me or another person in the library.

```
? ? ? ? ? ? ? ? ? ? ? ? ? ? ? ? ? ? ? ? ? ? ? ? ? ? ? ? ? ? ? ? ? ? ? ?

Are you looking for
     1. a particular document for which you have a title
     2. a particular document for which you have some number
        e.g., a bill number, a public law number, a House
        or Senate report or document number, a technical
        report number
     3. information or publications on some subject
     4. Maps

Select your choice by typing 1, 2, 3, or 4 and press RETURN
? 4

The Map Collection is located on the 3rd floor of the
Science and Engineering Library.  A useful overview of U.S.
government maps can be found in Chapter 17 (v.1 pg.117-121)
of:

Using Government Publications (Sears and Moody)
located in the Documents and Microforms Reference Collection
Doc Ref Z1223 Z7 S4 1985 v.1&2

* * * * * * * * * * * * * * * * * * * * * * * * * * * * * * * * * * *
* Press the RETURN key when you are ready for additional sources*
* * * * * * * * * * * * * * * * * * * * * * * * * * * * * * * * * * *

SuDoc numbers for some maps can be found using the subdivision
MAPS after headings for country or place names such as
AFRICA--MAPS or topics such as AIR-POLLUTION--U.S.--MAPS in
the subject index of:

Monthly Catalog of United States Government Publications
Doc Ref A1223 A18

Government Documents Catalog (MICRO MAX 800)
located on the service counter

* * * * * * * * * * * * * * * * * * * * * * * * * * * * * * * * * * *
* If you are still having difficulty in finding the appropriate *
* sources, please ask the librarian for assistance.             *
* * * * * * * * * * * * * * * * * * * * * * * * * * * * * * * * * * *

Do you have another question?
Please type 'yes' or 'no' and press RETURN
?
```

Figure 4.1. Sample output from POINTER.

These stipulations certainly influenced the design of the system in ways which imperiled its eventual classification as an "expert system." There are two aspects to these design choices: hardware and software. Looking first at hardware, the equipment available to me in the library was an IBM-PC microcomputer. Similar machines are becoming more and more prevalent in libraries. It seemed only prudent to design a system for export to other libraries on the basis of commonly held hardware. Furthermore, microcomputers provide fast response time, whereas a terminal running from a mini or mainframe computer located some distance away and connected by a phone line may be slower at times. There is also the expense of acquiring a terminal and getting it wired up.

And finally, personal computers are easy to program. All these factors—that we already owned the equipment, that such equipment was widely available in other libraries, that we could handle the necessary programming tasks ourselves to create a usable, fast system to help the students—led us to adopt the IBM-PC as the host hardware for POINTER.

Once the decision was made to go with the IBM-PC, we still had software choices to make. Since we had neither the time nor the money to shop for an expert system shell, we again went with what we had. A BASIC interpreter comes with the IBM-PC on the DOS disk. BASIC is a programming language widely used by people who have microcomputers, and as such, is a very suitable choice for a computer program designed to be modified by other librarians for use in their own libraries. It is a language we could deal with, whereas LISP or PROLOG would have had to be learned. So, although my programmer wrote the original program in LISP on a VAX minicomputer, she did so in a way that was easily translatable into BASIC. Not everything programmed in LISP is an expert system, nor does the fact that POINTER is not written in BASIC preclude it from being called an expert system. Neither the decision to use a microcomputer nor

```
171 LET Z1$ = "located on the service counter"
175 LET Z5$ = "located in the Documents Reference Collection"
1100 PRINT "Are you looking for"
1110 PRINT "   1. a document for which you have a title"
1120 PRINT "   2. a document for which you have some number"
1180 PRINT "Select your choice by typing 1 or 2 and press RETURN"
1190 INPUT T
1210 IF T=1 THEN GOTO 1510
1220 IF T=2 THEN GOTO 2590
1510 PRINT "In what year was the document produced?"
1540 INPUT Y
1600 IF (Y>1788) AND (Y<1972) THEN GOSUB 42270
1610 IF (Y>1971) AND (Y<1977) THEN GOSUB 42270:GOSUB 42450
1620 IF (Y>1976) AND (Y<1988) THEN GOSUB 42310
1630 GOTO 39600
2590 PRINT "Is the document for which you have a number"
2600 PRINT "     1. a bill"
2610 PRINT "     2. a public law"
2620 PRINT "     3. a House or Senate Report or Document"
2630 PRINT "Select 1-3 and press RETURN"
2640 INPUT N
2650 ON N GOTO 2800, 4400, 5000
39600 END
42270 PRINT "Cumulative Title Index 1789-1976"
42280 PRINT Z5$
42290 PRINT "Doc Ref Z1223 A115"
42300 RETURN
42310 PRINT "MICRO MAX 800"
42320 PRINT Z1$
42330 REM-- Autographics, Inc. rollfiche subscription
42340 RETURN
42450 PRINT "Cumulative Index 1976-1980 (microfiche)
42460 PRINT Z1$
42465 REM-- GP 3.8/3:976-80
42470 RETURN
```

Figure 4.2. Sample lines from the POINTER program.

the decision to use BASIC preempted us from designing a ''real'' expert system. However, presenting our rules as menu choices rather than as single questions was a more fundamental decision.

WHY USE MENUS?

One reason we decided to go with a menu-driven system was because it seemed so natural. In the process of categorizing the queries, we seemed to be developing some of the menus, and my way of thinking about reference books was easily translated into a menu-driven system.

There are several advantages to a menu-driven system. People often like to see all the options a system offers and are assisted by a menu which provides alternatives to choose from. Menus naturally help in progressing from the general to the particular and assist in windowing the question. A menu can be a teaching tool, laying out the categories or possibilities in a way that helps a person begin to relate to the documents collection like a documents librarian. This is particularly true when there are many options, all of equal value, so that there is no particular point in asking about one before the others. For example, when you have a dichotomy such as a specific item search versus a subject search, one question will get you started down the correct path. You can ask, ''Are you looking for a known item?'' and if the answer is NO, assume the person wants a subject search. But if your attempt is to fix a choice from among executive branch, legislative branch, and judicial branch publications, you would have to ask two, possibly three, direct questions if input is limited to YES/NO responses. We assumed that we should try to minimize the amount of typing required of the user, and numbered menu choices are certainly easier for the user than typing in whole words or phrases. They also make the programming easier. In the case of POINTER, we felt that the paths would be shorter and that we could get the person to the answer more quickly using menus than by asking a series of individual questions.

Disadvantages of a menu-driven system include the fact that it is inflexible and that it forces even experienced users to go through a proscribed procedure, although this is a more valid criticism in connection with database searching than for expert systems. Depending on the design of the menus, there is the danger of requiring too much reading. That is definitely the case with POINTER's ''subject'' menu. The user should probably not be expected to choose among more than five to seven possibilities. However, if the options are not well defined, the user may be in a quandary about which one to pick, not knowing where the choice will lead. A menu system can also be difficult to use if it does not match the user's own view of the request or needs and thus forces one to choose seemingly inappropriate categories from a rigid menu.

DIFFICULTIES ENCOUNTERED IN BUILDING POINTER

In retrospect, the primary difficulty encountered in putting POINTER together was the communication process and interaction between the expert and the knowledge engineer. I pretty much knew what knowledge I wanted included in the system, but I did not know how to configure it for the computer. My graduate student/computer programmer knew how to do things with the computer but felt she was really not interested in learning as much about librarianship as she would have had to in order to identify the aspects of librarian expertise involved in this type of public services work. We did not set up a mechanism such as interviews or observations that would have allowed her to isolate any heuristics I might be using while responding to reference questions. I was probably too impatient and she, too inexperienced. This difficulty was exacerbated by the fact that we were working under time constraints. It was perhaps unrealistic to think that we could accomplish all we set out to do in one summer. As a result, we have a computer program but not an expert system.

LIMITATIONS OF POINTER

We found during early testing that several additions and revisions to the program would be necessary. The students who tried it generally agreed that the initial screen was too full, so we divided that screen up into several screens. In addition, they felt that the top-level menu for those with no bibliographic information (i.e., the subject menu) was too long. I have not yet figured out the best way to divide it up, so that remains to be done. Information on how to find the cost and availability of government documents needs to be added to the knowledge base. Information on maps has been included but could be greatly expanded. Information about how to search for documents by author or agency could be added.

Several additional capabilities would be nice. A training or HELP feature to help patrons use the reference tools suggested by the system would be a great enhancement. These reference tools are quite complex, and information on their use should be incorporated into the system. The analysis of reference queries included many of the type where the given was a PUBLICATION and the wanted was GENERAL INFORMATION, such as:

1. Code of Federal Regulations/How to update a citation.
2. Census of Population/What categories of age and income are included?
3. Monthly Catalog/How to find the SuDoc number.
4. American Statistics Index/How to use it.
5. Publications Reference File/What is it?
6. 1970 Census/Why is income data for 1969 and not 1970?

Librarians get a lot of questions like these, but POINTER is not capable of handling them. Furthermore, if the person is looking specifically for one of the commercial reference books by title, POINTER will not help. The "real" question we are trying to deal with is not "Where is *American Statistics Index*?" but instead "What tools do I need to locate numeric data?" Whether users can jump that hurdle remains to be seen.

REFERENCES

Jahoda, G., & Braunagel, J. (1980). *The librarian and reference queries: A systematic approach*. New York: Academic Press.

Smith, K. F., Shapiro, S. C., & Peters, S. (1984). *Final report on the development of a computer assisted government documents reference capability; first phase* (Council on Library Resources Grant CLR 785-B). Buffalo: State University of New York at Buffalo.

5

A Model of Reference Librarians' Expertise: Reviving Refsearch on a Microcomputer

Howard D. White
Diana Woodward
College of Information Studies
Drexel University
Philadelphia, PA

INTRODUCTION

Our project is the overall design of an expert system, implementable on a microcomputer, for library reference work. We propose a system that supplies patrons with recommended sources for lookup of certain questions. Alternatively, the system can be used to teach students reference skills, or as a computerized aid for practicing reference librarians and information specialists.

The system, called Refsearch, incorporates a small indexing language that can simultaneously characterize a question and the desired work(s) that may answer it. The first author developed this language (with full scope notes) as part of an early expert system at the Institute of Library Research, University of California, Berkeley, during 1969 (Meredith, 1971a, 1971b). Soon after, a prototype version on a mainframe computer was tried in Berkeley's School of Librarianship (now School of Library and Information Studies) as a teaching aid in reference courses (Mignon, 1971; Maron & Sherman, 1971; Meredith, 1981). Because software was relatively primitive then, the prototype was rather taxing to use. (It involved translating language strings into numerical strings, often long, in order to search for desired reference works.) Current advances in software make it feasible to redesign the system so that it can use natural language and run on a microcomputer in libraries. (See Roysdon & White, 1989, for recent, related work.)

We propose to use the Refsearch language to describe approximately 100 works—enough to give us a test-bed for question-answering experiments in library (and possibly other) settings. These experiments are a future stage of the research. In the present project we want simply to create the expert system, involving reference librarians in the design process as consultants.

In the test bed, we will describe printed as opposed to online works, and reference as opposed to bibliographic works. (Some of our choices now exist in both online and printed versions.) Later, Refsearch may be tailored to accommodate types of sources omitted now.

At Berkeley, Refsearch was used by the first author to characterize about 145 works in the library school's general reference teaching collection. Experience gained there shows that many reference works have a fairly simple structure. They consist of files comprising records with standard fields in a standard order. When record structure is consistent throughout, entire works can be characterized through attribute-coding. In contrast, other standard reference works are congeries of files and tables of mixed types (for example, the *World Almanac*), and these do not lend themselves to coding as wholes. In this project we plan to avoid the latter, complex types of works, in order to concentrate on those that are readily describable as wholes.

Our long-range goal is to make the system sufficiently cordial, with menus, prompts, and conversational features, that it can be operated by patrons without the assistance of a librarian. We hope to create a model system that can be adapted by librarians and others as needed. Eventually it may be customized by library automation staffs so as to accommodate particular collections and types of queries. We may also be able to fulfill a goal unattained in the Berkeley project—the ranking of sources by whether they are more or less likely to contain an answer. The software to be tried includes Insight 2+ (Level Five Research, 1986), which incorporates expert system building tools, a Pascal compiler, and dBase III within the same shell on an IBM microcomputer.

NOTES ON THE DREXEL IMPLEMENTATION

A reference librarian makes use of two sorts of expertise in handling general reference questions: knowledge of procedures to be followed during question negotiation, and knowledge of types of information found in reference books. In the Drexel expert system, we have analogs of these two areas of expertise.

Insight 2+ allows us to model the librarian's procedural knowledge of how to conduct a question negotiation. We have approached the procedure of question negotiation as being essentially a diagnostic activity. The user is led by menus through a series of choices that help convert the "presenting question" into a sentence-like search string that retrieves sources. The menu-driven system prompts the patron in natural language and Refsearch terms at each point; the actual search on these terms involves programs transparent to the user.

We are using a rule-type knowledge base with backward-chaining inference. A rule-type knowledge base maintains the expert's knowledge as a series of rules in "if-then" form. This is well-suited to modeling the librarian's procedural knowledge of question negotiation. (Factual knowledge about reference books, on the other hand, is maintained separately in dBase III files.)

An inference engine allows an expert system to draw conclusions from the information in the database. A backward-chaining inference engine will test for all routes to the goal—retrieval of a particular work—and fire all sequences of rules it finds.

The Berkeley Refsearch project provided a database of facts about reference works on a mainframe computer. The Drexel system will maintain these facts in relational database form with dBase III.

Each record pertains to a single reference book. Most of the fields in each record are variables characterizing books in that file. Reference works, for example, have distinctive "entry points" (i.e., types of nouns with which they may be entered). We maintain a separate database file for each "entry point." The top menu determines the entry point and opens the appropriate dBase III file. Next, one proceeds to determine ways in which the user entry term is qualified, the service one wants the work to perform, and so on.

Unseen by the user, the fields contain numeric values representing a coder's judgment as to presence or absence of attributes of reference works, such as "enterable with the name of a real, living person." Codes are usually 0 (absent) or 1 (present), but may be decimal fractions, such as 0.5 (partially present). A Pascal program passes statements of desired attributes to dBase III, retrieves titles of works with nonzero values on these attributes, and totals the values. From summed attribute codes in the resulting display, a ranking is possible that shows which works are more or less highly recommended.

Simulating Librarians: The Refsearch Matrix

Refsearch simulates what sets reference librarians apart—their distinctive advice-giving capability. They have learned, first, a much larger repertoire of reference works than most people, and, second, the characteristics of these works. This knowledge is represented in the dBase III files just described—as matrixes on which retrieval operations are performed.

The files of Refsearch are entity-attribute matrixes (see, e.g., Martin, 1977). The entities are specific, printed reference works—dictionaries, directories, gazetteers, and so on–commonly included in the librarian's repertoire of titles, as developed in many library schools. Such works store general information on a huge number of topics, and collectively provide the content for a question-answering service in which speed in answering is the primary goal.

The attributes of these works—characteristics more or less known to librarians—are:

- The type(s) of nouns with which they can be entered
- The services they typically perform once entered
- Subject specialization (if any)

- Geographic focus
- Temporal focus
- Recency of publication.

We emphasize that operations on this matrix do not answer the patron's question. They merely yield a list of one or more plausible sources in which to look for the answer. In this, Refsearch simulates a reference librarian's mental process as he or she runs through the repertoire of known sources in order to make recommendations. Many years ago Wyer distinguished between reference service in the "liberal" mode, in which the librarian finds and gives an answer to a question, and the "conservative" mode, in which the librarian merely suggests a source (Wyer, 1930). Refsearch simulates the librarian in the conservative mode. Expert systems that simulate the liberal mode would have to be much more subject-specific.

No two librarians' minds being the same, we propose only a general model, still open to improvements, of what we think may be found there. However, once the model is explicit, it becomes a hypothetical librarian. Ours is Janus-faced, looking one way at reference questions, and the other at potential sources of answers. The Refsearch scheme lies between the faces, giving each the same vocabulary for describing what it sees.

A THEORY OF REFERENCE WORK

Refsearch is based, in fact, on a theory of how reference librarianship is done. We draw attention to its congruence with discussions of intermediation, such as Benson and Maloney's (1975), and its relevance in teaching reference skills (or public information work), irrespective of implementation on any particular computer. The "Janus-faced" nature of Refsearch reflects certain axioms. They are italicized in this section, which sketches our theoretical base.

The basic unit in the indexes and indexical arrangements of reference works is a single part of speech—the noun.

Indexable nouns appear as single words and as groups of words called noun phrases. The latter take various forms—for example, adjective and noun (Byzantine art), noun and adjective (Art, Byzantine), noun and noun (Theda Bara; Massachusetts, University of), verbal phrases used as nouns (Anointing the Sick), and so on. Numerical nouns are possible—for example, 1776. Long words or phrases are sometimes named by short-form nouns called abbreviations or acronyms.

Furthermore, every word in the dictionary, whatever part (or parts) of speech it normally is, functions as a noun in any question about it *as a word*. When a word is used to refer to (or name) itself, we show that it has noun status by special punctuation, usually quotation marks or italics. (For example, words ordinarily not nouns become nouns in the following: What does "fro" mean? When did "glitzy" enter English? Is there a Russian equivalent of "the"?)

Hereafter the term "noun" will mean not only single nouns, but noun phrases and non-nouns put in quotes for nominative use.

The basic unit of a question answerable within a reference collection is a single part of speech—the noun.

Ideally, this noun is not only explicit in the question, but used verbatim as an indexing term within the collection. The matter appearing with it, moreover, contains the answer we seek. The task of anyone searching for an answer is to match question-noun with index-noun and move thereby to the answer.

In practice, many patrons' questions do not permit this match as they are first posed (if ever). Their vagueness or opacity may sometimes be remedied by conversation between the patron and the librarian. Called "question negotiation" or "the reference dialogue," it is a way of making explicit what the patron has left implicit (Thomas, Hinckley, & Eisenbach, 1981). Even so, considerable translation from "question language" into "indexing language" may be needed by the librarian before the search can begin. The librarian may, for example, have to convert adjectives or verbs in the question into nouns, or substitute synonymous nouns for the originals, or draw on personal knowledge for a new tack, as when the patron asks something about *Tosca* and the librarian knows the answer will be found quickest under "Puccini." At other times, translations from the specific to the more general (or the reverse) will be in order.

These substitutions are complicated—so much so that only their aim is clear. That is to produce, from within the question, a noun that the librarian thinks will bring success as a search term.

People learn, through carrying out long and frustrating searches, what it is to have chosen the wrong term. Only experience can improve their judgment as to what are "likely" nouns on which to search. We have three suggestions for answering factual questions:

- It may be misleading to ask what the question is "about." It is "about" the unknown (i.e., the answer) as well as the known. Look to the known—the most specific, explicit noun the question contains and anything to be inferred from it and from the rest of the question—for a clue as to how to proceed to an index and the answer. Personal knowledge will of course sometimes supply additional clues that are not strictly inferable from the question.
- It may also be unwise to say, "This question is on such-and-such a topic," and then start pulling down works on that topic. Instead, ask: "If I extract a noun from this question, what works can I enter with it? What works have indexes or arrangements that allow me to look up nouns like this one?"
- Last, ask: "What do I want the work to do with respect to the noun once I'm past the index?"

Works vary as to what the nouns in their indexes (or indexical arrangements) refer.

We can put into different classes the different types of objects referred to by nouns. The names of these classes may be used to designate an important part of the structure of reference works. They tell, by referent, the kinds of nouns with which a work may—and may not—be entered; for example, nouns naming people or places or events.

The names of these classes also tell, by referent, the kinds of nouns from *questions* with which a work may—and may not—be entered. In other words, they can be used to classify search terms.

If index terms and search terms can be classed under identical headings, we have the beginning of a language that mediates between questions and the works that may answer them.

As noted above, one hopes the search terms will be indexed verbatim somewhere in the collection. But we do not want to search the whole collection each time an answer is sought; that would be absurdly wasteful of time. We want only those works whose index terms are in the same class as our search term; the rest we ignore. (For example, if one is looking for the founding date of Liberia, one ignores all works that cannot be entered with the name of a place.) Once we have created the classes that permit this match, we may develop other parts of our language that express other specifications, so that the works that meet all our specifications will be comparatively few.

As noted, we call our initial classes "entry points." Many reference works can be entered with index terms naming relatively clear-cut things, such as:

- Persons
- Organizations (corporate bodies)
- Places
- Artworks
- Products
- Events
- Temporal periods (years, eras, etc.)
- Languages
- Words.

Classes of less clear-cut entities from the Berkeley implementation were:

- Living objects
- Nonliving objects
- Human procedures
- Natural processes
- Laws
- Occupational fields
- Concepts.

In the present implementation of Refsearch it seems wise to start with the first group of entry points because they are reasonably easy for patrons to grasp without lengthy scope notes. All of the second group require rather lengthy glosses. For instance, Concepts are glossed as ideas named by words or phrases, rather than Words in the strict sense. Examples of Concepts (as defined at Berkeley) are T. S. Eliot's "objective correlative," Max Weber's "routinization of charisma," and abstract idea-systems such as "Marxism" or "Christianity." Some reference works deal with Concepts, and we must accommodate them eventually, but it is hard to distinguish them from the Words entry point without a short philosophical disquisition. Hence we will concentrate initially on the first group of entry points in the Drexel implementation.

After choosing an entry point, the searcher is asked to specify whether the entry term is a proper or common noun, whether the referent of the noun is real or imaginary, and so on, as needed. (Persons, Organizations, and Living Objects have their own further qualifiers.) Such qualifiers are not only derivable from search terms, but useful in characterizing the index terms in actual reference works. They help us divide the collection into sets of works to which the terms do or do not apply.

In making these distinctions, the searcher is partitioning potential sources of the answer into smaller and smaller groups. The better able to partition one is, the smaller the final number of works for examination. For example, comparatively few works in the general collection are enterable with names of imaginary beings, such as Othello, Pegasus, or Yggdrasil.

Works vary in what they do once the searcher is past the index.

In addition to analyzing works in terms of entry points, we can analyze them in terms of typical services they regularly perform once they have been entered with a particular noun or noun phrase. Works may:

- Identify
- Discuss
- Locate
- Date
- Evaluate
- Quantify
- Chronicle
- Give financial data.

If we know how these services are defined, we can often infer from a question what service a work must perform to provide an answer. Services are to entry points as output to input: We go in with a certain noun—the name of something—and come out with a one or more facts about it as a result of the service the reference work provides. It has been identified, or discussed, or located, or dated, and so on. The work must perform the service dependably (that is, for all or most of the items it covers)—to be coded positively on it.

A special class of reference works performs services with respect to Words (entities in quotation marks to show we are not using them in the ordinary way). Reference works enterable with Words may:

- Define
- Give pronunciation
- Give etymology
- Give synonyms
- Give usage
- Translate abbreviations
- Translate slang.

and so on; the list is not exhaustive. "Word books" such as dictionaries and thesauri can be easily handled with Refsearch, and we will include a number of them in the works chosen for the test bed.

Finally, we included terms for a number of "Special Services" that bring out useful question-answering features of a few works in any reference collection. These include provision of portraits, diagrams, and maps; provision of bibliographic data (writings by or writings about a person); provision of comparative and superlative ratings (to characterize, e.g., *The Guinness Book of World Records*); provision of genealogical tables, full texts of documents, and so on.

Combining services and entry points, we can build syntactical statements about works.

The Refsearch language lends itself to the creation of grammatical English statements, which makes it fairly easy to work with. A service will usually be related to an entry point as a transitive verb to a direct object. For example:

SUBJECT	VERB	DIRECT OBJECT
Work (Unknown)	*Service (Known)*	*Entry Point (Known)*
?	Identifies	Persons
?	Evaluates	Artworks
?	Dates	Events
?	Locates	Places
?	Locates	Persons

The grammatical subject of the sentence names what is unknown to the user—the source(s) of an answer. We want to use the two known elements to find this unknown. But by themselves the two knowns may apply to a large number of works, some of which we wish to rule out. We will, if possible, exclude them by adding further specifications to the string. Presumably some works that meet our first two specifications will fail to meet a later one. In relation to the "sentence" we are constructing, later specifications "qualify" or "delimit" the entry point.

Imagine, for example, that a searcher is trying to answer the question, "What do critics now think of *A Streetcar Named Desire*?" Assuming that someone knows this to be an American play of the late 1940s, the Refsearch sentence would be:

SUBJECT	VERB	ADJECTIVES(S)	DIRECT OBJECT	PREPOSITIONAL PHRASES
Work	*Service*	*Qualifiers*	*Entry Point*	*Delimiters*
?	Evaluates	Proper-name	Artworks	in Theater in U.S.A. in 1941–50 as of 1980–

The so-called "delimiters" include subcollection fields, geographical and chronological controls, and recency of publication of the reference work. These may not be known; if not, they may be omitted and the search is based on whatever is known. In that case, the list of sources retrieved may simply be larger because the search statement was less constrained.

"Subcollections" are broad subject groupings within a reference collection. (We would call them "subjects," but that is easy to confuse with the *grammatical* subjects of sentences that we also write of in presenting Refsearch.) In the Berkeley implementation we named about 20 subcollections—for example, Theater, Business, Sports, Politics, Medicine, Literature, Chemistry. In the Drexel implementation we may use a modified version of the main subject divisions of Sheehy's *Guide to Reference Books* (those with two-letter codes). Works are permitted to be in more than one subcollection.

"Geographic Controls" are the geographic boundaries beyond which a work does not refer, or enclosing an area in which the work has subject coverage. They are confined to a short list, based on literary warrant: USA, Canada, UK, Multinational, Continents, and World.

"Time Span" reflects the chronological coverage of the work, ranging from Antiquity through the modern centuries (named individually) through specific recent years (for yearbooks—e.g., 1981).

"Recency," on the other hand, reflects when the work was published. Thus a work may have been published in 1985 but deal with Antiquity.

Perhaps the most interesting thing about this scheme is that it builds in a syntax that derives from the syntax of normal English sentences. The attributes jointly constitute a faceted classification scheme for reference works. Familiar syntactical relationships seem the best way of linking the facets together. Given a string of terms naming attributes, it is not hard to cast them as a sentence, such as "What works *identify organizations* in *politics* in the *USA* in the *19th century*?" This syntactical element makes the terms and relations of the scheme easier to grasp and remember than if "random" order prevailed.

We further hold that Refsearch partitions a collection by a process much like a real reference librarian's. A good librarian runs through facets like those of Refsearch with the speed of thought. We are deliberately forcing the thought into slow motion so that the novice learns a method of searching step-by-step. Heretofore, in reference work as both practiced and taught, the method has been implicit. We are making it explicit—projecting it on a screen, so to speak—so that even those without serendipity as reference librarians can see what they need to do.

Incidentally, they are not shown what to do by librarians' standard tools, which do not function like Refsearch. For example, while entry-point information may be *present* in descriptions of reference works in Sheehy, Winchell, Walford, and so on, it is not *indexed* there so as to be a searchable attribute. Those well-known compendia are searchable only in conventional ways—by author, title, subject, and (to some degree) form and genre classes. Also not indexed in them are the routine services that reference works perform, or the other Refsearch facets. Refsearch thus nicely complements the standard tools.

Refsearch as an actualized language consists of all statements it has been used to make about reference works.

Refsearch terms are not complete in discrete, "thesaurus" form, but only when they have been cast in sentences to describe reference works. These descriptions of course should be true. Figure 5.1 gives four presumably true statements about a well-known reference work, the *Dictionary of American Biography*.

If not precisely true, Refsearch statements should be at least reasonably accurate, since coding for "certainty factors" admits of degrees of truth. For example, it is possible to include a work "truly" in a subcollection, such as Literature, by coding it as 1.00, and to exclude it "truly" by coding it as 0. The *Oxford Companion to American Literature* presumably would rate a 1.00; the *Handbook of Chemistry and Physics*, a 0. But one can also assign a work *partially* to the Literature subcollection—or to any value—by giving it a decimal fraction. For example, the *Encyclopedia Britannica*, which has many articles on writers and literature, might rate a 0.6 and *Who's Who*, which includes writers, might rate a 0.3. Another example: *Brewer's Dictionary of Phrase and Fable* should not be coded 1.00 on Imaginary Persons as an entry point, but it does contain some, and might rate a 0.6 as a possible source. Thus, works receiving certainty factors between 1.00 and 0 would not be excluded from retrievals; they would simply be ranked lower than works coded 1.00.

Subject	Verb	Adjective(s)	Direct Object	Prepositional Phrases
Work	**Service**	**Qualifiers**	**Entry Point**	**Delimiters**
DAB	Identifies	Real, Dead, Proper-name	Persons	in U.S.A. in 16th Century in 17th Century in 18th Century in 19th Century in 1901–10 in 1911–20 in 1921–30 in 1931–40 as of 1950
DAB	Discusses	"	"	"
DAB	Dates	"	"	"
DAB	Evaluates	"	"	"

Figure 5.1. Refsearch Analysis of *Dictionary of American Biography.*

QUESTION AND ANSWER: AN EXTENDED EXAMPLE

Suppose someone asks, "What is Linus Pauling's address?"

Here the patron starts with a "known"—the proper name of a person, Linus Pauling—and uses it as an index term to start the search for an "unknown," an address. Jahoda and Braunagel (1980) call these, respectively, a "given" and a "wanted." Mary Whouley, one of the originators of Refsearch at Berkeley, called the "known" or "given" a *handle*—a noun or noun phrase that can be extracted from a question and used to enter an index. It was her insight that reference works can be systematically coded on the types of nouns with which they can be entered.

We note in passing that as yet there is no algorithmic way to extract handles from questions. While human beings can usually do it well, no one, as far as we know, has programmed a computer to imitate their processes. For example, given the question, "How did Senator George Murphy of California vote on the Gun Control Bill of 1968?" it is not clear how persons reject "Senator George Murphy" and "California" in favor of "Gun Control Bill of 1968" as the initial noun phrase on which to search. General principles by which to extract good search terms from questions would, of course, be a major breakthrough in information retrieval, not to mention cognitive science.

To return to the Pauling question, the Refsearch translation would be: What works *locate real, living, proper-name persons* in *chemistry* in the *USA*? (The fact that Pauling is a living American chemist is presumed to be known to the questioner or the librarian. If it were not known, one could still ask for all works that *locate real, proper-name persons* without further qualification.)

Key words in this translation are entered into the computer, and it responds with the names of reference books that are positively coded on them. The search requires works that can be entered with proper names of persons who are living (as opposed to dead) and real (as opposed to imaginary). This alone partitions any reference collection into a relatively small subset. (For example, it rules out *Dictionary of American Biography*, which deals only with dead persons.) Further, the search requires that the reference work locate the person; again this partitions, because not all reference works enterable with living persons' names contain addresses. Finally, we constrain the search to persons in a particular subject field (chemistry) and a particular geographic locale (USA). By now the reference collection is partitioned to the point where only a few sources fill the bill—for example, *National Faculty Directory* or *American Men and Women of Science*. If no sources emerge, constraints such as the subject field can be dropped, thereby retrieving works not subject-specific, such as *Who's Who in America*.

The Pauling question, and indeed all questions when translated into Refsearch, are more or less elaborated forms of the basic "inverted file query" on a database in matrix form, as described in Martin (1977). Abstractly, that query is "What entity E has a value equal to V on attribute A?" The answer can consist of more than one entity, characterized by values on more than one attribute. The values will be implicitly or explicitly linked by Boolean operators, in this case AND. We specifically ask: What entities (in this case, books) have nonzero coding on the following italicized values: Service = *locates* AND Qualifiers = *real* AND *living* AND *proper-name* AND Entry Point = *persons* AND Subcollection = *chemistry* AND Geographic Control = *USA*?

With this input we retrieve the primary key for each record—that is, the title of the reference work, which is its unique identifier. Additionally, we would retrieve and print out its call number.

In summary, we envision a patron with a question about a known entity (a person, place, etc.) being led by computer prompts and menus to create a sentence that describes a work that may answer the question. The work can be entered with that kind of entity as an index term, performs a service suitable to answer the question, and meets any other specifications (geographical, chronological, etc.) that the patron sets. The computer will respond to the sentence by printing out all works meeting the search criteria, along with their call numbers, so that the patron can go to them on the shelves.

REFERENCES

Benson, J., & Maloney, R. K. (1975). Principles of searching. *RQ, 14*, 316–320.

Jahoda, G., & Braunagel, J. S. (1980). *The librarian and reference queries*. New York: Academic Press.

Level Five Research, Inc. (1986). *Insight 2 + reference manual*. Version 1.1. Indialantic, FL.

Maron, M. E., & Sherman, D. (1971). *An information processing laboratory for education and research in library science: Phase II* (ERIC document ED 060916). Berkeley: University of California, Institute of Library Research.

Martin, J. (1977). *Computer data-base organization* (2nd ed.). Englewood Cliffs, NJ: Prentice-Hall.

* Meredith, J. C. (1971a). *Reference search system (REFSEARCH) users' manual* (ERIC document ED 060918). Berkeley: University of California, Institute of Library Research.

* Meredith, J. C. (1971b). Machine-assisted approach to general reference materials. *Journal of the American Society for Information Science, 22*, 176–186.

* Meredith, J. C. (1981). Reference collection management. *The Reference Librarian, 1–2*, 69–72.

Mignon, E. (1971). Information science in the teaching of general reference service. *Proceedings of the American Society for Information Science, 8*, 143–146.

Roysdon, C., & White, H. D. (Eds.). (1989). *Expert systems in reference services*. New York: Haworth Press. (Also published as *The Reference Librarian, 23*.)

Thomas, D. M., Hinckley, A. T., & Eisenbach, E. R. (1981). *The effective reference librarian*. New York: Academic Press.

Wyer, J. (1930). *Reference work; a textbook for students of library work and librarians*. Chicago: American Library Association.

* Note: J. C. Meredith supervised the Refsearch project as an employee of the Institute of Library Research, University of California at Berkeley. However, none of the design of the Refsearch system at Berkeley was his. The originator of the ILR project was Mary Whouley (deceased), aided in 1968–69 by Edith Darknell and Howard D. White. White took over the project during April–September 1969 and created the intellectual entity reported in Meredith's publications. For example, four-fifths of the Refsearch Users' Manual (Meredith, 1971a) is White's verbatim and the rest paraphrases his spoken and written accounts. White intends to continue Refsearch as his own system in the future.

6
Implementation of Reference Models in Expert Systems*

James R. Parrott
The Library
University of Waterloo, Ontario

INTRODUCTION

This chapter begins by examining some concepts and techniques from the field of artificial intelligence (AI). It then describes briefly four reference-consultation expert systems. Next, it considers several theories of the reference process, and examines how certain features of the theories have been implemented in the four systems using the previously presented AI concepts and techniques. The analysis concludes with a list of suggestions for future development, emphasizing work on theoretical features that have been implemented only partially or not at all in the four systems described.

ARTIFICIAL INTELLIGENCE APPLICATIONS IN INFORMATION SYSTEMS

Linda C. Smith (1980) provided the following conceptual framework for studying artificial intelligence (AI) applications in information systems: pattern recognition, knowledge representation, problem solving, and learning by the system. Below, we shall discuss these four areas briefly.

Pattern Recognition

Pattern recognition involves determining that an object with a particular set of features belongs to some class. It is convenient to separate the process into two stages. In the first, a *feature selector* determines the values for a small set of features that characterize the object being scrutinized. Suppose, for example,

* Thanks are due to Linda Leger for her detailed comments and suggestions on this chapter.

that the object were a bibliographic reference. If the set included features such as "first piece of the reference," "second piece," and so on, then the values might be "author," "date," and so on, respectively, depending on the reference in question. In the second stage of pattern recognition, a *classifier* designates the object as a member of a particular class. In our example, the bibliographic reference might be assigned to the class of "periodical articles" or "technical reports." (A system called a "citation interpreter" that performs this sort of pattern recognition will be described in Chapter 9.) Smith pointed out that dividing a pattern recognition process into two stages has the advantage of separating the aspects of a problem that depend on subject matter (those handled by the feature selector) from those that do not (those handled by the classifier). In our example, this means the separation of semantic decisions, for example, about whether a piece is an author or a title, from decisions about class membership, for example, whether a reference is to a book or journal article.

Knowledge Representation

In order for an artificial intelligence system to function, it requires one or more bodies of knowledge, and it must have some way of representing that knowledge in computer form. The *Handbook of Artificial Intelligence* (Barr, Cohen, & Feigenbaum, 1981) considered several representation schemes, including semantic networks, production systems, and frames. Semantic networks employ nodes (representing objects, concepts and events) and links (representing their interrelations). They are especially useful in situations where the reasoning is based on a rather complex taxonomy. Production systems, by contrast, represent knowledge through rules (or productions) stating that if a particular condition holds, then a particular action should be performed. An example might be, "If a client is looking for a definition, then a dictionary or encyclopedia is a good place to start." These systems have the advantages that the conditions of applicability are explicit in the rules themselves, and that the knowledge embodied in one rule can be added to the system or deleted without affecting knowledge in other rules. Production systems are often used to represent knowledge about how people perform practical tasks; this is usually the case with expert systems. Finally, frames represent knowledge through frameworks of concepts that experience leads us to consider typical of certain situations. A framework will have "slots" for each concept that it considers typical of a given situation. Whether or not a slot is filled in depends on whether the concept has had a value assigned to it yet. They are particularly useful for representing expectations about objects or sequences of events, and are therefore helpful in processing natural language. Smith pointed out that, although the same knowledge can be represented using different schemes, the choice of representation has a strong influence on the ability of the system to solve the problem.

Problem Solving

Smith divided the area of problem solving for information systems into two broad fields: heuristics and inference, and human-machine communication. Problem solving can be effected by using either algorithms, which are procedures that are guaranteed to find a solution given enough time, or heuristics, which are rules of thumb that are not guaranteed to solve the problem, but which often do so in a reasonable amount of time. She emphasized that heuristics are indispensible in information systems, since algorithms for search strategy do not exist. The same might be said of strategy for the reference interview. Smith suggested that an especially useful form of inference for solving problems in information systems might be pattern-directed inference, in which the recognition of patterns in the input data causes the system to perform some action. This clearly would require the implementation of heuristics as rules saying that if a pattern exists, then an action should be performed. She noted that this form of inference has been used in expert systems. (In the following sections, heuristic rules used in expert systems for handling the reference interview and the reference search will be examined in the context of reference theory.)

Artificial intelligence research in human-machine communication, on the other hand, is aimed at making the system appear less rigid by providing an explanation facility, natural-language processing (to allow variations in acceptable input), and speech understanding (to keep track of what the conversation is about). Providing information systems with these sorts of enhancements is a promising area of research.

Learning by the System

Smith distinguished between short-term learning (in which the system modifies its responses to a particular user making a query) and long-term learning (in which the system makes an overall modification to its knowledge representation and heuristics based on the queries of many users). She found the approach of Elaine Rich to short-term learning particularly interesting. Rich (1979) set up a system, GRUNDY, that fits a particular user into a stereotype based on a small amount of information obtained from the user. GRUNDY then uses this information to suggest novels that the user might want to read. Rich's work has since formed the basis for a field called user modeling. P. J. Daniels (1986) provided an excellent review of its applications in information systems. Smith indicated, however, that long-term learning by information systems had received relatively little attention. She recommended that, if information systems were to gather statistics on searches, they might be able to form models of typical search techniques. Comparing these models with those of correct and efficient search techniques could generate a set of common mistakes, for which the system could watch and, if detected, could give advice.

EXPERT SYSTEMS FOR THE REFERENCE PROCESS

Many of the concepts discussed above—for example, pattern recognition, heuristic rules, semantic networks, natural-language processing and user modeling—have been explored in the development of reference-oriented expert systems in the past few years. In the present section, some brief information will be given on four such systems: ORA, POINTER, ANSWERMAN, and PLEXUS. The succeeding sections look at several theories of the reference process and examine how elements of those theories are implemented in these expert systems through the use of the above-mentioned AI concepts.

ORA (Online Reference Assistance) is a system developed at the University of Waterloo Library by a team of librarians (Parrott, 1986). Intended to simulate the services of an academic reference librarian for questions of low and medium level, it uses several technologies: a videotex-like database, computer-assisted instruction modules, and expert systems. Like other systems, it gives help in performing subject searches, but it also gives considerable assistance in tracking down publications for which the reference is already known. Perhaps its most interesting feature is an expert system called a "citation interpreter" that uses pattern-recognition principles to interpret bibliographic references and to help library clients fill out interlibrary loan forms. More information is given in Chapter 9.

POINTER is a system developed by Karen F. Smith (1986) at the Library of the State University of New York, Buffalo for aiding library clients in locating U.S. federal government publications. POINTER points to reference tools that will help the user find both specific publications and publications on a particular subject. It uses menus to narrow down the type of question being asked. In addition, it allows the user to enter a date to specify the time period of interest, when appropriate.

The National Agricultural Library, Beltsville, Maryland has developed an expert system called ANSWERMAN (Waters, 1986) to help library clients find answers to ready-reference questions. It uses a series of menus to narrow down the subject of the question and the type of tool needed (directory, encyclopedia, atlas, and so on). It has the capability of attaching estimates of confidence to its recommendations. Moreover, it can function as either a consultation system or as a front end to external online databases and CD-ROM reference tools.

PLEXUS is a system developed at the Central Information Service, University of London by Alina Vickery and Helen M. Brooks (1987) as a referral tool for use in public libraries. It is an ambitious creation incorporating several types of knowledge, including knowledge about the reference process, information retrieval, certain subject areas, reference sources, and library users. The system uses various forms of knowledge representation to handle these different kinds of knowledge: heuristic rules, frames, and semantic networks. It is notable for its inclusion of user modeling and its sophisticated deployment of natural language processing, frames, and semantic networks for handling the reference interview for subject queries. Although the subject domain is limited to gardening for the prototype phase, it is intended to be broadened in the second phase of development.

THEORY AND IMPLEMENTATION OF THE REFERENCE INTERVIEW

In a survey of the literature on the reference interview, Charles A. Bunge (1984) identified one of the most influential models of the reference interview put forward in the past two decades as that of Robert S. Taylor (1968). Bunge also pointed to an article by Geraldine B. King (1972) placing the Taylor model in the context of counseling techniques, as well as interesting alternatives to the Taylor model proposed by Mary Jo Lynch (1978), and Marilyn Domas White (1983).

Filters for Question Clarification

Taylor (1968) proposed five "filters" that help the librarian gather the information required in the clarification process. These five filters and their implementations in various reference consultation systems will be described briefly.

The first filter is devoted to determining the subject. It appears that most reference consultation systems have included some implementation of this filter. ANSWERMAN and ORA have implemented this filter using a series of menus. PLEXUS has employed instead a natural-language interface that uses semantic networks and frames. POINTER uses menus, except to determine the date, which the user types in.

The second examines the motivation and objective of the user. In some reference consultation systems, for example, ORA, this filter is implemented through a menu asking what kind of publication the user is preparing (short essay, term paper, thesis, and so on). PLEXUS, on the other hand, appears to deduce the motivation and objective of the user from the information gathered in the next of Taylor's filters, described below.

With the third filter, the librarian forms a model of the user, which covers such variables as previous library experience, subject background in the search area, thoroughness, frustration level, and so on. The field of user modeling is still rather new. PLEXUS is apparently the first reference consultation system to implement user modeling.

In the fourth filter, the librarian attempts to redefine the question so that it takes account of the way that information is organized in the library. (This filter overlaps with the process of constructing search strategy, as we shall see later.) ORA implements this fourth filter in answering subject-search questions by a sequence of menus. For example, one menu indicates that brief and introductory information (which can give some idea of what to expect later in the search) tends to be found in dictionaries, encyclopedias, and handbooks. The user is then asked whether this kind of information is desired. PLEXUS implements this filter by performing the search, and then indicating to the user the number of postings for each of the following categories: reference tools, organization names, databases, and human experts. The user is next asked to choose which categories are of interest.

Finally, the fifth filter is designed to determine the kind of answer that the user will accept. Although the user may have begun with clear ideas about acceptable amounts and types of information, these ideas may be altered by the time the fifth filter is reached. For example, the user may have learned that the search will be more difficult and time-consuming than originally expected. This filter is implemented indirectly in ORA by annotating suggested reference tools to indicate, for example, that one index is easy to use, but not comprehensive, whereas another is comprehensive but difficult to use. The user is then asked to choose which tools are of interest (all may be chosen).

Open and Closed Questions

King (1972) extended Taylor's model of the reference interview by suggesting that the first three filters (the subject, the motivation, and the user's characteristics) be negotiated by asking the user general "open" questions, in which the user is encouraged to talk about the information request. In order to simulate open questioning, it is necessary to add a natural-language interface at the appropriate points in the system. PLEXUS has done this for the first filter, the subject, by using an ingenious complex of semantic networks and frames. Because of the amount of time required for such a venture and also the indication in the literature (Lynch, 1978, p. 135) that only a fraction of reference questions may actually require open questioning, it was decided not to do this for the first version of ORA. King proposed that the last two filters (the relationship between the request and the library's file structure, and also the form and amount of information required) could be adequately handled by asking the user "closed" specific questions, in which the user has to choose among alternatives. Closed questions can be simulated by asking the user to choose from menus. All four systems surveyed use this technique for all the filters that they implement, with the exception noted above—that PLEXUS uses a natural language interface for the first Taylor filter.

Category Schemes for Reference Transactions

In a study of the reference interview in public libraries, Lynch (1978) adopted the following classification of transactions at the reference desk:

1. Directional (locations and services within a library)
2. Holdings (attempts to determine whether a library owns a specific item)
3. Substantive (factual information, complex subject searches, bibliographic verification)
4. Moving (type of transaction undergoes a change).

Lynch gave two category schemes for the reference interview (instead of Taylor's single set of filters), one for substantive transactions and one for holdings transactions.

Her categories for substantive transactions have many similarities to the Taylor filters, which were designed exclusively to handle substantive requests. Category 1, "subject definition," corresponds to Taylor's first filter. Category 2, "fact gathering," is similar to Taylor's second filter (motivation) but also includes some elements of his first filter. Category 3, "answer specification," is an interesting elaboration in (eight subcategories) of Taylor's fifth filter (acceptable answers). Subcategory (g), level of difficulty, might also be considered related to Taylor's third filter (user characteristics). Lynch's Category 4, "action taken," marks a significant departure from the Taylor filters. It examines the prior action that the user has taken in trying to answer the question. (It should be noted that subcategory (a), whether the user has ever used a specific tool before, might also fall under Taylor's third filter.) We see the beginning of an implementation of Category 4 in PLEXUS when its user-modeling facility asks, "Is this the first time you've asked anyone about the gardening problem you've got at the moment?"

Lynch's categories for holdings transactions are a major innovation; the Taylor filters, and consequently the King extension, do not apply to these transactions. Indeed, Lynch's article is one of few on the reference interview to take the holdings transaction seriously. She recognized that it is not so complex a transaction as the substantive transaction, but that it is an important function of reference service. Category 1, "bibliographic description," requests bibliographic details, spelling clarification, and source of information. The first of these subcategories is implemented in ORA's citation interpreter, an expert system using pattern recognition. Category 2, "function," asks what information is wanted and whether a different item might be useful. Category 3, "action taken," asks about prior actions taken in trying to find the item. Category 4, "location requirement," asks whether the user wants a circulating copy. Category 5, "other," asks if the user has had experience with the required item before. The last four categories do not yet appear to have been implemented.

Human Information Processing and Frames

White (1983) developed a theoretical model of the reference encounter that included concepts from the field of human information processing, especially the theory of frames, which embody expectations about certain situations that might occur. White indicated, for example, that a librarian might have a frame for clients in general. It would include a category having to do with the client's motivation (thus corresponding to Taylor's second filter). This category could have a default value (such as "writing a paper") and a procedure to ask the client how the information is to be used (which might alter the default value). The client would also have a set of frames for expectations about a reference encounter. Finally librarian and client would each have a "master frame" to structure the use of their set of frames for the reference encounter.

The theory that White proposed is obviously capable of incorporating devices such as the Taylor filters. It distinguishes itself from other theories of the reference process by its emphasis on considering the cognitive processes of not only the librarian but also the client. (As mentioned above, PLEXUS implements this kind of cognitive modeling.) But the White model also considers details of the interaction between librarian and client as they develop a common information base that will guide the search. It truly attempts to model the entire process. The implications of creating a knowledge base covering the entire reference process are explored by Parrott (1988), who concludes that such a knowledge base could be used to drive not only an expert system for client consultation, but also various intelligent computer-assisted instruction (ICAI) systems for both client and librarian.

THEORY AND IMPLEMENTATION OF THE REFERENCE SEARCH

An extensive review of research concerning the interaction of users with information systems and with skilled intermediaries to those systems has recently been authored by Nicholas J. Belkin and Alina Vickery (1985). In Chapter 7, *Search Strategy*, they devoted several pages to a consideration of search techniques, usually as handled by a skilled intermediary. Most of the literature that they reviewed applies mainly to situations in which:

1. The librarian has direct access to printed or online versions of various bibliographic files or source documents.
2. A computer intermediary has direct (or "front-end") access to such online files. (ANSWERMAN has this sort of front-end access to external online databases. Constructing expert systems that can also act as front ends to online catalogs, offsite databases, or CD-ROM databases promises to be an

exciting area of research.) Most of this literature concentrates on the proper choice of search terms to be used with particular files, and is not concerned with the preliminary step of choosing the files.

Some of the literature does, however, consider in detail the preliminary process of choosing the appropriate bibliographic files or source documents, a task that does not necessarily require direct access to external online databases. Because most expert reference systems (with the notable exception of ANSWERMAN) do not yet include front-end capabilities, only the latter search task, choosing appropriate tools, will be examined further here. The work of William A. Katz (1982) and Marcia J. Bates (1979) will be examined below as contributions to this literature.

Translation Devices

Katz (1982) provided an eight-step search process for reference questions. Although simple ready-reference questions usually require only the first two steps, more complex ready-reference questions and complex subject searches are likely to require the entire sequence. The first step is essentially an extension of the reference interview, in which the data gathered is used to determine the type of question. The second step involves translating the type of question into characteristics of the information system. Perhaps the most important such "translation devices" are procedures in the librarian's memory that link the type of question to forms of information sources. An example is a link from a request for an address to types of information sources like directories. In steps 3 and 4, Katz indicates that, if the question is sufficiently complex that these techniques are not useful, then appropriate sources will have to be determined by using bibliographical aids such as the catalog, bibliographies, indexes, and so on. (Presumably appropriate bibliographical aids are determined using links of the type suggested in step 2.) Further steps in the process require the actual consultation of information sources. They deal with negotiating the subject vocabularies and modifying or terminating the search based on the information found.

Translation devices of the type used in determining sources in the first four steps of the Katz model must be part of the heuristic rule structure for any reference-consultation system, since the latter must necessarily link the naive user's request with a library structure that the user does not necessarily understand. These devices are clearly used, explicitly or implicitly, in ORA, POINTER, ANSWERMAN, and PLEXUS.

Search Tactics

In her study, Bates (1979) labeled, defined, and grouped 29 search tactics into four categories: monitoring tactics, file structure tactics, search formulation tactics, and term tactics. We will examine five of those search tactics that are concerned with the choice of appropriate tools. They are labeled PATTERN, STRETCH, SCAFFOLD, WEIGH, and SORT.

To PATTERN is to recognize and use a pattern of search (e.g., the consultation of particular types of tool) that frequently helps with a certain kind of request. This corresponds to the Katz translation device mentioned above. To STRETCH is to use a source for a purpose that it was not intended. It seems that this can be considered a variation on "to PATTERN." All the expert reference systems under consideration appear to use heuristic rules based on PATTERN or STRETCH tactics.

To SCAFFOLD is to consult tools that will not themselves give the answer, but will give additional information that can be taken to other tools that will give the answer. This tactic can be considered in some sense a "second-order" heuristic procedure. Heuristic rules based on SCAFFOLD tactics apparently have not been used in any of the systems surveyed. It should be noted, nonetheless, that computing these SCAFFOLD pathways by matching the output values of one tool to the input values of another tool is the sort of thing that an expert system could handle more easily and consistently than a human intermediary. (Heuristic rules of this type will be considered in more detail in a later publication.)

To WEIGH is to assess the effectiveness and efficiency of using a particular procedure (e.g., a type of tool) to solve the problem. Each procedure is thereby assigned a weight. Finally, to SORT means to arrange those procedures according to the weights assigned them, in order to decide which sources to begin with and how far to go. Heuristic rules that perform functions similar to these WEIGH and SORT tactics are not uncommon in expert systems in general. WEIGH tactics are possible in ANSWERMAN, due to the provision there of factors representing the degree of confidence that an expert would have in finding the answer in a particular tool.

FUTURE PROSPECTS

From the analysis in the foregoing sections, it is clear that some features of the reference theories under consideration have been implemented only partially or not at all. The more important of these deserve examination in future research on reference-consultation systems. It is therefore suggested that:

1. More emphasis be placed on user modeling
2. More attention be given to determining acceptable answers (e.g., by implementing details of Lynch's Category 3 for substantive questions)
3. An attempt be made to deal with the problem of prior action by the user (see Lynch, 1978)

4. More attention be given to handling holdings transactions (see Lynch again)
5. The Bates SCAFFOLD tactic be implemented
6. Greater use be made of her WEIGH and SORT tactics
7. The knowledge base also be used to drive ICAI systems for instructing both users and librarians
8. More effort be made to allow reference-consultation systems to act as front ends to online facilities, like online catalogs, online bibliographic databases, and CD-ROM reference tools.

It should be noted that the last suggestion above is crucial, for once a reference-consultation system has a direct interface to other online facilities, it becomes possible to explore the implementation of the entire spectrum of Bates search tactics, instead of being restricted to those for choosing appropriate tools. Eventually, this should result in a convergence of two disparate lines of research: the one concerned with reference-consultation systems and the other with expert front-ends for online databases. Systems resulting from the blending of techniques from these two areas of research could combine the breadth of reference-consultation systems (which can address any problem in reference service, not just that of aiding the searching of online databases) with the depth of expert front-ends for online databases (which can address the important problem of vocabulary negotiation). Systems like this would be able to function as intelligent interfaces between the user and all online library tools, in the same way that reference librarians act as intelligent interfaces between users and printed library tools, and search editors act as intelligent interfaces between users and online bibliographic databases.

REFERENCES

Bates, M. J. (1979, July). Information search tactics. *Journal of the American Society for Information Science, 30*, 205–214.

Belkin, N. J., & Vickery, A. (1985). *Interaction in information systems: A review of research from document retrieval to knowledge-based systems* (Library and Information Research Report 35). London: British Library Board. (A supplementary volume, subtitled *Bibliography of research*, was published as a set of 4 microfiche sheets as British Library Research and Development Report 5846.)

Bunge, C. A. (1984, Summer). Interpersonal dimensions of the reference interview: A historical review of the literature. *Drexel Library Quarterly, 20*, 4–23.

Daniels, P. J. (1986, December). Cognitive models in information retrieval: An evaluative review. *Journal of Documentation, 42*, 272–304.

Barr, A., Cohen, P. R., & Feigenbaum, E. A. (Eds.). (1981–1982). *Handbook of artificial intelligence* (three volumes). Los Altos, CA: William Kaufmann, Inc.

Katz, W. A. (1982). *Introduction to reference work*. New York: McGraw-Hill.

King, G. B. (1972, Winter). The reference interview. *RQ, 12*, 157–160.

Lynch, M. J. (1978, April). Reference interviews in public libraries. *Library Quarterly, 48*, 119–142.

Parrott, James R. (1986, September). Expert systems for reference work. *Microcomputers for Information Management, 3*, 155–171.

Parrott, J. R. (1988). Simulation of the reference process. *Reference Librarian, 21*, 189–207.

Rich, E. (1979). User modeling via stereotypes. *Cognitive Science, 3*, 329–354.

Smith, K. F. (1986, September). Robot at the reference desk? *College & Research Libraries, 47*, 486–490.

Smith, L. C. (1980). Artificial intelligence applications in information systems. *Annual Review of Information Science and Technology, 15*, 67–105.

Taylor, R. S. (1968, May). Question-negotiation and information seeking in libraries. *College & Research Libraries, 29*, 178–194.

Vickery, A., & Brooks, H. M. (1987). PLEXUS—the expert system for referral. *Information Processing and Management, 23*, 99–117.

Waters, S. T. (1986, September). Answerman, the expert information specialist: An expert system for retrieval of information from library reference books. *Information Technology and Libraries, 5*, 204–212.

White, M. D. (1983). The reference encounter model. *Drexel Library Quarterly, 19*, 38–55.

7

Intelligent Computer-Assisted Instruction

Connie V. Dowell
Reference Department Library
University of California
Santa Barbara, CA

Phillip Crews
Hypergraphics Corporation
Denton, TX

INTRODUCTION

The Role of Instruction in the Library

Libraries are inextricably linked with the educational process. In the most direct sense, librarians within academic institutions often teach courses in research methods and work closely with faculty members to integrate library instruction into various curricula (Farber, 1974). In addition, most academic libraries have a brief orientation for new students which may be little more than a guided tour. On an ongoing basis, librarians must instruct clients at the reference desk in a one-to-one situation.

Furthermore, all entering the profession require specialized courses of instruction (MLS degree plan). Hopefully librarians follow this with a variety of continuing education experiences (e.g., the acquisition of specialized database search skills) to more productively perform their responsibilities.

Information, the very focus of libraries, is taking new forms (cd roms, microforms, data files) and its organization and dissemination now also takes many forms.This is evidenced by the number of media and computer centers housed within libraries. Some libraries are building extensive collections of maps and satellite imagery and acquiring the equipment to use them. Within these centers are materials that are actively instructional as opposed to the more passive books and journals which leave the reader to make her or his own inferences about the content.

Computer-Assisted Instruction

As with other areas of society, computers are having a profound impact on the instructional process. A number of benefits for the libraries are derived from computer-assisted instruction (CAI). These include:

1. *Instruction is more available.* When instructional materials are automated, they become available while the computer system is operational, not only when the librarian is available (e.g., after the reference desk closes). This enables a client to receive instruction based on her or his schedule regardless of the librarian's hours.
2. *Instruction is more accessible.* Through automation, instruction sequences may be replicated throughout the library at various workstations. Then, a client could go to one of these different stations instead of competing with other clients for access to a single librarian.
3. *Instruction is more formalized.* Just as every researcher is not a good administrator, every librarian is not a good teacher. Automation can formalize the instructional process by integrating the subject matter expertise of the most knowledgeable librarians with the teaching expertise of instructional design experts. The client should benefit from the incorporation of sound instructional theory.
4. *Instruction is standardized.* Automation can guarantee consistent delivery of the information. This insures that clients have mastered a designated level of skills, and could be a foundation for advanced or specialized courses.
5. *Client/library benefit from self-paced instruction.* Whatever the subject matter, the client can control the pace of the instruction which impacts his or her level of comprehension. For example, a client may have difficulty assimilating certain information and may need to spend extra time with that material. If the material ordinarily would be presented by a librarian, that professional may not have enough time to spend with the client without neglecting other responsibilities or clients. Thus the library benefits when a client can be better educated without placing additional demands on existing staff.
6. *Client/library benefit from the instructional medium.* The computer affords a sophisticated medium for providing instruction. Complex graphics, animation, and color can enhance the client's understanding (e.g., a map of the library with an illustrated path to a desired source is better than a list of instructions). The library benefits from the electronic medium which can easily be modified (as information changes) and distributed.
7. *Reduced cost of instruction.* Over a long period it is possible to amortize the cost of developing computer-assisted instruction plus achieve better results. This improvement is measured in terms of client satisfaction and better use of the library's professional staff.
8. *Improved staff morale.* Beginning levels of instruction can be redundant, lack challenge, and use the time of professionals that could be more productive. Computers are quite adept at delivering instruction and are not subject to boredom or frustration when presenting redundant, less challenging materials.

While this list of benefits is not intended to be comprehensive, it argues favorably for the integration of computer-assisted instruction into the instructional services of the library. However, at this point CAI has not really fulfilled its potential. Only a few programs such as the University of Illinois (Axeen, 1968) and University of Denver (Culkin, 1972) have successfully designed computer-assisted instruction. Several books have summarized the research on computer-assisted instruction in libraries (Renford & Hendrickson, 1980; Oberman & Strauch, 1982). Some authors have blamed this on librarians and computers not having enough common understanding of the other's problems and abilities to undertake the in-depth research required to successfully design library CAI (Culkin & Walker, 1984). One recent development at the University of Waterloo (Parrott, 1986) may be a giant step toward that in-depth research. Using experts systems technology, libraries may be on the road to applying artificial intelligence to library instruction.

INTELLIGENT COMPUTER-ASSISTED INSTRUCTION

In the balance of this chapter, significant advances in CAI will be explored in terms of its "marriage" with artificial intelligence. This new generation of systems, often referred to as intelligent tutoring systems or intelligent CAI (ICAI), embodies a number of new technologies designed to further advance the beneficial properties of existing CAI systems. A brief survey of existing ICAI systems will be presented, as well as the relative strengths and weaknesses of the different approaches.

ICAI is best understood when it is contrasted with conventional forms of instruction, specifically classroom (lock step) and traditional CAI. In traditional classroom instruction, students are treated as having the same background, aptitude, and interest. Empirical evidence suggests that student achievement (higher test scores and retention) is improved with CAI and/or individualized instruction afforded by small group (less than 15) tutoring (Ragosta, Holland, & Jamison, 1979). With CAI most of the benefits derive from the fact that a student can control the pace or amount of time she or he spends on each instructional sequence. Thus students can "slow down" and focus on topics they consider difficult and move quickly through materials that are perceived as being easy. Still, CAI course materials contain only a limited number of "preprogrammed" paths of instruction to accommodate different performance levels and, indirectly, the differences in background, aptitude, and interest. Clearly, individualized instruction in the form of a one-to-one student/teacher ratio can account for these differences but it is not cost-effective (even if an adequate number of qualified teachers were available). ICAI systems try to imbue the traditional CAI course development and delivery process with the codified intelligence of subject matter experts, instructional designers, and courseware developments with the intent of modeling the student/tutor interaction.

The Tutor/Student Paradigm

Gable and Page (1980) enumerate the characteristics of a human tutor that one would wish to impart to a computer.

These include:

1. The tutor will cause the problem-solving heuristics of the student to converge to those of the tutor.
2. The tutor will learn and adopt student problem-solving methods if they are better.
3. The tutor chooses appropriate examples and problems for the student.
4. When the student needs help the tutor can recommend solution choices and provide examples of how to apply the different techniques.
5. The tutor can work arbitrary examples selected by the student.
6. The tutor is able to adjust to different aptitudes, background, and interests of each student.
7. The tutor is able to measure student progress.
8. The tutor can review previously covered material as required.
9. The tutor is able to immediately detect student errors and give assistance while, at the same time, not impeding the student's creativity in solving a problem.
10. Once the student has solved a problem, the tutor can recommend a better approach.

Clearly, few human tutors possess all of these characteristics and the same is true for existing ICAI systems. However, experimental systems have been developed that, in limited subject domains, exhibit one or more of the attributes listed above with the exception of number 2 (the ability to learn from the student) and the ability to communicate with students using free-form, natural-language input. Existing systems can solve the latter problem by restricting the vocabulary of discourse which the student can use to communicate with the system. Nonetheless, the most fundamental and important rule for good instruction is handled exceptionally well by ICAI systems. That is, a good instructor knows the subject matter that she or he will teach.

The Conceptual ICAI System

The conceptual architecture used as a basis for most ICAI systems is specified by Clancey, Barnett, and Cohen (1982). They have defined three main components that functionally characterize the operation of an ICAI application as it delivers instructional material to a student. The first component, the expertise module, contains the subject matter to be taught. The second component is the student module which contains the recorded information that describes the student's current understanding of the domain material. Analysis of this data helps to uncover those topics a student is failing to learn and the causes that might be responsible. Given these learning deficiencies, the system can develop a teaching strategy to overcome the problem. This is the responsibility of the third component of the ICAI system, the tutoring module. By adding a fourth component, the authoring module, the ICAI architecture is complete in that both course materials construction and delivery are represented. This latter component is essential when one considers productivity issues in dealing with courseware development. The architecture and the relationship of its components is depicted in Figure 7.1.

Due to the complexity of the issues involved in developing ICAI systems, few, if any, current programs exhibit all of the characteristics prescribed for these modules. Nonetheless, the ultimate goal of researchers in the area is to fully develop all of the modules in a coordinated way that provides the most effective learning environment.

The Expertise Module

The expertise module contains both the subject matter to be taught (facts or domain knowledge) and procedural knowledge capable of generating and solving problems within the domain of discourse. This latter capability is a major factor in differentiating ICAI from traditional CAI approaches because teaching capability is separated from the subject expertise to be taught. To facilitate an "understanding" of the subject matter sufficient to be able to teach it, a number of different techniques have been employed to organize and structure the domain knowledge. These include: (a) semantic nets used to generate questions and answers involving causal or relational reasoning among facts contained in large databases (Carbonell & Collins, 1973; Laubsch, 1975); (b) procedural experts that incorporate methods of deduction that correspond to subskills which collectively represent the complete skill being taught (Brown, Burton, & Bell, 1974); (c) production rules that are used to construct modular representations of skills and problem-solving methods (Goldstein & Carr, 1977); and (d) a mixed organizational strategy that incorporates different representations such as semantic nets for causal reasoning and simulation procedures (procedural experts) to validate student responses (Brown & Burton, 1978).

When considering the tutor/student paradigm, the expertise module can assist with: selecting appropriate examples and problems for the student; providing alternative or better solutions to problems; providing help in solving problems; working arbitrary problems selected by the student; and explaining its own problem-solving heuristics. Again, not all ICAI systems possess these capa-

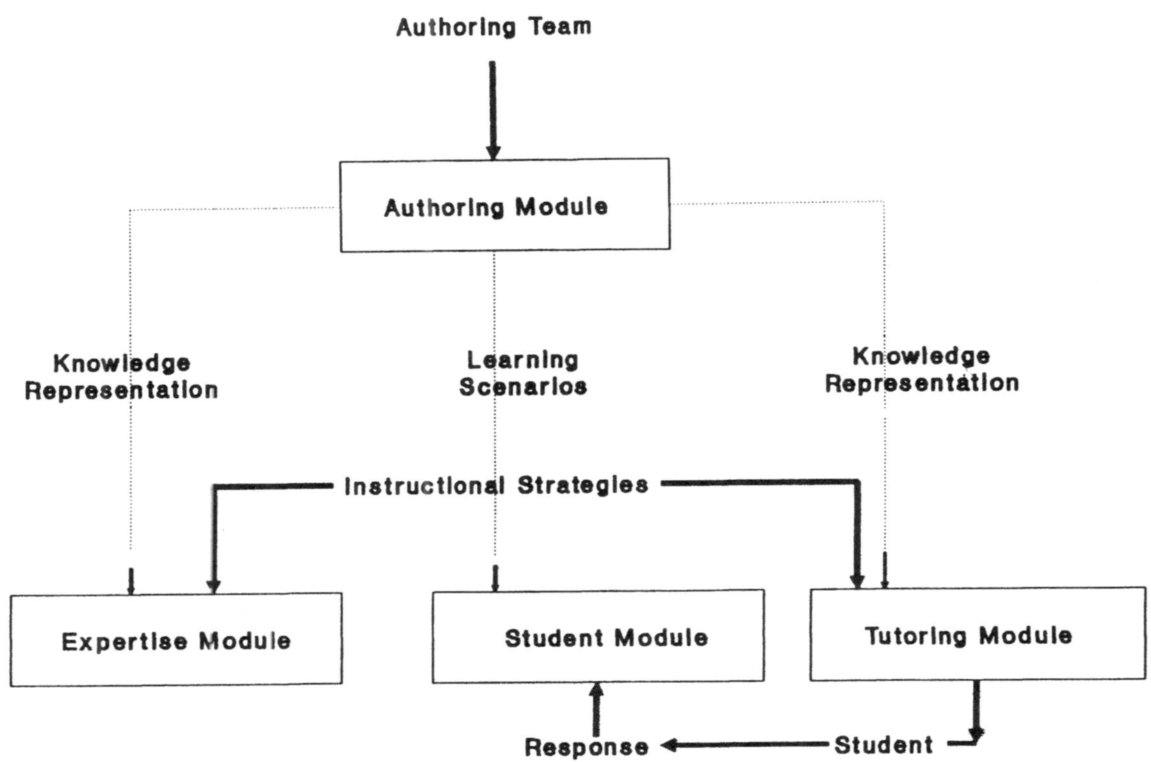

Figure 7.1 Conceptual ICAI System Architecture

bilities. For example, not all ICAI systems are articulate experts (those that can explain how they solved a problem).

In this case the ICAI system may use different problem-solving heuristics than those desirable to impart to the student, or the heuristics may not be sufficiently abstracted to be human intelligible. Nor can all ICAI systems solve all the problems they pose to the students. BIP (Barr, Beard, & Atkinson, 1975), the Basic Instructional Program, can teach programming techniques and use simple input/output pairs to evaluate the correctness of student programs, but it cannot synthesize or analyze programs.

In summary, the expertise module represents both the codified teaching strategy and subject matter data. Teaching and course information that must be codified includes the principles, rules, procedures, concepts, categories, and facts that define the knowledge required to teach a specific topic or set of topics. How this is accomplished profoundly influences the other components of the design. Knowledge representation will minimally influence the degree to which the system is generic (able to produce and deliver more than one specialized course), how adaptable and robust it is with regard to new authoring technology; and the general teaching philosophy of the system.

The Student Module

The student module is the component of the ICAI system that represents the current state of the student's understanding of the material being taught. With this information the system is able to make hypotheses about the student's performance, diagnose potential problems, and suggest corrective action. From the perspective of the tutor/student paradigm, this module enables the ICAI system to measure the student's progress and provide information so that the tutor can adjust to different student backgrounds, aptitudes, and interests.

The standard information for maintaining the student module is typically derived from a number of sources as opposed to the single question-response characteristic of traditional CAI systems. The different sources may be characterized as being either explicit, implicit, historical, or structural. Explicit information is solicited directly from a student through a consultation or test. Implict information is deduced by analyzing trends in student behavior over a period of time. Similarly, historical information contributes to an overall student profile that contains representation of a student's aptitude, background, and interests. This might include the student's preferred mode of interacting with the tutor, a general characterization of the student's level of ability, a list of previous areas of difficulty, and/or the student's objectives for taking the instruction. Finally, structural information describes attributes that characterize the various levels of difficulty for different instructional sequences.

The reasons for inadequate performance by a student are numerous and attempting to understand them is an active research question. In general, problems exhibited by a student may be cast into three categories. These include: misconceptions (overgeneralization, misfiled facts, missing information, etc.); learning abilities (understanding and following directions; language comprehension; and deductive skills) and attitudes (student's interest, initiative, and industriousness) (Gable & Page, 1980). To be completely successful, an ICAI system must deal with all three categories.

In diagnosing these problems early systems employed stochastic learning models but these proved to be inadequate (Laubsch, 1975). A more adequate model is formed when the system attempts to represent the student's knowledge as compared to that of the expert component of the ICAI system. In this approach, termed an overlay model, concepts (in the form of rules or entries in a semantic net) are marked when the system has confidence that the student understands the related material. Then, the measure of student understanding is cast as the difference between the expert model and that of the student (the marked versus unmarked rules) (Carr & Goldstein, 1977). In another approach (the "bug" model) the way in which a student model differs from the tutor is considered a deviation but not necessarily an error. In this approach the student is not presumed nor required to reason as the expert does.

As stated previously, a major characteristic that distinguishes ICAI from traditional CAI is the degree to which the system can adapt new approaches once a failed strategy has been uncovered. The development of a dynamic instructional strategy must be the product of informed judgment (a process which is improved by having more complete and reliable data upon which to make a decision). Typical CAI courseware is inflexible in this regard having only a few fixed strategies that it supports. ICAI, on the other hand, more flexibly develops learning strategies because it can better judge the reason that a particular strategy has failed and thus take more specific corrective action. Learning scenarios are incorporated for this reason; to provide tests, diagnosis, and feedback with the goal of collecting information that can be used to better match the instructional strategy with the learner's performance. Furthermore, a system that has an articulate expert component can explain to a student its reasons for selecting a particular topic which is an instructive process. This aspect is particularly important for reference referral.

The Tutoring Module

The tutoring module is the focal point for the student interaction with the system. Knowledge of natural language dialogues must be integrated with the teaching methods of the expertise module and student profile defined by the student module to implement the instructional strategies defined by the system. Instructional strategies encompass decisions that are concerned with how best to present training materials to the student. This includes issues such as how much material to present, the degree of student interaction with the system, the order in which the material is presented, as well as the depth and breadth of the presentation. In the context of the tutor/student paradigm, the tutoring module is able to communicate with the student, select problems and/or examples, monitor and criticize student responses, provide assistance upon request, and select remedial instructional sequences.

Similar to the student module, more research is required to better understand the relative effectiveness of different teaching strategies. To date, a number of approaches have been implemented. These include a diagnostic or debugging approach in which the system attempts to understand the student's misunderstanding by posing various tasks and evaluating the response; the Socratic method, in which the system attempts to question the student in a way that her or his own reasoning process will be revealed and thus be subject to modification; and a coaching method in which the student is engaged in some activity like a computer game or simulation to encourage skill acquisition and general problem-solving ability. A mixed strategy involves a form of dialogue management that enables the system to control the form of student interaction.

The Authoring Module

When trying to understand ICAI it is important to consider relevance of automated intelligence to both the development and delivery of course materials. The benefits of automation are best understood when one reviews the process of courseware development. The typical steps include instruction development, instruction delivery, and instruction evaluation.

Each step in the process reflects the need for a different form of expertise; specifically: authoring, presentation, and evaluation. Current ICAI systems focus on the delivery of course materials. An open and active research area is the development of knowledge bases that codify both instructional design and courseware development expertise that would guide (and thus make more productive) course development and improve its instructional quality. Within this scenario, an author/teacher less qualified in a particular subject area could enlist the support of these development experts to quickly construct high-quality instructional materials in the specific discipline.

At the current time, authoring technology is primarily concerned with the tools that are used to increase courseware development productivity and/or the instructional quality of the course. To that end, expert system shells that facilitate the development of course knowledge bases exemplify associated productivity tools although, as stated above, instructional design and courseware development knowledge has not yet been routinely codified.

The major success of ICAI currently involves the application of codified intelligence to instruction delivery. This manifests itself in two ways. The first area involves judging what materials are to be presented and at what level. Here, information involving a student's performance, aptitude, and background are utilized to develop the instructional sequences that comprise a lesson. This may be achieved at a number of levels and possibly by consulting more than one "expert" knowledge base. For example, at a very general level a cognitive model of a student may be utilized to select a general teaching strategy. However, as the course topics are presented deviations from the model may be observed that result in minor adjustments to the material selection. For example, a student that has a good record of performance in mathematics may be given a particular instructional sequence based on the fact that she or he had demonstrated a mastery of the required mathematics. However, as the sequence is presented and student feedback is gathered, it may be ascertained that the performance indicates a deficiency in this area, prompting a change in teaching strategy that would incorporate remediation in the necessary mathematics. The application of more fully informed judgment provides the qualitative difference between traditional CAI and this approach. Obviously, ICAI much more closely follows the human tutor/student paradigm.

A HISTORICAL PERSPECTIVE

The remarks that follow summarize the evolution of intelligent CAI presented in Goldberg (1973) and Gable and Page (1980) and the synopsis of representative systems discussed in Clancey, Barnett, and Cohen (1982). The interested reader is directed to those sources for a more comprehensive treatment of this topic. The earliest form of programmed instruction (though it did not use a computer) is attributed to Pressey (1926). In his approach, instructional materials were organized into frames and each frame had an associated question set. To progress to the next frame, the student had to demonstrate mastery (reflected in the scoring of the question set) of the current frame. There was no concept of branching or remediation.

If one views this as the lowest level of programmed instruction, then the next level, which incorporates branching and remediation, may be attributed to Crowder (1962). With his so-called "scattered textbook" approach a student could be directed to one out of a set of possible instruction sequences based on her or his response to the last question. For example, in response to a TRUE/FALSE question a student's answer could be classified as correct, incorrect but anticipated, or unanticipated. Three potentially different instructional segments correspond to each one of the answer classes. The disadvantage of this approach is that branching decisions are typically made based on a single piece of data (the student response) using simple pattern matching techniques. The evaluator has no real embedded "knowledge" of the subject matter being taught or the characteristics of the student previewing the materials.

The approach of applying "knowledge" of the student and subject matter in order to adaptively deliver the course materials represents the next level of sophistication for programmed instruction systems. This is the level at which the term "Intelligent CAI," applies. With "adaptive ICAI," different instructional strategies which control both the depth and breadth of the presentation are selected and revised based on the assimilation and analysis of sets of data values. For example, the system might "observe" a particular pattern in a sequence of student answers and infer that a specific deficiency exists. Similarly, the system may monitor student input and, because of a number of unanticipated inputs, decide that the student is becoming bored. In the former circumstance the system might invoke a different tutor to instruct the student in the remedial area. In the second scenario, the observation might trigger a different presentation strategy to hold the student's attention.

A different form of automated instruction is termed "generative ICAI." With this approach the knowledge of the subject is embedded in the algorithms that generate problems for the student and evaluate the responses. Because of their research nature and often novel approaches, ICAI systems are primarily experimental with a particular research focus. Of those systems reported in the literature, a number of distinct approaches can be identified. These include: theorem proving systems, information-structured systems, intelligent simulators, coaching systems, and systems employing student modeling.

Theorem-proving systems are exemplified by the work conducted by Goldberg (1973). His system was employed to teach theorem proving for algebra and simple predicate calculus. The system presents a theorem to a student that she or he must then solve by inputting a sequence of steps that constitute the proof. The knowledge of how to prove the theorem is represented internally as a binary tree where each node specifies a correct step or reduction in the proof. As the student proceeds, the system evaluates each proof statement but, more importantly, can give immediate advice if an incorrect step is taken. Another important aspect demonstrated by this system is the value of showing the student how the knowledge that drives the system is organized, since this constitutes an explanation of the proof as defined by the author.

Information-structured ICAI systems incorporate different organizational strategies to define relationships among various facts that constitute a subject area. Different pattern matching and search schema are used to extract related information to formulate problems and evaluate responses. Best known within this class of ICAI system is SCHOLAR (Carbonell, 1970). The system used a mixed initiative strategy (either the computer or the student can ask questions) to teach South American geography. Different facts concerning South America were associated by a set of common relationships (is-a-country-of, is-the-capital-of, has-population, etc.). in a semantic network. The network could then be traversed to formulate questions or respond to student questions.

In formulating questions, SCHOLAR utilized a simple Socratic tutoring strategy. The WHY system (Stevens, Collins, & Goldin, 1978), which instructs students in the causes of rainfall, began as an extension to SCHOLAR to better understand Socratic tutoring heuristics. Subsequently, the system architects explored global strategies employed by human tutors for dialogue management. Since this involved dispelling students' misconceptions, their work also contributed to a better understanding of student modeling.

Simulation is an important instructional tool because it enables students to freely experiment and learn about the system being simulated. However, in an unmanaged environment, students frequently have no idea about what experiments to try and so they often waste time conducting useless exercises. Also, many systems can easily be compromised when the students input faulty data. Adding intelligence to the simulation system overcomes these deficiencies because the system can provide different problems to solve and can monitor and filter the input accordingly. An example of this type of simulation system is SOPHIE (SOPHisticated Instructional Environment) (Brown, Burton, & Bell, 1975). With SOPHIE students are presented a schematic diagram of an electronic circuit which has a fault. Both the properties of the circuit and the measurement equipment used by a student to analyze a fault are simulated by the software.

After the student has taken various measurements, she or he can present a hypothesis regarding the fault which the system will analyze for consistency. During the experiment, the student can "replace" any circuit component if she or he can justify that it is faulty. Also, during the simulation the student may ask for help, at which time the system will formulate different hypotheses based on the student's measurements so far.

Coaching is a form of ICAI that employs a different tutoring strategy from both that of SOPHIE and SCHOLAR. In this approach students learn from participating in a computer game while the tutor attempts to infer a student's misunderstandings from observed behavior and give suggestions on how to overcome the deficiencies. Experimental systems in this area have tended to focus on the issue of how often the tutor should coach a student and what or how much to say during the coaching dialogue. Examples of these types of systems include WEST (Burton & Brown, 1979) which teaches students the appropriate manipulation of arithmetic expressions, and WUMPUS (Goldstein & Carr, 1977) which fosters a student's ability to make logical and probabilistic inferences from given information.

Student modeling is analogous to adaptive ICAI where different instructional strategies are employed to match the aptitude, background, and interest level of the student. Koffman and Blount (1975) have reported on such a system that uses a probabilistic grammar to generate questions and a scoring polynomial to choose the next concept to present. In this system concepts are represented by a hierarchical tree structure where each node contains the concept name and attributes. Attributes include a list of prerequisite concepts, level of complexity, and the names of routines that will generate an appropriate question set and evaluate the student response. Also included are use statistics such as the date/time the concept was last presented and the number of times it has been presented. This information is used by a scoring polynomial to ascertain the next topic to present.

Perhaps the most successful and most sophisticated ICAI system to date is GUIDON (Clancy, Barnett, & Cohen, 1982). Designed to instruct students in the diagnosis of infectious blood diseases, it utilizes the knowledge base rules of the MYCIN (Buchanan & Shortliffe, 1984) expert system as the subject matter to be taught. The MYCIN rules constitute the topics to be discussed and provide the basis for evaluating the student's behavior. However, GUIDON's teaching knowledge, also in the form of a knowledge base rule set, is wholly separate from those of MYCIN. While MYCIN's rules were not modified (which is important for separating instructional and subject matter knowledge), they were used in ways not intended by the original authors, for example, for forming quizzes, measuring student understanding, and summarizing evidence. The approximately 200 teaching rules of GUIDON guide the analysis of the MYCIN rules to effect the tutor/student dialogue, present diagnostic rules, construct the student model, and respond to the student's initiative. The separation of the teaching rules from MYCIN's infectious-disease knowledge base is also significant because, if the MYCIN diagnostic rules are replaced by those of another problem domain, GUIDON will be able to teach the new diagnostic concepts.

As a research system, GUIDON was designed to address two basic questions. The first involved evaluating how effectively the problem-solving rules of a particular expert system (MYCIN) could be used within an intelligent tutor; the second, what rules about teaching could be added to MYCIN to make it a more effective tutor. Several aspects of rules used in knowledge-based expert systems suggest they could form a good basis for teaching. First, they capture a significant part of the subject matter knowledge to be presented. Additionally, they are represented in a known syntax that can be parsed and analyzed so that conclusions can be drawn from their content. That is, the rules are data to the instructional component or system which can decompose them and reason about their purpose. Finally, expert systems by necessity have the capability to reveal their line of reasoning during a problem-solving exercise (if nothing else to convince the client of the reasonableness of the process). Because the rules are written to perform this function, they already possess a much better explanatory capability than comparable problem-solving algorithms. This facilitates the tutor/student dialogue.

Synopsis

All of the systems described above serve to validate the purported advantages that ICAI systems exhibit over "less intelligent" CAI programs. This is not to say there are no accompanying disadvantages. While each of these systems has been successful in a limited domain, the techniques are difficult to assimilate in less than an ad hoc fashion. This is particularly true of generative ICAI systems where, because the knowledge of the course is imbedded in the problem generation and evaluation algorithms, these procedures need to be changed with each new course. Scientists are not yet familiar enough with basic knowledge representation to be able to generalize the concepts. The best effort to date is realized in knowledge-based expert systems such as GUIDON.

EXAMPLE SET

A set of examples will help to illustrate the power of ICAI systems. The interactive tutoring sessions characterized below are extracted from a lengthier description of the dialogue management capabilities of SCHOLAR, WHY, and GUIDON discussed by Clancey et al. (Clancey, Barnett, & Cohen, 1982). In the following examples the statements made by the ICAI system are shown in bold face type, the student response is registered in normal type preceded by asterisks, and annotations regarding the dialogue are shown in italics.

Mixed Initiative Dialogues

As stated previously, the mixed initiative strategy enables either the student or the tutor (computer) to initiate the questions that will guide subsequent interactions. Practically, the student is limited to a restricted syntax and vocabulary since natural language processing is beyond the scope of any current system. The first example illustrates how a mixed initiative strategy allows the student to deviate from a prescribed learning path to explore answers to questions that she/he might originate. The interactive session was conducted using SCHOLAR.

[**Example 1**]

SCHOLAR initiates (or continues) the dialogue by posing a question.
What is the language of Argentina?
** Probably Spanish
Very good.
Approximately what is the area of Argentina?
Rather than respond to the question, the student elects to change the topic (a discussion of Peru), illustrating the mixed initiative approach.
** Tell me something about Peru
Peru is a country.
It is located in South America.
The capital of Peru is Lima.
Now answer the question you didn't answer before.
Having responded to the student, SCHOLAR returns to the original line of questioning which the student attempts to answer

** The area of Argentina is 1,100,000 square miles
Approximately true, but a more exact value is 1,200,000.

The eastern bordering country of Peru is ——.
The student's answer to this question is wrong and so SCHOLAR will correct it.

** Catholicism
Wrong. Catholicism is not a country but a religion.
The correct answer is Brazil.
Where is Peru?

The Socratic Tutoring Strategy

The WHY system will be used to illustrate the application of tutoring strategies to the ICAI system. Developed as an extension to SCHOLAR, it tutors students in the causes of rainfall which is a complex problem with a large number of interrelated factors, and where no single factor accounts for the process. It employs a Socratic teaching method which is appropriate for teaching complex subjects in which the student is attempting to generalize concepts from specific examples. WHY incorporates a number of heuristics, in the form of rules, that control the student/tutor interaction. For example, the heuristic rule that would force the student to consider the necessity of a particular factor is stated as:

IF
the student gives as an explanation of causal dependence one or more factors that are not necessary,
THEN
select a counterexample with the wrong factor and ask the student why her/his causal dependence does not hold in that case.

In the following dialogue the system will ask the student to suggest the causes of rainfall. When the student supplies a response, if it is not of sufficient generality, the system will look for a counterexample and force the revision of rule to account for it.

[**Example 2**]

Heuristic 1: Ask for a prediction about a specific case. Do you think the Amazon jungle has heavy rainfall or light rainfall?
** Heavy rainfall

Heuristic 2: Ask for prior causes.
Why does the Amazon jungle have heavy rainfall?
** Because it's near the Atlantic
Yes, the Amazon jungle is near the equatorial Atlantic.

Heuristic 3: Ask for immediate causes.
How does that affect rainfall in the Amazon jungle?
** The water in the current is warm.

Heuristic 4: Ask for subsequent causes.
What happens after the moisture-filled air reaches the land?
**I don't know.

Heuristic 5: Suggest a factor and ask if it is a cause. Do you think the Andes mountain range has any effect on the rainfall in the Amazon jungle?
** YES

Heuristic 3: Ask for intermediate causes.
How?
** The prevailing wind hits the Andes mountains and the air cools

Heuristic 3: Ask for intermediate causes.
How does the fact that the prevailing wind hits the Andes lead to air cooling?
Heuristic 6: Form a general rule from an insufficient cause.
Do you think any place with mountains will have heavy rainfall?
** YES

Heuristic 7: Pick a counterexample of an insufficient cause,
and

Heuristic 2: Ask for prior causes.
Southern California has mountains.
Why doesn't Southern California have heavy rainfall?

Student Modeling

The third example shows how an ICAI system utilizes the student model to structure the dialogue with the student and insure that learning objectives are met. In this excerpt the GUIDON system has accepted a student response which, in fact, is correct. However, by analyzing the student model in which marks have been applied to MYCIN rules the student has applied and is presumed to understand, GUIDON is not assured that the student really knows that the hypothesis is correct. Consequently, instead of just accepting the answer, the system requires the student to support the hypothesis and then tries to ascertain why other conjectures were rejected.

[**Example 3**]

In the initial portion of this dialogue the student has presented GUIDON with a hypothesis which is a part (subgoal) of the overall diagnosis. Since GUIDON supports a mixed initiative dialogue, the student may have volunteered this response or the program may be testing the student's understanding.

What is the type of the infection?
** Bacterial
The program asks the student to support this hypothesis either because it is incorrect or, as in this case, the student model indicates that the student may not know all the relevant rules.
(GUIDON changes the prompt for student input to \ssb^\‘‘>>’’ to indicate that specific input and student initiated options are not.)
What facts about this case tell you that the type of the infection is bacterial? (Enter one factor per line.)

The percent of PMNs in the CBC is not relevant for determining this type of infection.
>> PMNs in the CSF
>> Cerebral-fluid glucose value
>> Protein of the CSF
These factors are related to the rules used by MYCIN to conclude that the infection is bacterial, and the student model is updated accordingly.
You are right about the CSF protein, the percent of PMNs in the CSF, and the CSF glucose value; however, you should have mentioned the fact that the meningitis is partially treated, the WBC from the CSF, and the fact that the simultaneous blood glucose value is not known. Other hypothesis are then discussed.
MYCIN rejected some possibilities you did not mention:
What facts about this case tell you that the type of the infection is not viral?

EVALUATION OF ICAI SYSTEMS

Research into ICAI systems exemplified by the work described above helps to emphasize the potential for computer-based, intelligent tutoring. Realistically, though, only a small number of systems are commercially available for developing ICAI courseware (Crews, 1987; Patton, 1987). The discrepancy between research success and use in both academia and industry points to a number of problems that still must be overcome prior to widespread acceptance of the technology. Both this potential and current limitations of ICAI systems are discussed in more detail below.

Advantages and Potential of ICAI Systems

Reiterating an earlier point, the benefits of ICAI systems are easily seen when they are contrasted to traditional CAI systems or lock step education. Summarily, they are derived from the fact that ICAI systems more closely model the interaction between a single tutor and a student. The tutor is able to adapt to the background, interests, and aptitudes of the student and is more adept at uncovering student deficiencies and taking corrective action. Benefits also accrue from the research and development process in developing the "proof of concept" systems described above. These additional benefits are subsequently described.

Even though current ICAI systems are, for the most part experimental, the understanding derived from current research holds the promise of significant improvements in the future. Perhaps the most significant impact ICAI systems have shown to date is reflected in the conceptual architecture which unambiguously isolates several instructional functions. With this design research is better focused on knowledge representation of subject matter (expertise module); instructional strategies (the tutoring module); student characteristics (the student module); and, tutor/student dialogues. The advantage of this architecture is best represented by GUIDON which enables the subject matter and teaching expertise to be separated, thus providing a generic environment for courseware development.

The generic authoring capability indicative of the GUIDON system coupled with the emergence of high-level, knowledge-base development tools (collectively referred to as expert system shells (Schindler, 1986) has significantly reduced the time required to author ICAI courseware from 10–50 person years to one to three person-years (Roberts & Park, 1983). In turn this has led to the commercial availability of authoring systems that integrate the expert system shell with traditional CAI authoring software to produce a system capable of developing ICAI. As a consequence, a substantial growth in the number of ICAI systems and available courseware is perceived for the next decade that is commensurate with the growth of expert systems. It follows with this approach that, as expert system technology improves, the cost and time for developing ICAI will become smaller and the quality of the courseware will improve.

Parallelling the technological advances in both hardware and knowledge engineering (expert system) software will be an improved understanding of the instructional process that is afforded by ICAI research. For example, experience with the BUGGY ICAI system (Brown & Burton, 1978) corrected the longstanding belief held by a majority of educators that most arithmetic errors committed by students were random aberrations and not systematic. Many other relationships in the teaching/learning process are also made more clear as the effort to codify teaching expertise intensifies. Consequently, as technology and understanding of the teaching process converge, the goal of closely simulating the instructional environment characterized by the tutor/student paradigm will be realized.

Problems and Limitation

Existing ICAI systems have a number of problems and limitations by virtue of their experimental nature. The ones reported in the literature are generally prototype systems that are evaluating one aspect of intelligent automated instruction, such as a particular teaching strategy or learning model. While these papers often postulate approaches for solving existing problems within the framework of an integrated ICAI architecture, this is significantly different from having an operational system that solves the problems.

That is not to say that significant accomplishments have not been attained; only that additional research is needed to realize commercially viable, generic forms of these systems. Current research is focused in a number of areas which serves to point out the deficiencies of existing systems. One area of intense research involves student/computer dialogues. A long-standing research area within the artificial intelligence community has been understanding natural language. Because of the complexity of this issue, current systems are considerably more narrow than most natural environments. These systems often use a subset of natural language with a prescribed syntax to define a domain of discourse. The system cannot understand any dialogue that falls outside this boundary. More than anything this impacts the development of ICAI courses because of the need to always develop the dialogue component of the system. The use of expert systems shells with their dialogue management component helps alleviate the development problem but often restricts the form of the dialogue to one that is always computer initiated. The use of graphics is becoming a promising alternative to complete natural language interactions.

A second limitation of ICAI systems comes from the assumption that what a student knows is adequately represented as the difference between the expert and student models. Although cognitive scientists are making progress in this area, little is known about how to accurately model understanding. This impacts the accuracy of adaptive decisions that are the cornerstone of ICAI tutoring strategies. However, one can certainly argue that the current approach is better than making the decision based on the response to a single question.

A third limitation involves the extreme labor-intensive nature of ICAI systems development. In part this stems from the complicated task of acquiring and codifying both subject matter and teaching knowledge. Another aspect is the need to implement the knowledge structures and inferencing mechanisms that constitute the expertise, student, and tutoring modules. That the amount of time and effort required to build many of the ICAI systems described in this chapter often required many person-years underscores the magnitude of the development problem. However, expert system technology is beginning to have a dramatic impact on this process. An analogy can be seen with early CAI systems. Initially, CAI coursework was developed using programming languages and, as a rule, required approximately 200 hours of development for every hour of self-paced instruction. With the introduction of high-level authoring systems, the specification of course materials became significantly easier to the extent that the need to write computer programs was eliminated. As a consequence, the time needed to develop an hour of CAI dropped to approximately 15–20 hours. Similarly, the use of expert systems obviates the need to develop systems development. In part this stems from the complicated task of acquiring and codifying both subject matter and teaching knowledge. Another aspect is the need to implement the knowledge structures and inferencing mechanisms that constitute the expertise, student, and tutoring modules.

A final issue which is often cited as a limitation of the near-term usage of ICAI systems is the inherent cost of hardware and software. Most of the experimental ICAI systems require very powerful LISP processing machines to achieve reasonable performance. However, the newer systems that incorporate expert systems shells typically run on desktop computers as well. At a cost of $5000–$7000, these systems are attractive for use at multiple stations within a library. More importantly, computer hardware costs have a longstanding tradition of dropping dramatically. As the price drops more complex ICAI will be available at stand alone workstations. Libraries that utilize workstation computers comparable in power to the INTEL 80386 processor with a megabyte of main memory and 40 megabytes of fixed disk storage should have no difficulty in supporting ICAI applications.

CONCLUSION

While CAI is only beginning to be successfully applied to libraries, sound arguments can be made that automated instruction (CAI) itself could be improved by the application of artificial intelligence techniques (Kearsley, 1977). The experimental systems described above bear out that point by exploring how students learn and providing insight into the effectiveness of different teaching strategies. However, the research nature of these systems should not be diminished. Only now are commercially available ICAI authoring systems beginning to appear and these systems tend to have low-level author interfaces (expert system shells) for developing the tutoring, student, and expertise module knowledge bases. However, as these systems proliferate, which seems inevitable, the question of using ICAI in the library may become moot. In the final analysis the ICAI approach may be forced upon libraries as it becomes a prominent method for holding and disseminating information. In the interim, when addressing the bibliographic instructional needs of the library, one should accept the potential of ICAI systems but be realistic and moderate current expectations.

REFERENCES

Axeen, M. (1968). *Teaching library use to undergraduates: Comparison of computer-based instruction and the conventional lecture*. Final Report. Bethseda, MD. (ERIC Educational Document Reproduction Service, No. ED 014 316, 1968).

Barr, A., Beard, M., & Atkinson, R. (1975). A rationale and description of a CAI program to teach the BASIC programming language. *Instructional Science, 4*, 1–31.

Brown, J., & Burton, R. (1978). A paradigmatic example of an artificially intelligent instructional system. *International Journal of Man-Machine Studies, 10*, 323–339.

Brown, J., Burton, R., & Bell, A. (1974). *SOPHIE: A sophisticated instructional environment for teaching electronic troubleshooting (an example of AI in CAI)* (BBN rep. No. 2790). Cambridge, MA: Bolt Beranek and Newman, Inc.

Brown, J., Burton, R., & Bell, A. (1975). SOPHIE: a step toward creating a reactive learning environment. *International Journal of Man-Machine Studies, 7*, 675–696.

Buchanan, B., & Shortliffe, E. (1984). *Rule-based expert systems: The MYCIN experiments of the Stanford Heuristic programming project.* Reading, MA: Addison Wesley.

Burton, R., & Brown, J. (1979). An investigation of computer coaching for informal learning activities. *International Journal of Man-Machine Studies, 11*, 5–24.

Carbonell, J. (1970). AI in CAI: An artificial intelligence approach to computer assisted instruction. *IEEE Transactions on Man-Machine Systems, 11*(4), 190–202.

Carbonell, J., & Collins, A. (1973). Natural semantics in artificial intelligence. *International Joint Conferences on AI, 3*, 344–351.

Carr, B., & Goldstein, I. (1977). *Overlays: A theory of modeling for computer aided instruction* (AI Memo 406). Cambridge, MA: Massachusetts Institute of Technology, AI Laboratory.

Clancey, W., Barnett, J., & Cohen, P. (1982). Applications oriented AI research: Education. In A. Barr & E. Feigenbaum (Eds.), *The handbook of artificial intelligence* (Vol. II). Stanford, CA: HeurisTech Press.

Crews, P. (1987). Tbt EXPERT: a case study in integrating expert system technology with computer assisted instruction. In IEEE Computer Society (Eds.), *Proceedings of the Third International Conference on Data Engineering*, Los Angeles, CA.

Crowder, J. E. (1962). Intrinsic and extensive programming. In J.E. Coulson (Ed.), *Proceedings of Conference on Application of Digital Computers to Instruction*, pp. 58-66.

Culkin, P. B. (1972). Instructional materials: design and development. Computer-assisted instruction in library use. *Drexel Library Quarterly, 8*, 301–311.

Culkin, P. B., & Walker, E. (1984) Computers in user education. *Reference Services Review, 12*, 75–78.

Farber, E. I. (1974). Library instruction throughout the curriculum: Earlham College Program. In W. J. Lubans, Jr. (Ed.), *Educating the library user* (pp. 145–62). New York: Bowker.

Gable, A., & Page, C. (1980). The use of artificial intelligence techniques in computer assisted instruction. An overview. *International Journal of Man-Machine Studies, 12*(3), 259–282.

Goldberg, A. (1973). *Computer assisted instruction: The application of theorem Proving to adaptative response analysis* (Tech. Rep. No. 203). Stanford, CA: Stanford University, Institute for Mathematical Studies in Social Sciences.

Goldstein, I., & Carr, B. (1977). The computer as coach: an athletic paradigm for intellectual education. *Annual Conference of the Association for Computing Machinery*. Seattle, WA.

Kearsley, G. (1977). *The Relevance of AI research to CAI* (Rep. RIR-77-2). Edmonton, Alberta, Canada: The University of Alberta, the Division of Educational Research Services, Faculty of Education.

Koffman, E. B., & Blount, S. E. (1975). Artificial intelligence and automatic programming in CAI. *Artificial Intelligence, 6*, 215–234.

Koffman, E. B., & Perry, J. M. (1976). A model for generative CAI and concept selection. *International Journal of Man-Machine Studies, 8*, 397–410.

Laubsch, J. H. (1975). Some thoughts about representing knowledge in instructional systems. *International Joint Conferences on AI, 4*, 122–125.

Oberman, C., & Strauch, K. (1982). *Theories of bibliographic education: Designs for teaching*. New York: Bowker.

Parrott, J. R. (1986). Expert systems for reference work. *Microcomputers for information management, 3*(3), 155–171.

Patton, S. (1987). Intelligent CBT: Building knowledge bases. *Data Training, The 5th Annual Computer-based Training Conference and Exposition*, Atlanta, GA.

Pressey, S. (1926). A sample apparatus that gives tests, and scores, and teaches. *School and Society, 23*, 373–376.

Ragosta, M., Holland, P., & Jamison, D. (1979). *Computer assisted instruction and compensatory education: The ETS/LAUSD study* (No. 0400, 78-0065). Washington, DC: National Institute of Education.

Renford, B., & Hendrickson, L. (1980). *Bibliographic instruction: A handbook*. New York: Schuman.

Roberts, F., & Park, O. (1983). Intelligent computer assisted instruction: an explanation and overview. *Educational Technology, 23*, 7–12.

Schindler, P., Jr. (1986). Special report: AI wonderland. *Information Week*, (63), 24.

Stevens, A., Collins, A., & Goldin, S. (1978). *Diagnosing student's misconceptions in causal models* (BBN Rept. No. 3786). Cambridge, MA: Bolt Beranek and Newman, Inc.

Wexler, P. (1970). Information networks in generative computer assisted instruction. *IEEE Transactions on Man-Machine Systems, 11*(4), 181–190.

8

Scholar: A Scholarship Identification System in Prolog

Donald Nute
Department of Philosophy and
Artificial Intelligence Programs
University of Georgia

THE GOAL

There are hundreds of scholarships available to college students. Some of these are obscure awards with unusual eligibility requirements. I will describe an interactive system called SCHOLAR that uses information supplied by a student user to identify scholarships for which the student satisfies minimal eligibility requirements.

SCHOLAR was originally intended for use by advisors in the Office of Student Financial Aid at the University of Georgia to help students find ways to finance their educations. However, it operates very well as a stand-alone system, and it could be set up in a library or other suitable location where students could consult it without any supervision.

The original version of SCHOLAR was developed in about a month of intermittent work by three people. In that version, the rules for identifying scholarships were not clearly distinguished from the procedures for interacting with the user. Later a set of generic procedures for conducting the consultation was developed and collected in a package called XSHELL. In its current version, SCHOLAR has two components: the XSHELL user interface and an expandable knowledge base. By itself, XSHELL is a tool that can be used to develop other simple knowledge based systems.

Both XSHELL and the SCHOLAR knowledge base are written in Prolog. We will look at some reasons Prolog was selected for this project and at the basic features of Prolog. Then we will see how to construct special Prolog rules that XSHELL can use to identify scholarships. Finally, we will look at a sample consultation with SCHOLAR.

WHY PROLOG

Prolog (for *Pro*gramming in *Log*ic) is a programming language based on symbolic logic in much the same way programming languages like Fortran are based on arithmetic. Prolog allows us to program declaratively as well as procedurally. A procedural program gives the computer a list of steps to follow in a certain order to produce a solution to a problem. A declarative program provides some initial information about a problem and conditions that a solution to the problem must satisfy. Prolog constructs a logical proof that there is a solution to the problem. In the process, Prolog actually produces one or several solutions to the problem.

Two alternatives to Prolog were considered for this project. One was to develop SCHOLAR in LISP. The other was to use a commercially available expert system shell. We chose Prolog over LISP because Prolog has a powerful inference engine built into the language, while any needed inference engine must be constructed in LISP. We chose Prolog over commercial expert system shells because programming in Prolog gave us complete control over the format for the rules and questions in our knowledge base, the design of screen displays, and all other aspects of the user interface. Using a commercial expert system shell would have committed us to someone else's ideas about what the knowledge base and screen displays should look like and about how the dialog should develop. We felt that the tool should be modified to fit the job rather than the other way around.

Very good and inexpensive Prolog interpreters are now available for the IBM PC. Fast prototyping and good debugging facilities are also advantages of Prolog as an expert system development environment. Prolog has enjoyed wide use for expert system development in Europe and was selected as the programming language for the Japanese fifth generation computing initiative.

HOW PROLOG WORKS

There is no clear distinction between program and data in Prolog. Both are represented as sets of facts and rules.

A fact indicates that some individual has some property or that some individuals stand in some relation. For example, we can use the "fact" *blue(sun)* to say that the sun is blue, and we can use the "fact" *north_of(chicago,atlanta)* to say that Chicago is north of Atlanta. Although we call these statements *facts*, they may not be true.

A rule indicates that some fact is true if some other facts are true. For example, we can use the rule

```
north_of(X,Y) if in(X,canada) and in(Y,mexico)
```

to say that one thing is north of another if the first thing is in Canada and the second is in Mexico. In most Prolog implementations we replace the word *if* with the symbol **:-** and we replace the word *and* with a comma. Thus we rewrite the preceding rule as

```
north_of(X,Y) :- in(X,canada), in(Y,mexico).
```

In the fact *north__of(chicago,atlanta)*, we call *north__of* the predicate of the fact and *chicago* and *atlanta* the arguments of the fact. The arguments of a fact are like grammatical subjects and objects. They are what the fact is about. The predicate is what we use to say something about the arguments.

Predicates are usually specific in Prolog facts and rules, but arguments may be specific or variable. In Prolog, we represent anything specific by a single term or *atom* that begins with a lower case letter. Numerals, atoms beginning with lowercase letters, and any expressions between single quotes are called *constants*. So *north__of, sun*, and *chicago* are all constants. Atoms that begin with an uppercase letter are *variables* and can take on any value needed to complete a computation. So the rule

```
north__of(X,Y) :- in(X,canada), in(Y,mexico)
```

says that we can show that anything is north of anything else if we can show that the first thing is in Canada and the second thing is in Mexico.

Prolog does not know the meaning of *blue, north__of, sun*, or any of the other words we have used. Prolog can only tell by its position in a fact or a rule even that an atom is used as a predicate or as an argument. All it knows about the meaning of the terms is what it can discover from the facts and rules we give it. It does not know if *north__of (chicago,atlanta)* means Chicago is north of Atlanta or Atlanta is north of Chicago. The interpretation of this fact is left to us.

Suppose we give Prolog the following facts and rules:

```
in(toronto,canada).

in(juarez,mexico).

north__of(X,Y) :- in(X,canada), in(Y,mexico).
```

Then Prolog can prove *north__of(toronto,juarez)*. To do this, it looks for a fact or rule that matches what it is trying to prove. In this case, *north__of(toronto,juarez)* matches *north__of(X,Y)* in the rule if we let the variable *X* match *toronto* and we let the variable *Y* match *juarez*. Then Prolog knows that *north__of(toronto,juarez)* if *in(toronto,canada)* and *in(juarez,mexico)*. These facts are in its database, so it is finished.

Instead of *north__of(toronto,juarez)*, we might ask Prolog to prove that *something* is north of toronto. Then Prolog tries to prove *north__of(toronto,Something)*. Again, this matches *north__of(X,Y)* if *X* matches *toronto* and *Something* matches *Y*. Then Prolog needs to prove *in(toronto,canada)* and *in(Something,mexico)*. The first of these is a fact in the database, and the second matches a fact in the database if we let *Something* match *juarez*. So Prolog can prove *north__of(toronto,Something)*, if we let *Something* match *juarez*. Prolog will tell us that *juarez* is a *solution* to the goal *north_of(toronto,Something)*. This is how Prolog uses logic to solve problems.

Besides declarative programming, Prolog allows procedural programming. Prolog has built-in predicates that handle input and output functions, arithmetic, and other common procedures. We will not examine these, but they are used in the user interface package XSHELL. We will concentrate on declarative programming. Next we discuss the special formats for Prolog facts and rules, formats that the procedures in XSHELL can recognize and use. With a suitable set of facts and rules in a knowledge base, XSHELL will automatically conduct a consultation with a user.

PROPERTIES AND PARAMETERS

Remember that the purpose of SCHOLAR is to identify scholarships for which the user satisfies minimal eligibility requirements. We need rules that tell us when to identify particular scholarships for a student. An identification rule will tell XSHELL to identify such-and-such a scholarship if the student satisfies certain conditions. These rules will be ordinary Prolog rules with the basic form

```
xkb_identify(scholarship_name) :-
  conditions_for_scholarship.
```

The conclusion of every identification rule, the part that comes before :-, will have *xkb_identify* as its predicate. We use the prefix *xkb* here to remind us that these rules are part of an XSHELL knowledge base.

What kinds of conditions will we need in our identification rules? Let's look at a possible announcement for a new scholarship.

> The Robert E. Lee Award is a $1000 prize given annually to a descendant of a soldier who served under General Robert E. Lee in the Confederate Army. The recipient must be a resident of Virginia and must have completed one year of college. For further information, contact the Robert E. Lee Selection Committee, 1865 S. State Street, Appomattox, VA 12345.

There are three conditions for the award:

1. The recipient must be a descendant of someone who served under Lee in the Confederate Army
2. The recipient must be a resident of Virginia.
3. The recipient cannot be a freshman.

We will represent each of these as a separate condition in our identification rule.

The first condition requires that the recipient has a rather unusual property that we will call the *lee_soldier_descendant* property. XSHELL will determine this by asking the user a simple yes-or-no question we will supply. The condition *prop(lee_soldier_descendant)* tells XSHELL that to identify the Robert E. Lee Award, it must determine that the user has this property. Our rule becomes:

```
xkb_identify(robert_e_lee_award) :-

    prop(lee_soldier_descendant),

    other_conditions.
```

We record an appropriate question for the property as a fact in our SCHOLAR knowledge base.

```
    xkb_question(lee_soldier_descendant,
    $ Are you a direct descendant of anyone who fought under
    General Robert E. Lee in the Confederate Army?$).
```

Once again, the prefix *xkb* indicates that the question is part of an XSHELL knowledge base. The question is bracketed by dollar signs. Arity/Prolog allows us to display formatted text in this way. The message between the dollar signs will be printed exactly as shown, complete with spacing, carriage returns, and so on. Other Prologs do not support this representation, and XSHELL is written to accept and display questions written in other formats.

The second condition for the Robert E. Lee Award could also be represented using *prop*, but there is a better way. There may be many scholarships that require residency in a certain state. For example,

> The New England Sophomore Scholarship is given each year to a college sophomore with a B+ grade average who is a resident of New England. The amount of the award is $500. Contact the New Englanders, 14 Beacon Hill, Boston, MA 10101.

We could ask for the user's home state and use this to determine whether the user satisfies any of these conditions. Assuming that it is always better to ask one question rather than many, we will represent the second condition as a *parameter* that can take different values. We will call this parameter *home_state*.

We use the format *parm(home_state,a,'VA')* to tell XSHELL to find out if the value of *home_state* is Virginia. We enclose *VA* in quotes so Prolog will know it is a capitalized constant and not a variable. The middle argument *a* tells XSHELL to expect an atom of several characters as the response to the question. A *c* in this position tells XSHELL to expect a single character, and an *n* indicates a number.

We also need a question for *home—state*:

```
xkb_question(home—state,
$ Enter the two-letter postal code for your home state.
Use upper case letters only.$).
```

We ask the student for the class year and use this information to test many scholarships. If we allow the student to type the class year, there is a danger that the student might type 'junior,' 'Junior,' 'JUNIOR,' or even 'JR,' all meaning the same thing. We avoid this by using a short menu.

```
xkb_question(class,
$ What is (will be) your class standing?
(1) freshman
(2) sophomore
(3) junior
(4) senior$).
```

We want the Robert E. Lee Award to be identified if the parameter *class* does *not* have the property 1, that is, if the student is beyond the first year of college. Also, we want XSHELL to accept a single character as the response to this question. So our condition is *not parm(class,c,1)*, and our rule is

```
xkb_identify(robert_e_lee_award) :-
prop(lee_soldier_descendant),
parm(home_state,a,'1VA'),
not parm(class,c,1).
```

We expect more scholarships will depend on a student's state of residence or class year than on whether the student is a descendant of someone who served under Lee. In general, we should put the most common kinds of conditions at the tops of rules where they will be investigated first. If the student is not from Virginia, we do not need to ask about Lee at all. But we will want to know the student's home state for other scholarships. XSHELL remembers the answers to questions it asks and uses them later.

If the Robert E. Lee Award is identified, XSHELL will get a reporting phrase from the SCHOLAR knowledge base and display it together with the argument in the conclusion of the Lee Award identification rule. In this case, XSHELL reports

```
You are eligible for this scholarship:
robert_e_lee_award
```

If we want a more informative report, we can replace the argument *robert_e_lee_award* with whatever text we want.

Reordering the conditions and providing a more informative award description, our final rule for the Robert E. Lee Award is

```
  xkb_identify($
The Robert E. Lee Award.
The amount of the award is $$1000.
For further information contact
The Robert E. Lee Selection Committee
1865 S. State Street
Appomattox, VA 12345$) :-
  parm(home_state,a,'VA'),
  not parm(class,c,1),
  prop(lee_soldier_descendant).
```

Notice that we use a double dollar sign when we want a dollar sign to be printed as part of the report. Otherwise, Arity/Prolog will think that the dollar sign in $1,000 is the end of the formatted text.

RANGES AND SETS OF PARAMETER VALUES

XSHELL recognizes two other versions of the *parm* format for conditions in rules. To see how these formats work, let's look again at the New England Sophomore Scholarship. This scholarship has three eligibility requirements:

1. The recipient must be a college sophomore.
2. The recipient must have a B+ grade average.
3. The recipient must be a resident of New England.

Let's construct a rule for this scholarship.

The first requirement is easy: *parm(class,c,2)*. The second requirement is more difficult. We could treat it as a property, but other scholarships might also have a grade requirement. Or we could ask the student for a grade point average and use it to decide whether the student meets the requirement. Supposing the B+ range begins at about 3.3 on a 4-point grade scale, the student meets the requirement if the grade point average is 3.3 or higher.

Let's call this parameter *gpa*. We cannot represent requirement (2) as *parm(gpa,n,3.3)* because then a student with better grades would not qualify. Any value for *gpa* in the *range* 3.3 to 4.0 should be accepted. We represent this condition as *parmrange(gpa,3.3,4.0)*. The first argument is the name of the parameter, the second argument is the lowest acceptable value, and the third argument is the highest acceptable value. Notice that we do not use an *n* argument in this format because the input could only be numerical. When XSHELL sees this condition, it will get the value for *gpa*, remember it for later use, and then compare it with 3.3 and 4.0 to see if it falls within the proper range.

Condition (3) is clearly related to the parameter *home_state*. But there are six states that make up the New England region, so there is a *set* of six acceptable values for *home_state*. We represent this by *parmset(home_state, a,['CT','MA','ME','NH','RI','VT'])*. The first argument is the parameter name, the second tells XSHELL what kind of input to expect, and the third is the set of acceptable values. We represent the set using square brackets and commas.

When we supply suitable information about the scholarship, the identification rule for the New England Sophomore Scholarship looks like this:

```
  xkb_identify($
The New England Sophomore Scholarship
The amount of the award is $$500.
For further information contact
The New Englanders
14 Beacon Hill
Boston, MA 10101$) :-
  parm(class,c,2),
  parmrange(gpa,3.3,4.0),
  parmset(home_state,a,['CT','MA','ME,'
    'NH','RI','VT']).
```

We only need one new question for this rule:

```
  xkb_question(gpa,
$ What is your grade point average converted to a 4-point system?$).
```

MAJORS

A student's academic major is a very frequent criterion for scholarship eligibility. The *prop*, *parm*, *parmrange*, and *parmset* formats are the only standard formats used to write identification rules for XSHELL knowledge bases. We could use the *parm* format for major, but this presents two problems. First, a student might enter any one of "political science," "political sci.," "Political Science," and so on, for the same major. Constructing a menu of all possible majors would be a difficult and perhaps impossible task. The second problem is that a student might have more than one major. If major is represented using *parm*, XSHELL will remember the first answer it gets and never ask for other majors.

We could use *prop* and ask if the student's major is history, chemistry, biology, and every other major that shows up as a requirement for a scholarship. This will be tedious when the system keeps asking after the student has identified all majors.

We added a special format to SCHOLAR that is a compromise. It asks yes-or-no questions to determine a student's major until it gets a positive answer. The next time a major is a requirement, it asks if the student has more than one major. If the answer is no, the system never asks another question about majors. If the answer is yes, the system continues to ask about majors.

Let's look at a scholarship with a required major.

> The Bunsen Award is a $2500 scholarship for chemistry majors. Selection is based on scholarship and need. Contact Chemcorp, 22 Dioxin Drive, Stinking Creek, TN 55555.

Without more information, we set the minimal grade average at 3.0 when scholarship is a requirement. Where need is a criterion, we ask the student how much money is needed to continue school. Then we use *parmrange*, setting the minimum value for the parameter *need* at the amount of the scholarship and the maximum at the arbitrary limit of $10,000. A suitable rule for the Bunsen Award is:

```
   xkb__identify($
The Bunsen Award
The amount of the award is $$2,500.
For further information contact
Chemcorp
22 Dioxin Drive
Stinking Creek, TN 55555$) :-
   major(chemistry),
   parmrange(gpa,3.0,4.0),
   parmrange(need,2500,10000).
```

We need one new question for our rule:

```
   xkb__question(need,
$ What is the minimum amount of support you will need to continue school?$).
```

A SAMPLE CONSULTATION

Here is a sample dialog produced using only the identification rules for our three imaginary scholarships. In the sample consultation, the user's answers are in italics.

> SCHOLAR: An Expert System for Scholarship Eligibility
>
> This program will help a student identify scholarships for which s/he may be eligible.

Enter the two-letter postal code for your home state.
Use upper case letters only.
>*VA*

What is (will be) your class standing?
(1) freshman
(2) sophomore
(3) junior
(3) senior
>*2*

Are you a direct descendant of anyone who fought under General Robert E. Lee in the Confederate Army?
>*y*

You are eligible for this scholarship:
The Robert E. Lee Award.
The amount of the award is $1000.
For further information contact
The Robert E. Lee Selection Committee
1865 S. State Street
Appomattox, VA 12345

Press return when ready to continue.

What is your grade point average converted to a 4-point system?
>*3.2*

Are you majoring in chemistry?
>*y*

What is the minimum amount of support you will need to continue school?
>*3000*

You are eligible for this scholarship:
The Bunsen Award
The amount of the award is $2,500.
For further information contact
Chemcorp
22 Dioxin Drive
Stinking Creek, TN 55555

Press return when ready to continue.

I cannot reach a conclusion.
Do you want to conduct another consultation?
>*y*

SCHOLAR: An Expert System for Scholarship Eligibility

This program will help a student identify scholarships for which s/he may be eligible.

Enter the two-letter postal code for your home state.
Use upper case letters only.
>CT

What is (will be) your class standing?
(1) freshman
(2) sophomore
(3) junior
(3) senior
>2

What is your grade point average converted to a 4-point scale?
>3.7

You are eligible for this scholarship:
The New England Sophomore Scholarship
The amount of the award is $500.
For further information contact
The New Englanders
14 Beacon Hill
Boston, MA 10101

Press return when ready to continue.

Are you majoring in chemistry?
>n

I cannot reach a conclusion.
Do you want to conduct another consultation?
>n

The actual SCHOLAR knowledge base has rules to identify dozens of scholarships, and this knowledge base is growing. As we have seen, it is easy to convert announcements for scholarships into identification rules and questions.

9

Online Reference Assistance (ORA): An Expert System for Academic-Library Reference Assistance*

James R. Parrott
The Library
University of Waterloo, Ontario

MOTIVATION

The Problem

The serious overload at reference desks today is being blamed for an increasing incidence of "job burnout" among reference librarians (Neville, 1981; Ferriero & Powers, 1982). In a perceptive article, Miller (1984) examined a group of contemporary reference-service problems including job burnout. He concluded that staffing levels were generally too low to provide the personalized reference service required by library users. He proposed a number of solutions, preferring the use of alternative staffing arrangements. He considered that the use of online technology would probably not save the reference librarian much time, at least in the near future, the only exceptions being the use of word processors and database managers for the preparation of library publications, internal reports, and so on.

Online Simulation of Memory Processes

The advantages of using computers to assist in the preparation of library publications are too obvious to require enumeration. Word-processing software has proven invaluable in producing all kinds of publications from posters and flyers to more substantial ones. Database managers are equally indispensible in producing bibliographic publications. But are there advantages in having the computer play some role beyond that of assisting in the preparation of publications? Are there, for example, benefits to be gained from having the computer present

*Thanks are due to Linda Leger for her comments and suggestions on this chapter.

library publications in an online format? Probably the most evident would be the ease in updating information in the online publications. Another would be relief from the dilemma of having either to hand out publications containing outdated information or to discard them at sometimes considerable cost and prepare updated versions. A third benefit, of less obvious measurable value, but of probably greater potential, is that a series of online publications could be linked to a central index. Such an index could point to all sorts of information that is normally scattered over various posters, handouts, and other publications.

Online Simulation of Cognitive Processes

The database of information that is proposed above is essentially an online enhancement of the mechanical processes of writing and record-keeping used in preparing library publications. Writing and record-keeping represent the mechanization of a basic mental process, human memory; these mechanical extensions of memory are of considerable antiquity, reaching back at least several thousands of years. Mechanizing or simulating the full spectrum of human cognition, on the other hand, has been an elusive goal. It is only in the last few years that anything of significance has been achieved in this field—a field which has become known as cognitive science.

An important class of problems in cognitive science has to do with the simulation of interactions between people. To be sure, attempts to deal with these problems are not new. For example, they were to some extent addressed in programmed-learning texts, in which the interaction between student and tutor was simulated. But using a printed book to do this involved a lot of page flipping; it was not a convenient medium for such a simulation. With the advent of online technology, the field of computer-assisted instruction (CAI) began to provide useful simulations of the interaction between student and tutor. And in the last few years, the field of expert systems has done the same for the interaction between client and professional.

Because the interaction between library user and librarian in the academic environment has elements of the client-professional relationship as well as the student-tutor relationship, both expert systems and CAI offer useful online complements to a database of publication-type information. Library user-education applications of CAI have met with some success in the last two decades (Williams & Davis, 1982). In more recent years, expert systems for reference consultation have been announced: ORA (Parrott, 1986), POINTER (Smith, 1986), ANSWERMAN (Waters, 1986) and PLEXUS (Vickery & Brooks, 1987). This chapter is devoted to a detailed description of the current state of ORA, which combines expert systems, CAI modules, and databases of publication-type information.

BACKGROUND OF THE PROJECT

Task Group

The Online Reference Assistance system (ORA) was created by a task group that was struck in 1984 in the University of Waterloo Library, in Waterloo, Ontario. David Binkley, Maureen Carter, Gary Draper, Tom Eadie, Mary Ferguson, Linda Leger, Sue Moskal, James Parrott, and Susan Routliffe have served on the task group. Equipment and software were provided by Digital Equipment of Canada, and included several color graphics terminals, access to a VAX in the Waterloo Arts Computing Office using the VMS operating system, and the use of various software packages.

System Goal

The aim of the task group was not to apply a particular technology, but to try to deal with the problem of overload at the reference desks. The system, ORA, was therefore intended to simulate the services of a reference librarian for questions of low and medium-level difficulty. As it turned out, providing some relief from low-level questions required the construction of a videotex-like database of information pages and some computer-assisted instruction modules. Handling the medium-level difficulty questions entailed the construction of expert systems.

Software Development Tool

Software requirements for ORA included a database component with menu and subject access, computer-assisted instruction components, and expert systems. Since there did not appear to be a software package handling all of these, a computer-assisted instruction package, the Courseware Authoring System (CAS) was chosen, because it has a strong enough command language to allow database applications and expert system applications to be written as well. The command language, the Digital Authoring Language (DAL), is an extended subset of PASCAL, and is therefore a reasonably high-level third-generation language. It has indeed been possible to use DAL to write expert systems applications, but experimentation with PROLOG, a fifth-generation language, has since shown that it is much easier to write expert system applications in the latter. The problem with using a third-generation language like DAL is that the heuristic information (the knowledge base) in the system has to be expressed in rather elaborate code with several levels of nested IF statements to embody the particular logical conditions. In a language like PROLOG, the code is much easier to write, read, and alter.

Structure of the Chapter

ORA will now be examined, concentrating on medium-level questions. The chapter will be structured by type of reference transaction, following a classification scheme used by Mary Jo Lynch (1978) in a study of the reference interview:

- *Directional* transactions, which concern library locations, services and policies
- *Holdings* transactions, which involve determining whether the library owns a particular item
- *Substantive* transactions, which have to do with requests for factual information, for help in finding information on a topic, and so on.

DIRECTIONAL TRANSACTIONS

Scope

It is clear that directional transactions as described by Lynch are those that could be answered by library publications (such as a library handbook, posters, handouts, and flyers), with occasional human intervention. Although Lynch did not consider these true reference questions, they can hardly be avoided at the reference desk. Precisely because they are not true reference questions and because they are so repetitive, it was considered essential to have ORA handle as many transactions of this sort as possible.

Implementation

Most directional questions are handled in ORA by a section that constitutes an electronic version of the University of Waterloo Library Handbook. This consists of a set of information pages linked together in a tree structure with access by menus and by subject index. Other directional questions are handled by the command set at the bottom of all information pages. For example, the ''news bulletin'' command lists recent and forthcoming areas of development in ORA, and also general Library news (including book exhibits, orientation programs, major acquisitions, gifts, etc.). The ''hours'' command, on the other hand, calculates and displays which functions are currently open in the various campus libraries. It also gives the user a general schedule of hours of opening.

HOLDINGS TRANSACTIONS

Scope

Lynch describes holdings transactions as those in which a user wishes to know whether the library owns a particular item. The expertise required in answering transactions of this type can range from a low to a relatively high level. For a low-level question, such as a request for help in finding a simple book by author or title, ORA provides only an information page giving instructions in using the catalog for this purpose. For a somewhat more complex question, such as determining the form of entry for a journal title containing a corporate name, ORA asks for the data to be input, and uses natural language processing to construct probable forms of entry from it. For a question more complex still, such as finding a conference proceedings, ORA provides a expert system that not only makes deductions about which elements (conference name, editor, etc.) are valid search keys in the catalog, and suggests possible forms of entry for them, but also points to tools that will help in abbreviation expansion and in verification. Finally, for a situation where the user does not know enough about bibliography to recognize whether an item is a book, periodical article, conference proceedings, technical report, and so on, a more sophisticated system called a citation interpreter is used. In handling some transactions, ORA may use a cluster of modules of the types mentioned above.

In the next few pages, the structure and working of some of the holdings-transaction modules in ORA will be examined. To illustrate their working, we will refer to a particular holdings transaction of a type that occurs frequently, and that requires the use of a cluster of these modules. The modules in the cluster are called the citation interpreter (with an interlibrary loan option), form-of-entry transformer, and call-number locator. In the holdings transaction to be used as an example, the user wants to consult a copy of the item corresponding to the following bibliographic reference but does not even know whether it is a book, periodical article, technical report, and so on, much less how to determine whether the library owns a copy of it:

1894 Dewey, Frederick P. The accuracy of the commercial assay for silver. *Journal of the American Chemical Society*. 16(8):505–516.

Citation Interpreter

Introduction. Frequently users ask for assistance in interpreting bibliographic references. To help in this task, ORA has an expert system called a "citation interpreter" that employs pattern recognition. Essentially the system asks the user to examine a reference component-by-component and to identify from a sequence of menus whether the component in question is an author, title, date, and so forth. Where the user might not recognize the name for a particular type of component, an example is given. As the user identifies, one after the other, the type of component, the system constructs at the top of the screen either a sample reference or the actual reference. When the user is through, the system deduces the bibliographic form, using a set of heuristic rules, and labels the components of the reference, or transfers them to the appropriate spots on an interlibrary loan form. Because the citation interpreter gets help from the user, this is an example of machine-aided intelligence, rather than machine intelligence. Since the citation interpreter shifts the semantic burden to the client, and concentrates on using heuristic rules, the knowledge representation can be handled adequately using production rules rather than semantic networks. The system was therefore implemented as an expert system based only on production rules.

Building the knowledge base. Before describing the system in more detail, we shall briefly elaborate upon the building of the knowledge base for this system. Because references can be written in several styles and can represent several bibliographic forms (books, journal articles, conference papers, etc.), a particular kind of component (e.g., a title) can reasonably be expected to occur for different references in different places in the sequence of components. Therefore, in the citation interpreter certain components appear in several menus. Constructing the set of menus for the citation interpreter was done by examining a number of style manuals and analyzing the possible component sequences for every bibliographic form. After each bibliographic form had been analyzed, certain characteristic patterns in the component sequences were identified as implying with a high probability that the sequence corresponds to that particular bibliographic form. It was this information that was recorded in the knowledge base. For example, the occurrence and order of presentation of components like title, volume number, page numbers, and so on, were recorded in the knowledge base as the clues that identify a particular bibliographic form in a particular bibliographic style or styles.

Modes of operation. The system begins by giving the user the option of three modes: (a) having the system choose sample components, (b) having the user enter the value of the component at the keyboard, for example, typing in the author's name, or (c) doing the latter in order to obtain assistance in filling out an interlibrary loan form. After the mode is chosen, the pattern recognition process begins.

It should be noted that the first mode, in which the system chooses sample components, is faster for the user, since the latter is obliged only to identify the semantic type of the component, not to enter its value as well. In our example, this means that the user would only specify that the sequence of components is "date," "author," "first title," and so on. The user does not have to specify also that the respective values are "1894," "Dewey, Frederick P.," and so on. In the second mode, in which the user also enters the value of the component, the reference constructed at the top of the screen should be identical to the one the user has, not merely a reference of similar type. Although this mode is slower, and requires typing skills beyond simply entering numbers from a menu, it renders the interpretation of the reference easier for the user to understand, since the labeling is for the user's actual reference, not a similar one. The user does not have to reason by analogy in order to interpret the reference in question. The same considerations apply to the third mode, since it also requires that the user type in the value of each component. Clearly, in choosing the mode of operation, the user must weigh speed of operation against ease of comprehension.

Feature selector. The feature selector of this pattern-recognition system is the part that collaborates with the user to identify the semantic types of the components in the linear sequence that comprises the bibliographic reference. The menus with which the user is presented at each step in the process described above give a limited set of possible features (types of bibliographic components) to choose from. The set at any point is always a subset of all possible types of bibliographic components (author, title, date, imprint, etc.). The subset is chosen on a heuristic basis (types of components that are most likely to come after the previous type of component). As the user proceeds through the sequence of menus, the component sequence that is disclosed is stored to variables. In our example, that means that the sequence is stored as first-component = "date," second-component = "author," third-component = "first title," fourth-component = "second title," and fifth-component = "volume and paging." If the user has chosen the second or third mode, the system will also be storing the values of the components to variables. In our example, that means that the values are stored as first-value = "1894," second-value = "Dewey, Frederick P.," and so on.

Classifier. The classifier of this pattern-recognition system uses the above-mentioned set of heuristic rules matching certain ordered sets of features with certain classes of bibliographic forms. It does this by testing first to see whether the characteristic patterns for a particular bibliographic form are present in the component sequence that was disclosed. If not, it tests for another bibliographic form, and so on, until a match is found. The system is then able to announce the bibliographic form. In our "1894 Dewey . . ." example, the characteristic sequence of: "title," "second title," "year," "volume," identifies the reference as a periodical article.

The order in which the classifier tests for characteristic patterns is important. The classifier begins by checking for characteristic patterns that have the highest probability of yielding only one interpretation. Examples are the occurrence of "op. cit.," "ibid.," and so on, near the beginning of the reference. After ruling these out, the classifier tests for characteristic patterns that have the next highest probabilities of yielding only one interpretation. Examples are the occurrence in a title of a generic term for conference, such as "Conference," "Symposium," "Colloque," or "Tagung." The classifier continues to rule out interpretations and to test for patterns that have lower probabilities of yielding only one interpretation. Because it eliminates interpretations as it performs unsuccessful tests for patterns, therefore when it finally reaches patterns that yield several interpretations, only a very small number (usually one) remain as real possibilities.

Also, depending on the bibliographic form, the system may alter the names of some of the components. In our "1894 Dewey . . ." example, the "title" label would be modified to read "article title" and the "second title" label to read "periodical title." After this operation, the components of the reference can be labeled.

Form-of-Entry Transformer

Introduction. Because the transition from AACR to AACR-II cataloguing is far from over, and because the University of Waterloo Serials List has few cross references, users frequently have difficulty in locating serials in the Serials List when the serial title contains the name of a corporate body. An expert system, called a "form-of-entry transformer" allows the user to enter the title of a serial publication at the keyboard. This forms the dialog module of the system. The expert system then generates and displays various possible forms of entry, including one AACR and several AACR-II forms of entry. It does this by applying a set of heuristic rules to six databases of terms with equivalents in English, French, German, Italian and Russian.

Databases of generic terms. One of the six databases contains generic words for publication, such as "ABHANDLUNGEN," "BULLETIN," "COMPTES RENDUS," "DOKLADY," "JOURNAL," "PROCEEDINGS," "RENDICONTI," and so on. Another contains generic words for corporate body, such as "ACCADEMIA," "ASSOCIATION," "CONSEIL," "OBSHCHESTVO," "SOCIETY," "VEREIN," and so on. A third has generic words for meeting, such as "COLLOQUE," "CONFERENCE," "SYMPOSIUM," "TAGUNG," and so on. A fourth has prepositions; a fifth has articles; and a sixth has combinations of prepositions and articles, such as "DEGLI," "DELLA," "DELLE," "DES," "DU," and so on.

Heuristic rules. The expert system includes such heuristic rules as the following: IF the serial title contains generic words for a corporate body and for a publication, AND IF the pattern is publication-preposition-article-corporate body, THEN possible forms of entry include "corporate body. publication," "publication (corporate body)," and the original form of entry. In our "1894 Dewey . . ." example, the journal title is "Journal of the American Chemical Society." The form-of-entry transformer uses the heuristic rule quoted to generate from this the following possible forms of entry:

"American Chemical Society. Journal"
"Journal (American Chemical Society)" and
"Journal of the American Chemical Society."

Inference engine. Finally, the inference engine specifies the order in which the system checks for characteristic patterns such as the one mentioned in the last paragraph (i.e., publication-preposition-article-corporate body).

Call-Number Locator

Introduction. Finally there is an expert system called a "call-number locator" that helps a user transform a particular Library of Congress call number into a physical location in the library system. The dialog module asks the user for the location symbols (for the particular library and for the part of the library, for example, the periodical stacks) and then for the particular call number. The system then either gives an error message or calculates which face of which range the call number lies on and points to it on a map. It does this by using a small knowledge base and a larger database.

Knowledge base of error messages. The small knowledge base contains a set of heuristic rules to generate error messages of the type that any reference librarian would give. These messages are of the form "No call number begins with an I or an O." The inference engine functions by assuming that several errors have been made by the user, and by checking the input call number against the heuristic rules to see whether any of those errors have been made. If no match is found, control is passed to the database component.

Database of range-end call numbers. The database specifies the call numbers that fall at the ends of every stack range in the different sections of the library. A moderately intelligent interface takes the specified library, part of the library, and call number and calculates on which face of which range the call number lies. The calculation (using algorithmic rather than heuristic rules) is done by finding the highest and lowest range numbers possible for the first class letter, then, within that span of range numbers, finding the highest and lowest possible for the second class number, and so on. Although this system does not embody a particularly high level of expertise, since any reasonably intelligent user should be able to deduce this information from a detailed map and a few simple rules about the LC class schedules, it does mean that the user is required to perform fewer logical deductions.

SUBSTANTIVE TRANSACTIONS: READY-REFERENCE

Scope. This section of ORA is devoted to ready-reference questions, which are requests for factual information that can be satisfied by consulting a small number of reference sources. They include requests for such information as addresses, physical data, definitions, specifications, laws and regulations, biographical information, statistics, and expansions of abbreviations. Ready-reference questions that result from class assignments can often impose a severe burden on an already busy reference desk. A special part of the system is set aside for these questions.

Access. Katz implied (1982, Vol.2, pp. 41–42) that ready-reference questions rarely require a reference interview. Therefore, no attempt has been made to simulate one for this type of question. Instead, users indicate their question type to the system by employing a subject index or a menu-driven tree structure. Suppose, for example, that a user were looking for an address of a manufacturer of chemicals in the United States. The user could indicate the question type by invoking the subject index, entering the heading "manufacturers," and choosing from a list the subject heading dealing with U.S. manufacturers of chemicals. The user could also achieve the same effect by using the heading "chemicals." Alternatively, the user could indicate the question type to the system by making a series of choices from a sequence of menus. In our example, the sequence of menus begins: "FACTUAL INFORMATION," "INDUSTRIAL AND BUSINESS INFORMATION," "INDUSTRIAL AND BUSINESS ADDRESSES," "ADDRESSES OF MANUFACTURERS," and so on.

If the user is able to supply subject headings that match those that have been used in the system, the user will find the approach by subject index faster than by menu. If not, or if the user has misunderstood the scope of the system, then the approach by subject index will be slow and frustrating; the user may be reduced to browsing over subject headings. In such cases, the approach by menu will be preferable, since it reduces guesswork to a minimum by offering subject access through a hierarchical framework and by forcing the user to stay within the bounds of that framework. Hence, although menu access is often regarded as a slow form of access, it has distinct advantages when the user is unable to supply standard terminology as subject headings or does not have a clear idea of the scope of a system.

Heuristic search rules. Once the question type has been ascertained, the system uses a set of heuristic rules to prescribe search strategy. These rules point from the type of question to tools that are likely to help in locating the desired information. These rules can be considered as implementations of some search devices proposed by William A. Katz (1982, Vol.2, Chap.4, "The Search") and Marcia J. Bates (1979). Katz spoke of devices that aided the search process by translating the type of question to forms of information sources. Bates discussed 29 search tactics, among them the PATTERN and STRETCH tactics. Her PATTERN tactic involves recognizing and using a pattern of search that often helps in answering a certain kind of request. Her STRETCH tactic appears to be a variant of the PATTERN tactic: It involves using a tool for a purpose for which it was not intended.

For our example, finding an address for a U.S. manufacturer of chemicals, a heuristic rule corresponding to a Katz translation device or a Bates PATTERN tactic would be the following: IF the user wants an address for a U.S. manufacturer of chemicals, THEN use a directory for U.S. manufacturers of chemicals. A heuristic rule corresponding to a Bates STRETCH tactic would be the following: IF the user wants an address for a U.S. manufacturer of chemicals, but cannot find it in a directory of such manufacturers, THEN browse through trade magazines in the appropriate subject area. The latter technique is tedious, precisely because trade magazines are not intended to be used for this purpose, and therefore generally do not have cumulated indexes to their advertisements. It is nonetheless a technique that some users may find worthwhile.

SUBSTANTIVE TRANSACTIONS: COMPLEX SUBJECT SEARCHES

Scope. This section of ORA is designed to prescribe a search strategy (including the use of both library-produced bibliographic data bases and commercially published reference tools) to help a user with a complex subject search, that is, one requiring the use of several tools. Here the dialog module is intended to model the reference interview for a complex substantive query. The dialog module will be examined from the point of view of the best known theory of the reference interview, that put forward by Robert S. Taylor (1968). Taylor proposed five "filters" used by reference librarians to clarify the user's request in the reference interview.

First Taylor filter. The first set of menus in the dialog module narrows down the subject area, performing the first Taylor filter. The initial menu consists of nearly 50 broad subject areas arranged alphabetically. Secondary menus that further refine the broad subject areas are being prepared as required. Because of the amount of time involved, only areas that are asked for frequently at the information desks, and for which there are specialized reference tools, are being refined in this way.

Second Taylor filter. The second set of menus corresponds to the second filter, determining the motivation and objective of the user. Because ORA is designed for an academic environment, the motivation of the user is almost invariably the completion of a piece of writing. The writing can range in complexity from a very short essay to a dissertation or a research paper. The second filter is therefore implemented through a menu that attempts to determine the kind of writing that the user is trying to complete, and for which the information is required.

Third Taylor filter. The third filter, constructing a user model, is not yet implemented. It is planned to do so by using a series of menus to determine such characteristics as the user's level of familiarity with the subject area in question, with performing complex subject searches, with using the library, with using ORA, and with using computer systems in general.

Fourth Taylor filter. The fourth filter, redefining the question to take account of the way information is organized in the library, begins with a statement indicating that brief and introductory information is often found in dictionaries, encyclopedias and handbooks. The user is then asked if this would be useful. Next, the user is asked if more comprehensive material, such as that found in books might be useful. If so, the user is given some information about negotiating the subject vocabulary of the catalog. Finally, the user is informed that more detailed and up-to-date information can be located using abstracts and indexes. The user is again asked if this option sounds interesting.

Fifth Taylor filter. The fifth filter, determining what kind of answers will be acceptable to the user, is given an implicit rather than explicit implementation. The user is presented with bibliographic information on reference tools that might be useful, along with annotations indicating their scope and ease of use. The user is asked to choose which tools appear most useful. So, rather than being asked what kinds of answers will be acceptable, the user is provided with information about tools (such as comprehensiveness and ease of use) that can be weighed to make decisions about acceptability.

Search strategy. Once the nature of the user's request has been clarified, subject strategy can be constructed. (Incidentally, we have already considered this topic to some extent, since the last two Taylor filters overlap somewhat with the process of search strategy construction.) Katz indicated that for a complex subject search, it would be necessary to use not only translation devices of the type mentioned in the section on ready-reference questions, but also bibliographical aids to determine which additional library resources to consult. Both techniques are used in the section of ORA dealing with complex subject searches. The initial part of the search strategy formulation, which is concerned with finding brief and introductory material, is generally handled by Katz translation devices. For example, the user is referred to specific reference tools (such as dictionaries, handbooks, and encyclopedias) that will probably help the user start the search. If the user wants more comprehensive material, then bibliographical aids are suggested: beginning with the catalog and going on to abstracts and indexes.

CONCLUSION

A working system has been available for public testing since March 1987. It is being evaluated in order to help identify areas of such high use that they deserve further development, and to improve the user interface. Data for the evaluation is being gathered through an electronic suggestion box, transactional logging, and conversation with users. The purpose of the electronic suggestion box is to allow the active user to express specific concerns to the system designers. The user does this by invoking the suggestion-box command from one of the command bars at the bottom of most pages, and entering a message to the system. Transactional logging, on the other hand, allows information to be gathered regardless of the cognitive style of the user, since it tracks the paths of all users through the system. Conversation with users, although time-consuming, is probably the most probing method of data gathering, since a dialog permits considerable clarification of the basic problems a user may be experiencing.

Preliminary results indicate a great deal of interest from the public. Some very good feedback has already been received, resulting in several improvements to the user interface. For example, a major problem shortly after public installation of the system was that some users confused ORA with the much-anticipated, but not-yet-arrived online public catalog. Since that time, statements clarifying this point have been inserted just after the logo statement at the top of the system. (To do this, it was necessary to distinguish between reference service and the catalog, without actually using library terminology—not so easy as it might seem!) Unfortunately, not all interface problems that have been identified are so tractable. A case in point is the time taken to paint a screen, apparently a limitation of the color graphics terminals being used; the problem will probably require a financial solution.

On theoretical grounds alone (see the conclusions in the Chapter 6), there are clearly several useful structures that might be either introduced or improved in a system like ORA. Similarly, there are subject areas that might need more data. The challenge ahead lies in working with users to establish priorities for the further development of both appropriate structures and subject areas.

REFERENCES

Bates, M. J. (1979, July). Information search tactics. *Journal of the American Society for Information Science, 30*, 205–214.

Ferriero, D. S., & Powers, K. A. (1982, Spring). Burnout at the reference desk. *RQ, 21*, 274–279.

Katz, W. A. (1982). *Introduction to reference work.* New York: McGraw-Hill.

Lynch, M. J. (1978, April). Reference interviews in public libraries. *Library Quarterly, 48*, 119–142.

Miller, W. (1984, May). What's wrong with reference: Coping with success and failure at the reference desk. *American Libraries, 15*, 303–306, 321–322.

Neville, S. H. (1981, May). Job stress and burnout: Occupational hazards for service staff. *College & Research Libraries, 42*, 242–247.

Parrott, J. R. (1986, September). Expert systems for reference work. *Microcomputers for Information Management, 3*, 155–171.

Smith, K. F. (1986, September). Robot at the reference desk? *College & Research Libraries, 47*, 486–490.

Taylor, R. S. (1968, May). Question-negotiation and information seeking in libraries. *College & Research Libraries, 29*, 178–194.

Vickery, A., & Brooks, H. M. (1987). PLEXUS: The expert system for referral. *Information Processing and Management, 23*, 99–117.

Waters, S. T. (1986, September). Answerman, the expert information specialist: An expert system for retrieval of information from library reference books. *Information Technology and Libraries, 5*, 204–212.

Williams, M., & Davis, E. B. (1982). Computer-assisted instruction: An overview. In C. Oberman & K. Strauch (Eds.), *Theories of bibliographic education* (pp. 171–191). New York: Bowker.

10
Automating Descriptive Cataloging

Diane Vizine-Goetz
Stuart Weibel
William Oskins
Offices of Research and Technical Planning
Online Computer Library Center, Inc.
Dublin, OH

AUTOMATING DESCRIPTIVE CATALOGING

The centralization of technical services and growth of bibliographic networks such as OCLC have done much to improve library services. Shared cataloging has made cataloging faster, more efficient, and less labor-intensive. Despite these advances, cataloging remains a resource-intensive activity, requiring skills that are in demand. Furthermore, recent evidence suggests that the pool of qualified catalogers is decreasing significantly (Hill, 1985). Thus, efforts to further automate cataloging are particularly appropriate at this time and pertinent to OCLC's goal of reducing the rate of rise of library per-unit costs.

BACKGROUND

Cataloging is concerned with three separate but related activities:

1. Describing the item and choosing name and title access points
2. Assigning classification numbers
3. Assigning subject headings.

The first activity, called descriptive cataloging, is governed by a complex and detailed set of rules—the *Anglo-American Cataloguing Rules* (AACR2, 2d ed.)—that is a de facto international standard. Activities two and three, called subject cataloging, involve subject analysis. Wynar (1985) defines subject analysis as "the part of cataloging that deals with determining what the intellectual content of an item is 'about'." Recent attempts to automate cataloging through expert systems have focused on descriptive cataloging because it is considered rule-based (AACR2). Research is required to determine whether subject cataloging is also amenable to such automation.

Clarke and Cronin (1983) suggest two approaches for applying artificial intelligence techniques to cataloging:

- A human-machine interface as a first step towards expert-system cataloguing, where the intellectual effort is divided between the intermediary and the support system
- An expert system with full cataloguing capability linked into an electronic publishing system, so that as a text is generated on-line, it can be passed through an expert-system cataloguing process without any intellectual input from an intermediary.

Current research in automated cataloging described below reflects efforts in both directions.

Probably the first project that sought to automate cataloging using expert-system techniques was carried out by Davies and James (1984) at the University of Exeter, England. This study emphasized a software interface to Prolog rather than the creation of a knowledge base; consequently, a prototype cataloging system was never implemented.

Another attempt to use an expert system for cataloging was initiated at Linköping University, Sweden (Hjerppe, Olander, & Marklund, 1985). The project, ESSCAPE (Expert Systems for Simple Choice of Access Points for Entries), involved implementing a set of rules from Chapter 21 of AACR2 that deals with choice of access points. EMYCIN, a shell system for building expert systems, was used to implement the rules. This system prompts the user for a simple bibliographic description and then proceeds to establish access points. Although this effort was somewhat successful, the approaches are no longer being pursued. Instead, the HYPERCATalog project, concerned with the structure and design of an enhanced catalog, has been initiated.

Closer to the second approach is the AUTOCAT project in West Germany that seeks to generate bibliographic records of periodical literature in the physical sciences. This system requires that original documents be available in machine-readable form (Endres-Niggemeyer & Knorz, 1986).

In a related project, Harrison (1985) reported on the retrospective conversion of cataloging cards to full MARC format records using the optical scanning technology developed by the OPTIRAM Company of Great Britain. Although this effort is narrow in scope, it further exemplifies the growing interest in developing automated systems for cataloging and related activities.

The OCLC Automated Title Page Cataloging Project both extends and complements these approaches by using machine-readable files that capture the *image* of a title page. In addition to the text strings found on a title page, commonly used by other systems, our system also uses information about the typography and layout of the page to generate the elements of a first-level bibliographic description described in AACR2.

THE OCLC AUTOMATED TITLE PAGE CATALOGING PROJECT

Our interest in descriptive cataloging is limited to formulating the description (the part of the catalog entry that tells what the item looks like). Part I of AACR2 includes the rules for identifying and describing a work. The format for the description is based on the International Standard Bibliographic Description (ISBD). The ISBD format divides the data in the description of an item into eight areas:

1. Title and statement of responsibility
2. Edition
3. Materials (or type of publication) specific details
4. Publication, distribution, etc.
5. Physical description
6. Series
7. Note
8. Standard number and terms of availability.

If these elements occur in the item being cataloged, they are found in this order on the catalog entry. Some areas, however, are used only with specific types of materials. For example, the material-specific details area is used exclusively for cartographic materials and serials.

AACR2 also provides for three levels of detail in the description. The first level of description is the briefest, and is acceptable for identifying items in a small collection. The second level includes more detail and corresponds to Library of Congress cataloging practice. The third level includes all applicable rules.

Our study attempts to demonstrate the feasibility of developing an automated cataloging system whose input is machine-readable files containing information from title pages. The output is a first-level bibliographic description as defined by AACR2. Limiting the output to a first-level description reduces the amount of AACR2 rules to a number appropriate for a preliminary study. Success at this level would provide the foundation on which to build a system of broader scope, since the first-level description could be a basis for more detailed levels (i.e., the second-level description includes all of the information required in the first-level description, and so on).

The first-level description for monographs includes the following elements. Listed with these elements are the prescribed sources of information for each according to AACR2.

Element of Description	*Prescribed Sources of Information*
Title proper	Title page
First statement of responsibility	Title page
Edition statement	Title page
First publisher, etc., date of publication	Title page
Pagination	The whole publication
Note	Any source
International Standard Book Number (ISBN)	Any source

With the exception of the pagination, note, and ISBN elements, the information required to form the first-level description can usually be found on the recto (right-hand page) of the title page.

THE CHALLENGE OF AUTOMATED CATALOGING

> Ercegovac (1986) observes that [descriptive] cataloging has the unique property of being pseudoformalized, i.e., there is a large body of . . . rules that define and regulate the cataloging activity. [Yet,] . . . the process of cataloging is [a] far more subtle, experienced-based and example-driven domain.

What may initially appear as simply a matter of translating AACR2 into the knowledge base of an expert system is a far more complex problem. Consider, for example, rule 1.1B in AACR2 that states, in part, "transcribe the title proper exactly as to wording, order and spelling. . . ." This rule presumes the cataloger is able to identify the title proper of a work (an ability acquired through experience in recognizing titles) before the cataloging rule can be applied. As Hagler and Simmons (1982) point out, titles are not always presented in an unambiguous way:

> A title is a grammatical unit. It may incorporate words designating an author, publisher, date, or other information as well as what the average reader normally considers to be title words, as in the case of the titles *Shakespeare's Complete Works, The 1981 Proceedings of the Conference on Aging, The Barbara Kraus Calorie Guide, and Macmillan Bible Atlas.*

Likewise, AACR2 provides little guidance as to how subtitles are to be recognized. Although a subtitle often follows the title proper on the title page, there are exceptions to this general rule. Ultimately, it is the cataloger's interpretation of the layout of the title page that determines the words ascribed to the title or subtitle.

The first challenge of automating cataloging, then, and the one where we are focusing our efforts, is to ''understand'' bibliographic data as expressed on title pages. Only then can the rules found in AACR2 be applied.

METHODOLOGY

The automated title page cataloging project is organized into five activities:

1. Selecting a test sample of items
2. Creating machine-readable files for title pages
3. Identifying functionally related text strings from the machine-readable title page
4. Forming a rule interpreter and core set of rules to recognize basic bibliographic elements
5. Evaluating results.

Sample Title Pages

We considered a test sample of items necessary both for forming rules and testing system performance and generality. We produced the systematic random sample by selecting records from the OCLC database with the following characteristics:

1. Used for cataloging during May 1986
2. Three or more holdings symbols attached
3. English-language monograph.

These criteria produced a set of items that reflect current cataloging activity and are widely held by OCLC libraries. An average of 205 holdings symbols was attached per record. To make the task more manageable, we imposed the requirement that items also be English-language monographs. After the bibliographic records were selected from the OCLC database, the items were requested through interlibrary loan. In all 101 items were borrowed.

Machine-Readable Title Pages

Ideally, an automated cataloging system would be linked to an electronic publishing or optical scanning system that would provide information about the typography and text strings of title pages. For research purposes, however, it was deemed sufficient to capture title page images through a separate, manual step. The input to the automated cataloging system consists of manually prepared page composition files. The computer typesetting language (TeX) was used to prepare the files containing information from the title pages of the sample items. An original title page and a facsimile produced from a TeX page composition file are shown in Figure 10.1. The information in the TeX files includes the text strings and the following attributes for each string:

1. Font style
2. Font size
3. Location of the text string on a page

Our intent was to produce a close reproduction of a title page that would accurately describe the text strings in terms of their attributes on a page.

This approach is a first step toward a system that would handle the bibliographic elements of an electronically published document or scanned title page. The Library of Congress, among others, has expressed interest in a system linked directly to publishers (Schmidt, 1986).

Identifying Related Text Strings

Token formation. The first step in identifying related text strings is to form a token file from the page composition file. The token file is an ASCII file consisting of each space-delimited character string, or token, and attributes

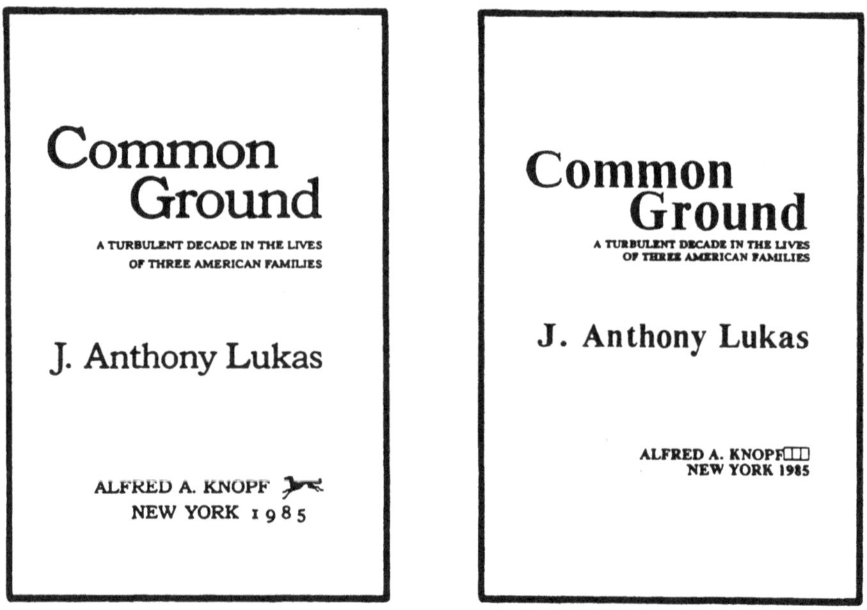

Common
Ground

A TURBULENT DECADE IN THE LIVES
OF THREE AMERICAN FAMILIES

J. Anthony Lukas

ALFRED A. KNOPF
NEW YORK 1985

Common
Ground

A TURBULENT DECADE IN THE LIVES
OF THREE AMERICAN FAMILIES

J. Anthony Lukas

ALFRED A. KNOPF
NEW YORK 1985

Original Title Page | Facsimile Produced Using TeX

Figure 10.1. An Original Title Page and a Facsimile Produced from a TeX Page Composition File.

describing the token's location on the page, font size, and font style. The token file is then read into a Prolog data structure and additional useful information is supplied. Case class, an element in the token data structure based on the idea of upper- and lower-case characters, is an example of useful information that has been derived for a token. Figure 10.2 illustrates several elements of the data structures used in the system. The element referred to as baseline is measured in millimeters from the top of a page and gives the alignment of the bottom of the characters in a token. The elements "start x" and "end x", also measured in millimeters, give the distance from the left-hand edge of the page to the first character of a token, and the distance from the right-hand edge to the last character in a token, respectively.

Compound token formation. The next processing step involves building functionally meaningful phrases, or compound tokens, that can be evaluated as bibliographic data. Compound tokens, which we call compounds, are built by adding tokens to a compound structure until one of the following occurs:

Automating Descriptive
Cataloging

Token Structure

Token ID	Character String	Base-line	Start X	End X	Font Style	Font Size	Case Class
1	Common	717	337	1054	Bold	48	UL
2	vskip	717	859	125	Bold	48	V
3	Ground	859	683	1307	Bold	48	UL
4	vskip	859	923	60	Bold	48	V
5	A	923	566	594	Bold	10	O
6	TURBULENT	923	606	850	Bold	10	U
7	DECADE	923	861	1024	Bold	10	U
8	IN	923	1036	1083	Bold	10	U
9	THE	923	1095	1177	Bold	10	U
10	LIVES	923	1189	1307	Bold	10	U

Compound Token Structure

Token ID	Character String	Font Size	Previous Vertical Distance	Next Vertical Distance	Case Class
1	Common Ground	48	0	60	UL,V,UL,V

Page Statistics Structure

Largest Font Size on Page	Left Margin	Right Margin	Top Baseline	Bottom Baseline	Mean White Space
48	337	1307	717	1676	.3833

Figure 10.2. Data Structure Elements

1. Font style changes
2. Font size changes
3. Vertical white space separating successive tokens exceeds a threshold.

These simple rules result in grouping tokens and their respective attributes into meaningful compounds. For example, from Figure 10.2 it can be seen that the tokens "Common" and "Ground" are formed into a compound that contains both. A new compound would be formed from the tokens that follow because the font size changes.

Page statistics formation. The last structure created describes the characteristics of the page including leftmost and rightmost margins, top baseline, bottom baseline, largest font on the page, and mean vertical gap between elements on the page. This structure provides an overall picture of the characteristics of a page for use in rule interpretation.

Application of Rules

Bibliographic elements are identified by applying a series of rules to each compound. Rules are specified as a Prolog structure having six arguments:

1. Rule number
2. Precedence class
3. Explanatory text
4. Confidence factor
5. Condition list
6. Resultant action.

The first argument is an integer that identifies the rule. When a rule succeeds for a particular compound, the rule number is recorded in the compound as part of the list of rules that has succeeded.

The second argument specifies the class of a rule. Rules are grouped in precedence classes to control their application by the rule interpreter. All low-precedence rules are applied before rules of the next higher level class. Only two levels of rule precedence are currently used; however, the simplicity of the control scheme lets us add classes easily. The third argument is a phrase that describes the rule. This information is used by an explanation facility to describe the rules that succeed for each compound. We use this capability to evaluate and modify the system's performance.

The fourth argument is a confidence factor that has a type value and a numeric value. For example, the confidence factor "ti(3)" implies that a compound is a title. The integer component of the term, (3), is a relative measure of the strength of the implication. When a rule succeeds, the associated confidence factor is recorded in a list in the compound with the confidence factors of any other rules that succeed for the compound. Confidence factors are a measure of the likelihood that the rule will correctly identify a compound.

The fifth argument specifies the condition or list of conditions that must be satisfied for the rule to succeed. Each of the terms in the list is subjected to a series of tests that either succeeds or fails. For example, "largest—font" is a procedure that compares the font size of the compound with the largest font argument of the "page—stats" structure and succeeds if they are equal. Multiple conditions in this list can be joined by an "and" or an "or" conjunction, as appropriate.

The last argument is the action list, consisting of the action that is to be executed if the rule succeeds. Currently, this action is simply to record the rule and associated confidence factor in the data structure for the compound.

To further illustrate the rule structure two rules for identifying titles are presented below:

Rule Element	*Definition*
rule(1,	rule id
free,	rule class
$First compound, largest font.$	explanatory test
[ti(9)],	confidence factor
[first—compound, largest—font],	list of conditions
[record—rule(1)]	action list
).	
rule(2,	rule id
free,	rule class
$Largest font.$	explanatory test
[ti(10)],	confidence factor
[largest—font],	list of conditions
[record—rule(2)]	action list
).	

Biliographic field resolution. After all rules for all precedence classes are tested, each compound will have a list of confidence factors associated with it. The first step of the field resolution process is to consolidate confidence factors of the same type. In this process, the values of confidence factors of the same type are added and then replaced by the sum of the individual confidence factors. Next, the list of confidence factors is sorted by the integer component or "weight" of the term. Thus,

[ti(4), sr(3), sr(5)]

becomes

[sr(8), ti(4)].

The method for identifying bibliographic elements consists of selecting the highest confidence factor from the list and identifying the compound as the corresponding element. Therefore, a compound with a confidence factor list of [sr(8), ti(4)] would be identified as a statement of responsibility. Figure 10.3 shows the results of the rule application and resolution for *Common Ground.*

```
Automating Descriptive
Cataloging


common.OUT
3-23-1987
9:54:33

Title Proper:
Common Ground
          Confidence Factor list = [ti(19)]
          Rules which succeeded:
          1: First compound, largest font.
          2: Largest font.


Other Title Information:
A TURBULENT DECADE IN THE LIVES OF THREE AMERICAN FAMILIES
          Confidence Factor list = [ot(7)]
          Rules which succeeded:
          8: After largest font, begins with article.


Statement of Responsibility:
J. Anthony Lukas
          Confidence Factor list = [sr(7)]
          Rules which succeeded:
          4: Strong name pattern (initial present).


Place, Publisher, and Date:
ALFRED A. KNOPF NEW YORK 1985
          Confidence Factor list =
[sr(7),pu(100),pl(8),da(100)]
          Rules which succeeded:
          4: Strong name pattern (initial present).
         10: Publisher name.
         11: Place name.
         12: Four character, all numeric, not largest font.

File completed:      9:55:37
```

Figure 10.3. Output from Automated Title Page Cataloging System for *Common Ground.*

Results

In our example, the title proper was identified by the successful execution of two rules, (a) the title proper is the first element on the page and is in the largest font size, and (b) only the title is in the largest font size. Rules such as these are not found in cataloging codes (AACR2, for example, gives no instructions about how to recognize titles) but represent our attempt to discover a technique for recognizing titles from the title pages of books. The result of applying our rules to 24 items from the sample is shown in Table 10.1.

Overall, 73% of the fields were identified correctly with under 20 rules. Further, the causes of many of the misidentifications were easily identified and can be remedied with simple solutions. For instance, the success rate for recognizing publishers and places could be improved if more complete authority files were used, and the three errors that occurred in the publication date element could be resolved by including a rule designed to recognize dates represented in Roman numerals. More difficult to resolve, however, are the problems of differentiating between titles and subtitles—these errors account for 43% of errors in title fields. For example, the system failed to identify the subtitle of the book *Terror in the prisons: Homosexual rape and why society condones it*, and combined the title and subtitle of the book *The novels of Nathalie Sarraute: Towards an aesthetic* into a single field.

Further success may be attained in a number of ways, including:

1. Adding more general rules dealing with the semantic information (words like "edited by" and "translated by") contained on title pages.
2. Extensive use of authority files for recognizing places and publishers.
3. Adding specific rules for particular types of documents (theses, technical reports, etc.).

We will perform a complete analysis of the system's performance when all items in the sample are processed.

Table 10.1. Results of Rule Application for 24 Items

Bibliographic Element	# Found on Title Page	# Identified Correctly	% Identified Correctly
Title Proper	24	15	63
Other Title Information	10	5	50
Statement of Responsibility	22	17	77
Edition Statement	NA	NA	NA
Place of Publication	21	17	81
Publisher	22	18	82
Date of Publication	12	9	75
All fields	111	81	73

SUMMARY

Despite what appears to be a moderate success rate (73% of the bibliographic elements were identified correctly), we are encouraged by the results achieved with only a small set of rules. This study demonstrates that it is feasible to automate much of the initial effort involved in descriptive cataloging.

REFERENCES

Clarke, A., & Cronin, B. (1983). Expert systems and library/informationwork. *Journal of Librarianship, 15*(4), 277–292.

Davies, R., & James, B. (1984). Towards an expert system for cataloging. *Program, 18*(4), 283–297.

Endres-Niggemeyer, B., & Knorz, G. (1986). Unpublished project description, personal communication.

Ercegovac, Z. (1986, May 6-8). Artificial intelligence and cataloging reasoning. *Proceedings of the 7th National Online Meeting New York*, pp. 109–117.

Hagler, R., & Simmons, P. (1982). *The bibliographic record and information technology*. Chicago: American Library Association.

Harrison, M. (1985). Retrospective conversion of card catalogues into full MARC format using sophisticated computer-controlled visual imaging techniques. *Program, 19*(3), 213–230.

Hill, J. S. (1985). Wanted: Good catalogers. *American Libraries, 16*(10), 728–730.

Hjerppe, R., Olander, B., & Marklund, K. (1985, July). *Project ESSCAPE—Expert systems for simple choice of access points for entries: Applications of artificial intelligence in cataloging*. Paper presented at International Federation of Library Associations (IFLA) 51st General Conference, Chicago, IL.

Schmidt, K. A. (1986). Technology at the Library of Congress: A summary of the proceedings of the LC/LITA Institute. *Information Technology and Libraries, 5*(4), 307–314.

Wynar, B. S. (1985). *Introduction to cataloging and classification*. Littleton, CO: Libraries Unlimited.

11
Selection of Main Entry: A Conceptual Model

Ann M. Sandberg-Fox
Library of Congress
Washington, DC

INTRODUCTION

The use of expert systems in the performance of cataloging tasks, specifically in the area of main entry selection, was pioneered in a doctoral study conducted by the author in the late 1960s (Sandberg-Fox, 1972). The aim of the study was to determine whether the human intellectual process of selecting main entry could be simulated by automatic, namely objective, nonintuitive, computer techniques. In view of the various dimensions of the topic, the study was addressed primarily to conceptual problems at the base of the entry process and the construction of a formalized model and set of heuristic procedures that would incorporate the design and objectives of this process. Technical feasibility with respect to the hardware/software aspects of implementing the model and heuristics was not within the scope of the investigation due to the exploratory nature of the study.

A corpus of AACR (1967) rules of entry and a counterpart corpus of ALA (Beetle, 1949) rules were selected in the study for characterization and testing of the following hypothesis:

> The corpus of AACR rules of entry would be more amenable to characterization and simulation by automatic techniques than its counterpart corpus of ALA rules of entry, because the corpus of the former (and, at that time, the most recent) cataloging code contained fewer rules; the rules were less complex, less redundant, and more explicit in specifying the bibliographic conditions operative for selection of entry.

Based on these factors, it was postulated that the conceptual model of AACR entry rules would be less complex and the heuristics applied to the model would generate the appropriate main entry assignment for a greater number of bibliographic items than the model and the applied heuristics representing the ALA entry rules.

In the case of both models and heuristics, tests of adequacy were conducted using a specially selected problem set of title pages of English language monographs. For details regarding the selection of main entry rules in the two codes, their characterization, testing, and findings, the reader is referred to the author's study. What is presented in the following pages is a reexamination of the process of selecting main entry as it is conceived and formulated in AACR2 (Gorman & Winkler, 1978) to assess its potential for characterization applying the method and heuristics used in the study to some of the title page data that were sampled.

CONCEPT OF MAIN ENTRY IN AACR2

The problem of selecting main entry is conceptually the same in AACR2 as it is in AACR and ALA in that it is a decision problem that requires of the cataloger: (a) maximum recognition of the presence or nonpresence of a particular set of bibliographic conditions, and (b) the need to decide the entry that is valid for these conditions. In a more formal sense, the process can be likened to an environment specified by a core of bibliographic principles which serve to govern the selection process, by a body of enumerative rules which defines the bibliographic conditions to which the governing principles apply, and by an unlimited quantity of bibliographic information which comprises the data for application of the rules and principles. Within this environment, the decision or selection process is accomplished through a series of logical, sequential operations which the cataloger performs with each bibliographic item. These operations can be envisioned as a sequence, or rather sequences, of questions, answers, and entry choices based on the cataloger's examination of the relevant bibliographic data. For instance, in the course of examining the title page to determine the presence of responsibility initially, a cataloger would presumably ask: "Is there an author name?" If there were two names, the typography would presumably be questioned: "Is one name in larger type?" and so on. In such a procedure, the questions presume two values, positive and negative responses or instances of authorship.

The content and structure of these operations were characterized in the study using directed tree diagrams. Directed tree diagrams are frequently employed in the design and analysis of computer operations, as well as in linguistic analyses of sentence structure (cf. Cullicover, 1982), and recently in the representation of bibliographic relationships in complex publication forms (Goossens, 1982). In selection of main entry, directed tree diagrams would serve to characterize the content and sequential operations of the process, and also act as operands on the bibliographic data presented or input to the system (topics which are discussed later in greater detail).

For the purpose of illustrating the method and heuristics discussed, the following basic rules of entry have been selected from Goman and Winkler (1978) for examination. Captions have been supplied to give an indication of their scope. For the text of the rules, the reader is referred to Chapter 21 (1978).

21.4A	(Works of single personal authorship)
21.5A,C	(Works of unknown or uncertain authorship or by unnamed groups)
21.6B1,2	(Principal responsibility indicated)
21.6C1,2	(Principal responsibility not indicated)
21.6D	(Shared pseudonyms)
21.7B	(Collections with collective title)
21.11A	(Illustrated texts)
21.11B	(Illustrations published separately)
21.14A	(Translations)
21.24	(Collaboration between artist and writer)
21.28B	(Related works)

With two exceptions (21.5C, 21.7B), these rules have identical or nearly identical counterparts in AACR. In the case of three rules, namely 21.4A, 21.6C1, and 21.11A, the author found their counterparts in AACR accounted for the highest percentage of cataloger usage. Thus, successful characterization of these rules would be optimal in accomplishing machine simulation of the entry process.

DEVELOPMENT OF THE CONCEPTUAL MODEL

The method of characterizing these rules is discussed in terms of a two-step process: the recognition of cataloging data on the title page, and on the basis of that recognition, the selection of the appropriate main entry.

Recognition Component

To give an account of the cataloger's ability to recognize the presence of an author (in this context, a person or corporate body) on the title page of a book is actually to describe his or her capacity to recognize a "name." Although a personal author, for instance, is defined in 21.1A1 as "the person chiefly responsible for the creation of the intellectual or artistic content of a work," the cataloger actually identifies the person as a name. Similarly, a corporate body is defined in 21.1B1 as "an organization or a group of persons that is identified by a particular name and that acts, or may act, as an entity." While there may be some question as to whether the name of the body qualifies as a "particular name," or that the body is acting as an entity, the cataloger is at least able to make the identification of the presence of some form of this name and to distinguish it from a personal name. There is perhaps no way of stating precisely how the identity of a "name" on the title page is established, but it is evident that in addition to perception, intuition, and other native capacities, the cataloger is greatly assisted by the physical and syntactic display of the bibliographic data. By physical is meant the position, typography, and composition (alphabet, numbers, etc.) of the data; by syntactic is meant those lexical units, words, of which the data are composed and the manner of their combination on the title page.

Taking the physical display, the most obvious way in which the title page assists the cataloger is in its design (the conventions of formatting, spacing, typography, etc.) which serves to identify and simultaneously distinguish parts or pieces of the data. Examples of the following three title page displays illustrate a common design.

(1)
THE YEAR
OF THE WHALE
BY
VICTOR B. SCHEFFER

(2)
PRINCIPLES OF
MATHEMATICAL LOGIC
By
D. Hilbert and W. Ackerman

(3)
THIRTY YEARS OF CHAMPIONSHIP GOLF
BY DAI REES
With John Ballantine

In terms of arrangement and distribution, the data are seen to comprise two physically distinct statements or strings, namely a title statement exhibited as the initial or first string in the display and an author statement exhibited as the second or substring in the display. Given this formatting, a characterization, for example, would recognize the author name(s) as being present in the substring. In a format where the latter were absent, there would be the recognition of a title statement or the initial string only. Certain complexities are introduced in author name recognition, for example, when the formatting displays a reversal in the sequence of data, that is, where the author statement occupies the first string and the title statement the second string:

(4)
MARTIN JOOS
THE FIVE CLOCKS

and when the formatting exhibits a conjoined title-author statement where the author statement is linked grammatically to the title statement or has the dual function of serving as the title statement:

(5) THE DIARY OF ANNE FRANK

(6) MATISSE

While there are devisable ways to construct a characterization to account for the formatting exhibited in (4), the problems exhibited in (5), (6), and other displays the author studied proved that the formatting of the title page data alone was insufficient as a means of recognizing all the author names that a title page may display. In addition to the formatting, the syntactic display of the data must be taken into consideration.

In terms of the syntactic display, the previous title pages exhibit the use of certain lexical units to signal the presence of a name. In the case of (1)–(3), the lexical unit BY introduces a name. In (2)–(3), the units AND and WITH are used to signal additional names in these displays. In (5), the unit OF is found in conjunction with a name. Likewise, in the case of BETWEEN, FROM, TO, ON, and 'S,S' the presence of an author name or names is signalled, as in the following examples:

(7) THE CORRESPONDENCE BETWEEN
BENJAMIN HARRISON AND JAMES G. BLAINE

(8) LETTERS FROM SAINT AUGUSTINE

(9) A Life in Fashion
By Tara Sarong
As Told To Betty Olsen

(10) LE CORBUSIER ON LE CORBUSIER

(11) NEWMAN'S BEST PLAIN SERMONS

An examination of hundreds of English language title pages showed a regularity in the use of these nine lexical units to signal names. As with the formatting of the data, certain complexities arise, one being the variety of contexts in which these units are used. For example, the unit BY can be used to express a relation in time (*by* the hour), a direction (we went *by* Champaign) and so on. On the other hand, it can be used in contexts to denote a particular function of a name (e.g., edited by, translated by) which would be important to recognize in the entry selection process. Thus, it is apparent that certain provisions must apply to take cognizance of the strings in which it occurs and, within the strings, the special contexts in which it appears in conjunction with a name. This is also true of the other lexical units.

Another complexity arises when the lexical units are omitted in the author statement. These omissions occur largely with BY and AND, where they are most certainly implied but physically absent in the author statement:

(12) THE HIDDEN DIMENSION
Edward T. Hall

(13) Introduction To Moral Education
John Wilson
Norman Williams
Barry Sugarman

or, in the case of AND, physically expressed in the form of a slash, comma, or ampersand:

(14) HOW TO GROW PLANTS—INDOORS AND OUTDOORS
BY
GERALD WHITNEY/JAMES GOOCH/DORIS ROYCE

(15) INTERIOR HOUSE DESIGN
By
Richard Locke, Susan Paige & Edward Gates

To account for these omissions or their substitute physical expressions, it is clear that techniques must be employed to facilitate these name recognitions. Despite these complexities, however, the association of the lexical units with author names, when used in conjunction with the formatting of the title page data, is seen to be a powerful cue for the characterization and perhaps, for the cataloger as well.

The characterization of the recognition component presented here was formulated in terms of the concept described above. The construction of the characterization based on this concept is summarized below.

CONSTRUCTION OF THE RECOGNITION COMPONENT

1. Central to the development and operational capacity of the characterization is the assumption that a scanning device exists that accepts the title pages of English language monographs and simulates the human reading of the printed characters on that page, namely, reading sequentially from left to right, top to bottom. However, it is important to point out that the characterization is not intended to constitute a model of the intellectual or intuitive processes of the cataloger. The fact that catalogers, for instance, can comprehend an unlimited variety of title page data and can judge their usefulness in formulating an entry choice immediately indicates that their capacities are quite different from a machine performing operations on the basis of printed characters presented or input to it.

2. The recognition component in the simulation of main entry selection in AACR2, as in the case of its predecessor cataloging codes, is characterized as a set of rules constructed out of eight of the nine lexical units identified earlier in the discussion as signaling devices for the presence of an author name: BY, AND, WITH, OF, FROM, BETWEEN, TO, and 'S,S.' (Constructing rules for the unit ON, as exhibited in (10), introduced an order of complexity into the characterization that was considered unfeasible for the few instances of these displays in which the unit appeared in association with an author name.)

3. The rules for these eight units identify the cataloging data on the title page as a sequence of two physically distinct and separate strings, of which the initial string is identified as the title statement and the second or substring as the author statement, each string being composed of as many physical lines of data as there are making up each statement. (With this abstraction of the title page, reverse formatting as exhibited in (4) can be accommodated only with special rules which, while possible to develop, were excluded in the characterization presented here.)

4. The rules consider each of the above strings to be in the form: #S#, in which the boundary marker # represents the physical breaks on the title page that come before, between, and after the title and author statements, and is a technique used by the rules to set apart and at the same time define the two strings, as for example:

#Introduction to Chemistry#	) #S1#
#By G. A. Dickinson#	) #S2#

5. Each rule is in the form: Recognize L (the lexical unit) in S, where to recognize is to identify the exact shape and form of the unit in S1, S2, or both strings as required. To accommodate main entry selection in the AACR2 rules selected for examination, author name recognition requires the following basic rules (with some exceptions), among other more special rules:

Recognize BY in S2
Recognize AND after BY in S2
Recognize WITH after BY in S2

The first rule, which has application to virtually all the AACR2 entry rules, would function to recognize each occurrence of BY in the author statement. Applying this rule to the title page display in (1), for example, would produce the recognition: #By Victor B. Scheffer#, which would be needed to accommodate entry selection under rule 21.4A. Similarly, application of this rule to the following displays would produce the name recognitions involving entry selection under rules 21.5A and 21.6D respectively:

(16) A TRIBUTE TO THE STATUE OF LIBERTY
By
Citizens of Long Island

(17) THE DETECTIVE SHORT STORY
A BIBLIOGRAPHY
By Ellery Queen

The second and third rules follow successive application after the first and would function to recognize the presence of additional names in the author statement, such as those exhibited in (2)–(3), which would be needed for entry selection under rules 21.6C1 and 21.6B1 respectively.

6. Because the lexical units, as noted, can occur in certain contexts to denote the function of an author name which figures importantly in the entry selection process, the rules provide for recognition of their contextual use by specifying the string and context in which they must occur. These rules are in the form: Recognize L in S1, S2 in the context of E (a specified environment), where "in the context of" means the environment occurs directly before or after the unit and is formally expressed in the rules as a slash,/. These rules are needed for name recognitions involving entry selection across a number of verbal rules in the corpus, notably 21.4A, 21.6C1, 21.7B, and 21.28B. One such rule is the following which recognizes the presence of any one of the units listed in conjunction with the specified environments (the three dots indicating additional environments) directly preceding it, the blank in the rule specifying the exact position of the units in the environment:

(18) Recognize OF, BETWEEN, FROM, TO, WITH in S1 when

```
{OF      }  /{Conversations   }
{BETWEEN }  / {Correspondence  }
{FROM    } /  {Diary(ies)      }     ________
{TO      } /  {Essays          }
{WITH    }/   {Letters         }
              {  . . .         }
```

This rule, for example, would produce the name recognitions in conjunction with the associated environments that are exhibited in (5) and (8) which involve entry under the verbal rule 21.4A and in (7) involving entry selection under rule 21.6C1. Another such rule takes recognition of the unit BY in association with the following contexts directly preceding it in the substring:

```
(19) Recognize {compiled          }   /
               {edited            }  /    ____________   BY
               {introduc(ed)(tion)} /
               {      . . .       }/
```

This rule, in particular, accommodates the name recognitions-environments needed for entry selection involving rules 21.7B and 21.28B. For example, applying the rule to the following title page display:

(20) ESSAYS ON THE EIGHTEENTH-CENTURY NOVEL
Edited by
Robert Donald Specter

would produce the recognition: #Edited by Robert Donald Specter#, involving entry selection under rule 21.7B. Although context-sensitive rules such as the above function to accommodate the various nuances of entry selection under the verbal rules, their application can also result in the type of nonname recognition that could work to obviate appropriate entry assignment. To illustrate, in the case of the unit 'S,S', the rule to recognize this unit when it occurs in the initial string in the absence of a substring produces successful recognitions for displays of the type exhibited in (11), which involves entry selection under 21.4A, but when applied to the following:

(21) A TREE'S LIMBS AND OTHER SCOTTISH TALES

produces a nonname recognition. Although these recognitions could not be avoided, the way in which the rule assisted in blocking a faulty entry assignment later was to have it recognize the unit in association with the definite or indefinite article which was almost always found to introduce the unit's association with a nonname. How these and other faulty recognitions were negated as entry choices is taken up in the next section.

7. With the exception of the units BY and AND, the units and the environments specified in the rules require identical physical expression in the string for name recognition to take place. In the case of BY and AND, the rules take cognizance of the condition of their being implied but physically absent in the author statement, as exhibited in (12)–(15) and "write "them in. The rule for BY, for example, calls for inserting the unit at the head of any substring in which it is physically absent. Application of this rule to the data exhibited in (12) would produce the recognition: #[BY] Edward T. Hall#, where the brackets are used by the rules to indicate the insertion. The rule for AND dictates insertion conditioned on a number of factors relating to its absence, its physical substitution, and the presence of other lexical units in the substring. For example, in applying the rule to insert AND after BY, [BY] at the end of each line except the terminal line, when this unit (or its substitute expressions) and the units OF, WITH, TO are physically absent, to the data displayed in (13) would result in the recognition: #[BY] John Wilson [AND] Norman Williams [AND] Barry Sugarman#. Through construction of the type of rules discussed above, the recognition component can be seen to provide the output, that is, the resulting name

recognitions and their environments, that is needed to facilitate the entry selection process. The second step in the characterization of this process is described below.

Selection Component

On the basis of the recognition component, the selection component functions to assign the appropriate main entry (a person or corporate body, or title), using the bibliographic conditions and specifications of entry contained in the corpus of AACR2 rules. In AACR2, as in its predecessor cataloging codes, the principles and rules of entry are formulated as sets of verbal instructions of the form: Enter a work, collection, and so on. These instructions specify which main entry is appropriate, taking into consideration the various configurations of responsibility and the various materials in which these configurations are displayed. The application of these instructions is, of course, dependent upon the cataloger, whose training and native capacities to understand and interpret their verbal import are essential to the component. To construct a characterization of the selection component then, it is necessary to devise some way to represent the content of these instructions and to somehow emulate the cataloger's ability to apply them.

Inasmuch as the instructions for entry selection in AACR2 are framed in terms of various roles of responsibility—single, shared, mixed, unknown, and so on, it might be expected that a characterization of this component would be constructed in a similar manner, taking into consideration the features and patterns of responsibility that comprise the content of the verbal principles and rules. A case in point would be 21.6B-C for shared responsibility, where the rules have the features of two or more persons or corporate bodies. In the four rules (21.6B1,2-21.6C1,2), the pattern is defined to apply to statements of responsibility where the names are found to be conjoined or linked primarily by ANDs (or its physical substitutes), WITHs, OFs, and TOs, as exhibited, for example, in displays (2)–(3), (7), (9), (14)–(15). To represent these rules in terms of the roles of responsibility they address, a characterization would utilize their explicit, that is to say, directly observable features and the constructs of the statements to which they are found to apply which, in the case of those noted above, could be abstracted in the form (the numbers indicating the displays):

(2)	BY X AND Y
(3)	BY X WITH Y
(7)	BETWEEN X AND Y
(9)	BY X TO Y
(14-15)	BY X [AND] Y1 [AND] Y2

(where the X and Y indicate the names in the abstractions). Each of these, along with other such abstractions, would be incorporated in the characterization as a representation of these particular rules.

Two difficulties that can be expected to arise in connection with this particular characterization are: (a) the number of abstractions which may be found to represent a given rule, and (b) the number of identical abstractions which may be found to represent different rules and main entry assignments. With respect to (a), it has already been seen from the examples above that there are several abstractions (and more) needed to represent the rules for shared responsibility. With respect to (b), it is sufficient to take a simple abstraction like BY X to illustrate this predicament. This abstraction is one of several that characterizes rule 21.4A as illustrated, for example, in (1). It is likewise an abstraction that is found to characterize rule 21.5A as in the case of (16) and the following statement of responsibility: By executives for leading retail stores. Whereas the former rule specifies main entry under the person, the latter specifies main entry under title. These difficulties point up the need to construct the characterization so that there will be an economy of abstractions to represent the verbal rules and a method of examining the abstractions to ensure appropriate main entry assignment.

In the way of defining its system of operation, it is expected that the characterization, given a name recognition produced by the recognition component, will apply an abstraction representing a particular rule or rules. In the case of an agreement, that is to say, where the name recognition would be found to "match "the abstraction, the selection of main entry would be considered to occur. To specify the main entry dictated by the rule, the name recognition would be examined for the presence of certain physical characteristics (e.g., typographical prominence of the names), plurality (e.g., citizens, executives), and so on, that are used by the verbal rules as indications of primary responsibility, the lack of a named corporate body, and so on. On the basis of this examination, an entry decision would be either specified or deferred for the application of other abstractions representing the same or other rules.

Much more is needed to define the system. In particular, some sort of heuristic procedure must be supplied which will enable the characterization to examine a name recognition for the above specifications and to produce the entry required for each alternative. Additionally, a heuristic procedure must be supplied, which will enable the characterization to apply the abstraction to a name recognition in an ordered sequence until one is found to apply. These procedures and the details of characterizing the selection component are summarized below.

CONSTRUCTION OF THE SELECTION COMPONENT

1. As with the recognition component, the selection component in the simulation of main entry assignment in AACR2 (as also in its two predecessor

codes) is characterized as a set of rules, which function to identify responsibility in the form of a name of a person or corporate body and to assign main entry either under one or the other name, or under title. For the purpose of distinguishing these rules from their verbal AACR2 counterparts, they are hereafter referred to as "experimental "selection rules.

2. Construction of the experimental selection rules proceeded in the manner and form described above. For the corpus of AACR2 entry rules selected, there is a set of experimental rules formulated as instructions of the form:

(22)

BY X - > A
Where A = X

with the interpretation that a recognition, where the statement of responsibility is BY . . . , goes to or is entered under author, where the author is X (name of person or corporate body). This particular rule, for example, would have application to cases of single personal authorship (21.4A) as illustrated in (1), shared pseudonyms (21.6D) as in (17), illustrated texts by one artist (21.11B) as in N.C. Wyeth's Illustrations for Robin Hood #By N.C. Wyeth#, and related works (21.28B) as in A Complete Concordance to the Iliad of Homer #By Guy Lushington Prendergast#, among other verbal rules in the corpus.

As previously mentioned, there are any number and variety of recognitions to which a single verbal rule may be applicable, which results in a multiplicity of experimental rules and at the same time an incomplete characterization of the verbal rule as there is obviously no way of knowing or anticipating all its abstractions. In essence, this would mean that the experimental rules would be restricted to apply only to those recognitions whose constructs are already known. To resolve this difficulty, the large number of special rules were rephrased in the form of fewer, more general type instructions. For example, given the following experimental rules needed for the recognitions applicable to 21.11A for illustrated texts, which specifies main entry under the writer of the text:

(23) BY X BY Y in S2 − > A, Where A = X
#By Naomi Lipetz
Illustrated by Lois Todd#

(24) BY X AND Y BY W in S2 − > A, Where A = X
#By Alfred Speye and Heidi Chubb
Illustrations by Anna Zipf#

it was found that the following general rule could be posited in place of these rules:

```
(25)        BY XZ in S2  – > A
            Where A = X
            And Z = anything or nothing
```

This rule has the interpretation that a recognition having any one of the above or any other abstraction goes to or is entered under a personal or corporate name, where the name to occupy the main entry is X, and Z in the abstraction is anything (any other name or names in the recognition) or nothing (no other name in the recognition). With the construction of this rule alone, an economy in the multiplicity of special experimental rules was achieved and, concomitantly, the successful characterization of parts of many of the AACR2 rules in the corpus, for example, in addition to 21.11A, 21.4A, 21.6C1, 21.6D, 21.11B, 21.14A, 21.24, and 21.28B.

3. As discussed in the development of the recognition component, the context in which a name occurs in a string figures importantly in the entry selection process, especially since in the case of the AACR2 rules noted in the discussion, selection of the appropriate main entry is largely predicated on the physical expression of these environments. For example, to accommodate selection of an A entry that is specified in 21.4A for the recognitions produced for (5) and (8) and in 21.6C1 for the recognition produced for (7), names in the context of "diary," "letters," and "correspondence" are explicit expressions of this entry assignment. In the selection component, these particular expressions are incorporated in an experimental rule of the form:

```
(26)
     {OF      }  /{Conversations  }
     {BETWEEN }  /{Correspondence }
     {FROM    } / {Diary(ies)     }——XZ in S1 - (in the
     {TO      }/  {Essays         }   absence of) S2 -> A
     {WITH    }/  {Letters        }
               /  {  . . .        }
   Where A = X
         Z = anything or nothing
```

As can be seen, experimental rules of this type were formulated largely by taking the environmental recognitions produced by the recognition component and specifying the main entry appropriate for the environment under application of the AACR2 rule.

4. For those AACR2 rules that were found to have identical abstractions but different entry assignments, exceptions were built into the existing experimental rules based on explicit syntactic data used to illustrate the entry choice. For instance, in the case of the identical abstractions for 21.4A and 21.5A noted earlier, an exception was incorporated into the general rule in the form of:

```
(27)  BY XZ -> A
      Where A = X
            Z = anything or nothing    }
      Unless X =   {(the)/(a) citizens  }
                   {          executives }
                   {            • • •    }
                   { ***                 }
                   { ! !                 }
      Then -> T
      Where T = title of monograph
```

with the exception being that where X is plurality expressed as "citizens," "executives," and so on, introduced with or without the definite or indefinite article, or where X is a nonalphabetic or nonnumeric character expressed as ***, !!, and so on, main entry is under title, which would apply to recognitions involving unnamed corporate bodies such as in (16) and those involving such indications of authorship as: #BY ***# under a subrule of 21.5C. However, recognitions such as in (1) and the following: #By a physician#, which have identical abstractions involving 21.4A and 21.5C respectively, would not qualify under the exception and would be entered under personal name (or the indication of one) as specified in these rules.

5. Exceptions in the form of the above were also constructed to take into consideration the typography, contextual data, and faulty recognitions which would result in inappropriate main entry choices. In the case of typography, the exception recognized the attribution of principal responsibility and subsequent main entry under the principal person or corporate body which is specified in rule 21.6B1. As in (27) above, it was built into the general rule as:

```
(28)  BY XZ in S2 -> A
      Where A = X
            Z = anything or nothing
      Unless Z is in larger type
      Then A = Z
```

With this exception, appropriate main entry choices could be accomplished in the following recognitions which characterize this rule: #By John Gavin with MARY SCHATZ#, #By Arnold Watson and associates#.

Additional exceptions incorporated in this rule applied to recognize the functional contexts of a name and the main entry assignments conditioned on their presence. The following exception applied to names in the context of "edited," "compiled," and "introduced," which are explicit conditions for entry under title specified in 21.7B for collections with a collective title:

```
(29)            BY XZ in S2 -> A
                Where A = X
                      Z = anything or nothing
                Unless X / {compiled      }
                           {edited        } BY— — — — —
                           {introduced    }
                Then -> T
                Where T = title of monograph
```

In the case of faulty recognitions, characterization of the selection component was successful in making appropriate entry assignments in most cases because exceptions, such as those above, applied to prevent their selection and, also, because the general mandate of the abstractions characterizing the AACR2 rules in the corpus dictated in the case of name (A) entries that main entry be under the first name. For example, the following faulty recognitions signaled by the lexical units AND, WITH, and OF (underlined for emphasis):

(30) #By Estelle Flood *And Colour Plates* by Marianne Moltz#
(31) #By S. Harley-Harris *With Selected Photographs#*
(32) #By Lord Ramsay *of Linlithgow#*

were of no consequence, as the abstraction of rules 21.6C1, 21.6B1, and 21.4A, among others involving these units, dictates entry under X (first name). Faulty recognitions signaled by the lexical unit 'S,S' noted in (21), however, necessitated the following special experimental rule:

```
(33) X 'S,S'Z in S1 - S2 -> A
     Where A = X
     Z = anything or nothing
     Unless X / ({the/a}) (definite/indefinite articles)
     Then -> T
     Where T = title of monograph
```

so that the name recognitions signaled by this unit, as in (11), would be selected for the main entry.

Where the lexical unit AND required insertion in the substring, faulty recognitions resulted in conjunction with statements of responsibility comprised of extraneous data, such as the following:

(34) By Edgar N. Koonz
Tulane University

Marvin T. Noonan
The American University

Recognition: #By Edgar N. Koonz [AND] Tulane University
[AND] Marvin T. Noonan [AND] The
American University#

Because the recognition rule operated to insert the unit at the end of each line of data in the absence of its physical expression and that of other lexical units, the faulty recognitions caused an inappropriate (T) main entry assignment under application of an experimental rule for 21.6C2, which specifies this entry assignment when responsibility is shared between four or more persons or corporate bodies, no one of which is attributed with having principal responsibility:

(35) BY X AND Y1 AND Y2 AND Y3 Z in S2 -> T
Where X, Y = author names
Z = anything or nothing
And where T = title of monograph
Unless X or Y1 or Y2 or Y3 is in larger type
Then -> A
Where A = name in larger type

For these faulty recognitions, as well as resulting ''zero'' or nonrecognitions in such displays as (6) and (10), the characterization would require additions of exceptions, ad hoc rules, and procedures which, although possible to develop, were not incorporated in this selection component.

6. To perform the application of the experimental selection rules described, there is a heuristic component, namely, a set of procedures that enables the rules to accept a recognition and to examine it for typography, and so on, that assist in selection of the main entry. In the characterization presented here, the experimental rules are represented graphically in the form of the tree diagrams mentioned in the introduction, and accomplish entry selection through the use of the binary (YES-NO) decision process discussed. For each experimental rule, there is a tree which has at the highest node the abstracted rule with positive and negative paths identified as YES-NO responses extending down to a pair of lower nodes. At each lower node is a specification that the recognition, in turn, must satisfy, positively or negatively. If a recognition should satisfy a specification, that Z is in larger type than X, for example, it would pass down the positive path to a still lower node for examination of another specification, and so on until an endpoint or leaf is reached. At the endpoint of a tree, the recognition would be assigned a main entry, A or T, with designation of the name or title of the monograph to occupy the entry, or be sent to the next experimental rule for matching and examination. The tree below for the special rule in (33) illustrates these heuristics.

Taking the abstractions for (11) and (21), each being found to match the rule would pass down the left (positive) path to entry under name X, where in the case

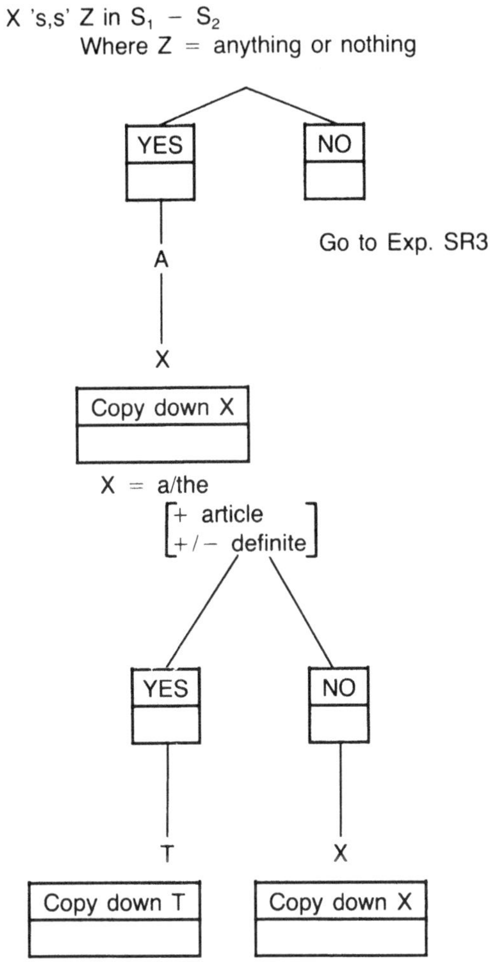

Figure 11.1. Directed tree diagram (33)

of (11), X would be copied down as "Newman's" and in (21) as "A Tree's." Upon examination for the specification X = (a/the) (presence or nonpresence of the definite/indefinite article), X in (11) not satisfying this specification would pass down the negative path to the endpoint in the rule which specifies Newman as the main entry, while X in (21), having a positive response, would pass down the positive path to the endpoint which specifies entry under title. Depending upon the extent of the specifications, branching (left and right) of the trees can be expected to vary as well as nodes and endpoints. A tree for the general experimental rule BY XZ -> A, for example, would have extensive branching, with nodes for syntactic data, typography, and environments. (The tree illustrated above, as well as all the trees in the characterization, are conceptual and do not represent the operations of a machine performing the entry selection process.)

7. Finally, with respect to their application, the experimental selection rules are arranged to be applied to a recognition in a given order. Application would start with rule 1 and would stop or continue with the application of successive rules until all the specifications are satisfied and an endpoint is reached. In the characterization presented here, order of application was determined by the degree of restrictiveness in the experimental rules, the first rules being considered the most restrictive in their application to the fewest or least number of recognitions (e.g., (26), (33), (35)), followed by successive rules of an increasingly less restrictive nature, ending with those which were least restrictive, or the most general rules, having application to the largest number of recognitions (e.g., (25)).

The above components consisting of the recognition rules and experimental selection rules, together with the heuristic procedures, form the conceptual model that was proposed for simulation of main entry selection in the AACR and ALA cataloging codes and has been presented here for its application to entry selection in AACR2. It is now possible to consider some of the practical implications regarding its further development and potential application.

PRACTICAL IMPLICATIONS

Because the AACR2 entry rules examined here have, as noted earlier, identical or nearly identical counterpart rules in the AACR code, characterization of their verbal content is found to differ minimally with respect to bibliographic conditions and assignments of entry. Differences arise principally with 21.5C and 21.7B where their respective counterpart rules 2C and 4A/5A specify different main entry assignments based on alternate considerations of what constitutes sufficient identification of a person or corporate body and what comprises a collection and editorial responsibility.

In most other respects, the characterization of the corpus of AACR2 entry rules replicates that of its counterpart AACR corpus. Consequently, observations relating to this code are consistent with many of the findings the author presented in her characterization of the latter code. One observation is that successful characterization of entry rules is dependent on bibliographic conditions of the rules being explicit, in the sense that they have physical expression and identification in the cataloging data. All the AACR2 rules examined supported characterization to some extent, with some being more amenable than others. For example, the conditions relating to editorial direction in 21.7B are considered to be more easily characterized than those in 21.5A and C which require highly specialized expressions on which to base main entry assignment. Regarding rules 21.4A, 21.6C1, and 21.11A (whose counterparts in AACR were noted as having the highest percentage of cataloger usage), most of the conditions in these rules supported characterization. However, one notable exception is the condition in 21.4A which calls for entering a work or works by one person under that person even though he or she is not named in the data. This condition completely faults characterization in that it utilizes examination of textual matter, reference sources, and so on that are external to the title page in order to assign an appropriate A entry.

Yet, it is also the case that conditions of the rules, although not supporting characterization, permit successful assignments of main entry choices. This phenomenon is attributed primarily to the redundancy in rules having specifications and assignments of entry that produce identical abstractions. This was noted earlier in connection with constructing the experimental rules where it was found that the many separate abstractions of the verbal rules in the corpus could be collapsed into the single experimental rule: BY XZ -> A.

Another observation is that successful characterization of entry rules is assisted by the design of the title page in both its presentation and display of data (kind and amount). For monographs, the title page serves as the chief source of information for determining main and added entries in AACR2; hence, its design assumes special importance. Differences in the physical ordering of the title and statements of responsibility restricted the characterization presented here to those title pages having the title presented first, separated and followed by the statements of responsibility. With additional procedures or other approaches, it is possible to resolve this problem. For instance, if these elements were tagged for or upon input, uniform sequencing could be obtained without imposing a defined physical sequencing of the data on the title page (e.g., using MARC tags, main entry assignment would be 1XX and always be sequenced before title (tag 245); yet, on the title page these elements could be reversed). However, identification of these elements would be more easily accomplished if they were strictly ordered on the title page.

In those cases where titles had the dual function of serving as statements of responsibility as in (6) and (10), no characterization was attempted. With no substring and no defined context in which the names are exhibited in the initial string (the lexical unit ON occurs infrequently in association with an author name), the experimental rules operated to make inappropriate entry assignment under title. By matching the initial string to a name authority database, names could be extracted, but then require ad hoc experimental rules of the number and type that are seen to compensate efficiency. Although these displays are infrequent, they could accommodate appropriate entry assignment if a substring were present. For example, in (6), the following statement of responsibility "By Matisse" with application of the experimental rule BY XZ -> A would assign main entry under the artist. Likewise, in the case of (10), where with the statement of responsibility "By Le Corbusier," the rule would apply to assign entry under the architect. Consistency in carrying a substring on the title page would also assist entry selection for conjoined title-author statements as in (5), (7), and (11), effecting a reduction in environmental-based experimental rules and, thus, greater simplicity in the construct of the model.

For those substrings with no lexical units in the data, inappropriate main entry assignments are more likely to occur, as noted in (34), based on faulty recognitions produced by the recognition component's insertion of AND. Again, ad hoc rules would be necessary to help resolve this predicament. However, more directly, the physical sequencing of the individual names (top-down) on the title page minus extraneous data (e.g., degrees, institutional affiliations) would work to allow the characterization to make appropriate entry assignments in these cases.

Other observations on the human and modeling processes of entry selection, while foregoing mention, point to the need for considerably more research in these areas. The expert system described here was limited in its design and construction to only a few AACR2 entry rules. More detailed examination of these rules, as well as the inclusion of more rules, is needed in order to give a fuller assessment of the code's potential for characterization of this process. Additionally, the assignment of added entries needs exploration. (The recognition component of this model functioned to identify many of the names used in these entries.) More extensive examination of the title page is also needed to determine the adequacy of its design to support characterization and subsequent automation of this process. (The design problems noted here indicate the need for a more structured display of data.) The conceptual model presented here also represents only one type of modeling; investigation should be made of other designs and constructs as well as other approaches. As models for the performance of other cataloging operations are developed, a prime concern will be their compatibility to operate interactively with each other and within the automated bibliographic environment.

REFERENCES

AACR. (1967) *Anglo-American cataloging rules, North American text*. Chicago, IL: American Library Association.

Beetle, C. (Ed.). (1949). *ALA cataloging rules for author and title entries*. Chicago, IL: American Library Association.

Cullicover, P. W. (1982). *Syntax*. New York: Academic Press.

Goossens, P. (1982). Hierarchical relationships in bibliographic descriptions. In A. H. Helal & J. W. Weiss (Eds.), *Hierarchical relationships in bibliographic descriptions* (pp. 13–128). Essen: Gesamthochschulbibliothek Essen.

Gorman, M., & Winkler, P. W. (Eds.), (1978). *Anglo-American cataloguing rules* (2nd ed.). Chicago, IL: American Library Association.

Sandberg-Fox, A. (1972). *The amenability of a cataloging process to simulation by automatic techniques*, Ph.D. dissertation, University of Illinois at Urbana-Champaign. (ERIC Document Reproduction Service, No. ED076225; University Microfilms, Ann Arbor, MI.)

12

The Selection of Search Keys

Raya Fidel
Graduate School of Library and Information Science
University of Washington
Seattle, WA

INTRODUCTION

One of the tasks carried out by reference librarians when performing an online search of bibliographic databases is the selection of search keys. To understand the nature of this task it is best to examine its place in the process of online searching.

Online searchers answer requests from library patrons: The patron presents the searcher with a request that reflects the patron's information need. Once a searcher feels she understands the request well enough to answer it, she performs an online search in the relevant databases. The outcome of an online search is typically an answer set that includes bibliographic citations.

Patrons' requests have two major aspects. The first is the topic of a request which presents the subject matter of concern to the patron. For example, "the analysis of students' behavior during final examinations to determine the difficulty of the examination" is a topic of a hypothetical request.

The second aspect includes request characteristics that do not relate directly to the topic but rather to the purpose of the request, or to how the information is going to be used. For example, a patron may need a comprehensive search that retrieves all the relevant citations (high recall search), or she may be interested in just a few highly relevant citations (high precision search). In addition, at one time the patron may agree to consider articles about any kind of examinations—not only finals—and at another time she may be satisfied to receive citations to articles dealing with the analysis of students' behavior during final examinations, whether or not the analysis is used to determine the difficulty of the examination (low specificity search).

A classic online search includes the following procedure. The searcher interviews a patron to clarify the topic and the characteristics of a request. The searcher then develops a plan for searching the request online—a search strategy. The strategy specifies which databases will be searched and which terms (or search keys) will be used in each database. It can also include a more specific plan that determines the flow of the search: the terms that will be entered first, when to review some results, and what to do if the results are not satisfactory. The actual session at the terminal follows the search strategy but searchers may deviate from their original plan if it does not seem useful. Some requests may require a number of terminal sessions because searchers may decide to log off and reconsider their strategy, possibly with the help of the patron. At some point the searcher will decide to terminate the search and print the answer set that is given to the patron.

This chapter focuses on one segment of the search process: the selection of search keys.

To begin, what decisions are involved in the selection of search keys?

Searchers must first break down a request into its individual components or concepts. The request about students' behavior, for instance, includes four concepts: (1) analysis, (2) students' behavior, (3) final examinations, and (4) difficulty of the examinations. Each concept requires a set of search keys for its representation. Thus, searchers look for search keys that will best capture the literature on the topic of each individual concept or of the request as a whole, and, at the same time, will retrieve an answer set that satisfies other request characteristics such as recall, precision, or specificity.

What are the options in the selection of search keys?

There are two distinct types of search keys. Searchers may enter any desired term or phrase and retrieve citations that include the term or the phrase in their text (free-text searching). Or, searchers may decide to use search keys from a thesaurus—a list of descriptors, or subject headings that are used for indexing and retrieval (descriptor searching). For many databases both options are available, and searchers can also use them in combination: A concept may be searched using free-text terms as well as descriptors.

Thus, one of the decisions that searchers make during an online search is what type of search keys to use. They decide this when they plan their strategy and also during terminal sessions when they revise their strategy. The significance of this decision is clearly demonstrated in a recent review article (Svenonius, 1986) which analyzes the large body of literature on the subject.

Expert systems that perform like online searchers may be called intermediary expert systems (IES) because they mediate between the patron and the databases he searches. Ideally, patrons would be able to present their requests to IES which then would make expert decisions about the search process, and in particular about the selection of search keys. IES should interrogate patrons to elicit request characteristics, but the systems will use their expertise to make decisions about matters that are beyond the knowledge of patrons. For example, such an expert system should ask the patron whether high recall or high precision is required, and will use this information to decide whether to use free-text terms or descriptors.

Various intermediary systems are already available for public access, such as

CITE (Doszkocs, 1983); others, such as CONIT (Marcus, 1983) or CAN-SEARCH (Pollitt, 1984) are still being tested in experimental settings. Through such systems, patrons are freed from encounters with many peculiarities in databases and search systems—such as ORBIT, DIALOG, or BRS—and yet can benefit from a large range of capabilities. In particular, patrons can enter a request in a loosely structured format, preferably in natural language, using a sentence-like expression. An intermediary system processes the request terms, displays information to patrons, and asks for feedback. The information displayed may be in the form of a list of subject areas, databases, search keys, or actual citations from which patrons are asked to make a selection, possibly in ranked order. Interactions of this nature usually proceed until patrons terminate the session.

Some intermediary systems are actually helper systems: they provide menu-driven interaction and thus free patrons from learning the command language while still requiring them to make most of the decisions during a search process; or, they drastically simplify searching by reducing the number of options to a minimum. CITE, for example, leaves the selection of search keys to the patron: It displays a list of search keys that can be used for a request component—both descriptors and free-text terms—and asks the patron to select the terms. In contrast, CONIT simplifies the selection of search keys because it searches each search key as a free-text term, and under certain circumstances (that depend on the search system, not on the request) also as a descriptor.

Intermediary expert systems, on the other hand, attempt a more powerful form of patron assistance: They replicate the performance of an expert in online bibliographic retrieval by incorporating the knowledge of an expert with rules for making inferences on the basis of this knowledge.

Most current attempts to build IES for interface with bibliographic databases are based on text analysis. This means that decisions these systems make are based on analyzing the text of the citations that are stored in them. Such a system may have, for example, a rule that states: if the number of citations retrieved for one request component is less than 20, enter a descriptor that is most strongly associated with the original descriptor. Thus, suppose the descriptor *Students' Behavior* retrieves 18 citations. The system then examines all the descriptors that have been assigned to these citations and discovers that 11 citations include also the descriptor *Elementary Education*. Following its rule, it will next retrieve citations to all documents about elementary education, regardless of whether or not the patron is interested in this area, or whether she needs high precision or high recall.

The primary limitation of building a knowledge base on text analysis alone, then, is that it can deal only with the topic but not with the other characteristics of a request: Aspects such as recall, precision, or specificity requirements cannot be addressed solely by text analysis. Yet, such aspects are extremely important for successful interaction and are thus central to search processes when performed by online searchers. It is desirable, therefore, to develop a form of IES that would incorporate a simulation of the knowledge that online searchers gained through experience.

To build such systems, one must first collect and present in a formal manner the searching behavior of online searchers. This chapter is a report of a research project that began to investigate the rules that online searchers apply when they select search keys.

THE METHOD

To examine the rules for the selection of search keys about 50 online searchers were observed performing their regular, job-related searches. Searchers who have been searching for more than two years were recruited from among librarians in all types of library, searching a wide variety of subjects. They were studied one at a time, and were asked to verbalize their thought processes during their searching to the degree that speaking out loud would not interfere with their performance. These verbalizations, including the creation of search strategy, were recorded. At the end of the observation period (between 5 to 10 searches), each searcher was interviewed to reveal and clarify information not accessible to observation.

Data collected for analysis were about 300 printed search protocols with transcriptions and verbalized thought processes and additional explanation from the final interviews.

Each instance in which searchers had selected a search key was then identified and the reason for the specific choice was explicitly noted. Analysis of the first 10 search protocols generated a preliminary list of conditions under which a particular selection was made. For example, a condition for choosing a free-text term is: to enter straightforwardly a specific concept which might not be a trustworthy descriptor.

All the search protocols were then analyzed against this preliminary list of conditions. Each instance in which searchers had selected a search key was listed under the condition to which it applied. Instances whose condition could not be found suggested a new condition to be added to the list. This analysis revealed that some conditions were considered by most searchers, others occur quite rarely, and a few conditions reflect searchers' individual idiosyncrasies.

The list of conditions for the selection of search keys is presented in Figure 12.1 in a form of a decision tree, and is explained in the next section. This set of decision rules is called here "The Selection Routine."

The Selection Routine describes the most commonly selected path, but there might be complications. As such, it cannot always accurately predict the selection of search keys unless other factors and their impact are known. This Routine groups together similar conditions so it could be presented in a decision tree, but it is not meant to represent a necessary sequence in the selection process.

THE SELECTION ROUTINE

Two questions are central to the decision about how to represent a request term:

1. Is it a "good" term for free-text searching?
2. Can the term be mapped to a descriptor?

To map a term to a descriptor is to select a certain descriptor as the representative of the term, whether or not the descriptor matches exactly the term.

The first question is a little more complex and requires some explanation. Searchers consider a term to be a "good" term for free-text searching if it (a) usually occurs in a particular context, (b) is uniquely defined, and (c) is specific in the concept it represents. Such a term will be called here a "single-meaning" term. On the other hand, a term that occurs in *more* than one context will be called a "common" term. For example, in the request about the analysis of students' behavior during final examinations to determine the difficulty of the examination, terms such as *students* and *behavior* are single-meaning terms. The term *examination*, on the other hand, is a common term; it can occur in a subject-related context ("the best way to take student examination"), or in a descriptive capacity ("examination of students' responses"), or still further, it can be used very loosely to represent the concept of an inquiry of any kind. Similarly, the term *analysis* is a common term because it is likely to occur in many abstracts, whether or not the articles report about actual analyses.

When a term is a common term, searchers most often do not have much choice in the selection of search keys: If it can be mapped to a descriptor, searchers almost always enter the descriptor as a search key [A] (i.e., option [A] in Figure 12.1) because, by definition, it is not desirable to use a common term as a free-text search key.

Only rarely, and under special circumstances, would searchers elect to enter a common term as a free-text search key if it can be mapped to a descriptor [B]. In the 300 searches analyzed for this study, such a selection was made only twice. In both instances, searchers were using a term to limit the retrieval and assumed that to require that a descriptor is assigned would be too limiting. A searcher may, for example, combine all the concepts of the request about students' behavior but the "analysis" concept. Looking at the retrieval she concludes that precision is not high enough. ANDing the set with the descriptor *Analysis* is likely to eliminate citations that are possibly relevant. ANDing it with the free-text term *analysis*, on the other hand, is likely to eliminate a smaller number of citations because the term is common in abstracts. Thus, precision is improved and recall is not reduced drastically.

The common term that cannot be mapped to a descriptor almost always results in unsatisfactory retrieval. Searchers have no choice but to enter a free-text key [C]. Under such conditions, they often combine the term with other search keys that represent additional request components, to retrieve citations, select some

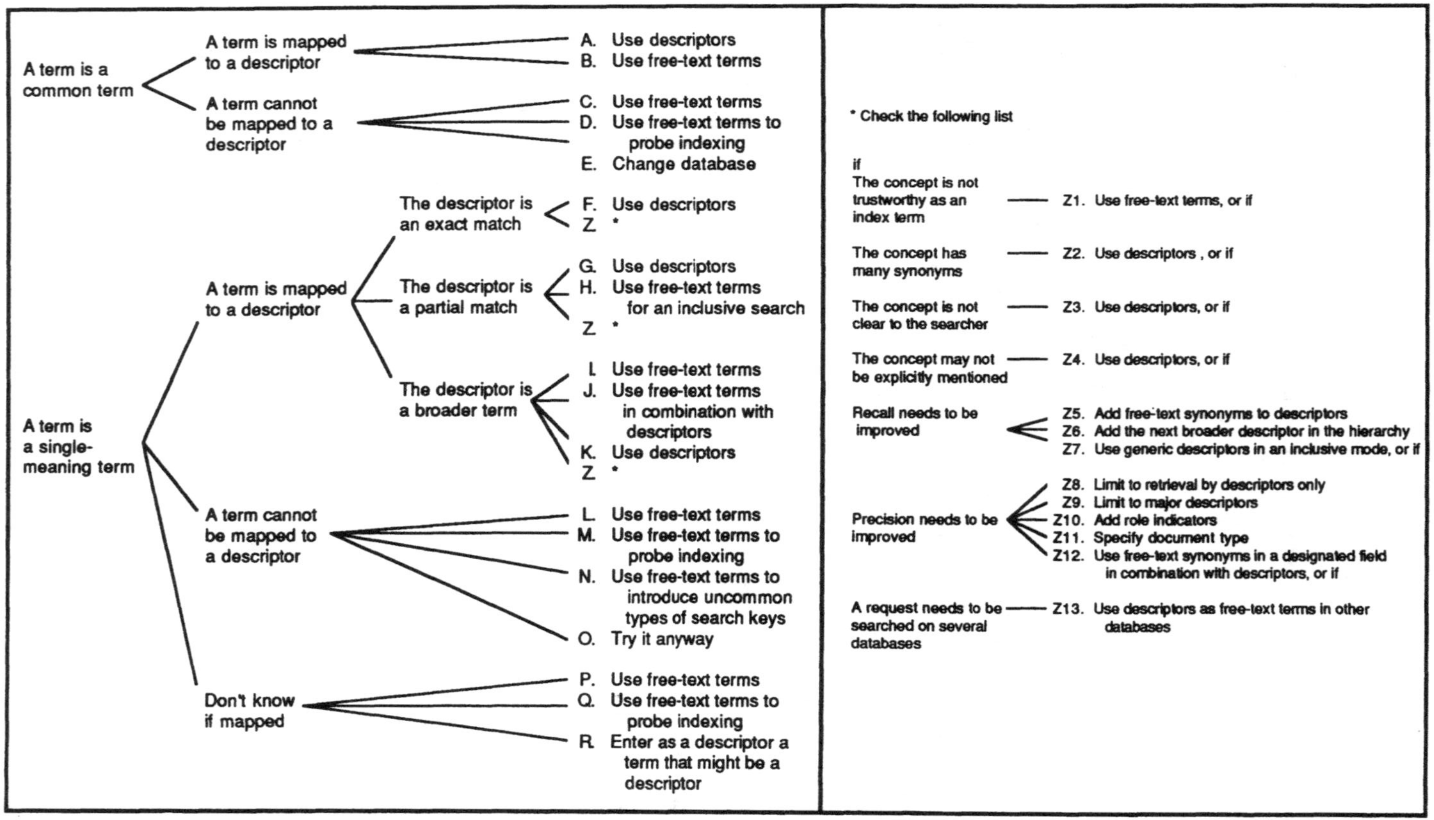

Figure 12.1. The Selection Routine.

relevant ones, and review their indexing in an attempt to find descriptors that might possibly be relevant [D]. For example, if the term *examination* cannot be mapped to a descriptor, one can AND the descriptors *Students' Behavior* and *Academic Difficulties* with the free-text term *examination*. Reviewing a sample of retrieved citations, one may find that all the relevant citations include the descriptor *Instructional Tests* in their indexing, thus suggesting that this descriptor is an appropriate choice for the representation of the concept *examination*.

Such probing does not always further the search and searchers may then decide to select a different database: one which does allow the common term to be mapped into a descriptor [E].

Single-meaning terms provide more options. If a single-meaning term cannot be mapped to a descriptor, searchers may enter a free-text term as the only search key [L], but they may also probe indexing of relevant citations to make sure that no adequate descriptor is overlooked [M].

In some cases, searchers may use a free-text key to search for a single-meaning term that cannot be mapped to a descriptor in a special way: They require that it occurs in a field other than the common ones, such as the journal title field [N]. Suppose a patron is interested primarily in the behavioral aspects of the request, and suppose the term *behavior*, or *students' behavior* cannot be mapped to a descriptor. Searchers may predict that searching for the occurrence of *behavior* in the text would retrieve a large number of irrelevant citations, and decide instead to retrieve citations to articles whose authors are affiliated with organizations which include the stem *behav* in their titles, or articles that were published in sources whose titles include this stem. If all else fails, searchers may enter a single-meaning term that is not mapped to a descriptor as a descriptor just to ascertain that their failure to map the term to a descriptor was not a mistake [O].

Another set of similar possibilities arises when searchers do not know whether a term is mapped to a descriptor. This may happen when the pertinent thesaurus is not available to searchers, or when they decide not to consult one. Here again, they can use free-text terms [P], they can use free-text terms to probe indexing [Q], or they can enter the term as a descriptor assuming that the term might be one [R].

The least problematic term is one that is single-meaning and also can be mapped to a descriptor. Such a term can be entered as a descriptor, as a free-text key, or as both. Here, searchers are free to deal with other request characteristics when selecting search keys. These characteristics are presented in the Z1-Z14 sequence. A single-meaning term that is mapped to a descriptor through any kind of match always includes a Z option. This option covers a variety of conditions, such as: The concept has many synonyms, recall needs to be improved, or a request needs to be searched on several databases. The Z options will not be discussed here; a somewhat dated but detailed explanation can be found elsewhere (Fidel, 1986).

A single-meaning term can be mapped to a descriptor through an exact match, partial match, or a term might be mapped to a broader descriptor. When a single-meaning term is mapped to a descriptor through an exact match, searchers may use the descriptor [F], or select to consider a variety of characteristics [Z].

Partial match usually implies mapping a request term to a narrower descriptor, or to a group of narrower descriptors. Searchers can always enter the descriptor, or the group of descriptors [G]. If suitable, however, they use a free-text key to inclusively search concepts that are not grouped together by the hierarchy of the controlled vocabulary [H]. If, for example, the request term *students* is mapped to descriptors such as *Foreign Students*, *College Students*, or *Undergraduates*, and a descriptor *Students* does not exist, the free-text key can be used to retrieve information about any type of student. It should be noted that in some search systems use of the free-text term *students* also would retrieve citations that are indexed with descriptors which include the term. This is a source for constant confusion for searchers who search a number of search systems regularly because the routine changes from one search system to another.

When a single-meaning request term is mapped to a broader descriptor, searchers may prefer to preserve the specificity of the request and use free-text search keys [I]. If they are concerned with the precision of the set to be retrieved, they enter free-text terms in combination (using the AND operator) with the broader descriptor to which it is mapped [J]. If, for example, the concept *final examination* is mapped to the descriptor *Instructional Tests*, searchers can AND this descriptor with the free-text term *final* and thus eliminate citations for articles about other types of examinations. Searchers, of course, may elect to enter just a descriptor even if it is broader than the original concept [K].

This concludes the description of the conditions and options presented in the Selection Routine. Our next question is how can this decision tree be used for the construction of IES?

APPLICATIONS TO EXPERT SYSTEMS

The Selection Routine presents the rules that searchers use when they decide which type of search keys to enter. The Routine by itself is not sufficient for an expert system to act like a searcher. IES needs more knowledge for that purpose. An expert system should be able to determine, for example, whether a term is a common term or a single-meaning one, if it is mapped to a descriptor and through what kind of a match, or when to ask patrons whether high precision or high recall is required.

This additional knowledge requires a variety of dictionaries, thesauri, and rules. A few examples of such knowledge and the manner in which it can be stored are discussed below.

Semantic Dictionaries

The most straightforward way for an expert system to check whether a given term is a common term or a single-meaning one is to consult a dictionary that would specify the status of each term. Unfortunately, such a dictionary does not exist and more research is needed before it could be constructed.

What are the issues that should be considered for the construction of such a dictionary?

From a linguistic point of view there are very few terms that are truly single-meaning. It is enough to browse through a regular dictionary to discover that most terms have more than one meaning. Thus the dichotomy common/single-meaning is not supported by linguistics, and most terms are neither the one nor the other.

On the other hand, searchers must make a decision whether or not a given term is "good" for free-text searching. For them the issue is a dichotomy, and they use their common sense and intuition to make the decision. Because the distinction between common and single-meaning terms is central to online searching, an expert system should also be able to make this distinction. Expert systems cannot use common sense or intuition, though, and one must devise rigorous routine for this decision.

Currently, we do not know what is the best way to determine for a given term whether it would be considered a common or a single-meaning term by online searchers. There are probably various methods to teach expert systems to make this distinction but the methods need to be tested and compared.

For example, one possible method to identify common terms for a database is to measure the frequency (the number of times) in which each term occurs in the database, and to designate terms that occur very frequently as common terms. Such a method is attractive because it is easy to implement and it does not require a full-scale dictionary. For each database an expert system needs to have a cutoff point beyond which a term would be considered a common term. A system may have a rule stating, for instance, that if the number of postings for a term is larger than 15,000 the term is a common term. While such a simple procedure is indeed attractive, we still need to test its validity. We need to examine whether common terms occur in high frequency and whether terms that occur in high frequency are always common terms.

Another method is to ask a panel of searchers-judges to consider each term in a database and to decide whether it is a common or a single-meaning one. While this method seems most reliable, it is too labor-intensive to be realistic.

As these examples illustrate, we are still in the dark: We have not found yet a method that is both feasible and reliable. Developing such a method requires extensive investigations. Since no such research is being carried out at present, either in information science or in linguistics, only the future can tell how soon will this issue be resolved.

Thesauri

Many databases have thesauri that list descriptors and lead-in terms: Terms that are not descriptors but are listed in the thesaurus and lead patrons—through "see" references—to descriptors. Searchers consult these thesauri when they are looking for descriptors. Expert systems can use the same thesauri to determine whether or not a term is mapped to a descriptor.

The thesauri to be used by IES, however, should be much more extensive than those used by human searchers, and may require special search algorithms. Ideally, patrons will present IES with requests expressed in natural language and in the form of a sentence. IES in turn should be able to identify the components of a request, and check the terms that represent each component in the thesauri of the relevant databases.

If an online searcher cannot find an entry to a given term, he can think about synonyms or other ways to represent a concept. To "think" about synonyms, expert systems require thesauri with extensive lead-in vocabulary that include any term that might be mentioned in a request.

In addition, the lead-in vocabulary would probably be more complex than that in a manual thesaurus. Some thesaurus look-ups are simple. Consider the concept *examinations* when it is not a descriptor. This term is an example of a simple case: a lead-in vocabulary is likely to have an entry for the term and guide a searcher to the right descriptor, say, *Instructional Tests*. Here, an online searcher and an expert system that can read the thesaurus would perform equally well. Suppose, however, that a request is about attitudes of students towards themselves. Here a searcher may pause to think about the best representation of the concept *attitudes towards themselves*. She may decide that another way to represent this concept is with the phrases *self image* or *self esteem*. In searching for descriptors, then, she would look under these phrases rather than under *attitudes*. An expert system should be able to make similar decisions.

For an expert system to consider different representations for a single concept, a sophisticated lead-in vocabulary with possibly the addition of some semantic rules are required. Like the distinction between common and single-meaning terms, thinking about various representations of a concept is guided by the searcher's linguistic abilities. A knowledge of the English language, and a special talent to manipulate the language, are considered by many an important requirement of online searchers. Expert systems can acquire this talent with the help of research in linguistics. Much research is being conducted in this area (natural language processing), but no conclusive prototype is available yet. It is possible, though, that such capabilities will be common to IES in the imminent future.

Options and Reasons

In addition to solving linguistic and semantic issues, searchers are looking for the search keys that would best satisfy a given request. An example can illustrate this function.

The Selection Routine does not provide a unique path for each set of conditions. For example, if a term is a single-meaning term and it is mapped to a broader descriptor, there are three options (in addition to the Z options): Searchers can use free-text terms [I], free-text terms in combination with descriptors [J], or they can use descriptors [K]. Suppose an expert system mapped a single-meaning term to a broader descriptor, how would it know which option to choose—which search keys to select?

To answer such questions, one must identify additional conditions that would determine under what circumstances should each option be selected. A substantial part of the study reported here was to uncover these additional conditions. It is beyond the scope of this chapter to provide a comprehensive description of these conditions, but one example can convey their nature.

The study found that searchers preferred to use free-text terms to represent a single-meaning term that is mapped to a broader descriptor under the following circumstances: (a) If a patron required retrieval with high precision, or (b) if they entered the broader descriptor and found that many of the citations retrieved were irrelevant. It was also found that the first condition occurred more frequently than the second one.

Alternately, searchers decided to enter a free-text term in combination with a descriptor (e.g., *final* AND *Instructional Tests*) only when they did not trust the indexing—thinking the descriptor was assigned loosely—and wanted to make sure that the specific term was present in the citations. This option, however, was rarely selected.

Searchers selected most often the third option: Once they had identified a descriptor for a single-meaning term, they entered it even if it was a broader descriptor. The most common reason for that selection was their knowledge that high recall was required. Another reason that was mentioned less frequently, but was still quite common, is the searcher's belief that it was better to search with descriptors. (It should be noted here that this argument was used consistently for particular databases.)

Three other reasons for selecting a broader descriptor that were mentioned by searchers relate to more specific situations. In a few instances searchers entered a broader descriptor after realizing that the free-text term had not provided enough retrieval. A few others used two broader descriptors that in combination represent the specific concept. For example, the descriptors *Instructional Tests* and *Graduation Requirements* are each broader than the term *final examinations*. Their combination with the AND operator, however, represents more closely the required concept. One searcher claimed that if the term is a single-word term, precision and recall would be improved if a broader descriptor was entered.

Once the reasons for selecting each option in the Selection Routine are laid out, one must ask: How can an expert system apply this knowledge when it selects search keys? IES will have a set of rules that will guide them in selecting options. To illustrate the nature of these rules, it is best to use an example.

An Example

Consider our sample request: "the analysis of students' behavior during a final examination to determine the difficulty of the examination." Suppose an intermediary expert system—named THE GOOD SEARCHER—has acquired the terminological and semantic talent needed for the analysis of requests. This system is able then to identify the components of the request, which are: (a) analysis, (b) students' behavior, (c) final examinations, and (d) examination's difficulty.

After looking in the thesaurus of an educational database the system finds out that:

1. The first concept, which is a common term, is mapped to the descriptor *Analysis*—an exact match.
2. The second concept is also mapped to a descriptor through an exact match.
3. The third concept is mapped to a broader descriptor—*Instructional Tests*.
4. The fourth concept cannot be mapped to a descriptor.

Following the Selection Routine, THE GOOD SEARCHER selects to represent the first two concepts with descriptors (options [A] and [F]). For the representation of the third concept, however, the system needs to make a selection among three options: [I], [J], and [K]. For that purpose it needs to know what are the precision and recall requirements, as described earlier. In response to the system's inquiry, the patron indicates that this is a high recall request. Following the reasons for the three options, THE GOOD SEARCHER decides to use the descriptor *Instructional Tests* (option [K]).

The last concept is a little more problematic because it is not mapped to a descriptor. While this condition raises four options ([L], [M], [N], and [O]), the system is programmed to always try option [M] first: use the free-text key to probe indexing.

The initial formulation of the request is then:

Analysis AND *Students' Behavior* AND *Instructional Tests* AND *difficulty*.

Because the first formulation was entered to probe indexing, THE GOOD SEARCHER asks the patron to provide some feedback. The system displays the 10 citations that have been retrieved and asks the patron to designate which citations are highly relevant. The patron marks six citations. The system's task now is to find descriptors that are assigned to these citations most frequently. It comes up with one descriptor: *Academic Standards*. The fourth concept of the request—examination's difficulty—can be now mapped to a descriptor.

The next decision the system is facing is whether to represent this concept only with a descriptor or whether to add the free-text term. Here, a general rule can be of help. It states: If more than 30% of the citations retrieved by the free-text key are relevant, use both descriptor and free-text; if less than 30% of the citations are relevant, use the descriptor only. Therefore, the system decides to represent the fourth concept with the combination: *difficulty* OR *Academic Standards*.

Using the modified formulation, THE GOOD SEARCHER finds 25 citations. Now it needs to find out whether the patron is satisfied with the retrieved set. After displaying the titles of the retrieved citations, it asks whether the retrieval seems relevant and whether there is enough. The patron is satisfied with the precision of the answer set but feels that some are missing: Higher recall is needed. Checking the options available to increase the recall of a retrieved set, the system discovers the rule: If a request has more than three components and higher recall is required, one request component should be eliminated. (This rule was not derived from the Selection Routine but from other stored knowledge about searching behavior.) The system cannot randomly select which concept to drop, however, and it asks the patron to rank the concepts in the order of their importance.

The patron response in decreasing order is: *students' behavior, final examinations, analysis*, and *examination difficulty*. Following its own rule, THE GOOD SEARCHER drops the fourth concept from the formulation and retrieves 53 citations.

To the system's request for evaluation of titles of retrieved citations, the patron asks that recall still be improved and expresses her satisfaction with precision. There are various options, and the system may select all or just some of them, depending on the specifics of the request. Under one situation it can add to the formulation the free-text term *final exam* [Z6], and under another it can retrieve all citations that have been indexed under a descriptor that includes the term *student*. (For simplicity's sake the specific situations are not explained here.) The system also considers option [B] for the concept *analysis* because it is a common term that is mapped to a descriptor, but it is not central to the request. In other words, *analysis* is a limiting factor—it qualifies the main subject of the request—and could be entered as a free-text term to increase recall.

After eliminating the other options to improve recall—through an interrogation of the patron—THE GOOD SEARCHER selects option [B] and retrieves 98 citations. At this point the patron is satisfied with both precision and recall, and the search is terminated.

CONCLUSIONS

What can we learn from the Selection Routine and its implementation for expert systems?

The first conclusion that stands out is that linguistic rules and semantic networks are essential to the operation of IES. No expert system could truly replicate the performance of human searchers before it can resolve semantic and linguistic issues.

Second, the Selection Routine demonstrates that once linguistic and semantic issues are resolved, IES can indeed be constructed to replicate the searching behavior of human searchers.

Third, such IES can identify which characteristics of a request are important to the success of a search and at which points in the search should the patron be asked about them. Most importantly, such IES can act on additional information they receive from patrons to improve search results.

Fourth, in some instances, such IES can *surpass* human searchers. IES have one substantive advantage over human searchers: They can process information much faster. Consider, for instance, the option [P]: to use free-text terms when it is *not known* whether a term is mapped to a descriptor. Obviously, it is better to know whether or not a term is mapped to a descriptor, but searchers decide not to check a term for descriptors because of various reasons. They may decide not to consult the thesaurus of a certain database because they think indexing—or the vocabulary itself—are not useful, because they are not available to them or because they have to search a request in a large number of databases.

While the first reason for avoiding a thesaurus look-up is justified under any circumstances, the rest are determined by cost-benefit considerations that are valid for human searchers but not for IES. An intermediary expert system should include all the thesauri of the databases it can search, and it should consult each of them for a request, regardless of the number of databases to be searched. While it probably should avoid consulting a thesaurus that is considered unreliable by most searchers, an expert system can perform better than a human searcher for a request that requires the use of a large number of thesauri.

In addition, IES are free from developing searching habits that might be counterproductive at times. A searcher may develop a habit of searching with free-text keys because most of the time this mode is required for the success of her searches. This searcher would probably elect to enter free-text keys, say, to search a database she rarely searches, even if a descriptor search is likely to produce better results. Because IES are based on the experience of a large number of searchers such individual idiosyncrasies are not likely to be incorporated into their knowledge. IES, then, can always select the path that seems most productive, free from individual habits.

Will IES replace human searchers?

Even though they can become very powerful, it is unlikely that the introduction of IES will eliminate the need for online searchers. It is obvious, however, that the role of online searchers will change and their expertise will be used differently. But this is another matter.

REFERENCES

Doszkocs, T. E. (1983). Automatic vocabulary mapping in online searching. *International classification, 10*, 78–83.

Fidel, R. (1986). Towards expert systems for the selection of search keys. *Journal of the American Society for Information Science, 37*, 37–44.

Marcus, R. S. (1983). An experimental comparison of the effectiveness of computers and humans as search intermediaries. *Journal of the American Society for Information Science, 34*, 381–404.

Pollitt, A. S. (1984). A "front-end" system: An expert system as an online search intermediary. *Aslib Proceedings, 36*, 229–234.

Svenonius, E. (1986). Unanswered questions in the design of controlled vocabularies. *Journal of the American Society for Information Science, 37*, 331–340.

13

Knowledge-Based Search Intermediaries for Online Information Retrieval

Mark H. Chignell
Department of Industrial and Systems Engineering
University of Southern California

Lee Jaffe
University Library
University of Southern California

Philip J. Smith
Deborah Krawczak
Stephen J. Shute
Department of Industrial and Systems Engineering
The Ohio State University

INTRODUCTION

The development of the computer, with its processing and mass storage capabilities, has allowed online storage of text, with resulting increased accessibility and availability of text. As a result, online information retrieval systems have developed. Artificial intelligence (AI) is the second technology of major importance to information science. AI has the potential to revolutionize the indexing strategies and, ultimately, the retrieval methods used in online retrieval by representing documents in terms of networks of concepts and topics rather than keywords and topical descriptions that stand alone.

Document retrieval is a knowledge-intensive process that stands to gain greater efficiency and wider usage from recent developments in information technology and artificial intelligence. A number of research projects are attempting to develop new methods of information retrieval that incorporate artificial intelligence techniques. In this chapter we will outline some of the problems that

*The EP-X project is supported by funding from Chemical Abstracts Services. Project Jefferson is supported by an equipment grant from Apple Computer and technical assistance from ABC-Clio. We would like to thank Robert Ledwith, Robert Strobaugh, and Chris Zeidner for their comments on an earlier version of the manuscript.

exist with current methods of online retrieval. Then we will review recent research aimed at developing improved methods of online information retrieval.

Information Retrieval and Library Research

The technology of information retrieval is in a state of transition. This dynamic process of change has been characteristic of information technology ever since the invention of writing. Initially, the emphasis was on the materials used to produce text, that is, paper and pens. With printing, mass production of texts became possible, and the emphasis shifted to that of making the printing process cheaper and more efficient. As the number of books available increased exponentially with the improved printing technology, the necessity to organize and classify the information became apparent, and library science and indexing schemes developed to meet the need. Information tools such as card catalogs, photocopying, and microfiche allowed people to access information through a combination of keywords and citation data. The development of online databases created new opportunities and challenges for information science (Salton & McGill, 1983).

Current online retrieval systems typically consist of a large database of stored document surrogates. Words and phrases which describe each document's contents (index terms) are selected from a controlled vocabulary of standard terms or freely. The index terms serve as descriptors of, or pointers to, the document they represent. The information need of a user is represented as a query. In the current paradigm the query is essentially phrased in the form "what documents do you have that conform to the following set of constraints?" The constraints are input as a search query which consists of a series of terms (keywords) combined in a structured query language often based on Boolean logic. The proper use of logical operators enables selective intersection, union, and exclusion operations on sets of documents whose index terms "match" the combination of keywords entered.

The Role of the Search Intermediary

Specialized expertise is usually required to understand the indexing policies employed in databases and to formulate search queries in the language of the database. Since most end users do not have this expertise, they require the aid of a search intermediary in carrying out a search. Librarians are often the intermediaries between information providers and information seekers. They identify sources of information; acquire information; organize the information; provide tools for searching through the information; and assist users with the minor and major questions relating to their information needs.

The role of intermediary is most obvious at the library reference desk. There the user is taught about, and assisted with, the library collection and the tools that fill reference rooms. Some of these tools have changed to electronic form—notably the online information services. With the advent of CD-ROM technology many more will soon follow. Though this newest generation of resources is a natural extension of traditional reference responsibilities, it makes for qualitative changes in the librarians' role.

The electronic services have removed the user further from direct access to needed information, emphasizing the librarian's intermediary role. With print tools, users always had the choice of circumventing the reference librarian and going directly to the source. Occasional users may find it difficult to search an online database directly, however, because of the expertise required and the costs associated with inefficient and unsuccessful searches. Thus, potential users will generally turn to a librarian who takes charge of the search process.

The existence of intermediaries has generally allowed system vendors to avoid the extensive interface development required for end user access. Most current systems are made for experts, information retrieval specialists whose job is to take the hurdles for the client. They are paid to know which database to search, how to develop a search strategy, and to work with the thesaurus and construct the search. In the ideal situation, the client is an expert in his or her field, with a working knowledge of the pertinent information resources. The librarian should be an expert in information retrieval, with at least a working knowledge of the client's general field. In many cases though, the intermediary may not have a good working knowledge of the relevant search topic, particularly if it is highly technical or specialized and the process of query negotiation must bridge the resultant gap. Though negotiations may differ as much as the many combinations of librarian and client allow, they all seek to resolve the perceived information need into an executable search query.

The immediate goal of the search intermediary is to choose the appropriate search tools and to turn the user's needs into concrete search terms. The first part requires assessment of the client's expertise and the scope of the information needed. Which sources contain the needed information in a form accessible to the client? The second part requires the skills of an interviewer and a translator. As an interviewer, the intermediary must extract synonyms and related terms from the client. As a translator, he must often deal with the problem of being less than intimately familiar with the language of the speaker. The translation process is often assisted by thesauri that map the terminology of the user onto that of the database. The intermediary endeavors to understand the basic knowledge needed to perform an intelligent search of the literature of the field. In turn, the client learns the basic concepts, plus the strengths and weaknesses of the different methods of information retrieval.

The client has to explain his or her information need to the librarian. The librarian asks questions to clarify the request and to translate the need in terms of selection of appropriate databases and the formulation of a search request. As an intermediary between the idiosyncratic language of the client and the various forms of database organization, the intermediary must strive to understand both as well as possible.

The role of the intermediary is multifaceted, as shown in Figure 13.1. The intermediary stands as an intelligent entity between the user and the online retrieval system (Chignell, Hancock, Smith, & Shute, 1986). In the terminology of information theory there are two communication channels in operation during

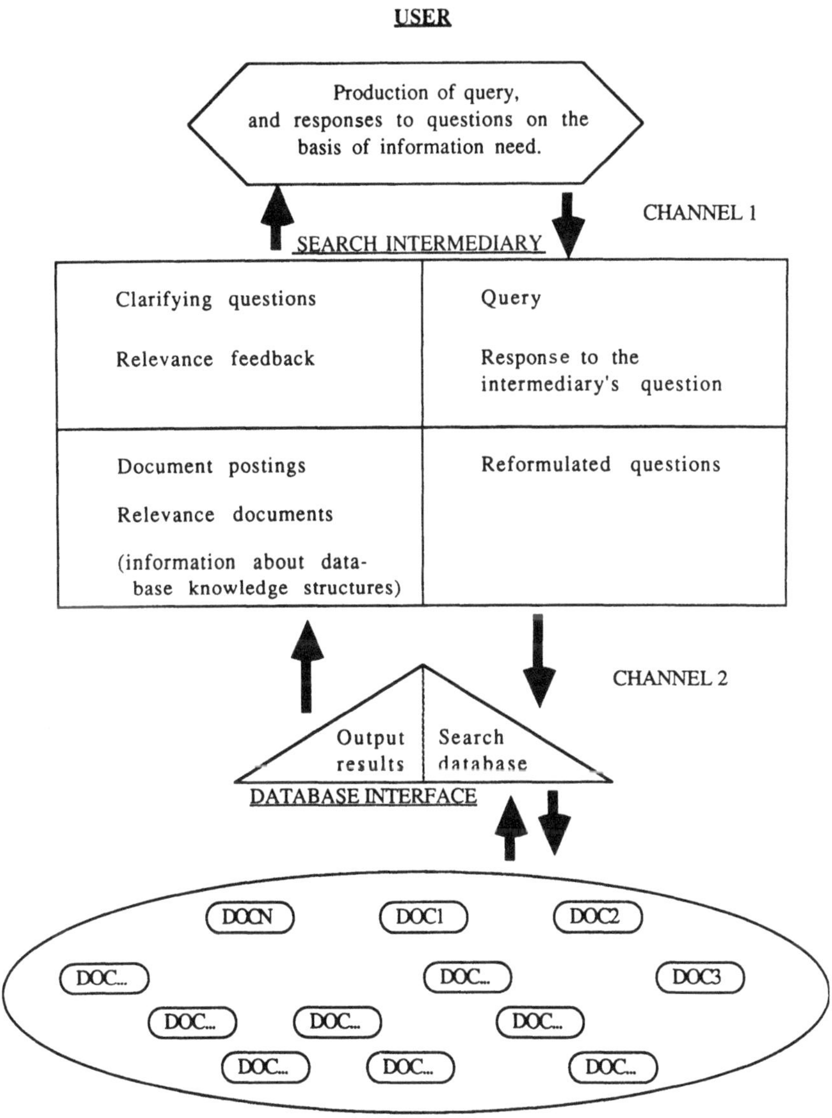

Figure 13.1. The Role of the Search Intermediary.

an online search. The first communication channel is used by the end user and search intermediary in formulating search queries. The second channel is used by the search intermediary in interacting with the online database. Faulty communication in either of these channels will result in poor retrieval performance.

Problems with Using Search Intermediaries

The search intermediary is an essential part of the current information retrieval paradigm due to his familiarity with current online systems and strategies for selecting files and reducing the costs associated with search. However, there are a number of problems associated with working through an intermediary:

1. The role of the intermediary is labor-intensive and costly. As information retrieval technologies mature, the cost of the intermediary's services will become a larger proportion of the total cost of information retrieval.
2. Many who wish to conduct bibliographic searches have access to information retrieval systems via remote terminals, yet do not have ready access to skilled intermediaries.
3. Knowledgeable though they are, human search intermediaries cannot be expected to have complete knowledge of all domains contained within the available databases. Furthermore, due simply to uncertainty and ambiguity in the use of language, critical nuances of end-users' topics can be lost or distorted during interaction with the intermediary.

Aside from these objective reasons, users are motivated to interact directly with online retrieval systems because they like the feeling of direct access (no need to make appointments and work through an intermediary) and they like to have a feeling of control and direct involvement. Although some institutions subsidize the cost of online retrieval, cost is a factor for most users when choosing whether or not to use intermediaries. For instance, some systems are cheaper to use at night when intermediaries generally aren't available and this leads to dilemmas where the user trades off cheaper connect time at night against more efficient searching in the day. Intermediaries too may be dissatisfied with the current mode of interaction which places an undue burden on librarians as they seek to reconcile information needs with the realities of what is available while in the midst of a commercial transaction.

In our view, the need for search intermediaries, in spite of the problems associated with mediated information retrieval, is indicative of inappropriate structuring and indexing of online databases which leads to inadequate software interfaces for online retrieval. Consider the following query in the area of environmental pollution:

WASTE(W) (TREATMENT OR REMOVAL)
AND (PRECIPITATION OR PPTN) AND
(METHYLMERCURY OR CADMIUM)

This example demonstrates several problems with the use of Boolean search strings, the predominant method of expressing online search queries at present. First, the user must anticipate the various synonyms and abbreviations that may have been used. For PRECIPITATION, this list might include PRECIPITATE, PPTN, and PPTG. Second, the user must be aware that a specific character string may have more than one meaning. Even in the limited domain of environmental pollution PRECIPITATION refers both to airborne water such as rain or snow and to a waste removal process. Third, in some databases such as the *Chemical Abstracts*, documents are indexed at only the most specific level. Therefore, a user interested in a broader topic such as heavy metals must enter this term along with all terms naming specific heavy metals. Otherwise he will only retrieve documents specifically indexed under a topic like HEAVY METALS and not, for instance, those that are indexed under instances of that topic such as CADMIUM. These problems are compounded by the need to identify concepts in the form of Boolean statements. There is consistent evidence that the formation and comprehension of logical expressions exceeds normal human information processing limitations for the population at large (Hildreth, 1983; Tversky & Kahneman, 1974; Wason & Johnson-Laird, 1972). Selection and placement of appropriate logical operators has been found to be difficult even for expert searchers (Oldroyd & Schroder, 1982). Effects of order and scope of activation of logical expressions, and use of negation have proven especially troublesome in the context of online retrieval systems. These findings indicate that effective unmediated online search should either provide user assistance in the construction of search queries, or else make the process transparent to the user.

The Nature of Search Intermediary Expertise

An improved understanding of the components of online retrieval search skill is a necessary prerequisite in building knowledge-based systems which incorporate search expertise.

In order to conduct an effective bibliographic search, at least five broad classes of knowledge are necessary:

1. Procedural expertise in the use of computer systems is needed in order to initiate and sustain an effective pattern of communication with the retrieval system. In addition, a higher-level component of procedural expertise involves the user's developing an internal representation of user-system interaction, permitting successful prediction of system behavior under a

variety of conditions. Ideally, an online retrieval system should require a minimum of procedural expertise since this is not directly relevant to the actual content of the retrieval task.

2. Domain knowledge, consisting of knowledge about the concepts, relationship among concepts, and terminology in the database domain is necessary. For example, knowledge of the database domain of environmental pollution encompasses such concepts as pollutants, affected organisms, geographic locations, methods for removal, media, and the effects of particular pollutants.
3. Strategies for query formulation, both general and data-base-specific, represent a substantial body of essential expertise. A vital component of the skilled searcher's expertise lies in her facility in combining logical operators with keywords. Indeed, expert searchers demonstrate considerable skill in using such operators.
4. Knowledge of database-specific construction and indexing policies is also needed, and may have implications for deciding which search strategy is most promising in the context of the particular database.
5. Higher-level search decisions appear to be a major part of search expertise. Hawkins and Wagers (1982) delineate four approaches to search, selection of the best method being contingent upon such aspects as the breadth of the initial search topic. Tradeoffs must be carefully weighed. For instance, the building block approach involves the formulation and executing of a separate search for each concept, with the results of each subsearch combined to yield a final document set. This logically constrained approach does not lend itself well to the exploration of unanticipated interesting paths (e.g., browsing). The best general search strategy frequently depends on the characteristics of the particular database, such as indexing policies.

Expert System Search Intermediaries

One answer to the problems identified above is to incorporate components of these classes of knowledge in an expert system search intermediary for online retrieval. Expert systems are generally defined as computer programs that solve problems of commercial and scientific importance using knowledge and inference procedures. The development of an expert system requires that there be a human expert who can act as a source of the expertise that will be built into the program. In contrast to this rather narrow view of expert systems some have used the alternative term "knowledge-based systems" to reflect the fact that the same general methods can be used to create intelligent behavior whether or not the rules and inference procedures are explicitly modeled on those of a corresponding human expert (e.g., Davis & Lenat, 1982).

In the case of information retrieval, the question arises as to whether it is appropriate to mimic exclusively the methods used by human search intermediaries in expert systems. The memory-intensive nature of the information retrieval task may favor computer representations of the task in some cases.

In addition to the question of what search expertise should be incorporated within an expert system search intermediary (c.f., Kinnell & Chignell, 1987), there is the prior question of whether or not it is appropriate to try and build expert system search intermediaries. There are a number of features of expert systems that seem ill-suited to applications in online information retrieval. These include the following:

1. An expert system is restricted to a narrow knowledge domain.
2. Expert systems are interactive and should have a relatively fast response time.
3. Expert systems are knowledge-intensive and the task of constructing expert systems (known as knowledge engineering) is fairly onerous.

It will be difficult to build expert system search intermediaries that attempt to deal with all possible knowledge domains. By their nature, expert systems utilize the expertise of one, or a few, experts in a *limited* domain. Thus, in applying expert systems techniques to the online retrieval task, it will initially be advisable to target specific knowledge domains such as environmental pollution or the U.S. Constitution. Even with a narrow domain, the concept of an expert system must be tailored further to meet the needs of online information retrieval. Whereas conventional expert systems work with facts directly, information retrieval is concerned with indirect access to information. As Paice (1986) has pointed out, search intermediaries do not generally have expert knowledge in the fields for which they are responsible. Yet it seems to be this domain knowledge, expressed in both the language of the user and the language of the database, that is the most important element of online retrieval.

The major components of an expert system are the knowledge base, inference engine, and user interface. As we discussed above, it is probably not appropriate to construct the knowledge base for an expert system search intermediary based on rules of search expertise. Instead, the knowledge-based system should represent and organize the domain knowledge in a way that allows users to express queries accurately and efficiently. Thus, the knowledge base for an online retrieval intermediary will not consist of rules in the form of a production system such as OPS5 (e.g., Hayes-Roth, Waterman, & Lenat, 1983), but will instead be a topic hierarchy (similar to the architecture used in the MDX system; Chandrasekaran & Mittal, 1983). The inference engine, too, will be modified with the user having more control of the reasoning process than typically occurs with expert systems. While the system may make suggestions about broadening or narrowing the topic, and point out ambiguities and errors, it is the user who has to be in charge of where to go next during query formulation because it is his information need that is being discussed. This again creates an unusual situation for expert systems because the user has critical information upon which the success of the interaction depends and the expert system can only get that information by interacting with the user. Thus, knowledge based-search intermediaries are not going to be expert systems in the usual sense. Instead, they are going to be like roadmaps of knowledge, with signposts about where to go next and intelligent hints about what to do.

Knowledge-based Search Intermediaries

While it is difficult to build expert system search intermediaries which explicitly model the multifaceted expertise of human search intermediaries, there are a number of ways in which useful features of a search intermediary can be built into online retrieval interfaces. We refer to an interface which has these features as a knowledge-based search intermediary because it uses various types of knowledge to assist the user without incorporating many aspects of the expertise used by human search intermediaries.

In the remainder of this chapter we will discuss some of the features that can be incorporated in knowledge-based search intermediaries using examples from two ongoing research projects. The first project is being carried out in the Industrial and Systems Engineering Department of the Ohio State University with the support of Chemical Abstracts Services. EP-X (Environmental Pollution Expert) is a prototype knowledge-based system that assists users in conducting bibliographic searches of the environmental pollution literature. Although not a natural language understanding system per se, EP-X (Krawczak, Smith, Shute, & Chignell, 1985) assumes that the user initially represents her topic internally as a natural language request, then asks the user to map her topic into a list of keywords or keyword phrases and enter them using an alphanumeric keyboard. EP-X then displays a natural language interpretation of the user's topic. This type of inference from the user's list of keyword phrases is made possible by the restricted domain, pollution, that is covered by the database. The interaction with EP-X creates a mapping of a topic of interest into a set of appropriate keywords, with iterative keyword entry and interpretation as the means toward obtaining agreement between what the user believes her topic to be, and how the system interprets it.

The architecture of EP-X is based on a "divide-and-conquer" strategy for online retrieval which was inspired by prior studies of expert human searchers. That is, a search in EP-X consists of two parts, first the user finds the neighborhood of interest, and then the user interacts with the system in increasing recall and precision (Figure 13.2, redrawn after Shute, Smith, Krawczak, Chignell, & Sater, 1986).

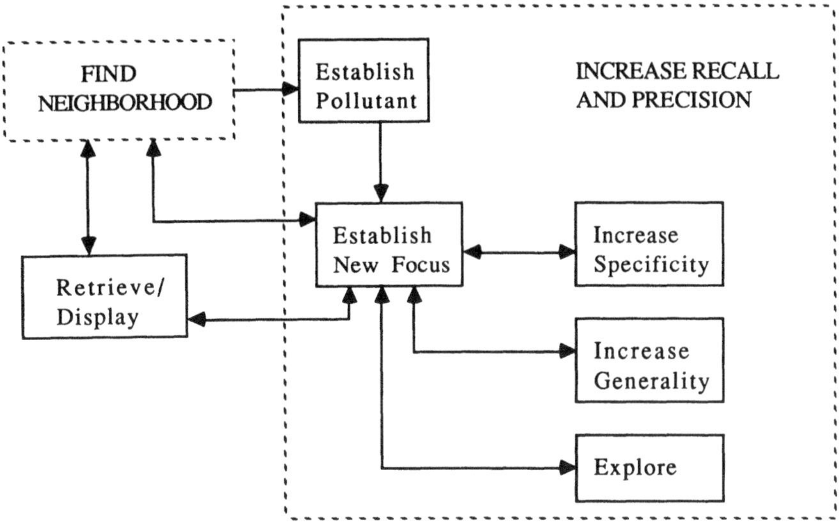

Figure 13.2. The EP-X System Architecture.

In contrast to EP-X, which deals with environmental pollution, the online retrieval system being developed by Project Jefferson at the University of Southern California deals with a humanities topic in an educational setting. Project Jefferson is a joint research project being carried out by the Industrial and Systems Engineering Department, the University Library, and the Freshman Writing Program at the University of Southern California with the support of Apple Computer and ABC-Clio. This project is designed to build a curriculum and set of aids that will assist undergraduates in understanding the Constitution and in researching and analyzing issues related to the Constitution. A major component of Project Jefferson is the development of a knowledge-based search intermediary to be used by the students in their research.

Knowledge Representation Strategies

Ideally, the knowledge base of the intermediary should represent knowledge in a form which is as complete, rich, and readily-searched as that of the human domain expert. The development of knowledge-based systems to act as intermediaries in online retrieval requires that the concepts which make up the domain knowledge can be indexed appropriately. Concepts would be represented in a form that allows easy access during querying. Hierarchies represent one form of knowledge that meets this requirement. To illustrate, consider the partial concept hierarchies shown in Figure 13.3.

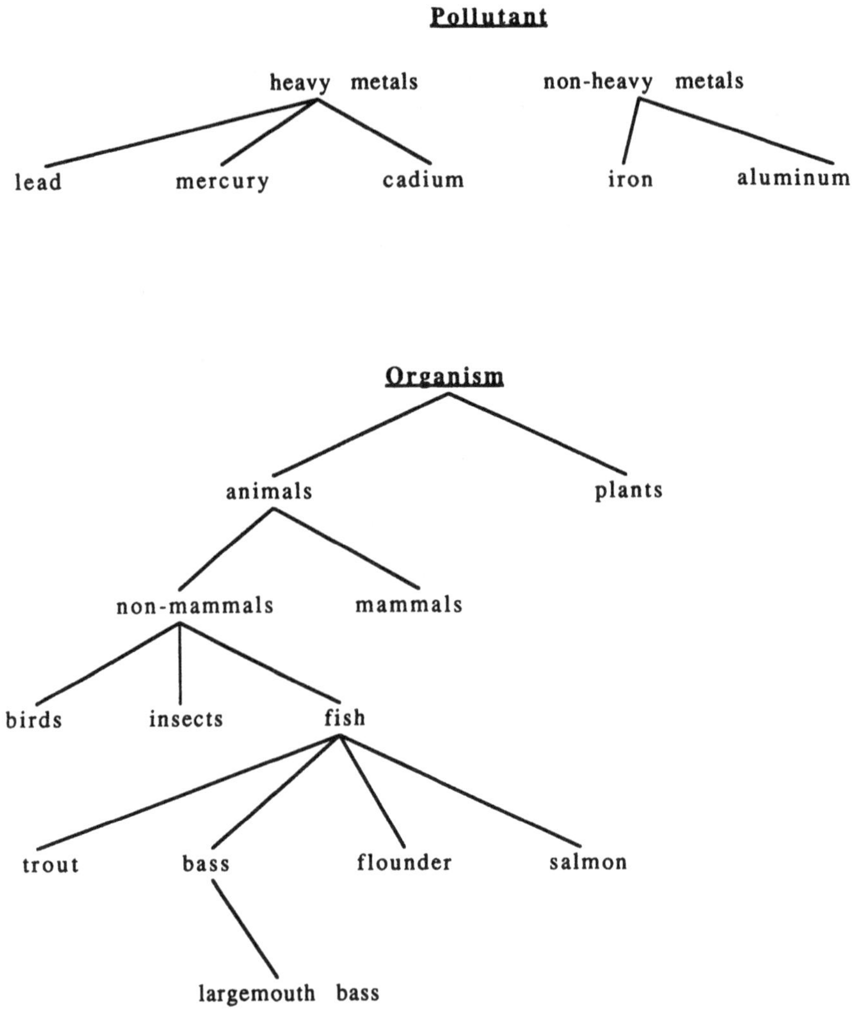

Figure 13.3. Partial hierarchies for the pollutant and organism concepts.
(Source: Krawczak, Smith, Shute, & Chignell, 1985)

Each node of the hierarchy is a particular instance of the concept that labels the entire structure. Each subordinate node is a more specific instance, and each super-ordinate node a more general instance. By implementing each node as a frame (Minsky, 1975), properties of each instance can be stored locally with that instance, and can also be propagated down the hierarchy to the successors. Most importantly, critical semantic relationships among instances are preserved, and can be used to structure search.

One of the features of frames is that they can carry out inheritance. Inheritance is based on the idea that objects tend to form groups and that members within a group tend to share common properties. In environmental pollution, for instance, we know that cadmium is a type of heavy metal, which in turn is a type of metal. Thus, we expect cadmium to retain all the basic properties of metals and heavy metals, but with further restrictions. We can make assumptions about some of the characteristics that cadmium has based on our knowledge about heavy metals in general. Thus, if we don't have any information to the contrary, we might assume that cadmium is a toxic substance since heavy metals in general are toxic.

Representation of knowledge in an online retrieval interface should incorporate a number of constructs that aid search and retrieval. These include unambiguous semantic primitives which define the vocabulary of the knowledge base, contextual information that specifies the roles of semantic primitives in the topics discussed by particular documents, descriptions of class relationships, and triggers which can be used to identify ambiguity, provide advice, and make suggestions to the user.

Semantic Primitives

Knowledge-based search intermediaries require an explicit representation of domain knowledge. The basic units of the knowledge are specific concepts which we refer to as *semantic primitives*. In EP-X, for instance, ATMOSPHERIC PRECIPITATION, and PRECIPITATION AS A WASTE REMOVAL PROCESS are separate semantic primitives. In general, ambiguity can be avoided by creating separate semantic primitives for each sense of ambiguous words such as PRECIPITATION. In Project Jefferson, the various types of discrimination that can occur must be similarly disambiguated. Thus, separate semantic primitives are developed for RACE DISCRIMINATION, SEX DISCRIMINATION, REVERSE DISCRIMINATION, and so on.

Contextual Information

A knowledge-based search intermediary needs more than just semantic primitives existing in isolation. To capture knowledge about topics, contextual information can be added by specifying the role that each semantic primitive can play in a document. In the knowledge domain of EP-X, mercury may be referred to as a pollutant, or as an ingredient in vapor lamps used to treat bacterial pollutants. Similarly, in the domain of Project Jefferson, the concept of due process may refer to supposed reverse discrimination in graduate school admissions or to the admissibility of evidence given while under hypnosis. When frames are used for knowledge representation, the effect of context can be indicated by the type of slot that a semantic primitive fills within a frame. Documents discussing the treatment of bacterial pollutants in EP-X, for instance, will indicate that mercury is being discussed as a constituent of a mercury vapor lamp, rather than as a pollutant.

Class Relationships

The knowledge representation should be capable of describing class relationships, in addition to its use of frames, slots, and semantic primitives. The system should know that TROUT and FLOUNDER are kinds of fish or that the AMERICAN CIVIL LIBERTIES UNION is a kind of organization. Such class relationships can be represented in frame hierarchies, as is done in both EP-X and Project Jefferson. A number of useful features of a knowledge-based search intermediary stem from this use of frame hierarchies. For instance, instead of having to recall all species of fish to increase recall, a knowledge-based system using frame hierarchies like EP-X (Krawczak et al., 1985) can use semantic relationships between concepts to infer that the user is interested not only in fish, but in all species of fish as well, and add documents discussing them to the active list.

Identifying Contexts

Other information besides properties of particular instances can be stored in each frame within the hierarchy. Synonyms may also be stored locally at each hierarchy node. So for example, the term "quicksilver" could activate the *MERCURY* node in the pollutant hierarchy in Figure 13.3. This property can help to resolve the problem of synonymy where the same concept can be expressed using a number of different words or phrases. At other times, uncertainty over the current context may lead to clarification from the user. In a system such as EP-X where the user can input keyword phrases, an input such as New York has to be disambiguated, since it can refer both to a state and a city. There are a number of types of concept clarifications that can be useful in working with frame hierarchies. Quicksilver and mercury, or U.S., U.S.A., and United States are examples of equivalence relationships which involve simple mappings of multiple keyword phrases to single concepts, whereas the New York example refers to disambiguation of nested terms within the same hierarchy.

Control Processes

Knowledge representation is a fundamental prerequisite for a knowledge-based search intermediary, but control processes are needed to allow the user to interact with the knowledge in formulating a query. Different control processes will be appropriate for different user goals and subgoals. One of the major goals for a knowledge-based search intermediary will be to assist the user in identifying a well-defined topic for the query. The control process for selecting a query topic with a frame hierarchy can be generally characterized as:

1. Select the frame of interest.
2. Identify the relevant slots for the current context.
3. Identify the corresponding slot fillers.

In Project Jefferson, for instance, the relevant frame might be the Fourteenth Amendment. Relevant slots might be COMPLAINANT, DEFENDANTS, GEOGRAPHIC LOCATION, and BASIS FOR COMPLAINT. Relevant slot fillers might be a prospective medical student, the defendants might be the University of California Board of Regents, the location might be Davis, California, and the basis for the complaint might be perceived reverse discrimination.

Increased recall and precision can be achieved by using other control processes that allow the user to move up (generalizing the search) or down (focusing the search) the frame hierarchy. The process of generalizing a search can be illustrated with an example (extracted from Krawczak, Smith, & Shute, 1987).

A user is interested in the topic "pollution of natural waters including lakes, rivers, etc., by radioactive substances such as Radon-222, Cesium-137, or Strontium-90." As the user enters each new keyword phrase, EP-X places it in the box at the top of the screen (see Figure 13.4). During this transaction, EP-X must infer that:

1. The term pollution is uninformative since all the documents in the database discuss pollution.
2. The semantic interpretation of the concept NATURAL WATERS includes subconcepts such as lakes, rivers, oceans, and bays.
3. Radon-222, Cesium-137, and Strontium-90 are all specific pollutants.

Once the keyword phrases are entered to the user's satisfaction, the system indicates that the current query represented by those keyword phrases will retrieve 14 documents. The user wants more than 14 documents and chooses the BROADEN option. Before giving the user a chance to select a keyword to broaden, EP-X makes any reasonable suggestions based on its knowledge (see Figure 13.5). In this case, EP-X notices that RADON-222, CESIUM-137, and STRONTIUM-90 are all specific concepts that fall under the more general term RADIOACTIVE SUBSTANCES.

The process of narrowing will be illustrated with an example from Project Jefferson. Figure 13.6 shows a prototype version of the Project Jefferson interface. A file cabinet is used as a graphic device to represent the text structure of the Constitution. The drawers in the file cabinet represent the various articles and

ENTER KEYWORD LIST

Your keyword list currently consists of the following:
POLLUTION
NATURAL WATERS
RADON-222
CESIUM-137
STRONTIUM-90

Type your next keyword or keyword phrase and press RETURN.

If you are done entering your keyword list, just press the RETURN key.

ENTER KEYWORD:

If you want to get further explanation, type HELP and press RETURN.

If you want to start a new search, type RESTART and press RETURN.

If you want to stop the search, type STOP and press RETURN.

Figure 13.4. Entering the Keyword List in EP-X.

amendments. Article V is highlighted to show that it is currently being added to the query (the "Find These" box). Article III is grayed out to show that it has already been added to the query and the postings prior to the addition of Article V to the query are shown in the "These Found" box (i.e., 15 postings). In the Project Jefferson interface, the suggestions for broadening and narrowing the topic are made by the librarian, which is a context-sensitive help system. The librarian is activated by double-clicking on the icon.

Consider the case of a user who is interested in the Equal Rights Amendment and related issues. The user may have begun in the Amendments draw but then found that most of the documents there refer to freedom of speech, due process, and related issues. The user then opens up the Article III draw (judicial power and the Supreme Court) to examine cases relating to women's rights. The search can then be narrowed by focusing on cases pertaining to the Equal Rights Amendment. The librarian assists in narrowing by suggesting that Article V (the creation of amendments) be opened. The librarian is able to make this suggestion

SUGGESTION FOR BROADENING

Radon-222, cesium-137 and strontium-90 are all radioactive substances
If you broaden your topic to include all radioactive substances as pollutants
an additional 73 documents will be added for a total of 87 documents.

Do you want to:

1 **BROADEN** your topic as suggested above

2 **IGNORE THIS SUGGESTION** (leaving your topic unchanged)

ENTER CHOICE: 1

When appropriate type either HELP, RESTART or STOP and press RETURN.

Figure 13.5. A Broadening Suggestion in EP-X.

because the user had previously looked under the Equal Rights Amendment in the Amendments draw. Another version of the system might have led the user directly to Article V after he had attempted to use the Amendments draw. The disadvantage of this approach might be that narrowing on the Equal Rights Amendment occurred too quickly and that the search might have benefited from considering relevant legislative cases.

This example illustrates an important issue in the development of knowledge-based search intermediaries. There are many different ways to represent and use knowledge in a particular domain. Ultimately, the selection of how to organize the knowledge and link topics will depend on the conceptual framework that is adopted and on empirical analysis (i.e., what works best in practice).

Building a Knowledge-based Search Intermediary

EP-X was built after careful study of the *Chemical Abstracts* database and after observing the performances of indexers and searchers (e.g., Chignell, 1984; Smith, Chignell, & Krawczak, 1984; Smith, Shute, Chignell, & Krawczak,

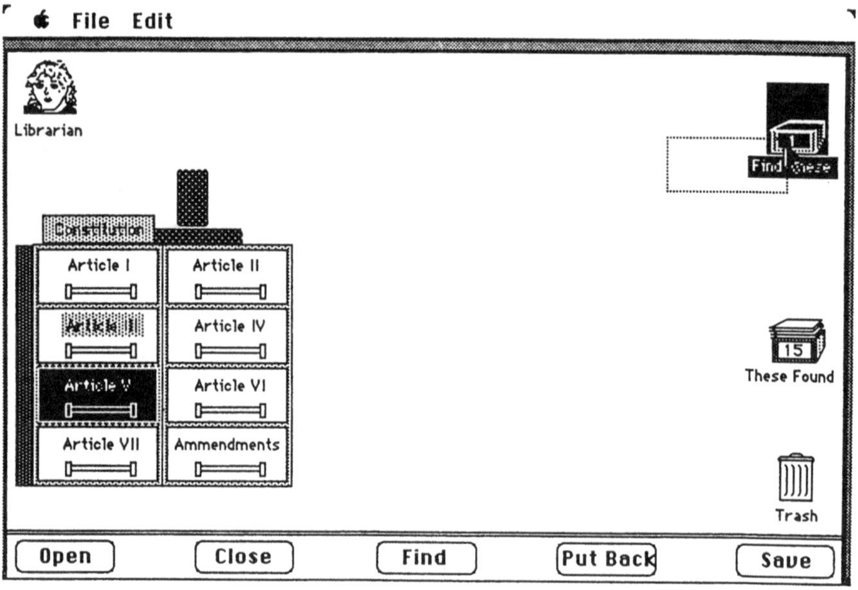

Figure 13.6. A Screen from an Early Prototype of the Project Jefferson Interface.

1987). In these studies it was found that the domain of environmental pollution can be divided into a relatively small number of stereotyped, general topics. A simple example of a general topic is: the uptake of a *pollutant* by an *organism* in a *geographic location*.

Each document in EP-X's database is indexed according to the topics that EP-X knows about. Consider, for instance, a document on environmental pollution which describes the effects of heavy metals from industrial waste on trout populations in Lake Erie. Using a keyword indexing strategy, the following frame entry is placed in the database in addition to the standard bibliographic information:

Document XXX

Polluted Medium:	Water
Pollutant:	Heavy Metals
Source:	Industry
Transportation Process:	Leaching
Location:	Lake Erie
Effect:	Unknown
Organism Accumulating Pollutant:	Trout
Concentration:	Unknown

This frame is then an instance of the following general topic:
<Polluted Medium> where <Pollutant> from <Source> is transported by <Transportation Process> to <Location> and results in <Effect> on <Organism Accumulating Pollutant> with level of <Concentration>.

In some ways the development of an appropriate knowledge representation for EP-X was fairly straightforward because there were already a large number of searchers and end users working with an existing online database. This allowed the EP-X team to construct the frame hierarchy based largely on existing practice. At the time when Project Jefferson began, however, online searches relating to the Constitution were much rarer and, as a result, the structure of the knowledge domain seemed less clear.

A domain expert participated in a series of interviews aimed at building a conceptual representation of the Constitution. The outcome of these interviews was a simple template for analyzing constitutional issues. This template (model) was based on the assumption that the best way to understand the Constitution is to examine the way in which specific cases are analyzed and interpreted. Each controversy or case can be analyzed with this template into the basic constitutional values that are involved, along with the evidence and arguments that support each side. A query can then be expressed by filling in each of the windows in the template. The concrete model of a court case was used to assist the students in recognizing the structure of the model. Filling in the template (i.e., instantiating the model for a particular query) involved answering questions such as the following:

- Who is the judge?
- What event created the current controversy (court case)?
- What were the background circumstances leading to the conflict?
- Who are the two sides in the cases?
- What action does the defense want to take?
- What alternative is proposed by the prosecution?
- What is the "real" motivation of the defense?
- What is the "real" motivation of the prosecution?

This approach was eventually discarded when informal study indicated that students could not use the model effectively (Kinnell & Chignell, 1987). In response, we used an alternative approach, building the interface around the text of the Constitution. Documents relating to constitutional issues were described in terms of the articles, sections, or amendments that were salient. The interface was then constructed so that the user could describe a topic by name (e.g., freedom of speech) or by amendment (e.g., the First Amendment). One lesson that might be drawn from this experience can be briefly summed up as "don't build a superfluous conceptual model if there is an adequate model already in use." In this case, we built an abstract conceptual model which appealed to the experts but which served mainly to confuse those who would use the system.

Experience with EP-X and Project Jefferson illustrates a key point about the development of knowledge-based search intermediaries. The intermediary must be built with a clear view of the eventual user in mind, as well as the knowledge domain. The EP-X team did not have to worry about the fact that the users of their system would lack basic knowledge in chemistry. In contrast, the Project Jefferson team were dealing with students with prior models of the Constitution (which may be incorrect, fuzzy, or just plain different), which differed from the "true" model described by experts in the field. This meant that while the basic elements of the search intermediary were similar in the two projects, a greater emphasis was placed on training the users about the important topics and concepts in the knowledge domain in Project Jefferson. It became clear in Project Jefferson that it was not enough just to build a knowledge-based search intermediary that *could* be used effectively, steps had to be taken to ensure that the interface *would* be used effectively by the user population. In response to the need for training potential users of the online retrieval interface, the Project Jefferson team began developing a hypertext (Nelson, 1981) representation of the Constitution to provide training. Hypermedia (Yankelovich, Meyrowitz, & van Dam, 1985), where the hypertext is augmented with graphics may also be an appropriate interface for online retrieval in its own right, but that topic is outside of the scope of this chapter.

Another feature of both EP-X and the Project Jefferson interface is the use of *interactive postings*. In a conventional retrieval system, once users or intermediaries make a query to the database, they are informed of the number of postings for the query (i.e., how many documents in the database match the query). However, the user has no way of knowing how many documents are within the scope of the query until it is formulated and submitted to the database. *Interactive postings* tell the user how the number of relevant documents is changing as the user formulates and changes the query. Both EP-X and the Project Jefferson interface use reports of document postings freely as part of the interaction with the user. This allows the user to observe directly the effects that broadening and narrowing have on the number of document postings.

CONCLUSIONS

The current paradigm of information retrieval refers to documents as collections of keywords, perhaps reflective of the information within the document. The indexing strategy used constrains the inherent possibilities of the information retrieval system. It is clear that keywords do not fully index the knowledge contained within a document. On the other hand, natural language understanding is not yet at the stage where the document can serve as its own index entry and retrieval can be done on the basis of full text analysis. Further, given current and near future computing capabilities, it is likely that full text analysis in information retrieval will be too burdensome computationally to merit extensive implementation. Thus, information science appears to be confronted by the two extremes of keyword and full text indexing. In this chapter we have examined a third alternative lying between these two extremes, which we refer to as topic-based indexing.

Knowledge-based search intermediaries, and the associated indexing and search methods are a major part of the new information retrieval paradigm. This paradigm shift will change the way in which online retrieval systems function. Current research on interactive (Humphrey & Miller, 1987) and automated (Vieduts-Stokolov, 1987) indexing is creating the capabilities that will be needed in restructuring online databases to meet the demands of the new paradigm. The most obvious change for users will be in the nature of the interface between them and the information retrieval system. To compensate for the increased burden on the user, the system will know more about the subject matter and will be able to respond to errors better, both on operational levels and subject-matter levels. Frame-based systems such as EP-X, Project Jefferson, and ÇoalSORT (Monarch & Carbonell, 1987) appear to be promising forerunners of the interfaces that are needed. Syntax in the new interfaces should eventually become transparent. Users will take on a more active role as they search through the relevant domain knowledge in formulating queries rather than handing over much of the search activity to an intermediary.

Knowledge-based systems can be developed that allow the user to build his query directly, thus permitting searchers to conduct searches unaided by human intermediaries. The ultimate goal of systems such as EP-X and Jefferson is to remove the emphasis on search strategy and replace it with emphasis on subject knowledge. This gives more control to the subject specialist (or student) who is the information seeker. Online retrieval should benefit greatly from the development of knowledge-based systems that act as intermediaries by providing a model of the domain knowledge that can be explored as part of the process of query formulation.

REFERENCES

Chandrasekaran, B., & Mittal, S. (1983). Conceptual representation of medical knowledge for diagnosis by computer: MDX and related systems. *Advances in Computers, 22*, 217–293.

Chignell, M.H. (1984). *Knowledge-based information retrieval.* Unpublished Master's Thesis. Department of Industrial and Systems Engineering, Ohio State University, Columbus, OH.

Chignell, M.H., Hancock, P.A., Smith, P.J., & Shute, S.J. (1986). Information retrieval: An intelligent interface perspective. *Proceedings of the IEEE International Conference on Systems, Man, and Cybernetics*, pp. 372–377. Atlanta, GA.

Davis, R., & Lenat, D. (1982). *Knowledge-based systems in artificial intelligence*. New York: McGraw-Hill.

Hawkins, D., & Wagers, R. (1982). Online bibliographic search strategy development. *Online, 6*(3), 12–19.

Hayes-Roth, F., Waterman, D.A., & Lenat, D. (1983). *Building expert systems*. Reading, MA: Addison-Wesley.

Hildreth, C. (1983). To Boolean or not to Boolean? *Information Technology and Libraries, 2*, 235–237.

Humphrey, S.M., & Miller, N.E. (1987). Knowledge-based indexing of the medial literature: The indexing aid project. *Journal of the American Society for Information Science, 38*, 184–196.

Kinnell, S.K., & Chignell, M.H. (1987, May). Who's the expert?: Conceptual representation of knowledge for enduser searching. *Proceedings of the National Online Meeting*. New York.

Krawczak, D.A., Smith, P.J., & Shute, S.J. (1987). EP-X: A demonstration of semantically-based search of bibliographic databases. *Proceedings of the ACM SIGIR Conference*, pp. 263–271. New Orleans, LA.

Krawczak, D.A., Smith, P.J., Shute, S.J., & Chignell, M.H. (1985). EP-X: A knowledge-based system to aid in searches of the environmental pollution literature. *Proceedings of the Second Conference on Artificial Intelligence Applications*, pp. 552–557. IEEE Computer Society.

Minsky, M. (1975). A framework for representing knowledge. In P. H. Winston (Ed.), *The psychology of computer vision* (pp. 211–280). New York: McGraw-Hill.

Monarch, I., & Carbonell, J. (1987). CoalSORT: A knowledge-based interface. *IEEE Expert, 2*(1), 39–53.

Nelson, T. (1981). *Literary machines*. Ann Arbor, MI: XOC Inc.

Oldroyd, J., & Schroder, J.J. (1982). Study of strategies used in online searching: 2. Positional logic—an example of the importance of selecting the right Boolean operator. *Online Review, 6*, 127–133.

Paice, C. (1986, October). Expert systems for information retrieval? *ASLIB Proceedings*, pp. 343–353. London, England.

Salton, G., & McGill, M.J. (1983). *Introduction to modern information retrieval*. New York: McGraw-Hill.

Shute, S.J., Smith, P.J., Krawczak, D.A., Chignell, M.H., & Sater, M. (1986). Enhancing cognitive compatibility in a knowledge-based information retrieval system. *1986 Fall Industrial Engineering Conference Proceedings*, pp. 111–115. Institute of Industrial Engineers, Norcross, GA.

Smith, P.J., Chignell, M.H., & Krawczak, D.A. (1984). Development of a knowledge-based bibliographic information retrieval system. *Proceedings of the International Conference on Cybernetics and Society*. Halifax, Nova Scotia: IEEE.

Smith, P.J., Shute, S.J., Chignell, M.H., & Krawczak, D.A. (1987). *The role of the human factors engineer in designing the interface to a knowledge-based system*. Unpublished manuscript, Department of Industrial and Systems Engineering, Ohio State University, Columbus, OH.

Tversky, A., & Kahneman, D. (1974). Judgment underuncertainty: Heuristics and biases. *Science, 185*, 1124–1131.

Vieduts-Stokolov, N. (1987). Concept recognition in automatic text-processing systems for the life sciences. *Journal of the American Society for Information Science, 38*, 269–287.

Wason, P.C., & Johnson-Laird, P.N. (1972). *Psychology of Reasoning: Structure and Content*. Cambridge, MA.: Harvard University Press.

Yankelovich, N., Meyrowitz, N., & van Dam, A. (1985). Reading and writing the electronic book. *Computer, 18*(10), 15–30.

14

MedIndEx— The Medical Indexing Expert System

Susanne M. Humphrey
National Library of Medicine
Bethesda, MD

INTRODUCTION

Research on expert systems for indexing is being conducted at the Lister Hill National Center for Biomedical Communications (LHNCBC), the research and development arm of the National Library of Medicine (NLM). The prototype MedIndEx (Medical Indexing Expert) System is a knowledge-based system designed to provide interactive computer assistance to indexers of the periodical medical literature. The knowledge base consists of medical facts needed for indexing and the indexing rules. First, we present background on indexing from a thesaurus, showing that knowledge-based indexing is an extension of thesaurus-based indexing. Second, we present a tutorial on frames, which are data structures particularly suited for knowledge-based systems. Finally, we describe the prototype, highlighting the features of frame systems which have been explained previously: explicit relationships between frames represented as *frame-slot-value*; procedures and rules attached to slots; inheritance of slots, values, and attachments through the hierarchy of frames; creation of instantiation frames that inherit from the knowledge base; and internal retrieval of values from other slots.

BACKGROUND: THESAURUS-BASED INDEXING

The National Library of Medicine has been indexing the world's periodical medical literature since 1879, when the first issue of *Index Medicus*™, a periodical subject-author index to medical journal articles, was published. At that time, NLM's official designation was *Library of the Surgeon-General's Office (Army)*, although even then it was sometimes called the *National Medical Library*. The first computerized *Index Medicus* was the August 1964 issue, prepared by the new computer-based system, MEDical Literature Analysis and Retrieval System

(MEDLARS®). The computerized index, MEDlars onLINE (MEDLINE®), roughly the equivalent of *Index Medicus*, became searchable online in October 1971. The database available for online retrieval consists of more than 20 years of indexed medical literature, beginning in 1966. These and other achievements of NLM have been reviewed on the occasion of the Library's sesquicentennial year, 1986, by Lindberg (1987), NLM's director.

The heart of the MEDLINE system is the indexing activity (maintaining and applying the indexing rules), and maintaining the computerized thesaurus which indexers use, Medical Subject Headings (MeSH®). Indexing is the process of assigning to a document the indexing terms from MeSH which best describe the content and substance of the document. Descriptions of indexing at NLM and development of the MeSH thesaurus have been published by Bachrach and Charen (1978) and Humphrey and Miller (1987).

NLM uses a system of *coordinate* indexing. This is achieved by assigning to a document:

- A descriptor/qualifier expression.
- A pre-coordinate descriptor.
- Two or more descriptors or descriptor/qualifier expressions.

For example, Figure 14.1 displays a typical citation to a document in the MEDLINE database. The elements of this citation have two-character labels (UI = Unique Identifier; AU = Author; TI = Title; AB = Abstract; SO = Source; MH = MeSH Heading). The descriptors and qualifiers which index the document are labeled MH. The asterisk is a weight indicator which identifies a central concept. *Clubfoot/DIAGNOSIS*, *Prenatal Diagnosis*, and *Ultrasonic Diagnosis*

UI 85140931
AU Benacerraf BR ; Frigoletto FD
TI Prenatal ultrasound diagnosis of clubfoot.
AB Five cases of congenital clubfoot diagnosed prenatally by ultrasound are reported. The incidence of clubfoot may be higher within an affected family and may be associated with other structural anomalies or chromosomal abnormalities. Identifying a clubfoot in utero should therefore alert the sonographer that other anomalies may be present and should lead to a detailed structural survey.
SO Radiology 1985 Apr;155(1):211-3
MH Abnormalities, Multiple/DIAGNOSIS
MH Chromosome Abnormalities/COMPLICATIONS/DIAGNOSIS
MH Clubfoot/*DIAGNOSIS/COMPLICATIONS/FAMILIAL & GENETIC
MH Female
MH Human
MH Pregnancy
MH *Prenatal Diagnosis
MH *Ultrasonic Diagnosis

Figure 14.1. Citation in the MEDLINE Database.

index the main ideas in this document. *Clubfoot/DIAGNOSIS* is an example of coordination by descriptor/qualifier expression. *Chromosome Abnormalities* is a precoordinate descriptor, coordinating *Chromosomes* with *Abnormalities*. The set of descriptors and descriptor/qualifier expressions pointing to this document exemplifies the remaining method of coordination.

The purpose of storing these indexing terms is to allow searchers to retrieve citations by entering search statements while connected to the MEDLINE database via an information retrieval system (e.g., DIALOG, BRS, NLM). Computerized index searching, which is the basis of the major retrieval systems, has been described in detail by Salton and McGill (1983) and Humphrey and Melloni (1986). To illustrate, the citation in Figure 14.1 would be retrieved by the following search statement, using the Boolean AND operator for intersection: *Clubfoot/diagnosis AND Prenatal Diagnosis AND Ultrasonic Diagnosis*. This statement would also retrieve other citations to documents about the same topic, including the following titles:

- Sonographic diagnosis of clubfoot in utero.
- In utero sonographic detection of hand and foot deformities.
- Antenatal sonographic diagnosis of clubfoot.

These various titles, all retrieved by the identical search statement, illustrate the supreme advantage of indexing using a thesaurus, namely, that an indexing term uniquely locates information about the idea that the term represents regardless of the words and phrases in the citation.

Indexing consistency studies measure the degree to which searchers ultimately may rely on the assignment of like headings to like concepts, and has been accepted as a measure of indexing quality (Funk & Reid, 1983; Leonard, 1975). Numerous studies on indexing consistency/variability of the 1960s and 1970s have been cited by White (1973) and Leonard (1977). White reviewed 41 reports published from 1961–71. Leonard reviewed and summarized 34 studies resulting in one 1954 report and 31 reports published from 1961–75.

A number of indexing consistency studies of the NLM system has been performed (Funk & Reid, 1983; Leonard, 1975; Lancaster, 1968; Marcetich & Schuyler, 1981). All used Hooper's measure of indexing consistency (Hooper, 1965). In the Lancaster study, consistency percentages did not exceed 46.1%; in the Leonard study, 48.2%. Funk and Reid calculated consistency for nine categories of indexing term. The consistency percentage for descriptors, excluding geographic descriptors and check-tag descriptors (a small set of high-volume descriptors, like *Review*, *Human*, *Animal*, *Female*, *Comparative Study*), was 48.2%. The percentage for descriptors with central concept indicators was 61.1%. Consistency percentages for descriptor/qualifier expressions was 33.8%, in general, and 43.1% for central concepts. All the studies of the NLM system corroborate Lancaster's findings of lower consistency for descriptor/qualifier expressions than for descriptors regardless of qualifier.

Marcetich and Schuyler (1981) investigated the use of the Associative Interactive Dictionary (AID) developed by Doszkocs (1978). The AID system displayed occurrence frequencies in order of decreasing frequency for the number of times in the database a heading was assigned to documents about a particular topic indicated by the presence of a word for that topic in some part of the document, typically its title. Resulting measures showed that indexing consistency in assignment of descriptors, excluding check-tags and disregarding qualifiers, increased from 39% to 43% with the use of the AID; for indexing central concepts, consistency increased from 48% to 55%.

In our research we are introducing the element of a *standard* for indexing. The standard we are using is the version of indexing that conforms to the thesaurus, the indexing rules, and to the practice of those indexers who write the rules and train and revise others in their application. Promoting *expert indexing*, that is, indexing consistent with a standard, seems a sensible approach to promoting consistent indexing, and is in fact, as indicated earlier, a basic premise of thesaurus-based indexing systems.

In addition to promoting expert indexing, our research is concerned with modeling indexing. Protocol studies of expert indexers have been performed by researchers from Carnegie-Mellon University, under contract to NLM (Crain, 1985). The clauses of the transcripts of these sessions (two indexers each indexed four documents in a single session) were encoded according to 32 activities, categorized as Reading and Writing, Goal Setting, Evaluatory, and Other. For one of the indexers, out of 315 clauses altogether, 90 were encoded by one of the following activities:

- Decide to go to reference tool.
- Decide to search for item in reading.
- Verbalization of plan for indexing task.
- Metacomment on indexing process.
- Recall of knowledge about indexing.

Many of the clauses encoded by these five activities indicated that indexers regularly consult medical references and indexing tools, and draw on personal recollections of knowledge and rules. They appear to have preconceived notions of the indexable entities and relations in medical documents, and they use these to form expectations as they index a document. The system being developed in our research encodes some of this expertise in a knowledge base, and uses it to interactively guide the indexing of documents.

The MeSH thesaurus contains over 14,000 descriptors, and is published in three forms: *Medical Subject Headings Annotated Alphabetic List, Medical*

Subject Headings Tree Structures, and *Permuted Medical Subject Headings*. The *Alphabetic List* includes *see related* cross-references between descriptors, and *see* cross-references from entry terms (synonyms and near-synonyms) to descriptors. The *MeSH Trees* provide hierarchies, beginning with general categorizations, for example, disease (category C), procedure (category E), anatomical structure (category A), substance (category D), and extending to seven levels of specificity within subcategories, for example, musculoskeletal system (subcategory A2). Figure 14.2 shows the *Leg Injuries* hierarchy in subcategory C21, *Injuries, Occupational Diseases* and *Poisoning*. The entries in the *Permuted MeSH* are all the individual words in the descriptors and cross-references in the thesaurus. For example, the entry for *Surface* is shown in Figure 14.3.

According to accepted standards (American National Standards Institute, 1980) MeSH is certainly a thesaurus but it is not, strictly speaking, a *knowledge base*. By this, we mean a *computerized* knowledge base, which is a collection of facts and rules for applying these facts to perform an intellectual task, in this discussion, indexing the medical literature. To be sure, the current system does provide state-of-the-art automated assistance for thesaurus-based indexing. Three types of assistance furnish simple authority control, verifying that the preferred form of heading has been stored and establishing synonyms in the entry vocabulary that are automatically replaced by respective preferred forms:

- Verification that the indexer's entry is a MeSH descriptor, entry term (referred-from term of *see* reference), or entry version (official abbreviation or other alternate form of MeSH descriptor).
- Replacement of entry term or entry version by corresponding MeSH descriptor.
- Replacement of MeSH descriptor/qualifier expression by corresponding precoordinate descriptor.

A fourth form of computerized assistance implements or suggests the application of certain simple indexing rules when a descriptor has been assigned. An

LEG INJURIES	C21.866.558
FEMORAL INJURIES	C21.866.558.276
HIP FRACTURES	C21.866.558.276.425
FEMORAL FRACTURES	C21.866.558.276.425.278
HIP DISLOCATION	C21.866.558.418
KNEE INJURIES	C21.866.558.554
TIBIAL FRACTURES	C21.866.558.857

Figure 14.2. Portion of MeSH Tree Structures.

SURFACE
ANTIGENS, SURFACE
BODY SURFACE AREA
HEPATITIS B SURFACE ANTIGENS
IMMUNOGLOBULINS, SURFACE
RADIOTHERAPY, SURFACE see BRACHYTHERAPY
SURFACE-ACTIVE AGENTS
SURFACE ANTIGENS see ANTIGENS, SURFACE
SURFACE MARKERS, IMMUNOLOGICAL see ANTIGENS, SURFACE
SURFACE PROPERTIES
SURFACE TENSION

Figure 14.3. Portion of Permuted MeSH.

example of the former is automatic assignment of the descriptor *Human* when an indexer has assigned an age-group descriptor such as *Child*. An example of the latter: When the indexer tags the descriptor *Angiography* with a central concept indicator, the system reminds the indexer that this descriptor is usually NIM (not tagged for publication in *Index Medicus* under this descriptor), meaning that the concept is usually not the main idea of a document.

Fifth, and finally, MEDLINE verifies the allowability of MeSH descriptor/qualifier expressions. For instance, the qualifier *cytology* may be appended only to descriptors in MeSH category A (anatomy) or B (organisms). *Lung/cytology* is thereby acceptable, whereas *Lung Diseases/cytology* is not.

The last two types of assistance are more knowledge-based than the first three. In particular, qualifier allowability employs a mechanism common to knowledge-based systems, known as *inheritance*, whereby a rule applied to the parent term in a hierarchy is applied by default to the children of that term. For example, a rule that allows the qualifier *cytology* to be appended to a descriptor is associated with MeSH category *A*. Therefore, according to inheritance, *cytology* may be appended to *Lung* since this descriptor is encoded as *A4.411*. In fact, whenever an indexing rule applies to each descriptor in a hierarchy, the rule can be said to be *inherited* from the top node of the hierarchy by its descendants.

Portions of the *Neoplasms* hierarchy in MeSH, shown in Figure 14.4, will be used for illustrating inheritance of indexing rules. In the display, "NON MESH" indicates the term cannot be assigned to a document, but merely names a node in the tree. According to the *MEDLARS Indexing Manual*, a neoplasm is indexed in two places, under the site-neoplasm descriptor, for example, *Kidney Neoplasms*, and under the histologic-type-neoplasm descriptor, for example, *Adenocarcinoma*. In addition, the rule is repeated as an annotation to each specific site-neoplasm descriptor in the *MeSH Alphabetic List*, as the indexing instruction, *coord IM with histol type neopl (IM)* (as explained earlier, "IM" means "as central concept for *Index Medicus*"). The other part of the rule is annotated to

NEOPLASMS	C4
...	...
NEOPLASMS BY HISTOLOGIC TYPE (NON MESH)	C4.557
...	...
NEOPLASMS, GLANDULAR EPITHELIAL	C4.557.576
ADENOCARCINOMA	C4.557.576.36
...	...
CARCINOMA, RENAL CELL	C4.557.576.36.270
...	...
...	...
NEOPLASMS BY SITE (NON MESH)	C4.588
...	...
UROGENITAL NEOPLASMS	C4.588.945
...	...
UROLOGIC NEOPLASMS	C4.588.945.947
...	...
KIDNEY NEOPLASMS	C4.588.945.947.535
...	...
...	...
...	...

Figure 14.4. MeSH Hierarchy to Illustrate Inheritance of Indexing Rules.

each histologic-type-neoplasm descriptor, as the instruction, *coord IM with precoord organ/neopl term (IM)*.

Although these annotations exemplify inheritance, in a knowledge-based system, the rule would be attached only to the top node of the hierarchy to which it applies, and thereby automatically inherited by each of its descendants, making it redundant to explicitly attach the rule to each descendant. For example, the instruction to coordinate with *histol type neopl* need only be attached to *Neoplasms by Site (Non Mesh)*, and not also to *Kidney Neoplasms* or any of the other descendants. A more specific rule may override the inherited rule. For example, the rule for the histologic-type-neoplasm descriptor *Carcinoma, Renal Cell* is *coord IM with KIDNEY NEOPLASMS (IM)*, as this histologic type apparently occurs only in the kidney.

The degree of computer assistance to indexing can be greatly enhanced by developing knowledge-based systems. However, a knowledge base implies not only naming the concepts in a subject domain, but also the relations, and explicitly linking the concepts according to these relations. In the next section, we will describe the data structure and computer language we are investigating at NLM for representing knowledge to assist in indexing the medical literature.

TUTORIAL: FRAMES FOR REPRESENTING KNOWLEDGE

In the previous section, we have provided background about indexing and thesauruses, and the need for engaging the computer to provide *expert*, or *knowledge-based*, indexing, which is not currently being provided in any major indexing system for information retrieval. Before describing the research being performed in the MedIndEx Project at NLM in the next section, this section will present a tutorial on *frame languages*. A *frame* in a knowledge base is analogous to a *record* in a computerized thesaurus. Frames are a common type of data structure in high-level programming languages, known as *knowledge representation languages*, for building knowledge bases. Knowledge representation languages are usually extensions of artificial intelligence programming languages, like LISP and PROLOG.

Original use of the word *frame* for computerized structuring of knowledge is usually attributed to Minsky (1975). Two of the earliest experimental frame-based knowledge representation languages are Knowledge Representation Language (KRL) (Bobrow & Winograd, 1977), developed at Xerox Palo Alto Research Center, and Frame Representation Language (FRL) (Roberts & Goldstein, 1977), developed at the Massachusetts Institute of Technology. Frame systems are now available commercially. However, a simple frame system may be implemented using the LISP programming language (Winston & Horn, 1989). This tutorial uses an experimental LISP-based knowledge representation language, FrameKit, as originally developed by Carnegie-Mellon University under contract to NLM (Carbonell & Joseph, 1985).

The tutorial will examine the parts of a frame, demonstrate functions which return values from frames, and explain four important features of frame languages: *inheritance, internal retrieval, instantiation* and *restrictions*. We have shown in the previous section that inheritance is already familiar to indexing. Instantiation is exemplified by the indexing process itself. When an indexer assigns a descriptor to a document, for example, *Clubfoot* to *document 85140931*, the indexer is thereby linking this descriptor, which stands for the *idea* of *clubfoot*, to a specific case which has been described in this document. In effect, the indexer has created an *instance* of the idea of *clubfoot*, and labelled this instance *clubfoot 85140931*. This point will be reemphasized at the end of the tutorial.

In this tutorial we will behave as users of the knowledge base, and enter commands, known in FrameKit and LISP in general as *functions*. [We will sometimes refer to the commands as *expressions* instead, in order to avoid confusion with a frame relation having a similar name.] User entries will be on the same line as the arrow prompt, –>. The system's response will follow on subsequent lines. Figure 14.5 shows a sample knowledge base in frames. Do not be concerned about understanding the computer code in detail. Please refer to these frames throughout the tutorial. To begin, note that the knowledge base which we will use for this tutorial contains ten frames. This knowledge base has been entered previously, using FrameKit's *make-frame*. This and other functions which we will use in this tutorial are listed in Figure 14.6.

To examine the leg frame more closely, we will use *ppf* (for *prettyprint frame*) to display the frame:

```
(make-frame |body area|
   (inv+is-a (value axilla neck pelvis leg knee foot))
   (function (if-needed (or
            (get-value (car (get-value !frame 'part-of)) 'function)
            (prompt)))))

(make-frame axilla (is-a (value |body area|)))

(make-frame neck (is-a (value |body area|)))

(make-frame pelvis (is-a (value |body area|)))

(make-frame leg (is-a (value |body area|))
   (has-parts (value foot knee))
   (function (value locomotion)))

(make-frame knee (is-a (value |body area|))
   (part-of (value leg)))

(make-frame foot (is-a (value |body area|))
   (part-of (value leg)))

(make-frame |lymph node|
   (body-area (restrictions (member !filler '(axilla neck pelvis nil)))
            (if-needed (prompt))))

(make-frame |foot abnormality|
   (inv+is-a (value clubfoot))
   (body-area (value foot)))

(make-frame clubfoot (is-a (value |foot abnormality|)))
```

Figure 14.5. Knowledge Base for Tutorial on Frames.

```
-> (ppf leg)
(setq frame:
      '(leg (is-a (value |body area|))
      (has-parts (value foot knee))
      (function value locomotion))))
leg
```

The frame itself begins with the name of the frame, *leg*. The frame has three slots, *is-a*, *has-parts*, and *function*, which name relations that link *leg* to the

FrameKit functions:

make-frame	building individual frame
ppf [prettyprint frame]	displaying individual frame
get-immediate-value	directly retrieving the actual slot value
get-value	retrieving the inherited slot value
get-value-demons	internal retrieval of a slot value by demons
add-to-value-demons	adding a slot value, including checking restrictions

Lisp functions added to FrameKit:

outline	displaying frames according to specified relation
show-restrictions	displaying the allowable slot values
prompt	prompting for a slot value

Figure 14.6. FrameKit and Lisp Functions for Tutorial on Frames.

respective slot values. As shown in each slot of the frame, the label *value* names the *value facet* of a slot, and precedes one or more terms, for example, (*value foot knee*). In the code a multiword term is delimited by vertical bars, for example, |*body area*|. Other facets will be introduced later in the tutorial. This frame states that the leg is classified as a body area (*is-a* relation), and has as its parts the foot and knee (*has-parts* relation), and its function is locomotion (*function* relation).

The *knee* and *foot* frames are also classified as body areas, having the same *(is-a (value |body area |))* as the *leg* frame. We will display the *is-a* classification of *body area* and the *has-parts* classification of *leg*, using *outline*:

```
-> (outline '|body area| 'inv+is-a)
|body area|
- foot
- knee
- leg
- pelvis
- neck
- axilla

-> (outline 'leg 'has-parts)
leg
- knee
- foot
```

The system returns values directly from a slot in a frame when we use *get-immediate-value*:

```
-> (get-immediate-value 'leg 'function)
(locomotion)
```

To illustrate inheritance, we will enter the following expressions:

```
-> (get-immediate-value '|foot abnormality| 'body-area)
(foot)
-> (get-immediate-value 'clubfoot 'body-area)
nil
-> (get-value 'clubfoot 'body-area)
(foot)
```

The *body-area* of *foot abnormality* has been returned directly by *get-immediate-value*, just as the *function* of *leg* was returned earlier. However, the same expression applied to the *clubfoot* frame was not successful, having returned *nil*. Yet the *body-area* of *clubfoot* is in the knowledge base as an inherited value—inherited from the *foot abnormality* frame by virtue of the *is-a* link between these two frames. *Get-value* returns inherited values, and has returned the *body-area* of *clubfoot*. In general, *get-value* preferentially returns an immediate value if there is one. If it fails, it attempts to return the inherited value (that is, the immediate value of the same slot in the frame of its parent). If it still fails, it tries the parent of the parent frame, and so forth, up the *is-a* hierarchy.

Note that *get-value* for retrieving *function* of *knee*, shown next, did not return either an inherited or an immediate value. This is not surprising, as the *knee* frame has no *function* slot, and its parent in the *is-a* classification, *body area*, although it has a slot named *function*, does not have a *value* facet for this slot.

```
-> (get-value 'knee ' function)
nil
```

get-value-demons will, however, return a value for the *function* of *knee*:

```
-> (get-value-demons 'knee 'function)
(locomotion)
```

This value was returned because of the expression *(get-value (car (get-value !frame 'part-of)) 'function)* found in the *function* slot of the frame corresponding is the *is-a* value of *knee*, which is *body area*. We will enumerate the steps that have taken place:

1. The system first attempted to return an immediate value for the *function* of *knee*. It failed because the *knee* frame does not have a *function* slot.
2. The system then attempted to return the inherited value for the *function* of *knee*. It failed because the parent of *knee*, *body area*, does not have a *value* facet for the *function* slot.

3. The system next looked in the *function* of the *body area* frame for another facet, the *if-needed* facet.
4. When the system found the *if-needed* facet, it processed the *get-value* expression in this facet, *(get-value (car (get-value !frame 'part-of)) 'function)*. This sort of expression is known as a *demon*. This if-needed demon applied the rule, "Return the immediate or inherited value of the *function* slot of the immediate or inherited value of the *part-of* slot of the current frame." The system thereby returned the immediate value of the *function* slot of *leg*, which is the immediate value of the *part-of* slot in the *knee* frame.

Demons often combine internal retrieval with inheritance. That is, a demon is an expression which returns a value from another slot (possibly from another frame), plus the demons themselves are usually inherited by descendant frames. The advantage of this internal retrieval is that it consistently applies the same rule (for returning a value from another slot) and it reduces redundancy in the knowledge base. For example, if the demon in the *function* slot had not existed, a value would need to be represented explicitly in a *function* slot of each descendant of the *body area* frame. Less redundancy in a knowledge base usually implies less maintenance of the knowledge base. The tradeoff is that employing this sort of *procedural knowledge*, rather than returning values directly, takes more time, which is of major concern in the design of interactive systems.

However, slot values are not always present or retrievable in a knowledge base. For example, the possible value for the location of a lymph node may be one of a set of body-areas or it may be unspecified. This membership list is found in the *restrictions* facet of the *body-area* slot of the *lymph node* frame: *(restrictions (member !filler '(axilla neck pelvis nil)))*. *Show-restrictions* returns a list of restrictions for a slot:

```
-> (show-restrictions '|lymph node| 'body-area)
(axilla neck pelvis nil)
```

The *restrictions* on a slot value may be inherited, and are particularly useful in the *instantiation* of knowledge base frames. In the ensuing discussion of instantiation, recall that indexing is a form of instantiation.

Suppose we have a specific document, *document 40* for example, which discusses lymph nodes. Just as we might assign the MeSH descriptor *Lymph Nodes* to index this document, in effect, instantiating this descriptor from the thesaurus, we can instantiate the *lymph node* frame, by making an *instantiation frame* linking the frame term to the document number:

```
-> (make-frame |lymph node 40| (is-a (value |lymph node|)))
|lymph node 40|
```

and then use *ppf* to display it:

```
-> (ppf |lymph node 40|)
(setq frame: '(|lymph node 40| (is-a (value |lymph node|))))
|lymph node 40|
```

We will illustrate inheritance of restrictions by displaying the restrictions on the *body-area* slot of this instantiation frame:

```
-> (show-restrictions '|lymph node 40| 'body-area)
(axilla neck pelvis nil)
```

Suppose *document 40* discusses *pelvic* lymph nodes. According to the input system established in the knowledge base, we can use *get-value-demons* to prompt us for the body-area value:

```
-> (get-value-demons '|lymph node 40| 'body-area)
body-area
  value:
```

As explained earlier, *get-value-demons* runs the demons in the *if-needed* facet. In this case, the demon associated with the *body-area* slot is simply the *prompt* expression. This demon is called from the instantiation frame, *lymph node 40*, which inherits the *body-area* slot from the *lymph node* frame because *lymph node 40 is-a lymph node*. As shown earlier, the restrictions are inherited as well. To illustrate, we will enter an unallowable value, *foot*, in response to the prompt:

```
-> (get-value-demons '|lymph node 40| 'body-area)
body-area
  value: foot
Failed restrictions check on: lymph node 40 body-area foot
nil
```

Now we will enter an allowable value:

```
-> (get-value-demons '|lymph node 40| 'body-area)
body-area
  value: pelvis
(pelvis)
```

Any of the *get* expressions can be used for returning the value that has been added, and the value can also be displayed by *ppf*:

```
-> (get-immediate-value '|lymph node 40| 'body-area)
(pelvis)
```

```
-> (get-value '|lymph node 40| 'body-area)
(pelvis)

-> (get-value-demons '|lymph node 40| 'body-area)
(pelvis)

-> (ppf |lymph node 40|)
(setq frame:
  '(lymph node 40: (is-a (value |lymph node|))
                   (body-area (value pelvis))))
|lymph node 40|
```

Prompt, shown earlier, not only displayed the prompt and read the user's entry, but also processed an *add-to-value-demons* expression, which attempted to add to the slot the value that was read. It is the *add-to-value-demons* expression, within *prompt*, that performs the restrictions check. It may also be used directly:

```
-> (add-to-value-demons '|lymph node 40| 'body-area 'foot)

Failed restrictions check on: lymph node 40 body-area foot
nil

-> (add-to-value-demons '|lymph node 40| 'body-area 'pelvis)
(pelvis)
```

RESEARCH: KNOWLEDGE-BASED PROTOTYPE INDEXING SYSTEM

The MedIndEx Project at NLM is investigating a knowledge-based approach to indexing the periodical literature. A prototype MedIndEx System has been developed on NLM's VAX 11/780™ minicomputer under the UNIX™ BSD 4.3 operating system. The University of Maryland Window Library, written in C, (Torek, 1985) has been adapted for the user interface in the initial prototype described here.

The system is designed to interact with trained MEDLINE indexers. For each input, consisting of a MEDLINE citation to a document, there will be two forms of output describing the subject content of the document:

- A set of inter-related instantiation frames, which we refer to as *indexing frames*, created by an indexer using the system.
- A set of MeSH indexing terms, generated automatically by the application of knowledge base rules to the indexing frames.

A *knowledge base frame*, similar to the frames in the tutorial in the previous section, not only names a medical concept, but also names the relations this concept has to other concepts. An *indexing frame* links a knowledge base frame to a specific document. For instance, as mentioned earlier, the frame term *clubfoot 85140931* is the name of an indexing frame for *document 85140931* titled *Prenatal ultrasound diagnosis of clubfoot*. We will describe how an indexer might create this frame using the system.

First, we will show the *generic* document frame in Figure 14.7. Several of the slots of this frame correspond to the fields in the MEDLINE citation in Figure 14.1. This frame serves as a template for *document 85140931*, shown in Figure 14.8, which is a document instantiation frame that *inherits-from* the generic document frame. Instead of the slot name *is-a*, we use the slot name *inherits-from* for the parent(s) of a frame, and its iverse, *inv+inherits-from*, for the child(ren) of a frame. We will return to the *contents* and *indices* slots at the end of this section.

Let us begin showing some of the actual screens of the interface in the MedIndEx System as if we were indexing the clubfoot document. We select *rad8504* from a journal selection menu, shown in Figure 14.9. We then select the document from a manu by entering *931*, the last three digits of the unique identifier, as shown in Figure 14.10. We are now ready to index the document we have selected. The next screen displays the citation and two windows, labeled *Disease Process* and *Procedure*. The system presents these as the initial categories appropriate to the medical domain for the prototype, which is clinical research. We select option *d* to enter the *Disease Process* window, as shown in

```
(document (unique id) (author) (title) (abstract) (source) (pagination) (contained-in) (status)
        (contents) (indices))
```

Figure 14.7. Generic Document Frame.

```
(|document 85140931| (inherits-from (value document))
        (unique-id (value 85140931))
        (author (value (Benacerraf BR |;| Frigoletto FD)))
        (title (value (Prenatal ultrasound diagnosis of clubfoot.)))
        (abstract (value (Five cases of congenital clubfoot diagnosed prenatally by ultrasound
            are reported. The incidence of clubfoot may be higher within an affected
            family and may be associated with other structural anomalies or chromosomal
            abnormalities. Identifying a clubfoot in utero should therefore alert the
            sonographer that other anomalies may be present and should lead to a detailed
            structural survey.)))
        (pagination (value 211-213))
        (contained-in (value |journal rad8504|))
        (status (value unindexed))
        (contents)
        (indices))
```

Figure 14.8. Document Instantiation Frame.

```
-------------------------[ MedIndEx Prototype ]-------------------------
|                           Journal Selection                           |
|=======================================================================|
|                                                                       |
|                       Journal Issues Available :                      |
|                                                                       |
|  journal       source                        total docs    partially |
|                                             (no. indexed)   indexed  |
|                                                                       |
|  rad8505       Radiology 1985 May;155(2)       29 (2)          2     |
|  rad8504       Radiology 1985 Apr;155(1)       27 (0)          1     |
|                                                                       |
|=======================================================================|
|Options: journal, journal s[ee], e[xit]:  rad8504                      |
|_______________________________________________________________________|
```

Figure 14.9. Journal Selection.

```
------------------------[ MedIndEx Prototype ]------------------------
|                     Unindexed Document Selection                     |
|======================================================================|
|                                                                      |
|  ---------[ Unindexed documents available for indexing : ]--------- |
| |                                                                 | |
| |  85140932: Radiology 1985 Apr;155(1):215-9                       | |
| |            Chronic pancreatitis: ultrasonic features.            | |
| |  85140931: Radiology 1985 Apr;155(1):211-3                       | |
| |            Prenatal ultrasound diagnosis of clubfoot.            | |
| |  85140928: Radiology 1985 Apr;155(1):197-200                     | |
| |            The spine and spinal cord during neurosurgical        | |
| |  85140927: Radiology 1985 Apr;155(1):193-6                       | |
| |            Parathyroid aspiration biopsy under ultrasonic        | |
| |            guidance in the postoperative hyperparathyroid patient| |
| |  85140926: Radiology 1985 Apr;155(1):192-3                       | |
| |            Videodensitometric ejection fractions from intervanous| |
| |            digital subtraction left ventriculograms: correlation | |
| |            with conversational direct contrast and radionuclide  | |
| |            ventriculography.                                     | |
|  ------------------------------------------------------------------ |
|                                                                      |
|======================================================================|
| Window Commands: u[p], d[own] or q[uit]:                             |
| Options: p[revious] menu, w[indow], selection:  931                  |
|______________________________________________________________________|
```

Figure 14.10. Document Selection.

```
------------------------[ MedIndEx Prototype ]------------------------
| Frame: document                              Document: 85140931 |
|===================================================================|
| --------------------------------------------------------------- |
|| AU :  Benacerraf BR ; Frigoletto FD                            ||
|| TI :  Prenatal ultrasound diagnosis of clubfoot.               ||
|| AB :  Five cases of congenital clubfoot diagnosed prenatally   ||
||       by ultrasound are reported. The incidence of clubfoot    ||
||       may be higher within an affected family and may be       ||
||       associated with other structural anomalies or            ||
||       chromosomal abnormalities. Identifying a clubfoot in     ||
||       utero should therefore alert the sonographer that other  ||
||       anomalies may be present and should lead to a detailed   ||
||       structural survey.                                       ||
||  SO : Radiology 1985 Apr;155(1):211-3                          ||
| --------------------------------------------------------------- |
|    -----[ Disease Process ]-----  --------[ Procedure ]--------  |
|    |                           |  |                          |   |
|    |                           |  |                          |   |
|    |                           |  |                          |   |
|    -----------------------------  ----------------------------   |
|===================================================================|
| Window Commands: u[p], d[own] or q[uit]:                         |
| Options: s[doc sel], w[indow], d[is], p[roc], q[uit]:  d         |
|__________________________________________________________________|
```

Figure 14.11. Initial Category Selection.

Figure 14.11. Even though the abstract is displayed, indexing is based on the full text of the document on paper.

In order to avoid imposing a new indexing vocabulary on indexers, the system is designed to accept MeSH terms. Each allowable entry is mapped to a frame term in the knowledge base. We enter the initial indexing term, *Clubfoot*, in the *Disease Process* window, as shown in Figure 14.12. This *Clubfoot* entry causes a *clubfoot 85140931* frame to be created. The system then presents the relations associated with this indexing frame as prompts. These prompts are called from the knowledge base by *if-needed* demons. This is the same mechanism that was illustrated in the tutorial by the *if-needed* demon containing the *prompt* expression, which prompted for a *body-area* value for the *lymph node 40* instantiation frame. The indexing frame, with the first prompt, is shown in Figure 14.13.

```
|    -----[ Disease Process ]-----  --------[ Procedure ]--------  |
|    |                           |  |                          |   |
|    | Clubfoot                  |  |                          |   |
|    |                           |  |                          |   |
|    -----------------------------  ----------------------------   |
```

Figure 14.12. Initial Frame Term Selection.

```
------------------------[ MedIndEx Prototype ]------------------------
| Frame: clubfoot                                  Document: 85140931 |
| -----------[ Frame ]--------------      -----[Originating Frames]---- |
||intervention                          | |nil                         ||
||   value:                             | |                            ||
||                                      | |                            ||
||                                      | |                            ||
||                                      | |                            ||
||                                      | |                            ||
||                                      | |                            ||
||                                      | |                            ||
||                                      | |____________________________||
||                                      |  ---[Retrieved Values for:]--- |
||                                      | |intervention                ||
||                                      | |                            ||
||                                      | |    None                    ||
||______________________________________| |____________________________||
|                                                                      |
|======================================================================|
|                                                                      |
|______________________________________________________________________|
```

Figure 14.13. Indexing Frame with First Prompt.

How does the system know to display in *intervention* prompt? The indexing frame, *clubfoot 85140931*, has an *inherits-from* link to the *clubfoot* frame in the knowledge base. The chain of linkages is as follows: *clubfoot 85140931 inherits-from clubfoot inherits-from abnormality inherits-from disease process*. These linkages can be seen in Figure 14.14 as the *inherits-from* and *inv+ inherits-from* slots and values. Other parts of these four frames are shown as well. For now, note the *if-needed* facet of the *intervention* slot in the *disease process* frame. It contains demons which prompt for slot values. It is these which are inherited by the *clubfoot 85140931* frame, and cause the *intervention* prompt on the screen.

In using the system we may, at any slot value prompt, request a display of allowable values. We do this by entering the command, *^r* (^ indicates the control key on the keyboard), as shown in Figure 14.15. This restrictions request is equivalent to *show-restrictions* in the tutorial. In response, the system overlays a window for displaying the restrictions hierarchically, as shown in Figure 14.16. In this case, the restrictions have been inherited from the *restrictions* facet of the *intervention* slot of the *clubfoot* frame, as shown in Figure 14.14. Terms in hierarchical displays (see Figures 14.16 and 14.17) which are upper-case preceded by a slash are qualifiers in MeSH. These forms may seem quite natural for indexers, but perhaps not others viewing the displays. Note in Figure 14.14 that both the *disease process* and *clubfoot* frames have restrictions in the *intervention* slot. This means that the restrictions in the *clubfoot* frame are to override the restrictions in the *disease process* frame. If the *clubfoot* frame did not have these restrictions, they would be inherited from the same slot in the *disease process*

```
(|disease process| (inv+inherits-from (value abnormality))
  (body-part
    (restrictions (member !filler (get-hierarchy '|body part|))
    (if-needed (<demons retrieving values, suggesting candidate
            values, displaying prompts for values>)))
  (body-area
    (restrictions (member !filler (get-hierarchy '|body area|))
    (if-needed (<demons retrieving values, suggesting candidate
            values, displaying prompts for values>)))
  (intervention
    (restrictions (member !filler (get-hierarchy 'procedure)))
    (if-needed (<demons retrieving values, suggesting candidate
            values, displaying prompts for values>))
    (if-added (cond (!filler
            (add-heading !filler)
            (<demons adding subheadings>))))

(abnormality (inherits-from (value |disease process|))
  (inv+inherits-from (value clubfoot)))

(make-frame clubfoot (inherits-from (value abnormality))
  (inv+inherits-from (value |clubfoot 85140931|))
  (body-part (value joint))
  (body-area (value (joint foot)))
  (intervention
    (restrictions (member !filler (list 'procedure (get-hierarchy 'imaging) 'surgery)))))

(|clubfoot 85140931 (inherits-from (value clubfoot)))
```

Figure 14.14. Linked Indexing Frame and Knowledge Base Frames.

frame, through the *abnormality* frame, which also does not contain overriding restrictions.

The restrictions on the *intervention* slot in the *disease process* frame are the *procedure* hierarchy in the knowledge base. We display this hierarchy by using another feature of the system, which is to request a hierarchical display of the knowledge base by entering the command, ^[, at any slot value prompt, just as ^*r* was entered in Figure 14.15. The ensuing interaction is shown in Figure 14.17.

```
-----------------------[ MedIndEx Prototype ]-----------------------
| Frame: clubfoot                                Document: 85140931 |
| ----------[ Frame ]-------------      -----[Originating Frames]---- |
||intervention                        | |nil                        ||
||   value: ^r                        | |                           ||
||                                    | |                           ||
||                                    | |                           ||
||                                    | |                           ||
```

Figure 14.15. Restrictions Request.

```
------------------------[ MedIndEx Prototype ]------------------------
| Frame: clubfoot                                 Document: 85140931 |
|====================================================================|
|                                                                    |
|  ------------------------ Restrictions ------------------------   |
|  |         procedure (non-MeSH)                              |   |
|  |           imaging (non-MeSH)                              |   |
|  |             /RADIOGRAPHY                                  |   |
|  |               Angiography                                 |   |
|  |               Tomography, X-Ray Computed                  |   |
|  |             /RADIONUCLIDE IMAGING                         |   |
|  |             Ultrasonic Diagnosis                          |   |
|  |           /SURGERY                                        |   |
|  |                                                           |   |
|  |                                                           |   |
|  |                                                           |   |
|  |                                                           |   |
|  -------------------------------------------------------------   |
|                                                                    |
|                                                                    |
|====================================================================|
| Window Commands: u[p], d[own] or q[uit]:                           |
|____________________________________________________________________|
```

Figure 14.16. Restrictions Hierarchy Display.

We have requested only two levels be displayed. Terms that have further children are followed by (+).

As we have seen in the tutorial, the system disallows slot values that fail the restrictions check. When we attempt to add to the *intervention* slot */DRUG THERAPY*, which, according to Figure 14.16, is not in the restrictions hierarchy for this slot, the system immediately erases the value and displays an error message, shown in Figure 14.18. We now enter a slot value appropriate to the document, *Ultrasonic Diagnosis*, as shown in Figure 14.19.

At the second slot value prompt, we enter the *^u* command to display the current frame, *clubfoot 85140931*, shown in Figure 14.20. Note that it contains data that we have not entered. The system has displayed the *body-part* and *body-area* slots and their values inherited by this frame from the knowledge base *clubfoot* frame (see Figure 14.14). The *ultrasonography* value in Figure 14.20 is equivalent to the value which we have added to the slot, *Ultrasonic Diagnosis*, in Figure 14.19.

For simplicity, in this example there are no further slot value prompts. The system now prompts us for a decision to store the frame, not store the frame, or display the frame, as we have just done. We enter *y*, as shown in Figure 14.21. This response causes the system to prompt us to go to the next frame or a previous frame or return to the document selection menu. We select *n*, as shown in Figure 14.22. If we selected *d*, indexing of the current document would be interrupted, and the indexing frames for the document that have been completed would remain stored. We might then continue indexing this document later, by

```
------------------------[ MedIndEx Prototype ]------------------------
| Frame: clubfoot                                  Document: 85140931 |
| -----------[ Frame ]-------------     -----[Originating Frames]----- |
||intervention                        | |nil                          ||
||   value:                           | |                             ||
|  _______________________________________________________________    |
||       Enter the term for which you wish to see the hierarchy.      ||
||       Options : term or q[uit] :                                   ||
||____________________________________________________________________||
|                                                                     |
||                                    | |intervention                 ||
||                                    | |                             ||
||                                    | |    None                     ||
||____________________________________| |_____________________________||
|_____________________________________________________________________|

|  _______________________________________________________________    |
||       Enter the term for which you wish to see the hierarchy.      ||
||       Options : term or q[uit] : procedure                         ||
||       Number of levels : d[efault all], number[1-7], q[uit] : 2    ||
||____________________________________________________________________||
|                                                                     |

------------------------[ MedIndEx Prototype ]------------------------
| Frame: clubfoot                                  Document: 85140931 |
|=====================================================================|
|  ------------------------- Hierarchy --------------------------     |
|  |  medical entity (non-MeSH)                                 |    |
|  |is the parent of: procedure (non-MeSH)                      |    |
|  |                    /ADMINISTRATION & DOSAGE                |    |
|  |                      /DRUG THERAPY                         |    |
|  |                    imaging (non-MeSH)                      |    |
|  |                      /RADIOGRAPHY (+)                      |    |
|  |                      /RADIONUCLIDE IMAGING                 |    |
|  |                      Ultrasonic Diagnosis                  |    |
|  |                    radiation administration (non-MeSH)     |    |
|  |                      /RADIOTHERAPY (+)                     |    |
|  |                    /SURGERY                                |    |
|  |                       Lymph Node Excision                  |    |
|  ---------------------------------------------------------------    |
|=====================================================================|
| Window Commands: u[p], d[own] or q[uit]:                            |
|_____________________________________________________________________|
```

Figure 14.17. Knowledge Base Hierarchy Options and Display.

```
|=====================================================================|
|            Failed restrictions check on:  /DRUG THERAPY             |
|_____________________________________________________________________|
```

Figure 14.18. Failed Restrictions.

```
------------------------[ MedIndEx Prototype ]-----------------------
| Frame: clubfoot                                   Document: 85140931 |
| -----------[ Frame ]-------------      -----[Originating Frames]---- |
||intervention                         | |nil                         ||
||   value: Ultrasonic Diagnosis       | |                            ||
||   value:                            | |                            ||
||                                     | |                            ||
||                                     | |                            ||
```

Figure 14.19. Adding an Allowable Value.

selecting from a "Partially-Indexed Document Selection" menu, similar to the "Unindexed Document Selection" menu in Figure 14.10. Revising previously-stored frames, the *p* option, is discussed later on.

The completed and stored *clubfoot 85140931* frame has *ultrasonography* as the value for the *intervention* slot (see Figure 14.20). The system has therefore instantiated this value as a subsequent frame to be completed. This *ultrasonography 85140931* frame, displayed in Figure 14.23, will be used for highlighting the two windows on the right of the screen.

First, note the "Originating Frames" window. The entry there shows the origin of the current frame, specifically that *ultrasonography 85140931* came into existence because *ultrasonography* is the value for the *intervention* slot in the stored indexing frame for *clubfoot*. The *[A]* in this window indicates that this

```
------------------------[ MedIndEx Prototype ]-----------------------
| Frame: clubfoot                                   Document: 85140931 |
|======================================================================|
|                                                                      |
| ----------------------[ Current Frame ]------------------------     |
||                        clubfoot 85140931                           ||
||                     -------------------------                      ||
||  body-part                                                         ||
||    value: joint                                                    ||
||                                                                    ||
||  body-area                                                         ||
||    value: (joint foot)                                             ||
||                                                                    ||
||  intervention                                                      ||
||    value: ultrasonography                                          ||
||                                                                    ||
||                                                                    ||
||                                                                    ||
||____________________________________________________________________||
|                                                                      |
|======================================================================|
| Window Commands: u[p], d[own] or q[uit]:                             |
|______________________________________________________________________|
```

Figure 14.20. Current Frame Display.

```
------------------------[ MedIndEx Prototype ]------------------------
| Frame: clubfoot                                    Document: 85140931 |
| -----------[ Frame ]--------------       -----[Originating Frames]---- |
||intervention                       |  |nil                            ||
||   value: Ultrasonic Diagnosis     |  |                               ||
||   value:                          |  |                               ||
||                                   |  |                               ||
||                                   |  |                               ||
||                                   |  |                               ||
||                                   |  |                               ||
||                                   |  |                               ||
||                                   |  |_______________________________||
||                                   |   ---[Retrieved Values for:]---  |
||                                   |  |intervention                   ||
||                                   |  |                               ||
||                                   |  |    None                       ||
||___________________________________|  |_______________________________||
|=======================================================================|
| Options : ^u [see current frame], y [ store frame] [^u y/n]  y        |
|_______________________________________________________________________|
```

Figure 14.21. Prompt at Completion of Frame to Store or Display Frame.

```
|=======================================================================|
| Options: n[ext] frame, d[ocument sel], p[revious frame] [ndp]:  n     |
|_______________________________________________________________________|
```

Figure 14.22. Prompt to Proceed to Next or Previous Frame or Another Document.

```
------------------------[ MedIndEx Prototype ]------------------------
| Frame: ultrasonography                             Document: 85140931 |
| -----------[ Frame ]--------------       -----[Originating Frames]---- |
||problem                            |  |1) clubfoot                    ||
||   value:                          |  |intervention     [A]           ||
||                                   |  |                               ||
||                                   |  |                               ||
||                                   |  |                               ||
||                                   |  |                               ||
||                                   |  |                               ||
||                                   |  |                               ||
||                                   |  |_______________________________||
||                                   |   ---[Retrieved Values for:]---  |
||                                   |  |problem                        ||
||                                   |  |    Clubfoot                   ||
||                                   |  |                               ||
||___________________________________|  |_______________________________||
|                                                                       |
|=======================================================================|
|                                                                       |
|_______________________________________________________________________|
```

Figure 14.23. Originating Frames and Retrieved Values.

value (or an equivalent) has been *added* to the slot. The other possibility is *[R]*, which would indicate that the value is *retrievable* (the *internal retrieval* feature will be discussed next). The values in this window correspond to an *originating-frame* slot in the *ultrasonography 85140931* frame, that is *(|ultrasonography 85140931| (originating-frame (value (|clubfoot 85140931| intervention added))))*.

The "Retrieved Values for:" window in Figure 14.23 displays the retrieved value for the current slot, which is the *problem* slot. This slot is inherited from the *procedure* frame in the knowledge base, since *ultrasonography 85140931 inherits-from ultrasonography inherits-from imaging inherits from procedure*, similar to the inheritance linkages from *clubfoot 85140931* to *disease process* shown in Figure 14.14. The slot has an *if-needed* demon that uses the value in the *originating-frame* slot. In this example the rule says, in effect, since *ultrasonography* is an *intervention* in the *clubfoot* indexing frame, then *clubfoot* should be retrieved as a *problem* in the *ultrasonography* indexing frame. It is important to note that *Clubfoot* has not been physically added to the *problem* slot of *ultrasonography 85140931*. In fact, when we attempt to do so, the system immediately erases it and displays an error message at the bottom of the screen, as shown in Figure 14.24.

The *originating-frame* slot has two important uses by the system. First, its values automatically provide *candidate* slot values. An example of this is the automatic display of the *body-part* as we continue completing *ultrasonography 85140931* in Figure 14.25. The running of an *if-needed* demon of the *body-area* slot has caused the automatic appearance of *Joints*, based on the body-part of the originating frame, the *clubfoot* indexing frame (see Figure 14.20, which shows *joint* as the inherited *body-part*). The demon has actually been inherited by *ultrasonography 85140931* from the *procedure* frame, and has made the inference that the *body-part* of the *originating-frame* (e.g., the *clubfoot* indexing frame) may well be the body-part of the current frame. We may confirm the candidate value (in effect adding it to the slot), over-write it, or erase it. The system will not present a candidate value unless it passes the restrictions for the current slot.

We will now explain the other use of *originating-frame* in the revision of previously-stored frames (option *p* in Figure 14.22). This is based on the principle that, except in the initial frame, the absence of an *originating-frame* will cause the frame to be erased. For example, if we completed and stored *clubfoot 85140931* (see Figure 14.21) and *ultrasonography 85140931*, and later returned to *clubfoot 85140931* and erased *Ultrasonic Diagnosis* from the *inter-*

```
|=====================================================================|
|   This value has already been retrieved for the current slot.       |
|_____________________________________________________________________|
```

Figure 14.24. Error After Attempt to Add a Retrieved Value.

```
------------------------[ MedIndEx Prototype ]-----------------------
| Frame: ultrasonography                         Document: 85140931 |
| -----------[ Frame ]--------------     -----[Originating Frames]---- |
||problem                            | |1) clubfoot                 ||
||   value:                          | |intervention     [A]        ||
||                                   | |                            ||
||body-part                          | |                            ||
||   value: Joints                   | |                            ||
||   value:                          | |                            ||
||                                   | |                            ||
||                                   | |                            ||
||                                   | |____________________________||
||                                   |  ---[Retrieved Values for:]--- |
||                                   | |body-part                   ||
||                                   | |                            ||
||                                   | |    None                    ||
||___________________________________| |____________________________||
|                                                                    |
|====================================================================|
|                                                                    |
|____________________________________________________________________|
```

Figure 14.25. Automatic Presentation of Candidate Value.

vention slot, the *ultrasonography 85140931* frame will be erased as well since it originated only from *clubfoot 85140931* (see Originating Frames window in Figure 14.23). If, however, there were a second *originating-frame* in *ultrasonography 85140931*, the system would erase the *clubfoot* entry from the *originating-frame* slot, and it thereby would no longer appear in the Originating Frames window of *ultrasonography 85140931*. In that case, the *ultrasonography 85140931* frame would not be erased since presumably *Ultrasonic Diagnosis* had also been added to the indexing frame remaining in the Originating Frames window. Of course, the erasing of frames has a domino effect since the disappearance of values of the erased frames may lead to erasure of *their* corresponding indexing frames.

The last feature we will describe is the automatic assignment of MeSH indexing terms to the document. We may enter, at any slot value prompt, the *^n* command to overlay a display of the MeSH terms so far. For example, suppose we had done this on a second pass through *clubfoot 85140931* (see Figure 14.21). The resulting display is shown in Figure 14.26. The initial value, *Clubfoot* (see Figure 14.12), automatically became the first indexing term. The rules for adding further MeSH terms are in the *if-added facets* of slots and are known as *if-added demons*. This facet is inherited through the *inherits-from* links, just as are slot values, restrictions, and if-needed demons. A simple *if-added* demon is *add-heading*, which, when attached to a slot, causes the slot value to be appended to the list of MeSH terms for the document. The demon *(add-heading !filler)* caused the system to append *Ultrasonic Diagnosis*, the *!filler* argument of the demon, to the indexing terms. The *clubfoot 85140931*

```
------------------------[ MedIndEx Prototype ]-----------------------
| Frame: clubfoot                               Document: 85140931 |
|==================================================================|
|                                                                  |
| ---------------[ Indices so far for the document ]-------------- |
||   MH - Clubfoot/DIAGNOSIS                                      ||
||   MH - Ultrasonic Diagnosis                                    ||
||                                                                ||
||                                                                ||
||                                                                ||
||                                                                ||
||                                                                ||
||                                                                ||
||                                                                ||
||                                                                ||
||                                                                ||
||                                                                ||
||________________________________________________________________||
|                                                                  |
|==================================================================|
| Window Commands: u[p], d[own] or q[uit]:                         |
|__________________________________________________________________|
```

Figure 14.26. First Display of Automatically Assigned MeSH Indexing Terms.

frame has inherited this demon from the *intervention* slot of *disease process* (see Figure 14.14).

Note in Figure 14.26 the MeSH subheading *DIAGNOSIS*, which has been appended to the MeSH term *Clubfoot*. This has occurred because the *intervention* slot contains another demon, known as *assign-subheading*. This demon used the knowledge that the value of the *purpose* slot in the *ultrasonography* knowledge base frame is *diagnosis*. Therefore, the demon assigned the subheading as soon as *Ultrasonic Diagnosis* was added to *clubfoot 85140931*. However, if the system does not know (from the knowledge base) the purpose of the intervention, the demon will not assign a subheading until the purpose of the intervention is known, when the purpose slot of the filler indexing frame (e.g., *ultrasonography 85140931*) is itself filled.

Another *if-added* demon is illustrated by the last indexing frame, *patient 85140931*. A *patient* indexing frame is always created, since the slot (*patient (value patient)*) is in the *disease process* and *procedure* frames in the knowledge base. Figure 14.27 shows values we have added to the *gender* and *age* slots. When we again display the MeSH terms, we see that a new indexing term, *Prenatal Diagnosis*, has been appended, as shown in Figure 14.28. The *if-added* demon of the *age* slot of *patient 85140931*, inherited from the *patient* knowledge base frame, says, "If the purpose of a procedure is diagnosis, and the age of the patient is a prenatal age, then append *Prenatal Diagnosis* to the MeSH terms." This demon illustrates that, in addition to automatically assigning subheadings, the system also makes inferences for adding certain MeSH descriptors.

```
------------------------[ MedIndEx Prototype ]-----------------------
| Frame: patient                                  Document: 85140931 |
| -----------[ Frame ]--------------      -----[Originating Frames]---- |
||gender                              | |1) ultrasonography          ||
||  value: Female                     | |patient      [R]            ||
||  value:                            | |2) clubfoot                 ||
||                                    | |patient      [R]            ||
||age                                 | |                            ||
||  value: Fetus                      | |                            ||
||  value:                            | |                            ||
||                                    | |                            ||
||                                    | |____________________________||
||                                    |  ---[Retrieved Values for:]--- |
||                                    | |age                         ||
||                                    | |                            ||
||                                    | |    None                    ||
||____________________________________| |____________________________||
|                                                                    |
|====================================================================|
|                                                                    |
|____________________________________________________________________|
```

Figure 14.27. The Last Indexing Frame for a Document.

```
------------------------[ MedIndEx Prototype ]-----------------------
| Frame: patient                                  Document: 85140931 |
|====================================================================|
|                                                                    |
| --------------[ Indices so far for the document ]---------------  |
||   MH - Clubfoot/DIAGNOSIS                                        ||
||   MH - Female                                                    ||
||   MH - Human                                                     ||
||   MH - Prenatal Diagnosis                                        ||
||   MH - Ultrasonic Diagnosis                                      ||
||                                                                  ||
||                                                                  ||
||                                                                  ||
||                                                                  ||
||                                                                  ||
||                                                                  ||
||                                                                  ||
||                                                                  ||
||__________________________________________________________________||
|                                                                    |
|====================================================================|
| Window Commands: u[p], d[own] or q[uit]:                           |
|____________________________________________________________________|
```

Figure 14.28. Second Display of Automatically Assigned MeSH Indexing Terms.

```
(|document 85140931| (inherits-from (value document)) ...
        (title (value (Prenatal ultrasound diagnosis of
            clubfoot.))) ...
        (contents (value |clubfoot 85140931| |joint 85140931|
                |ultrasonography 85140931|
                |patient 85140931|))
        (indices (value (Clubfoot /DIAGNOSIS) (Female) (Human)
                (|Prenatal Diagnosis|)
                (|Ultrasonic Diagnosis|))))
```

Figure 14.29. Document Instantiation Frame with Contents and Indices Values.

When a slot value is modified, the MeSH terms list may also be modified. After a value has been modified, the system runs a procedure known as *generate-all-indices* next time we request the indexing terms display. This function simply runs all the *if-added* demons of all the slots of all the indexing frames up to that point.

Finally, we return to the *contents* and *indices* slots of *document 85140931*, shown originally in Figure 14.8. At the completion of indexing this document, the system will automatically have added values to these slots, as shown in Figure 14.29.

CONCLUSION

After presenting background information about thesaurus-based indexing, and a tutorial on frames, we have described the prototype MedIndEx System we are developing at NLM. Further details of this research are in a report by Humphrey, Kapoor, Mendez, and Dorsey (1987). A follow-up report by Humphrey and Kapoor (1988) describes the prototype developed in the windowing, mouse-driven workstation environment of the Sun-3™ family machines. We are continuing to expand the knowledge base and design the interface. In particular, the immediate task is defining the slots and structuring the slot values needed to develop the inferencing rules, and maintaining a computerized environment which facilitates the testing and revision of the rules.

REFERENCES

American National Standards Institute. Subcommittee 25 on Thesaurus Rules and Conventions (1980). *American national standards quidelines for thesaurus structure, construction, and use*. New York: ANSI.

Bachrach, C. A., & Charen, T. (1978). Selection of MEDLINE contents, the development of its thesaurus, and the indexing process. *Medical Informatics (London), 3*, 237–254.

Bobrow, D., & Winograd, T. (1977). An overview of KRL, a Knowledge Representation Language. *Cognitive Science, 1*, 3–46.

Carbonell, J., & Joseph, R. (1985, October). *FrameKit+: A knowledge representation system* (Preliminary draft). Pittsburgh, PA: Carnegie-Mellon University, Department of Computer Science.

Crain, C. J. (1985, December). Protocol study of indexers at the National Library of Medicine. In J. G. Carbonell, D. A. Evans, D. S. Scott, & R. T. Thomason (eds.), *Final report on the automated classification and retrieval project: The MedSORT Project, Carnegie-Mellon University* (Appendix A.4). Pittsburgh, PA: Carnegie-Mellon University, Departments of Philosophy and Computer Science.

Doszkocs, T. E. (1978). An Associative Interactive Dictionary (AID) for online bibliographic searching. In E. H. Brenner (Comp.), *Proceedings of the ASIS annual meeting, 41st annual meeting, New York, November, 1978* (Vol. 15, pp. 105–109). White Plains, NY: Knowledge Industry Publications.

Funk, M. E., & Reid, C. A. (1983). Indexing consistency in MEDLINE. *Bulletin of the Medical Library Association, 71*, 176–183.

Hooper, R. S. (1965). *Indexer consistency tests: Origin, measurement, results, and utilization* (TR95-56). Bethesda, MD: IBM Corporation.

Humphrey, S. M., & Kapoor, A. (1988, July). *The MedIndex System: Research on interactive knowledge-based indexing of the medical litarature* (LHNCBC 88-1). Bethesda, MD: United States National Library of Medicine. (National Technical Information Service, No. PB88-243902/AS).

Humphrey, S. M., Kapoor, A., Mendez, D., & Dorsey, M. (1987, March). *The indexing aid project: Knowledge-based indexing of the medical literature* (LHNCBC 87-1). Bethesda, MD: United States National Library of Medicine. (National Technical Information Service, No. PB87-175790/AS).

Humphrey, S. M., & Melloni, B. J. (1986). *Databases: A primer for retrieving information by computer*. Englewood Cliffs, NJ: Prentice-Hall.

Humphrey, S. M., & Miller, N. E. (1987). Knowledge-based indexing of the medical literature: The Indexing Aid Project. *Journal of the American Society for Information Science, 38*, 184–196.

Lancaster, F. W. (1968, January). *Evaluation of the MEDLARS Demand Search Service*. Bethesda, MD: United States National Library of Medicine.

Leonard, L. E. (1975). *Inter-indexer consistency and retrieval effectiveness: Measurement of relationships* (Ph.D. Thesis). Champaign, IL: University of Illinois, Graduate School of Library Science.

Leonard, L. E. (1977, December). *Inter-indexer consistency studies, 1954–1975: A review of the literature and summary of study results* (Occasional Papers No. 131). Champaign, IL: University of Illinois Graduate School of Library Science.

Lindberg, D. A. B. (1987). National Library of Medicine: The view at 150 years. *Journal of the American Society for Information Science, 38*, 34–39.

Marcetich, J., & Schuyler, P. (1981, June). *The use of AID to promote indexing consistency at the National Library of Medicine*. Paper presented at the Eighty-first Annual Meeting of the Medical Library Association, Montreal.

Minsky, M. (1975). A framework for representing knowledge. In P. Winston (Ed.), *The psychology of computer vision* (pp. 211–277). New York: McGraw-Hill.

Roberts, R. B., & Goldstein, I. P. (1977, July). *The FRL Primer* (Memo 408). Cambridge, MA: Massachusetts Institute of Technology, Artificial Intelligence Laboratory.

Salton, G., & McGill, M. J. (1983). *Introduction to modern information retrieval.* New York: McGraw-Hill.

Torek, C. (1985). *The Maryland Window Library.* College Park, MD: University of Maryland, Department of Computer Science.

White, L. (1973, November). *Minimizing variabilities in indexing* (Research Report). Tucson, AZ: University of Arizona, Arid Lands Information System. (National Technical Information Service, No. PB-237-989).

Winston, P. H., & Horn, B. K. P. (1989). *LISP* (3rd ed.). Reading, MA: Addison-Wesley.

15

Applications of Knowledge-Based Systems to Classification in Libraries

Irene L. Travis
Information, Technology and Facilities Dept.
World Bank
Washington, DC

INTRODUCTION

Classification is the fundamental activity in the organization of knowledge. For this reason it is prominent in all systems for organizing knowledge in libraries and information centers and also in the knowledge bases of knowledge-based systems (KBSs), such as expert systems (ESs) and systems that understand natural language text. Classification may be defined in two ways. First, it may be defined as:

1. Creating categories or classes of like objects, actions, or concepts that are useful for some defined purpose and arranging these classes into a conceptual structure based on the relations among them.

For convenience we will refer to these objects, actions, and concepts as entities and to the conceptual structure as a classification system. A familiar example of classification under this definition is the creation of library classification schemes and subject heading lists, such as the Dewey Decimal Classification (DDC) (Dewey, 1989) and the Library of Congress Subject Headings (LCSH) (U.S. Library of Congress, 1986). Another example is the creation of database indexing languages, such as the NASA Thesaurus (U.S. National Aeronautic and Space Administration, 1982).

However, classification may also be defined as:

2. Identifying individual entities as instances of classes in an existing classification system.

Determining that an item should be assigned to a particular class or subject category from a published classification scheme or indexing language, such as those mentioned above, is an example of classification in this second sense. Following the practice of many people who study classification, we will distinguish between these two classification activities by calling the first activity classifying and the second classing. Similarly, we will refer to someone engaged in classifying as a classifier and to someone engaged in classing as a classer, indexer, or cataloger.

CLASSIFICATION

We begin by looking at classification as a general phenomenon. The reason for this apparent digression will become clear when we turn our attention to KBSs. As mentioned above, classification is widely employed in constructing knowledge bases. Moreover, some of the first successful KBSs were used for classing; simple medical diagnosis is an example of a classing problem. Both facts bear on the suitability of KBSs for the support of library activities involving classification.

Following this discussion of classification generally, a brief overview is provided of classification as it is now incorporated into library activities. Although the focus on classification in libraries will be in the classical sense, it will be acknowledged that all methods for collection and database description involve aspects of classification. A thesaurus or a subject heading list may be presented in an alphabetical order, rather than a classified one, but it still incorporates a structure that reflects a relational analysis among the classes represented by the index terms, particularly the analysis of generic/specific or hierarchical relationships. The construction of any such tool involves classifying by our definition, and, similarly, indexing in this context is simply another form of classing.

Because the use of specific terms will be used frequently in the rest of the discussion, some definitions will be given at this point. Earlier, the conceptual structure derived from the organization of classes was defined as a classification system. In this discussion an indexing language will be considered as a classification system for library materials. We consider an indexing language to be a language because all such systems have a grammar that defines the permissible heading structures, and a semantic component or vocabulary that determines the concepts that can be expressed in the language. Library classification schemes, subject heading lists, and thesauri are types of indexing languages which are defined as follows:

- A classification scheme is an indexing language with the terms or class descriptions arranged in a systematic order: that is, with classes arranged by their semantic, rather than their alphabetic, proximity. To implement this order, the classification scheme includes a filing code or notation. The notation for an individual class is the class number.

- A subject heading list is an alphabetically arranged indexing language that is a list of subjects developed for manual card or book catalogs, particularly the LCSH.
- A thesaurus is an alphabetical indexing language devised primarily for in-depth indexing to construct bibliographic databases for mechanized retrieval systems.

Thesauri are distinguished from subject heading lists in several ways. First, their entries are restricted primarily to one- or two-word phrases or terms, and these terms are entered in natural language order (e.g., elementary education). By contrast, subject heading lists may have quite complex heading structures and may invert terms in order to group like subjects in a quasiclassified arrangement (e.g., Buildings, Commercial; Buildings, Industrial; Buildings, Residential). Moreover, when a cataloger or indexer classes with a subject heading list, a single subject, such as "the history of industrial architecture in France," is supposed to be expressed by a single subject heading. To use a thesaurus, by contrast, indexers break complex subjects down into component parts, such as France and Industry and Architecture and History, using as many index terms as needed to express the complete idea.

A patron searching a manual catalog created from a subject heading list looks up one heading at a time. A patron or searcher using an automated system to search a database that has been indexed with a thesaurus combines the simple thesaurus terms to express a request, most often using Boolean logic. The subject heading list is precoordinated (complete subjects are specified before indexing or searching) while the thesaurus supports postcoordination, synthesizing subjects at the search stage.

Classifying

Turning first to activities within the scope of definition (1), it is noted that classifying is essential to cognition. Much of our understanding of the world consists of our mental ability to categorize and to recognize relationships among classes of physical objects, events, and other phenomena, thereby imposing a structure on our experience. It is therefore a ubiquitous intellectual activity. For instance, classification is an essential part of science and engineering. Taxonomies of plants and animals are particularly well known results of classifying, but there are many other examples, such as taxonomies of diseases in medicine and fault trees for diagnosing equipment failures in electrical engineering. Taxonomies are often embodied in library classification schemes and also occur prominently in KBS knowledge bases.

Relations used in classifying. Relations that serve as the basis of a conceptual structure of classes of entities (i.e., a classification scheme) can have a variety of strengths and origins. They can be derived from the definition of the classes (semantic relations) or they may result from events and situations in the world that associate classes of entities with each other (pragmatic relations). For example, the relationship between the concepts "buildings" and "highrise buildings" is definitional or semantic, while the relationship between "highrise buildings" and "crime" is pragmatic. Although the distinction between semantic and pragmatic relations is not hard and fast, the distinction affects the way that both library classification systems and KBS knowledge bases are constructed.

The most widely exploited semantic relation is the generic/specific one between classes of entities (e.g., residential buildings are a kind of building). Relations of this sort are very useful because most attributes of the parent class also pertain to the subclasses and individual members. That is, things that are true of all buildings, for instance, are generally true of residential buildings; things that are true of all residential buildings are generally true of single-family houses. Inheritance also extends to relations between an individual and a class. Most things that are true of single-family houses in general are true of my house. These relations thus establish conceptual hierarchies in which subclasses may "inherit" attributes from the broader classes. Links that support property inheritance are labeled as ISA (i.e., "is a") or, alternatively, AKO (a kind of) relations in knowledge bases and "narrower term" or NT in most modern thesauri. Older indexing languages, such as LCSH, do not properly distinguish NT relationships from other types that do not support inheritance.

In KBSs the mechanism of inheritance supports default inferences about objects based on their class membership. That is, the system can reason about a new subclass or individual it encounters based on what it knows about the parent class. It also allows information about classes of entities to be stored at the most general level to which it applies, obviating the need to repeat it for each subclass or individual that shares the attributes in question.

Apart from generic/specific links, there are other kinds of semantic links that are important, such as quasi-generic/specific relationships where some, but not all, entities of one kind are members of a broader class. All commercial buildings, for example, are buildings by definition, but they may or may not be recreation sites. One would not want to assume that a hospital had any attributes in common with the local sandlot. Commercial buildings and recreation sites are overlapping classes, but one is not subsumed by the other. Therefore, where inheritance is concerned, each case must be looked at on its own merits.

The exact nature of relations between classes is not always specified in classification systems. In many indexing languages, for instance, the hierarchical "broader term"/"narrower term" relations are specifically labeled, but all other links are simply designated as "related terms." This designation is applied regardless of whether the related term represents a part of a whole (buildings/framing), a related discipline (buildings/civil engineering), a related activity (buildings/climate control), a contrasting concept (commercial buildings/

residential buildings), the product of a process (buildings/construction), or any of the other numerous identifiable semantic relationships among entities and concepts. Since in indexing applications the primary role of related terms is to suggest alternatives to human searchers and indexers, narrow identification of the relations is usually regarded as an unnecessary source of complexity and error. By contrast, automated natural language understanding (NLU) requires exact specification of the nature of these links.

Ordinarily relationships other than generic/specific ones cannot support inheritance. Even in part/whole relationships, where some attributes may be shared, most attributes are not. A light fixture in a mobile home, for instance, does not have much in common with it except its physical location. One exception is in biological systems, such as systems of the human body. In this case many attributes of the parent system, such as the circulatory system, are also attributes of its parts, such as the veins and the capillaries. Another is geographic locations. Many things that are true of a state will also, for instance, be true of municipalities in that state. Intuitively, we can see that interchangeable parts, such as screws, are likely to have much less in common with their parent systems than parts that are in no way interchangeable and are linked only to one system.

Thus far, a description has been given of links between concepts that are largely definitional and semantic in nature, whether hierarchical or not. They are relatively permanent and are the bulk of those shown in library classification schemes and indexing languages, dictionaries, and lexicons. Events and situations also link entities in the real world pragmatically. Class concepts especially may be linked in the "subjects" of library materials, which are grammatically noun phrases, or through sentences in a text or knowledge base. Consider, for example, the subject, "the use of microcomputers for estimating costs in small construction companies," or the sentence, "Microcomputers have allowed many small construction companies to estimate their costs more accurately." Here, there is no semantic link between "microcomputers" and "cost estimation by small construction companies," but the phrase and sentence both define a relationship between them. In this case the microcomputer is a tool to solve the cost estimation problem for companies that can afford only minimal overhead. Relations among individuals (a particular microcomputer and a particular small construction company) are even more highly pragmatic.

Pragmatic relationships among classes are expressible in some indexing languages and classification schemes for libraries, but much less commonly than semantic ones. Moreover, as we will see below, these links are not usually explicitly listed in the classification scheme or indexing language, but are introduced by the indexer or classer at the time a particular item in a library collection is indexed or classed, much as terms for individual entities were created above. An example would be a code indicating the role of a concept in a subject, such as being a catalyst in a chemical reaction. KBSs, such as ESs and NLU systems, by contrast, need to represent this kind of association, just as they also required a greater level of discrimination among the semantic relations mentioned above.

Structures used in classifying. An inverted tree structure, in which one universal class is divided according to the values of successive attributes or principles of division into increasingly narrow classes, is the classic model of a classification structure that many of us carry in our heads, as shown in Figure 15.1a. It is suitable for instances in which a subclass can be viewed as having only one parent, such as in phylogenic (evolutionary) classification of animals. However, in libraries and in KBSs physical entities or concretes, as the Indian classification theorist, S.R. Ranganathan, called them (Ranganathan, 1967) are often not viewed from a single perspective. A highrise building can be viewed as a type of building defined by its physical configuration; however, it can also be defined by its use (residential, commercial), its material (glass buildings), or its period (art deco buildings)—to name only a few. Further afield, it could be viewed as an agent for social change, a subject area for science fiction, a cause of traffic congestion, or a subject for the graphic arts. It is clear that a tree is an awkward form for showing all these links, and, furthermore, it cannot link all the occurrences of the concept "highrise buildings" that might occur in the tree to each other. In Figure 15.1a, for instance, the term Highrise Buildings occurs under both Commercial Buildings and Residential Buildings. These occurrences of a concrete that are scattered throughout a classification structure are called distributed relatives.

Looked at another way, we can say that tree structures are unidimensional; that is, we can order the classes in a single linear sequence (Figure 15.1b), as is done for shelving purposes in libraries. However, when we are not constrained by the need to have a single fixed sequence of classes, multidimensional structures are possible, where each class can be linked to any number of others to form a semantic network. A thesaurus that displays multiple broader and related terms for each entry is an example of such a structure. Figure 15.2 shows a set of thesaurus entries and a portion of a semantic network representing the same information. Such structures, where one term can have many broader term linkages, are sometimes called tangled hierarchies. The origin of the term is graphically illustrated in the semantic network representation.

In practice many tree structures compensate for their limited linkage by the use of indexes that can show all the occurrences of a concrete that has occurred in multiple contexts in the classification scheme. The Relative Index to the DDC is a well known example of a systematic attempt to show all of the potential contexts (hierarchies) for a concrete class. Figure 15.3 shows a section of a relative index. The index is usually not available to the public; however, the subject catalog serves much the same function, although in a less systematic fashion. Figure 15.4 shows a portion of a subject catalog in the LCSH style. Subject catalogs also tend to bring together the concretes, such as highrise buildings, that a discipline-oriented classification scheme will scatter.

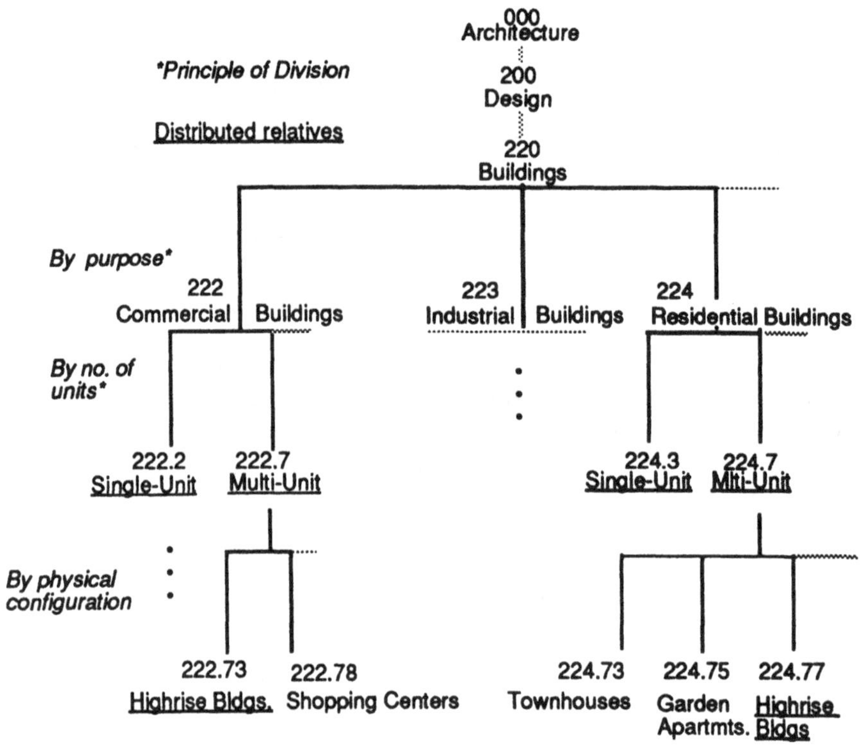

Figure 15.1a. Inverted Tree Structure.

000 Architecture
.
.
200 Design
  220 Buildings
    222 Commercial Buildings
      222.2 Single-Unit
      222.7 Multi-Unit
        222.73 Highrise Buildings
        222.78 Shopping Centers
        .
        .
    223 Industrial Buildings
        .
        .
    224 Residential Buildings
      224.3 Single-Unit
      224.7 Multi-Unit
        224.73 Townhouses
        224.75 Garden Apartments
        224.77 Highrise Buildings
        .
        .

Figure 15.1b. Linear Sequence of Classes.

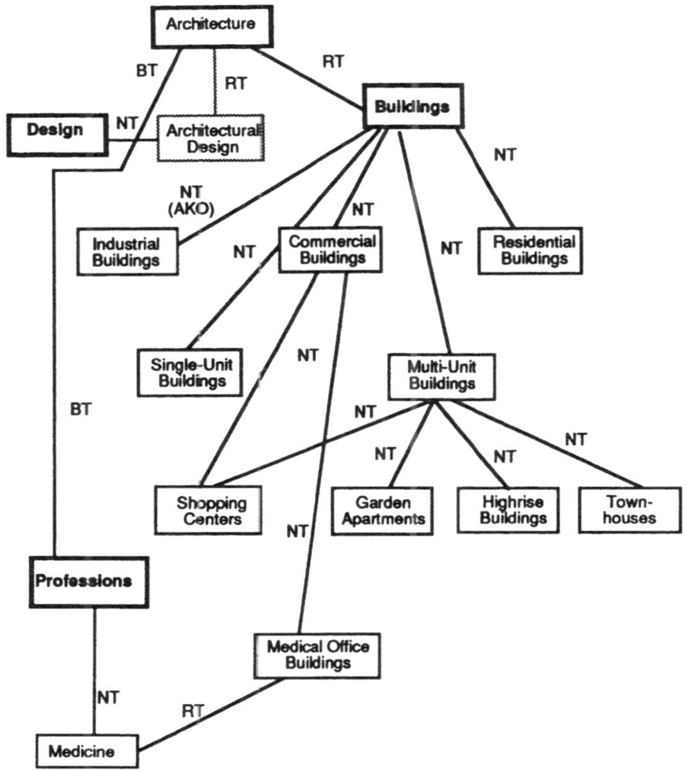

Architectural Design
  Use Architecture and Design

Architecture
  BT Professions
     Disciplines
  RT Buildings

Buildings
  RT Architecture
  NT Commercial Buildings
     Industrial Buildings
     Multi-Unit Buildings
     Residential Buildings
     Single-Unit Buildings

Commercial Buildings
  BT Buildings
  NT Shopping Centers
  RT Highrise Buildings
     Industrial Buildings
     Residential Buildings

Design

Garden Apartments
  BT Multi-Unit Buildings
     Residential Buildings

Highrise Buildings
  BT Multi-Unit Buildings
  RT Commercial Buildings
     Residential Buildings

Industrial Buildings

Medical Office Buildings
  BT Commercial Buildings
  RT Medicine

Medicine
  BT Professions
  RT Medical Office Buildings

Multi-Unit Buildings
  BT Buildings
  NT Garden Apartments
     Highrise Buildings
     Shopping Centers
     Townhouses
  RT Single-Unit Buildings

Professions
  NT Architecture
     Medicine

Residential Buildings

Shopping Centers

Single-Unit Buildings

Townhouses

Figure 15.2. Semantic Network with Corresponding Thesaurus Entries.

Buildings	220
Commercial Buildings	212
.	
.	
Highrise Buildings	
Commercial	222.73
Residential	224.77
.	
Single Unit Buildings	
Commercial	222.2
Residential	224.30

Figure 15.3. Relative Index.

Automatic procedures for classifying. Although there are programs to help with the clerical side of building classification schemes and to help in maintaining their referential consistency, very little work has been done to date to automate semantic analysis. There is, however, a well developed area of study known as automatic classification, which is based on a different approach to the problem. It originated in biology as numerical taxonomy (Sokal & Sneath, 1963) and can be found in many other applications, including artificial intelligence (AI).

We will illustrate these techniques using the most pertinent case, document classification. The usual approach in this instance is to create a vector to represent each document in a collection, as shown in Figure 15.5. The elements of the vector are the number of instances of each of the words that occurs in the document except certain very common words that may be on a stoplist. These counts may be weighted by the number of times the word occurs in the collection as a whole. The distance between each document vector and every other document vector in the collection is then computed using a distance measure and a threshold for that measure to create groups of documents whose word profiles are more similar to each other than they are to those of other groups. Such groups are usually called clusters.

Clustering is more flexible than an analysis of likeness based on a single attribute or, even, a fixed set of attributes. The members of a cluster do not have to have any single attribute in common. The groups created by these pragmatic, word-based techniques, however, often have no satisfactory intuitive semantic

Buildings, Commercial
See also Buildings, Highrise; Buildings, Industrial; Buildings, Residential; Shopping Centers; and buildings used by particular kinds of businesses and professions, such as Buildings, Medical; Retail Stores, etc.

.
.

Buildings, Highrise

.
.

Buildings, Medical
See also Hospitals ;

.
.

Buildings, Residential
See also Buildings, Commercial; Garden Apartments; Buildings, Highrise; Buildings, Industrial; Townhouses

.
.

Townhouses

.
.

Figure 15.4. Subject Headings.

interpretation. There are various problems with the stability and efficiency of the classification algorithms, which tend to be computationally intensive.

Because groups of individual entities, rather than a hierarchy of headings, are the output of the clustering process, clustering both classifies and classes simultaneously. The group is defined only by its membership. Under some methods, the database must be reclustered every time a new document is added to it if the clusters are to be valid. Most systems, however, include methods for adding new documents to existing clusters, at least up to a point. A rapidly changing environment will, however, destabilize these groups just as it will destabilize a

DOCUMENT TEXT

Document 1: The last decade has seen the transformation of McLean, Virginia. Highrise commercial and apartment buildings have sprung up, containing hundreds of thousands of square feet of office space, while the local shopping center has doubled its size. The many small farms within the town borders are now rows of expensive townhouses.

Document 2: The amount of commercial footage available in West Coast cities has grown phenomenally in the last 10 years. Highrise commercial buildings have changed the face of San Francisco, Los Angeles, Portland, and Seattle. Townhouse parks in the suburbs house professional offices, and massive shopping centers dominate the landscape.

Document 3: Tenants and landlords, homeowners and developers are all awaiting the effects of the new tax laws. Developers of vacation and resort properties are particularly concerned about the loss of mortgage interest on second homes as a tax deduction. Beach-side highrises and townhouses at the bottom of the ski lift may go begging as their actual cost...

Document 4. Commercial investors are becoming increasingly alarmed over the surplus of commercial space in across the country. Cities in parts of the US affected by the oil bust are, of course, especially hard hit. In those areas, hundreds of commercial buildings - from high rises to office blocks and townhouse clusters - wait for better economic times. However, even ..

WORDS	DOCUMENT VECTORS 1	2	3	4
apartment	1	0	0	0
.				
buildings	1	1	0	1
.				
center(s)	1	1	0	0
.				
cities	0	1	0	1
.				
commercial	1	2	0	3
country	0	0	0	1
.				
highrise(s)	1	1	1	1
.				
home(s)	0	0	2	0
house	0	1	0	1
hundreds	1	0	0	1
.				
office(s)	1	1	0	1
.				
properties	0	0	1	0
resort	0	0	1	0
.				
shopping	1	1	0	0
.				
space	1	0	0	1
.				
tax	0	0	2	0
tenants	0	0	1	0
.				
town	1	0	0	1
townhouse(s)	1	1	1	0
transformation	1	0	0	0
US	0	0	0	1

CLUSTERS

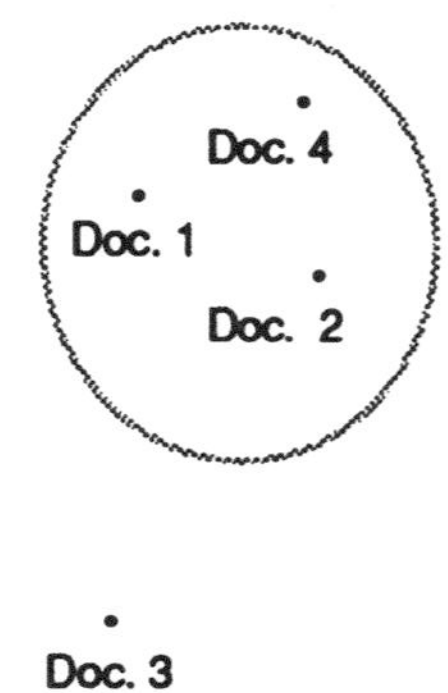

Figure 15.5. Document Clusters.

conventional system with a resulting need to recompute the classes. For an extensive discussion of clustering see Salton and McGill (1983).

Although there is frequently a problem with naming or interpreting clusters, such a step is often not required. Clustering can be useful, for example, for organizing the storage of a bibliographic database, so that documents that are likely to be retrieved together are stored together. The user need not be aware of the clusters or interact with them in any way. This purpose is identical to one of the principal motivations for shelving items in a classified order in libraries with closed stacks. Although most users cannot browse the collection, retrieving books from the stacks will still be much more efficient because books that are used together are more likely to be shelved together.

Classing

Classing (i.e., assigning objects to a particular class) is generally accomplished by matching the values of the attributes of an individual entity to those defining the classes in the classification scheme. Matching is frequently not straightforward either because the entity does not exactly match the class or because we lack sufficient information. The first case, inexact match, can have three basic causes. First, individual entities can vary in the degree to which they possess a particular attribute or value: some red objects are less red than others. Second, the meaning of some adjectives, and of some classes, is completely situation-dependent. "Recent" means one thing in the context of superconductor theory and quite another in the context of geology. Fuzzy set theory (Zadeh, 1965) is one method for handling these problems. It assigns weights based on the degree to which the individual exhibits the attribute and allows the subjective definition of functions to describe concepts like "recent." In the third case, a particular exemplar may lack some of the attributes usually associated with a class or have different values for those attributes. A platypus lays eggs, for example, even though most mammals bear live young, while a dog that has lost one leg is still a dog. We may have to make a decision based on overall likeness rather than on a single set of defining attributes. This case is clearly a possible application for the kind of matching used in automatic classification, as described above.

In addition to inexact matching, classing can also be difficult because the classer has insufficient information. In this case, weights on class assignments, such as index terms, can be interpreted as probabilities (i.e., "given these clues, the probability of class x is y"). The difference between fuzzy and probabilistic approaches in information retrieval is explained by Bookstein (1986) in a particularly lucid fashion. Alternatively, weights on class assignments can be interpreted more broadly as certainty factors and can be computed by other methods than the probability calculus.

The simplest case of classing involves assigning an entity to a single class. This may be accomplished either by going down a list, trying each class to see if it fits the case in point, or by organizing and indexing the classification scheme in such a way that it may be searched more directly for candidate matches. The appropriateness of the search procedures depends on the size and complexity of the classification scheme. In a thesaurus, for example, indexers and searchers use the alphabetical arrangement to find an initial candidate term, and then move around in the vocabulary looking for more appropriate alternatives by following the references for synonyms and broader, narrower, or related terms. Similarly, in classing with the DDC, catalogers use the relative index to find the appropriate area of the classification scheme, and then browse within that area to find the most appropriate heading. They may also approach the scheme through the schedule synopses, which give, in effect, a table of contents for the scheme. The hierarchy of the scheme allows the catalogers to browse it at a high level, only going into detail in areas that seem likely to contain the target classes. The DDC, for example, has three synopses showing the broadest 10, 100, and 1000 classes.

The single assignment model is not always realistic. In many cases entities to be classed may have several correct assignments in a scheme. This case is particularly true of writings, which may discuss a number of different subjects, or even of medical patients or malfunctioning equipment that may, in fact, be suffering from several conditions simultaneously. In the worst case, the conditions may be interacting to confuse the attributes of the conditions to be classed.

Such complications lead to the establishment of rules and guidelines for classing that cover such factors as how to make a single assignment in a scheme when there are multiple possibilities, how to make multiple assignments when that is permitted, when to class at a narrower class than the one being considered, when to class at a broader class, and when to move to another part of the classification scheme to try alternative possibilities. These are the kinds of procedures that must be somehow incorporated into a KBS that classes.

CLASSIFICATION IN LIBRARIES

In the previous section we employed a number of examples drawn from the use of classification in libraries because we could assume that the reader is familiar with library use. In this section we will survey classification in libraries more systematically and at a more technical level.

While a number of points are made that relate directly to issues involved in applying expert systems to these activities, the reader knowledgeable about the construction and application of indexing languages and classification schemes may wish to omit this section or read it very selectively. The discussion of knowledge-based systems is continued in the section headed Knowledge-Based Systems and Classification.

Classification is, of course, fundamental to the description and organization of library materials for retrieval. However, because cataloging, classification, and the development of indexing languages are expensive activities and sometimes must be done by subject or language specialists, a relatively small amount of such work is now done in general libraries. Such institutions minimize in-house cataloging activities by utilizing cataloging data from the Library of Congress or commercial agencies, as well as that of libraries with which they have cooperative arrangements. Libraries with specialized collections are more likely to build their own systems for indexing or classing for internal use and for specialized databases to be vended to the wider information community. Searching, however, also heavily involves classification, as we shall see. In this form, classification is widely practiced by librarians and patrons alike.

Classifying in Libraries

In our approach to classification in libraries, we will maintain the distinction between classifying and classing developed above. As above, we will also begin here with classifying—in this instance, building classification structures to organize library materials. We will first concentrate on the best known products of this activity, the major classification schemes and alphabetical indexing languages. Some knowledge of these systems is essential for understanding how library catalogs and bibliographic databases are created and searched. This understanding, in turn, is a prerequisite for exploring the application of knowledge-based approaches to enhancing these processes.

The Library of Congress is the primary center for maintaining the indexing languages most generally used in the United States for describing library collections. These basic tools for organizing materials in general libraries—the LCSH, the Library of Congress Classification (LCC), and the DDC—are products of the late 19th or early 20th century, although they are continuously updated. They were invented to exploit the possibilities of card catalogs and open stacks. They strongly reflect that technology.

Modern languages take more account of mechanization and automation and are significantly different. Some of these languages have features that we will later associate with knowledge bases. They, therefore, merit attention, even though the more complex ones are not in common use. Large libraries are conservative in practice because of their huge investment in existing catalogs, and the Library of Congress, which is by far the largest library in the United States, is the major influence on cataloging in this country. This fact and the economics of standardization and cooperation inhibit the adoption of new approaches to subject access. As a result, more is understood about designing bibliographic databases for automated retrieval than is reflected in the library catalog systems commonly in use, whether manual or automated. On this ground as well, then, there is justification for reviewing types of indexing languages that are outside the mainstream of library practice in the United States.

Characteristics of indexing languages. To complete our understanding of classifying in libraries, we need to review how indexing languages are constructed. All indexing languages provide alphabetical access, classified access, or both to users. In fact, both elements are almost always present, but one is usually emphasized. For example, information in libraries has traditionally been organized to offer these two complementary approaches to the user. Classified arrangement is most often used in U.S. libraries for shelving. It facilitates browsing and serendipitous discovery, but the users need some means to find their way into the scheme and to see groupings that cannot be accommodated by the single linear sequence provided in a shelving scheme. This need is fulfilled for the public by the alphabetical subject catalog, which organizes subjects alphabetically, as its name implies. Our previous examples in Figures 15.1b and 15.4 illustrate this difference by showing first how subjects would appear on the shelves, and then how they would be grouped in the subject catalog. One facilitates browsing and the other, direct access through alphabetical look-up, a uniform and universally understood approach. Since the focus of this chapter is classification, we will begin our discussion with indexing languages that emphasize classification and then turn to alphabetical languages.

Classified retrieval systems. When classification is mentioned, the retrieval mechanism that springs to mind, at least for library users in the United States, is shelf classification—the organization of library materials by subject for browsing. This device provides a valuable but limited retrieval capability. On the other hand, in Europe, particularly in Great Britain, classified catalogs are fairly commonly used either instead of or in conjunction with shelf classification. In a classified catalog, the entries are arranged in classified order as on the shelves. However, since actual materials are not involved, only their surrogates, there may be multiple entries for the same item. These entries may either be multiple subjects pertaining to the item or different aspects of the same subject. A book on Georgian residential architecture might be entered, for example, under class numbers for both "the Georgian period in architecture" and "residential architecture." This file is accessed by an alphabetical index, which replaces the alphabetical subject catalog that is common in the United States and is closely coordinated with the classified file to complement the classified catalog. Figure 15.6 shows a classified catalog and its index.

Many advances in bibliographic classification theory in this century have been made in the context of classified catalog applications. Their greater flexibility and the problems involved in optimizing the form and content of their alphabetical indexes have motivated a number of innovations. Moreover, research in this area has helped change the perception that alphabetical systems and classified systems are competitive. This view was common until fairly recently. The current view of them as complementary systems is an important insight that

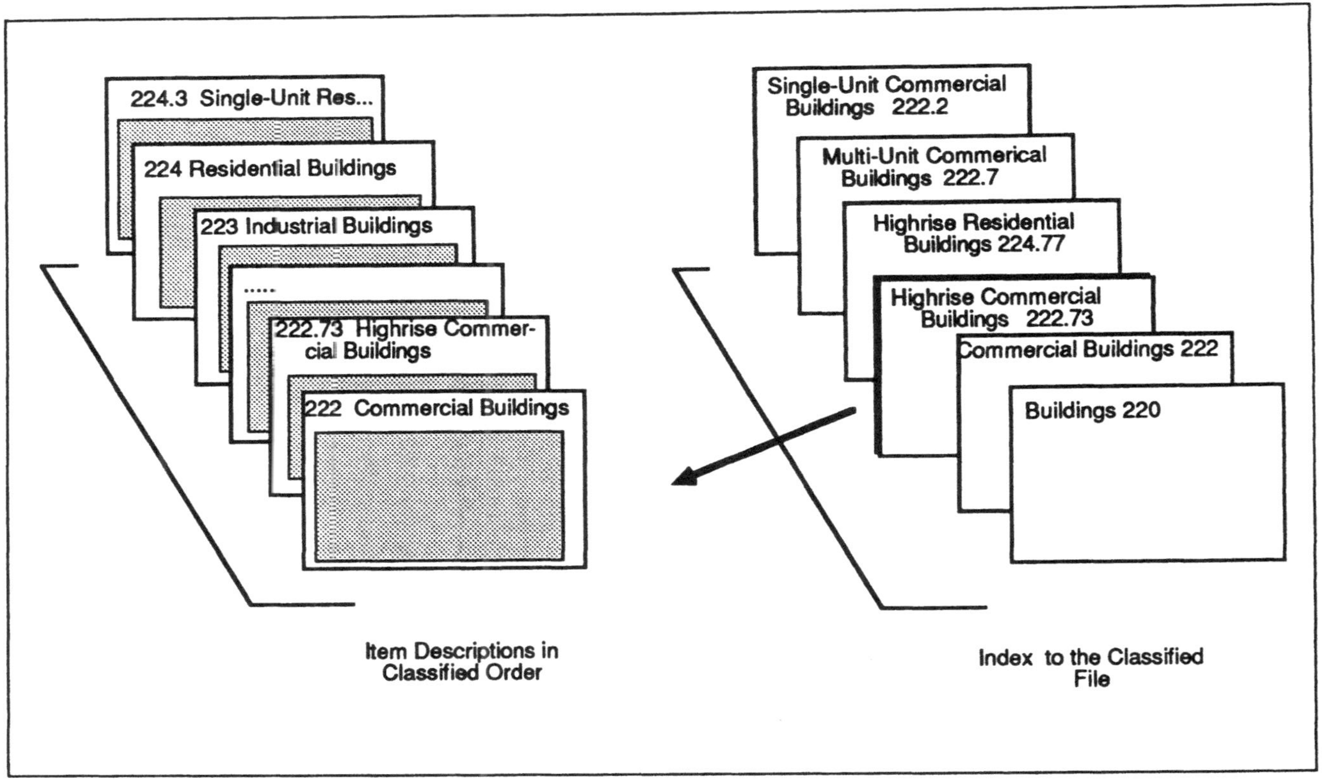

Figure 15.6. Classified Catalog.

allows us to see all indexing languages as a single family with different forms that have developed in response to different physical retrieval system media and different user requirements. The classified catalog comes closer to being a model for what online browsing by class number can be like than the much more familiar, but limited, shelving implementations. Classified card catalogs do not provide the flexibility of automated systems, but they certainly provide more options than are possible solely through the physical arrangement of library materials.

LCC: an enumerative classification scheme. Among the indexing languages used for shelf classification and classified catalogs, the simplest languages from a structural point of view are the enumerative classification systems like LCC. By enumerative we mean basically that all possible subjects are listed in the scheme. In contrast, when using synthetic languages, the cataloger builds new subjects by combining concepts from the classification schedules according to prescribed procedures. This distinction will be clearer when we have looked at synthetic languages in more detail.

LCC, like all other general or universal classification systems, is divided into major disciplines. Within each discipline there is quite a bit of hierarchical structure, as well as numerous form headings (periodicals, treatises, etc.) that conform to a prescribed pattern. However, in the case of the LCC the notation of the system, the code for filing the library materials, does not reflect any of this structure except the major discipline subdivisions. In effect, classes are simply numbered in sequence with numbers skipped to allow for expansion. TL1496 [Fluid dynamics in space] is not a subdivision of TL1490 [Radiation shielding of space vehicles]: It is only further down the schedule (U.S. Library of Congress, 1983, p. 71). They are, in fact, two coordinate classes under the heading "Environmental engineering in space. Space environment" which, as is typical of LCC, has no notation itself. TL1489 [Environmental engineering in space—General works] is the first class in the sequence. Also, in many cases, subjects are simply arranged alphabetically by topic, rather than being systematically organized. For instance, consider the following section of the schedules (U.S. Library of Congress, 1983, p. 74.):

TL709.5 [Details and parts of jet engines, A-Z]
.B6 Blades
.D5 Diffusers
.F8 Fuel Systems
.H42 Heat Generators etc.

In other words, the class number for "jet engine fuel systems" would be TL709.5F8. The arrangement is quite arbitrary. However, these features mean that the system is relatively easy to update and that the changes, while continuous, have been incremental.

Information in the classification schedules could definitely be of assistance to users of online catalogs if it could be properly displayed. For browsing purposes, the user need only find some access to schedules, whether through a class number that they have found or through keyword searching of the headings; however, proper presentation of the information requires considerable design effort (Cochrane, 1982).

LCC class numbers also cannot be decomposed into separate aspects or facets. For example, the notation TL1490 for "Radiation shielding of space vehicles" cannot be broken into identifiable notational components for "Radiation," "Shielding," "Space," and "Vehicles," as is possible in some of the synthetic schemes described below. The advantage of decomposition is that the facets can be reordered into in a new classified sequence. The user of a synthetic scheme in an online environment could select, for example, all items that had "space" as a component concept in their subject, and reorder them by the disciplines in the systematic order provided by the classification scheme (e.g., all books on space arranged by psychology, geography, social sciences, law, literature, medicine, technology, etc.). Of course, there is little motivation for this decomposition capability in a shelving scheme like LCC: The items in a collection can be shelved in only one sequence.

Since this ability to regroup items would be useful for online retrieval, it is interesting to consider whether LCC could be retrofitted, so to speak, to include it. There are some possible approaches, but the regrouping would have to be done on the verbal plane rather than the notational plane, to use, again, S. R. Ranganathan's terminology. That is, we could pull together all the classes that include the concept history, and then display them in class number order, but we would have to search the class descriptions for the word "history" and its synonyms, rather than searching using the notation representing the concept.

Moreover, it is not an easy task to discover all the classes that do in fact include any given concept. If we examine Figure 15.1b again, which is similar to the display one would see in a classification schedule without the definitions, instructions, and other information that would accompany many headings, we see that the headings associated with the class numbers are quite abbreviated. They are always scanned in context; therefore, the information carried by the headings in the hierarchy above the class in question is not ordinarily repeated for that class. For instance, the description for the entry "224.73 Townhouses" in Figure 15.1b does not tell us that this class number also incorporates the concept "residential buildings." Discovering which classes include which concepts is, therefore, nontrivial. In addition, the vocabulary is not constant from heading to heading, especially in a large classification scheme, and the LCC schedules occupy several linear feet of shelving. Such schemes are worked on in pieces over a long period of time, and vocabulary control is not regarded as particularly essential because the primary purpose of the language is to facilitate browsing, not alphabetical look-up of subjects.

On the other hand, the technology for creating complete headings from the abbreviated representations in classification schemes is well understood, since this same process is used to create the alphabetical indexes for classified catalogs as seen in the index entries in Figure 15.6. The best known method is chain indexing (Mills, 1955). Chain indexing, however, is a procedure, not an algorithm. It involves considerable judgment and considerable "tweaking." It might, however, be a suitable target process to automate, or partially automate, with a knowledge-based system. The feasibility of chain indexing the LCC was explored by Immroth (1971). Problems of adapting LCC and other classification schedules, which are written for indexers, for display to online users and the benefits of class number browsing are discussed in Cochrane (1982).

The Library of Congress is, of course, well aware of these problems. They are now planning to convert LCC to a machine-readable database from which the scheme would be generated for publication or for online use, as has already been done for the DDC. The background study for this project strongly recommends that extensive editing of the scheme be done at the time to make it more usable in an automated environment (Williamson, 1989).

Synthetic classification schemes: Faceted classification and the DDC. Unlike enumerative classification schemes, synthetic classification schemes do break subjects down into concepts. They represent each concept with a notational element, and then synthesize a class number by ordering the concepts in a prescribed sequence. In a purely synthetic scheme, the notation can be freely manipulated to reorder the file on any attribute. We will see examples of this feature presently. There are many levels of synthetic capability in existing schemes. In order to maximize the contrast with LCC, we will look first at faceted classification schemes, which are highly synthetic, and then at the much more familiar DDC, which also has synthetic features.

Faceted classification schemes. In faceted classification schemes, such as Ranganathan's Colon Classification (Ranganathan, 1963), the subjects in a field are analyzed to determine the patterns of conceptual roles that occur in them (e.g., agent, material), the most desirable facet to file under for a subject having several roles, and the preferred sequence of roles in filing. That is, where a single choice must be made, should a book about ceramic coatings for semiconductors be filed under semiconductors or under ceramics? Should a book about the history of semiconductors be shelved before or after a book about semiconductor manufacturing technology?

After this analysis has been performed, the concepts are organized by the roles they assume in the subject field. These roles are the facets of the faceted classification scheme. The terms associated with each role are called the foci of the facet. Each concept is then given a notation that reflects its facet assignment and the overall notation is worked out to produce the proper filing sequence. Figure 15.7a shows our familiar architecture example as a faceted scheme, while Figure 15.7b shows how a sample of items would be classed using the scheme.

Architecture

By architectural activity	
.	
Design	Bn
By class of structure	
Buildings	Cf
Landscapes	Cn
.	
.	
By physical configuration	
Townhouses	
Dd	
Garden Apartm'ts	Dn
Shopping Centers	Dp
Highrise Buildings	Dr
By size	
Single-unit	Gd
Multi-unit	Gn
By purpose	
Commercial	MF
Add the notation in Table 3 to Mf	
Industrial	
Mg	
Add the notation in Table 3 to M	
Residential	Mp
.	

Table 3: Businesses, Industries and Professions	
Wholesale	334
.	
Retail	335
.	
Communications	336
.	
Service Industries	337
.	
Restaurants	337.3
Professions	34
Medicine	345
.	
Sports & Entertainm't	35
.	
Mining	362
.	
Manufacturing	364
.	

Figure 15.7a. Partial Schedule for a Faceted Classification Scheme.

The class notation is usually put together "from the bottom up" as shown here so that the most specific aspect of the book will be its filing key. We will continue to, refer to strings of characters representing a synthesized class, such as "MpCfBn," as "class numbers" by convention, even when, as in this case, the code is purely alphabetical. The alphabetical codes here have no mnemonic significance. Letters are often used instead of (or with) numbers in classification notations because the alphabet provides a larger coding base, and, thus, more information in a shorter code.

As shown in Figure 15.7a, subjects are still usually treated within the framework of a particular discipline, as in traditional schemes. This context is created

Houses into Offices
MfGdDrBn

Highrise Architecture: Buildings and Landscape
MfGnDrBn

Restaurant Design
Mf337.3CfBn

Industrial Building Design
MgCfBn

Residential Architecture
MpCf Bn

Multi-Family Residential Architecture
MpGnCf Bn

Apartment Towers
MpGnDrCfBn

Figure 15.7b. Examples of Items Classed Using the Faceted Scheme.

either because the faceted classification is limited in scope or because the general scheme has already been broken into disciplines, such as Music or Medicine, and the facets have been derived within that subject area. The reason for this practice is simple: Different subjects have different facets that are important. Music is concerned with form, period, country of origin, school, instrumentation, acoustics, pedagogy, and the like. Medicine, on the other hand, is concerned with such facets as the attributes of the patient, the location of the disease, the disease itself, and its treatment. Time and place, which are so important in music history, play a much less significant role in medicine. There have been a number of attempts to devise universal faceting formulas, but these are more valuable as guidance to the classifier than as rigid principles (Foskett, 1971).

Some concepts are found in a wide variety of subject areas. These include primarily geographic locations, time periods, and bibliographic and literary forms. There are, however, many others, such as people by age, race, socio-economic group, or occupation that can recur in more limited contexts. Tables of such concepts, technically called tables of common isolates, can be created and referenced by a particular facet. They are not facets themselves because they have no predetermined role. "Table 3" in Figure 15.7a is such a table. These occupations could be used in a variety of facets throughout the schedules of a general classification scheme. A table of common isolates can reduce repetition and introduce a common notation for these frequently recurring concepts.

In a thesaurus, all component terms are listed alphabetically, and the indexing practice also is to assign a list of terms to a document without indicating how they are to be combined. In a faceted classification system, as we see in the examples, the terms are preassigned to facets (e.g., the term "Commercial" to the "By purpose" facet), and, by contrast, the order in which the terms are to be combined is specified. In classified catalogs, where an item may have a number of entries, this string of codes may be rotated to allow entry under different parts of the class number.

Within each facet, the terms are ordinarily arranged hierarchically, and the notation often reflects both the facet from which the term was drawn and its level in the hierarchy. Notations that carry information of this sort are called expressive notations. The notation in Figures 15.1 and 15.7 show hierarchy, for example, while the notation in Figure 15.7 also shows where concepts have been synthesized and which facets have been combined.

Expressive notation is informative; however, it is also often long and cumbersome. It is likely to be only a nuisance in shelving where most of the information is lost, since few users can "read" the class numbers. However, in an automated system, the information carried by the notation can be exploited to allow the user to move around in the hierarchy, to create new orderings of the items, or to allow the system to show the role of each term in a document description so that, for instance, oxygen as a product of a chemical reaction is not mistaken for an input.

In Figure 15.7a the facet structure is arranged to duplicate the arrangement in Figure 15.1b, which groups materials according to whether they are about commercial, residential, or industrial buildings, but scatters material on, for instance, buildings of particular physical configurations, like highrises. With a faceted classification, we can easily change this ordering. In the first place, we can retrieve all material on concepts such as *highrises* or *restaurants* wherever they occur because they have a specific notation that we can search on. Moreover, by changing the order of the facets in Figure 15.7a so that, for instance, buildings "by purpose" and buildings "by physical configuration" switch places, we can cause the items on highrise buildings to file together, although items on residential and commercial architecture will now, of course, be scattered. These goals can be accomplished without the user having to understand the notation because it can be entirely internal to the system (Travis, 1982).

Faceted schemes also have more flexibility to express new subjects than the enumerative schemes because the cataloger can combine existing concepts to create new classes, even though the framework is still fairly rigid. As an example of rigidity, concepts cannot assume roles with which they were not associated at the time the system was devised. For example, in one early faceted scheme for education, teachers could evaluate students, but students could not evaluate teachers because students were always conceptualized as the recipients of the action. Terminology for new concepts still has to be added continually. The degree of structure, such as the preassignment of terms to categories, makes the system relatively inflexible compared to an alphabetical language and difficult to update whenever some radical shift takes place in a subject field, as the above example about the students suggests.

To clarify the concepts introduced relating to the components and microstructure of languages Figure 15.8 illustrates the differences between subjects, concepts, terms, headings, roles, facets, foci, classes, and class numbers. It reveals (a) how subjects are broken into concepts, which may (optionally) be mapped into predetermined roles and (b) how the concepts and roles are mapped to the four major kinds of indexing languages: enumerative classification schemes, synthetic classification schemes, alphabetical subject heading lists, and indexing thesauri.

Since pure faceted classifications are not in common use, this discussion would be academic but for two important links to the main thrust of our discussion. First, the notions associated with faceted classification are pertinent to our pending review of the DDC, which is, of course a very widely used system. Secondly, the notion of a subject being made up of predetermined facets is virtually identical to the "frame" construct used for knowledge representation in some KBSs.

The Dewey Decimal classification. The DDC is in wide use all over the world and is updated and reissued in a new edition about every seven years with substantial changes. Indeed, the Lake Placid Club Foundation, which maintains it in conjunction with the Library of Congress Dewey Office, regularly introduces "Phoenix" schedules as part of the new editions in which outdated sections of the scheme are completely reworked. These facts are both strengths and weaknesses of the scheme. On the one hand, the DDC has been able to grow and to stay acceptably current for a hundred years, which is remarkable considering how structured it is and how much the structure of knowledge has changed in that interval. On the other hand, with each change libraries must either reclassify extensively, stay with an older edition, or temporize in some way. All three

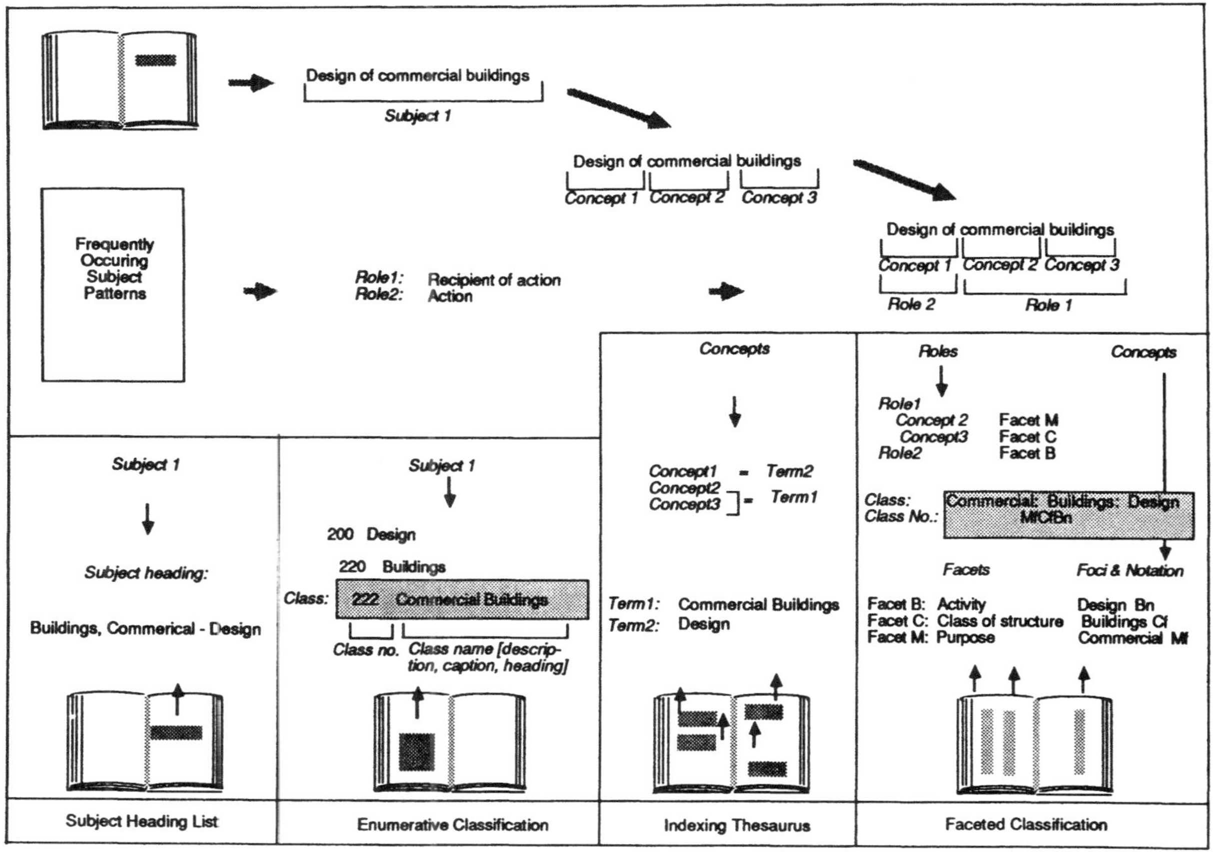

Figure 15.8. Indexing Language Terminology.

"solutions" are common. As a result, while the scheme is widely used, there is considerable variation from library to library in how it is applied, far more so than with LCC.

The DDC has always had certain features that have been exploited and extended by subsequent classification theorists, whose ideas and experience, in turn, have been fed back into the scheme and influenced certain aspects of its development. Expressive notation and synthesis, called "number building" in the DDC, are two such features. Users of the DDC are very familiar with tables of bibliographic forms, dates, and places, where each has a standard code. These are tables of common isolates in the sense defined above. The DDC has gradually extended their scope and use. Similarly, the literature schedules are highly synthetic. Experienced Dewey users have always been able to "read" many Dewey numbers. In addition, while there are many inconsistencies, the DDC notation basically reflects the scheme hierarchy: that is, 110 is a subclass of 100.

The difference between the DDC and the faceted schemes is one of degree. In the DDC there is a base number that may express several facets with some additional synthesis possible, rather than full faceting. The cataloger is usually limited in the number of facets of the subject that can be expressed. The purpose for which the DDC, like LCC, was designed was to group materials on the shelves, not to indicate the detailed subject of the item in the class number. Moreover, while various numbers are permanently assigned to concepts (e.g., 73 for the United States), this assignment is not one to one. The number 73 can occur in many contexts unrelated to the concept of United States. The digit 0 is generally used to indicate that something has been added to the base number, but it carries no information as to what type of synthesis occurred.

In a faceted scheme, on the other hand, there is usually either a unique facet divider for each facet or a unique code for each concept that disambiguates each part of the notation. Faceted class numbers are therefore simpler to break down into their component parts for purposes of creating new groupings not shown by the basic shelf ordering and can be more fully expressive of the subject.

Alphabetical indexing languages. We will not dwell on alphabetical languages here, because they primarily manifest the problems we have already discussed with a different emphasis. In alphabetical indexing languages, the focus is on the direct access offered by the alphabetical approach, rather than on the useful sequence of classes provided by a classification scheme. Anyone constructing an alphabetical language will have to lay out at least a partial hierarchy in order to control the reference structure. Some languages are even a conscious joining of the two approaches, with a classified display showing the thesaurus term hierarchies and an alphabetical section that provides an index to the classified listing but also carries information about term relationships that are not hierarchical, including synonyms for the terms used in the classification. For a thorough discussion of alternative layouts for thesauri and other indexing languages, see Soergel (1974).

Because of its prominence, we will now briefly discuss the LCSH. An extensive discussion of this complex system is contained in Chan (1978). In its older editions, the LCSH featured many multiterm headings showing a wide variety of structures and often inverted multiterm headings so that they would file under the prominent concept to improve the collocative features of the catalog, for example, "California, Southern" vs. "Southern California." Moreover, until the most recent edition (U.S. Library of Congress, Subject Cataloging Division, 1988), the list also did not distinguish directly and clearly between broader or narrower terms and related terms, although it was possible for catalogers to infer which were which. LCSH also made and makes very heavy use of subdivisions—some customized to the subject and some for general use. In the more recent editions, considerable effort has been made to move to standardized subdivisions, where possible, and to present them as tables, in a fashion that is directly analogous to the tables of subdivisions and common isolates in the DDC and other classification schemes. There has also been some move toward less complex headings and direct entry, that is entering a phrase in its natural-language order. Direct entry makes it easier for users to find a heading because they do not have to guess how it might have been inverted, but does not necessarily group headings in a useful way. Seen another way, heading inversion introduced another level of classification into the catalog over and above the broader/narrower/related term reference structure. In moving away from this type of classification toward a more strictly alphabetical sequence and in the explicit labeling of broader, narrower, and related terms, the later editions are adopting practices closer to those of indexing thesauri. As with LCC, however, the age of the scheme, its size and complexity, and its very wide-spread use, have made it difficult to introduce radical changes.

For alphabetical languages in an automated environment, the actual wording that is used to represent a concept is not as important as it is in printed lists and card catalogs. In these media, the users must find the preferred form of a heading in order to find information about an item, and moving around in the catalog is physically inconvenient. It is best, therefore, if the user's first guess is correct. In this environment the user is always conscious of the existence of preferred forms, and constructors of indexing languages spend a great deal of effort deciding on the best wording for an entry.

This aspect of vocabulary control loses some of its prominence in the much more flexible environment of an online system, although choosing preferred forms of headings may still be a useful practice. What does continue to be important is the display of the relations among the terms, including synonymy—

thesaurus information in Roget's sense. It is not as necessary to choose a single term to express a concept as it is to link all the terms that might be used for that purpose and to show the relations among the conceptual groupings.

Looking at the other side of the question, the notion that the terminology of the headings is not important seems untenable, given the technology of the last half of the 20th century. We have seen several circumstances under which classification headings need to be turned into searchable alphabetical headings, such as for creating scheme indexes, creating indexes to classified catalogs, and exploiting the information in the classification scheme for online searching.

To conclude classification in alphabetical languages, we would be remiss if we did not look at one further language type. Up to this point we have left the impression that alphabetical subject languages were either subject heading lists with precoordinated strings of terms or thesauri, and that they include no relationships between the terms other than broader term/narrower term, and related term. In fact, some postcoordinate indexing languages have always allowed capabilities like those of faceted classification in that they have permitted the indexer to tag the role of the term and/or to show which concepts were linked together in a document to form a single subject. In recent years, another form of indexing language with close ties to faceted classification has evolved, originally for book catalog use. These "string languages" assign the concepts in a subject to a fixed set of general roles and order them according to a prescribed formula in a way very similar to the way that the facets were combined in Figures 15.7b and 15.8. These ordered concepts or strings are then rotated in a quasi-algorithmic fashion to make a number of entries for each subject under the significant concepts in the heading. Figure 15.9a shows a subject transformed into a string with the various headings that would be derived from it. Figure 15.9b compares string languages to the other types of languages we have considered. PRECIS, the best known string language, which is used at the British Library and by the British National Bibliography, is described in Richmond (1981).

Constructing indexing languages. The above discussion has already given us some clues as to the processes involved in building indexing languages. The different types of languages suggest many of the variables to be resolved in the design: the relative weight of alphabetical vs. classified arrangement; the degree of synthesis to be provided; the specificity of the language; the amount of information to be provided in the notation, if any; the alternative access methods to be available; and the forms of headings to be allowed.

In this section we will look at some other topics such as the sources used for a new indexing language and the structuring of term relationships. These two aspects have particularly close analogs in the knowledge engineering process. We cannot treat this topic in much depth here, however. There are several major and excellent books devoted to index language construction, such as those by Soergel (1974) and Lancaster (1986).

Subject: Effect of highrise buildings on neighborhood crime rates

Coded string:

Passive system:	Neighborhoods
Up-reading connective	in
Part	Rate
Difference	Crime
Action	Effect
Up-reading connective	on
Down-reading connective	of
Agent	Buildings
Difference	Highrise

Index entries:
1. Neighborhoods. Effect of highrise buildings on crime rate.
2. Crime rate in neighborhoods. Effect of highrise buildings.
3. Highrise buildings. Effect on crime rate.
4. Buildings. Effect on crime rate.

Figure 15.9a. Coded String with Example Headings.

INDEXING LANGUAGE CHARACTERISTICS	LANGUAGES				
	String Lang.	Enum. Class.	Faceted Class.	Subjct Headg	Indexng Thesrus
Classes synthesized by classifier	no	partly	no	partly	no
Classes synthesized by classer	yes	partly	yes	partly	no
Classes synthesized only by searcher	no	no	no	no	yes
Translates subjects as a whole	yes	yes	yes	yes	no
Isolates concepts	yes	no	yes	no	yes
Term roles indicated in headings/nos.	yes	no	yes	yes	infreq.
Terms/foci pre-assigned to roles	no	yes	yes	no	no
Notation used	no	yes	yes	no	no
Permutation of terms/facets possible	yes	no	yes	no	no
Designed for exhaustive indexing	poss	no	poss	no	yes
Designed for online retrieval	no	no	no	no	yes

Figure 15.9b. Comparison of String Languages with Other Indexing Language Types.

When a new indexing language is to be constructed, an important issue is the sources and methods that will be used to gather terminology and to make decisions regarding preferred terminology and the identification of term relationships. For instance, should the classifiers simply examine the items to be indexed and build the vocabulary from their content, or should they, at the opposite extreme, only consult reference sources and build a system that represents the generally accepted structure of knowledge in the area, fitting the documents into this framework? There is, of course, no single answer to this question.

On the one hand, the structure of knowledge changes so quickly, particularly in the sciences, that the major problem for librarians is to build retrieval systems that are not immediately obsolete. Moreover, many bibliographies and databases exist precisely to provide interdisciplinary or mission-oriented coverage that is very collection-specific and does not conform to, for example, the structure of university curricula or encyclopedias. For these reasons, complete reliance on reference sources is not possible or advisable.

On the other, there are many relationships among concepts that are relatively permanent and, whether permanent or temporary, should be correctly represented. Particularly in classification schemes it is very important to have an overview of the area being represented that goes beyond the information in an initial set of documents. Such a set can only be a sample of what is to come. Indeed, without some clear knowledge of the scope, purpose, and coverage of a scheme, a representative sample for initial analysis cannot even be collected. An intellectually respectable representation of the domain of an indexing language thus requires sources of expertise beyond the documents being classed, including other indexing languages, reference books, and human experts.

Classifiers often begin by collecting as many terms as possible from the sources mentioned above, noting their source and their relations to other terms that the source provides. However, at some point they must begin the process of producing order out of chaos. This includes grouping synonymous terms, and choosing the word or phrase that will represent the resulting concept. Since there are few true synonyms, the classifiers must make fundamental decisions about the degree of discrimination that the language will allow its users.

In building a thesaurus, the classifiers must also determine whether a concept that is usually expressed with more than one word will be divided into several terms or left as a phrase. Reasons for keeping a concept name as a phrase include those cases where the words taken separately do not mean the same thing as the phrase, for example, "heavy metal" when applied to rock groups. Other grounds include the case where each word in a phrase has a very general meaning, and an unmanageable number of documents might be indexed under the terms individually; however, when taken together, their meaning is quite specific. Examples include phrases like operating system, or, to turn to our previous examples, commercial buildings. Another case is where one word is used metaphorically, as in "butterfly nuts." Yet another counter indication for dividing a phrase is the presence of a term, like nuts, that has many different meanings.

Once the terms or classes have been defined, analyzing their relations in order to create references among them is a complex task. Even determining which terms are broader and narrower terms of a given term is by no means straightforward. It is easy to become confused between generic/specific relations and part/whole relationships, quasigeneric relationships, and many others that are not legitimate broader-term/narrower term links. Consider architecture and design (part/whole) or commercial buildings and highrise building (quasigeneric/specific) from our previous examples. On the other hand, it is also easy to forget relations that should be quite obvious. For instance, one might link guide dogs to aids for the handicapped because the term was found in that context, while forgetting to make the link to dogs. The larger and older the scheme, the more difficult it is to keep track of these possibilities when new terms are added. Establishing other kinds of links is even more difficult and judgmental. Methods such as semantic factoring (guide dogs = dogs + blind persons + guidance) help make the linking process more systematic.

To give a further flavor to the classifier's job, Figure 15.10 lists a few of the questions that occurred to the author in the course of devising the "simple" examples of indexing languages used in this chapter. Others have no doubt occurred to the reader.

Maintaining indexing languages. Before leaving our discussion of indexing languages, we must mention an over-arching problem for languages and systems developed with them: namely, obsolescence of headings and terminology and the problems of coping with updates.

For our purposes, there are really two cases of obsolescence: those where the name of the concept has been changed, for instance, "Great War, 1914-1918" to "World War I," and those where the structure of the concepts and their relationships require updating. While the first case may seem to pose few difficulties, the second case requires reindexing or reclassifying part of the collection. Even the former sort of change is not easy in a large catalog.

Automation will eventually take care of the concept name-change problem, but conventional techniques cannot do much in the case in which the materials must be reexamined in order to be properly classed in the new scheme. These cases can range from simple instances where headings are newly subdivided to cases in which whole discipline areas are completely reworked. This problem primarily affects large research libraries that keep older materials permanently. There is some question, for instance, not only about whether biology books written in the 1920s can be reclassed according to the current paradigms in biological science, but even about whether they should be, given that their primary use may be by historians of science. In any event, whatever the

FIGURE 1	FIGURE 2 (con.)
1. Are commercial, industrial, and residential (and religious, government, etc.) the classes of buildings I want as the fundamental categories? 2. Is single-unit and multi-unit a fine enough division? What happens to duplexes, triplexes, apartment houses: Are they "physical configurations?" 3. Is a notation with 10 slots on each level enough? What happens if there are more than 10 classes? **FIGURE 2** 1. Should "Commercial Buildings" and "Industrial Buildings" be broken into "Commerce," "Industry," and "Buildings?" If so, what happens to "Residential Buildings?" 2. Is "highrise" one word or two words? 3. Why are "Single-Unit Buildings" and "Multi-Unit Buildings" listed as NTs to "Buildings" rather than to "Commercial Buildings?" 4. Why is "Design" an RT rather than an NT to "Architecture?" 5. Why isn't "Buildings" an NT of "Architecture?" 6. Why is "Shopping Centers" an NT under "Commercial Buildings" while "Highrise Buildings" is an RT?	7. Do "constructed terms" like "Single-Unit Building" and "Multi-Unit Building" that seem quite natural in the tree display in Figure 1a make any sense in an alphabetical language? Would anyone who was searching ever think of them, as compared, for example, to a commonly used term like *single-family house (home, residence)*? Will someone looking up *single-family house* see "Single-Unit Building?" Do I need these concepts at all? **FIGURE 4** 1. Should it be "Commercial Buildings" or "Buildings, Commercial?" Do I want all the "Buildings" headings together to facilitate browsing at the cost of an "unnatural" indirect heading structure? **FIGURE 8** 1. Do I really want the concepts to combine (file) in this order? 2. If I indicate special purpose buildings by using Table 3, am I really going to be able to express concepts like *stadium, theater, service station.* etc. in a satisfactory way? Is it enough simply to include such things under commercial buildings for sports and entertainment or retail sales? What about the difference between a medical office building and a hospital? Can I distinguish them? Do I need to distinguish them? 3. How am I going to be sure that there is a one-to-one correspondence between concepts and notation?

Figure 15.10. Fourteen Questions about Four Examples.

intellectual merits of reindexing or reclassing, most libraries cannot afford to do it at present because it is very labor-intensive. As a general rule, however, the less structured the language, the easier it is to update. The problems of updating an alphabetical indexing language that incorporates a minimal amount of classification are an order of magnitude less than the problems of revising a highly structured language like the DDC.

Obviously these practical problems involved in updating retrieval systems have a great effect on the user. If outdated terminology has not been changed, or at least cross-referenced, the user may have great difficulty finding the term the system uses for the concept he has in mind. He may be puzzled, and, indeed, often offended by the headings in old catalogs that reflect the social values of the time at which they were created. Much has been made in recent years of racist and sexist headings or otherwise offensive headings (Berman, 1971). A few examples from a supplement to the LCSH (U.S. Library of Congress, 1984, xvi) show that as of that date (1982) there were still socially outmoded headings in the list (Figure 15.11).

In addition, materials may be scattered by heading changes or classed under headings that do not really match the subject of the item very well. Users may find that even fairly recent material relating to a topic of current interest, such as life styles, cannot be found through the catalog because the concept does not exist.

Indexing languages—conclusion. In short, while the different indexing languages support different technologies and facilitate different kinds of searching to varying degrees, the notions underlying indexing languages apply across all types. The emphasis on various elements—vocabulary control, the analysis of semantic or pragmatic relationships, the degree of precoordination, the use and expressiveness of notation—vary with the application. Moreover, these classification systems are forms of knowledge representation, and they have much in

Old	New
Altar boys	Acolytes
Divorcees	Divorced women
French-Canadian dialect	French language - Canada
Jews – Rites and ceremonies	Judaism – Customs andpractices

Figure 15.11. ***LCSH*** **Heading Updates (1982).**

common with the other forms of knowledge representation now being developed for KBSs.

Classing in Libraries

Classing is an essential activity both to searching library retrieval systems and to creating them. In this section we will consider both activities and their relationship.

Retrieving by using classification. The exact procedures used to search retrieval systems vary considerably with the type of system, differences that we will presently consider. However, some parts of the search process are constant across most search situations—except, perhaps, shelf browsing—and are very similar to the operations performed by indexers or catalogers in adding material to a retrieval system. The process includes the following steps:

1. Conceptualizing the subject of the search
2. Conceptualizing an approach or strategy for finding materials on a subject
3. Translating the queries that implement the strategy into the vocabulary and query structures of the retrieval system
4. Evaluating the results
5. Modifying the query to improve the search.

Each step involves classing operations and interactions with the system.

Search operations in general. Oddy (1977) and others have pointed out that one of the most difficult things in searching is not to formulate a formal query, but to define what will satisfy it. That is, the less a user knows about an area, the harder it is to have a clear conceptualization of what one is seeking. The classification structure of the indexing language can provide a means for browsing in the system. In conjunction with retrieved relevant and irrelevant documents, it can help users move around in the system and sharpen the focus of their search.

Experienced users develop a strategy for finding materials. This strategy may range from a decision to browse through a subset of the collection to a set of decisions covering all aspect of a search. These might include databases to be searched; initial probes to be devised; the order in which information-gathering procedures are to be carried out; the types of vocabulary to be used in the search requests (free text or controlled or some combination of the two); and methods for broadening or narrowing a search depending upon the results of initial explorations. By free text we mean that each word in a title, abstract, subject heading, or other descriptive information associated with the document can be searched. When the full document is available for free-text searching, the resulting procedure is called full-text searching.

When a collection has been indexed using an indexing language, the classification structure also helps translate concepts from the user's formulation of an information need to the language of the system. Both the synonym references and the other references between terms (BT,NT,RT) help users match their terminology to the system's usage. That is, if users can find some match for the concepts in their queries in the retreived system, the system can help guide them to the most appropriate heading or headings.

Using classification in different retrieval environments. In considering further how classification is used in retrieval, it is necessary to make some distinctions between manual systems, online catalogs using the indexing systems originally devised for card catalogs, and online database systems with indexing that takes automated retrieval into account.

Manual systems. In a small general library, patrons may use an overview of the DDC to find the section of the library they wish to browse. In a large collection, particularly where patrons have a relatively fixed information need, using the subject catalog both as source of references in itself and as a guide to the stacks is essential. The patron uses classification actively in moving around in the catalog and passively in browsing the shelves.

Automated versions of manual systems. Moving next to online catalogs whose databases are still conventional subject cataloging and classification data, the situation is already somewhat more complex in that a number of new options can be provided still utilizing conventional technology. These include the following extensions:

- Creating new ad hoc groupings of materials by searching on the keywords in subject headings and subheadings that were not filed together in the catalog. For instance, one could find all of the headings that contained a particular geographic place name in them, even though in the catalog the place name might sometimes have been the main heading and, at other times, a subdivision. For example, books about the history of Arlington, Virginia, in a catalog compiled using the LCSH would be listed under "Arlington, Va.—History." However, a book about the Iwo Jima Memorial in Arlington would be under the name of the memorial with Arlington, Va. only as a modifier, for example, "Iwo Jima Memorial, Arlington, Va." Finally, a book about tourism in Arlington would be under "Tourist trade—Virginia—Arlington." A free-text search facility allows all these items to be brought together by someone needing to search comprehensively for information on the area.
- Browsing through the collection in class number order, which will show all the materials in the collection, not just those that happen to be on the shelves on a particular day or those that happen to be suitable for open shelving. Browsing through the classification schedules themselves is also possible and can help the user find new areas of the collection to search. Finally, where the

classing has been planned for online use, there can also be multiple class numbers for the same item, which helps overcome the principal limitation of shelving as a retrieval system.

Allowing manipulations that are extensions of the cycling procedure described above. Online systems can facilitate search expansion (or contraction) with special browsing aids, such as those proposed by Oddy. He proposes to allow the user to browse by searching on the characteristics of items that the user has found to be of interest, such as those by the same author or those indexed under the same subject heading. In addition, online systems can use basic information about the co-occurrence of subject headings and class numbers to compute statistical measures of relatedness to generate ranked lists of alternative terms or class numbers so users can find materials relevant to information already located (Doszkocs, 1983). For example, a user might be searching under a subject heading like "Hotels—Fires and fire prevention." The system might then suggest the class numbers of the books with that subject heading where there might be additional materials of interest that had not been indexed under that heading. It can also suggest subject headings that have been used with "Hotels—Fires and fire prevention" that are pertinent, but not cross-referenced from that heading, such as "Fire sprinklers," "Inflammable textiles," or the names of particular hotels where there have been major fire disasters.

Online storage and retrieval systems. When the database has been exhaustively indexed or classed using a modern thesaurus, online systems permit some additional uses of classification in the search strategy. Whereas traditional library subject heading lists precombine terms into subjects (e.g., "Computers—History"), modern indexing languages used to index databases generally keep combination to a minimum. They would use two terms ("Computers" and "History") to express the subject that would be combined into a single heading in the traditional library subject catalog. A searcher approaching a subject in such an environment must break it down into its component facets, each represented by a term. Such a decomposition is always required, followed by the construction of a query from the components. For example, "Computers AND History," where AND is a Boolean operator that requires that both terms be present in a document in order for it to be retrieved. However, the request is now ambiguous. Whereas the original heading clearly meant the history of computers, this formulation could also retrieve material about the use of computers in historical research or the impact of computers on the history of civilization.

In addition, some searchers use their knowledge of the role or function of each term, that is, of the relations among them, to build their search strategy (Fidel, 1982). For example, a user might be looking for material on reinforcing highrise buildings against earthquakes. There is an action (reinforcing), an active system (earthquakes), and the recipient of the action (highrise buildings) specified in this request. Some searchers aiming at high recall (i.e., finding as many relevant items as possible, even if many that are not relevant are also retrieved) would identify highrise buildings as the principal topic and begin a search by compiling a comprehensive set of items on this concept. They would then narrow the search by adding terms representing the other facets after they had discovered the best way to represent these concepts in the system's indexing language.

We see a clear trend that increasing levels of automation and of information description provide the user with more options and more potential to explore the library's resources. If the user is not given a great deal more assistance than is provided in manual systems, the user's effectiveness with the "better" system may be even worse than it is with manual ones (Janosky, Smith, & Hildreth, 1987). Automatic systems that still usually show only a few lines on a screen make it much more difficult, in fact, for the user to gain a comprehensive view of a library's collections than do manual ones, unless they are very carefully engineered.

Systems without indexing languages. Many informal systems have no indexing language or, at most, simple lists of folder subjects. Some systems rely on uncontrolled keywords that are supplied by the authors of the items in them, or that are simply extracted from the text by some means.

There are, also, formally designed retrieval systems with no controlled vocabulary. Even though their relationship to classification in libraries is tangential, there are two major classes of such systems that must, at least, be mentioned. The first are the free- and full-text retrieval systems. To implement free- or full-text searching, all words in the parts of the document that are searchable are indexed except certain words that may be placed on a stop list. The user can combine terms, not only using the Boolean AND, OR and NOT operators, but also such devices as proximity operators (term x and term y within the same paragraph, sentence, etc.).

On the one hand in these systems, the user no longer has to second-guess the indexer, but on the other, the user has to second-guess all of the authors. For example, all four of the "documents" in Figure 15.5 are clearly about aspects of real estate development in the United States. Yet, the term *United States* appears in none of them, and the term *US* appears in only one (Document 4). In the first two documents we know that they concern the United States because they mention particular towns, cities, or regions of the country. An indexing language that allows a user to automatically expand a search for *United States* to encompass all its subdivisions can solve this problem.

However, in the third document, there really is no direct word-level clue that this document concerns the United States. As a matter of world knowledge and of the pragmatics of where the article might have appeared (a magazine in the United States), we assume that "the new tax laws" means the new tax laws in the United States. But there really is no way that a user can retrieve this article as being about real estate investment in the United States using only word searching. As things stand at the present, unless a human indexer had assigned the heading representing the concept United States to that document, it could never be retrieved under that concept. The user, instead, would have to look at all the documents about investment and manually select those that were about the United States in order to find this one.

The more abstract the concept being searched, the more difficult it becomes to search without human indexing. For instance, initial findings by Fidel (1987, personal communication) in her most comprehensive studies of searcher behavior to date, reveal that search intermediaries searching engineering databases almost never use controlled vocabulary, even when such indexing is available, while searchers in the humanities rarely use free text.

In passing we mention that, while the examples in Figure 15.5 were made up by the author, they were not made up to illustrate this particular point. From the point of view of this discussion, they are simply ordinary text passages that have not been manipulated or contrived. The problem was accidental, but it is an exact replication of what actually happens in free text.

Of more theoretical interest are the systems based on the statistical properties of word occurrences in documents. In Figure 15.5, which illustrated classification based on word co-occurrences, documents are represented as vectors. The distance between these vectors can be computed. If we now think of a query as simply another piece of text, which can be represented in exactly the same way as a document, we can compute the difference between the query and all the items in the collection, retrieving those that fall above a certain threshold. In practice, to make such an operation more feasible, the documents are clustered as they are in Figure 15.5, and a vector is computed that is representative of the cluster. The initial matching is then done hierarchically against the representative vectors, and then against the individual documents in the appropriate clusters.

These systems, which are completely automatic, represent a different line of system development from that common in libraries today. They have not had a significant practical impact on libraries or commercial retrieval systems even though they have been in the laboratory for more than 20 years, and it is difficult to predict whether they will. Nonetheless, over time researchers in this area have evolved an impressive body of theoretical and experimental results. Many of these researchers, for instance Bruce Croft (Croft & Lewis, 1987), are also experimenting with knowledge-based extensions to this technology. However, the relationship of these systems to classification is more elusive than that of the other systems we have discussed, since they are not based on the semantic analysis of term relations, but rather solely on the distribution of words in text.

Searching and system information. When users match subjects against a subject heading in a catalog or a term in a thesaurus, they are classing their requests in exactly the same way a subject cataloger classes an item, but often with far less knowledge of the system. Catalogs, indexes, and online databases are constructed using tools and procedures. However, the user rarely sees these tools or the policies that support their use. Rather, they see only their products.

Patrons and intermediaries have little access to the indexing and abstracting rules that were used to create online databases or even the library catalogs and hard-copy bibliographies, unless they have specialized training from the creator of the data. In short, all retrieval systems, both for organizing library collections and for organizing bibliographic databases, have indexing and classing rules, and these rules are usually a great mystery and great source of confusion to library patrons.

Classing with indexing languages. Manual classing with indexing languages is a multistage procedure. First, the classer must determine which concepts from a document are to be represented in the document indexing, classification, or subject cataloging. Second, the classer must match the identified subjects with the terms or classes in the indexing languages. In some cases the process stops at that point, but in others the indexer must then carry out various types of synthesis, such as the addition of subheadings or the concatenation of facets either on the verbal or the notational plane.

Determining subjects. Of all the operations that are carried on in libraries, the one that is the most difficult to describe is the process by which a classer decides that a piece of text or equivalent unit in other media is about a particular subject and, in some cases, the weight that one subject has relative to others. The most extensive philosophical analysis of this process was carried out by Wilson 20 years ago (Wilson, 1968). From this analysis he concluded that "being about something" in a library system probably meant something akin to being the kind of writing that the system's categorization processes assign to this heading, rather than having some more abstract interpretation.

Indexing based on the identification of the principal subjects of a work is paramount in systems that must select only one, or at most four of five, headings or class numbers to describe an entire book or other complex item. It also comes into play in many forms of exhaustive indexing (i.e., indexing that attempts to cover all topics discussed) where an effort is usually still made to determine the overall thrust of a journal article or other item that is being indexed in depth. This practice ensures that the primary subjects are well covered.

The selection of significant words or phrases from a text within the local context of a sentence or paragraph is a somewhat lower-level cognitive activity than is a decision about the subject of large pieces of text. This kind of selection is practiced in exhaustive indexing of text. While it is not found in manual systems, such as card catalogs and printed bibliographies in libraries, it is widely used in online bibliographic databases and back-of-the-book indexes. Even here, however, some sophisticated, intuitive language processing is taking place. This processing includes the ability to recognize noun phrases, synonyms, the referents of pronouns and elliptical expressions, and the relative importance of concepts. Recognizing the relative importance of concepts means being able to recognize that a concept is occurring in a passage of text at far beyond an expected rate or to recognize the technical use of common terms, such as spin or charm in physics.

The ultimate extension of this type of indexing is the relatively trivial mechanical process of indexing all of the words in a text, or all of the words except some selected "stop words" to form a concordance or index to all word occurrences. Laboratory work has indicated that term weighting is an important factor in improving retrieval, but most commercial implementations do not include it. Gerard Salton at Cornell is especially associated with the advocacy of term weighting in documents and queries, like that previously shown in Figure 15.5. Such weighting allows retrieved documents to be ranked and allows queries to be adjusted by automatically altering the weights on the query terms. Salton and his students have published very widely on these topics (Salton, Fox, & Vorhees, 1985).

There has been far more concentration to date on remedying indexer inconsistency at the level of choosing terminology for concepts, as described below, than at the level of selecting the concepts. However, indexing policies and quality assurance checks, check lists, and suggestions to the indexer of terms used to index other similar documents in the past can have some effect.

Matching concepts. In indexing with an indexing language, one has to translate the selected subjects or isolated concepts into the language. Entry vocabulary, references, alternate displays, and other devices are meant to help the classer arrive at the best possible representation. This involves far more than matching words. In fact, relying on word matching is a major source of error. In any general scheme there are terms with many possible homonyms, like bridge or bank, that may have a completely different meaning in the context of the indexing language from the one the indexer had in mind. The broader the coverage of the language, the worse the problem.

In a previous example we noted that a highrise building could be discussed from several points of view including its architectural design, its construction, its community impact, or as a topic in literature or the arts. In a particular scheme highrise buildings might be listed as a specific entry only under architectural design. However, if an item is about the effect of highrise buildings on crime rates, then it needs to be classed under the most specific heading available in sociology, in order to put it in the proper context. It needs to be classed there even if there is no heading specifically for highrise buildings in that schedule, and the exact words appear elsewhere in the scheme. A little reflection on the nature of shelf browsing will provide the justification for this rule. Presumably, the user does not want to find materials on sociology in the middle of the architectural design section, nor would a person looking for materials on crime want to miss some of them because they had been shelved in a slot solely because the class description happened to contain the term "highrise buildings," a fact that the user might never suspect.

On the other hand, if an item is about several aspects of highrise buildings, it must still be shelved in only one location, which illustrates the limitations of shelving as a retrieval mechanism. Many of the problems which are part of the term-matching phase really have to do with choosing among possible subjects or aspects of a subject to be expressed when the system limits the possibilities. This step is definitely part of the translation process, and the classer must refer to the specific indexing language, as well as to the item being classed, in order to carry it out, as we will see presently when we look at some examples of the rules that are generally used to handle the problem.

Even in post-coordinate indexing languages (thesauri), the indexer should remember to indicate the orientation of an item (e.g., design); otherwise, users will find it impossible to specify a search that does not retrieve a great deal of irrelevant material. The difference between these systems and the shelving schemes is that, if a user really does want material on all aspects of highrise buildings, one can omit the contextual terms in the query. Users are not bound to the discipline orientation imposed by the general shelving classification schemes.

Synthesizing subjects and class numbers. After the right headings or classes have been identified, it may still be necessary to construct the final heading or class number. This construction may involve adding subheadings or the notation for standard subdivisions to a listed heading or class number, as we saw above. It may also involve ordering the concepts into an approved form in a faceted classification or ordering a string of terms in a string language. The procedures for this step may be fairly complex. Proper synthesis of class numbers in DDC, for example, is algorithmic, but requires considerable practice. Similarly, knowing which subdivisions can, or in some cases, must, be applied to a main heading can require referring to separate tables, to worked-out examples, or to classing policies. There is also a judgmental aspect, in that a small library may decide to describe items less specifically than a large one, because the more general description is all that is required to create manageable groups of items. They might, for instance, not apply date subdivisions to history numbers for countries for which they only had, and only expected to have, one or two books. In fact, an abridged edition of the Dewey Decimal Classification (Dewey, 1979) exists for smaller libraries, as does a subject heading list (Sears List of Subject Headings, 1986) that is basically a subset of the the LCSH.

Rules and procedures. Classing involves rules and procedures at all stages of the process. These include the following examples for classification schemes:

- Class at the most specific heading that covers the item.
- If an item discusses two subtopics under a heading, class at the dominant one; if there is no dominant one, class at the first one listed.
- If an item discusses three specific topics under a generic heading, class the item at the generic heading.
- Class under the most specific (distinguishing) facet of a subject.

The indexing done for traditional alphabetical subject catalogs very strongly resembles classing in an enumerative scheme without the notation. However, the number of subject headings assigned may be greater than one, although the intent in card catalogs was to create a single entry. Nonetheless, up to three subject headings may be conventionally assigned if required to cover the scope of an item at the level of the entire book, journal set, film, or other physical item. If multiple headings are assigned, they supposedly cover the item as a whole. For example, if a book only covered three types of buildings—that is, monasteries, convents, and cathedrals—a subject cataloger could assign the three types as headings. If the book discussed more than three types or the vocabulary lacked the specific headings, she would have to use the next most specific heading representing ecclesiastical architecture or whatever was available.

Millions of records exist in the Library of Congress's MARC (machine readable catalog) format. The LCSH is also machine readable. This enormous achievement, made possible by the foresight and effort of thousands of librarians over a period of 20 years, forms the backbone of library automation. Without it, automated processing, whether conventional or knowledge-based, would be impossible. Nonetheless, this database still represents the conversion to machine-readable form of a card-based system. Many of its characteristics, such as the fact that the average number of subject headings per item is less than two, pose major limitations to the exploitation of the database for subject searching. Much of what we will have to say about knowledge-based systems in the subsequent sections of this chapter will be inherently conservative in that it will assume that this database is a fact of life and proceed from there.

However, the existence of this cataloging database in its present form does not mean that it cannot be augmented or supplemented. Continued improvements in optical character recognition devices are making the conversion of printed text to machine-readable form much less costly than it has been. We can, then, build around the MARC databases, adding additional information from texts and additional semantic information to the front-end of the retrieval system. Bates (1986) presents a very cogent argument for this approach. In addition, advances in automatic classification and indexing may make updates and upgrades of subject analysis more feasible.

Automated classing by conventional methods. Automated indexing and classing have been the subject of experiment for 30 years. To date, only the relatively indiscriminate extraction techniques have had any commercial success. The first of these were KWIC/KWOC rotated title indexes, followed eventually by the free-text search systems described above. The statistical systems also create their databases by automatic indexing of the text, as we saw in Figure 15.5. Basically they invert every word, as do the free-text systems, but they also do some additional manipulations, such as creating groupings of rarely occurring related terms, and adding weights to the index term assignment. There have also been attempts to extract the most significant subject phrases from a document, but these have never had commercial viability.

Far fewer systems have tried to assign items to predetermined categories, that is, to class under the definition in this chapter. The "brute-force" method is to try to compile all the phrases that can trigger the assignment of a subject heading or class number. A variant on this method, but one that uses sophisticated techniques to match the input strings to the indexing language, has been developed by Klingbiel (1973) and used in the production of indexing by the Defense Technical Information Center (DTIC). It is also used by the NASA Scientific and Technical Information Center for the less ambitious task of mapping DTIC subject headings into the NASA Thesaurus as part of reformatting DTIC records for use in their bibliographies and online databases (Klingbiel, 1985).

Another approach, first defined by Maron in the early 1960s (Maron, 1961) is based on probability. Basically one tries to identify words or phrases that are good clues to class assignment and then assesses the probability of a class based on those clues. This technique has been used primarily for assigning items to one broad class from a relatively limited list (i.e., a few hundred categories). The method is inexpensive, but the accuracy attained still mandates human review. Review is also desirable for the products of the brute-force method. However, the problem with reviewing the machine output is that the indexer has to look at the document in most cases to judge the indexing, and the review may be as time consuming as the indexing.

Classing in libraries: A summary. In this section we have looked in detail at how classification pervades the areas of library activities that involve the subject description and retrieval of materials. We have considered the major approaches to classification, indexing, and retrieval only at a general level. The detailed study even of any one of the major indexing languages is a topic for a book in itself.

We hope, however, to have accomplished several things. The first is to provide an idea of the potential scope for the application of KBSs to classification. The second is to provide some idea of the complexity of the problem of describing and searching unformatted information, such as texts, and the diversity of the current solutions. We have emphasized these aspects for two purposes: (a) to help the reader to understand what is involved in automating the intellectual aspects of the description and retrieval processes and, (b) to provide some idea of what will be involved in building and maintaining the even more complex KBS knowledge bases being proposed as part of ES and NLU systems.

KNOWLEDGE-BASED SYSTEMS AND CLASSIFICATION

Certain similarities between KBSs and retrieval systems bear upon the suitability of KBSs for classification applications, but also highlight the strengths and shortcomings of both types of systems as they presently exist. After a brief review of the types of KBSs most pertinent to our problems, their data structures, and their functions, we consider these similarities in somewhat more detail.

KBS Techniques

Among the various types of KBSs, ESs and NLU systems are the ones most directly applicable to library automation. The central role of NLU is evident when we observe that language is what many expert librarians have expertise in. They know the sublanguages of subject areas and the artificial languages of indexing and classification systems. On the other hand, ESs are the most highly visible form of applied AI in the marketplace. The state of the art in language processing is probably of greater significance to AI in libraries. Its current limitations introduce barriers to a number of potential KBS applications, particularly in general libraries.

Expert and natural language understanding systems. Expert systems simulate an expert's approach to solving a particular kind of problem. Their special role has been to extend conventional data processing techniques to handle cases where data is missing, where uncertainty exists, and where human mental processes efficiently reduce the number of possibilities considered, and bring information to bear on the decision that is not obtainable from manuals, textbooks, or other standard sources. ESs technology is also, at this point, a set of programming tools and techniques which may be used to build systems that could be handled by other means but which are more conveniently built with ES tools. We will try to concentrate on instances where the added facilities of an ES seem to be required.

In early ESs, most information was incorporated in the form of rules. However, as systems have grown more sophisticated, additional data structures have come into use. For small systems with very small numbers of rules, structuring the knowledge base is not a major concern, just as a collection of documents must grow to a certain size before most people will bother to organize it. However, just as the thought and overhead involved in keeping a library accessible grows as the collection grows, the need to organize a knowledge base also grows with the size of the system. Knowledge engineers will necessarily become more and more preoccupied with the organization of knowledge, and their problems will sound very familiar to librarians.

At one time ESs and NLU were quite separate fields of reseach, even though both types of systems require a knowledge base. The separation of the research community and the differences in research emphasis still largely obtains, but these two kinds of systems are now being integrated in a number of ways in KBS environments. For instance, an NLU system may provide the user interface to an ES, or it may generate part of an ES knowledge base. These two relationships are the most common kinds of marriage. Other kinds are possible, however. For instance, the NLU system might be used on an "as needed" basis. An expert search system that was attached to a statistically based retrieval system might, for example, use an NLU system to screen output or to help reformulate a query when the word-based statistical techniques were not performing adequately.

Turning to NLU systems specifically, we note that their first commercial use has been as query languages, not for knowledge bases, but for database management system (DBMS) interfaces. DBMSs present a structured universe in which vocabularies are limited and terms are preassigned as values to particular attributes. These features reduce the problems associated with the semantic interpretation of database queries in comparison to querying unformatted text.

For instance, both text and database systems that use Boolean operators in their query languages need to be able to distinguish between query terms that the user considers to be synonymous or alternatives for the same concept and ones that represent different concepts. The former are ordinarily linked by a Boolean OR and the latter by a Boolean AND in both text and structured data base searching; for instance, "(Apartment houses OR Highrises OR Garden apartments OR Condominiums) AND Design."

As is well known, English queries are ambiguous in that users frequently use the word *and* for both the logical OR and the logical AND relationships. Since structured systems have their terms (values) presorted into fields (attributes), they have a basis for determining when terms are synonyms or alternatives in the particular domain of that system. Natural language interfaces OR values of the same attribute and AND those from different attributes, providing a user override for exception handling. And there are certainly exceptions. For instance, a user—to delve up an example much favored by writers on database systems—may want a supplier who can provide both gadgets and widgets. Since gadgets and widgets would both be values of a "parts" attribute (class), the system would automatically OR them, assuming that gadgets and widgets were alternative in the sense that the user would be satisfied by suppliers who could provide either one or the other, as well as both. The user would have to override the system in this case to get it to interpret the *and* in his natural language query correctly.

For unstructured text, we would like to have the same defaults, but terms are not precategorized unless we are dealing with a faceted classification, so semantic analysis is required. A recent article by Das Gupta (1987) outlines a method based on analysis of terms through conventional dictionaries. He encountered a fairly high error rate, but for interfaces where users can correct the system's assumptions some error rate is tolerable.

For the reasons outlined above, the first NLU systems to become commercially available are those, such as Intellect* and Themis** as described in Rauzino (1983), that are used to interface DBMSs. Text understanding systems,

*Intellect is a trademark of Artificial Intelligence Corporation.

**Themis is a trademark of Frey Associates.

such as those that translate military message traffic or newspaper stories into formatted databases, are less well known and more experimental. They are also, however, more pertinent to our discussion.

There are many different approaches to text understanding. Systems vary, for example, in the extent to which they carry out a full syntactic analysis of a sentence in the course of interpreting it. To briefly illustrate the state of the art in these systems, we will describe an eclectic system that has combined techniques from many different approaches into a single, modular system. Developed by Loatman (1987) and his research associates at Planning Research Corporation, this system represents the state of the art in systems designed to interpret short texts, such as those news stories and messages mentioned above.

As Loatman explains, the PRC Adaptive Knowledge-based Text Understanding System (PAKTUS) integrates several approaches that have had some success in the past and adds a sophisticated set of tools for building grammars and lexicons. Figure 15.12 gives an overview of the PAKTUS system. The system itself is within the large box, while the arrows into and out of the box indicate interfaces to its external environment. In the lower right hand corner, the figure shows output to a message routing system, a knowledge base, or a database. Moreover, the matcher/router that can output to a message handling system could equally well output indexing to a bibliographic system. The specifications for matching index terms would replace the user profiles shown as input to the matcher.

After a stream of text in electronic form enters the system, as shown at the top of the figure, the preprocessor decomposes it into individual words, sentences, and messages. The words identified are then mapped to entries in a lexicon that contain information about their meaning and usage. When PAKTUS encounters a new word, which often happens, it tries to analyze the word morphologically, using information about 138 prefixes and suffixes. If this analysis does not allow it to match the word with a root that it knows and therefore arrive at a meaning, it deduces as much as it can from the syntactic and semantic context. It later verifies its deductions through a mixed-initiative interaction with a dictionary officer (a person who knows the structure and function of the PAKTUS lexicon).

The next step in processing the text is to parse the sentences syntactically using a grammar embodied in an Augmented Transition Network (ATN), a technique originally developed by Woods (1970) for the NASA moon rocks question-answering system. The syntactic structures are then converted to language-independent conceptual frames. A frame is a data structure that corresponds to an object or an action and contains slots that have information about that object. They correspond roughly to the records, attributes, and values of databases, but are more flexible.

The conceptual frames in PAKTUS represent a proposition about the world (a state, process, or action) and contain pointers to the entities that fill the various roles in the frame, such as agents, actions, places, and starting or ending times for an event. Parses that cannot be mapped into any conceptual frame are

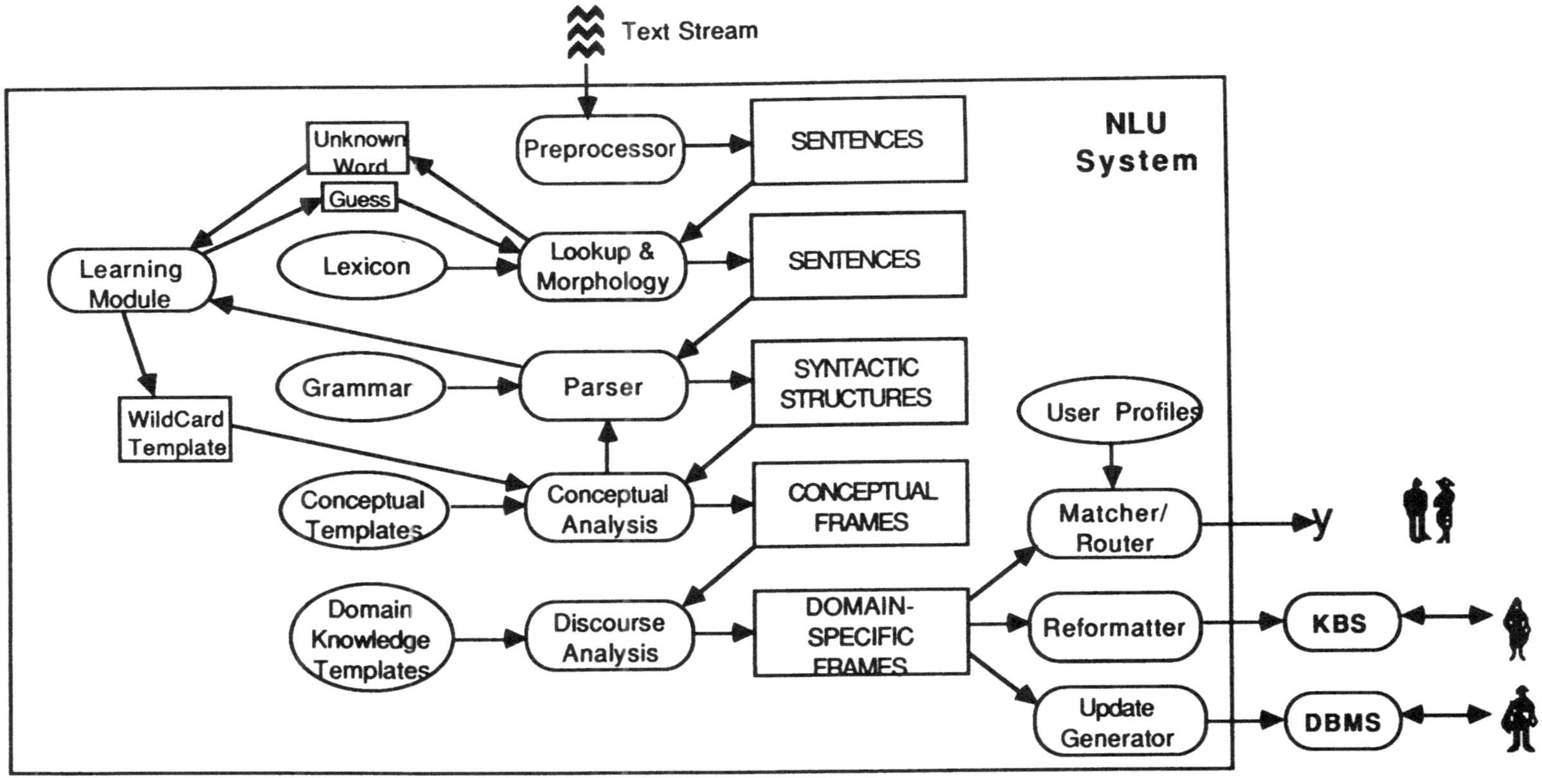

Figure 15.12. PAKTUS Overview.

rejected, and the parser generates alternative parses. A frame usually corresponds to the information in a clause.

After the message has been processed and one or more conceptual frames have been filled, the frames representing the text are collected by a discourse analysis component that uses a paradigm similar to that of the Dyer's Boris system (Dyer, 1983) to fill in the blanks in the patterns they contain. Pattern matches are specified by "demons" in concept templates developed specifically for each application. These demons apply knowledge about the particular application domain to integrate all the information in the conceptual frames, both explicit and implied, into structures that are meaningful and appropriate for the particular application being supported by PAKTUS. As mentioned above, these applications can include data or knowledge base generation, selective dissemination of information, or indexing.

Figure 15.13 reveals the output of these various processes. The unprocessed message is at upper left with the output of the preprocessor next to it. Immediately below is the parse tree for the first sentence followed by the two conceptual frames generated for the two sentences. One corresponds to "Ask" and the other to "Begin." The "Ask" frame contains another conceptual frame for the physical transfer of objects (PTRANS), in this case, light bulbs. Each concept has roles, as shown, such as "Experiencer." Finally, at the bottom of the figure we see a concept template that has synthesized the information that was needed for a particular application from the concept frames.

While systems like PAKTUS are beginning to be genuinely useful for certain types of applications, it still requires a great deal of human input to construct one for a particular domain, much like that required to build and maintain an indexing language. Because of this requirement and because problems like ambiguity become steadily more difficult as the range of subject areas broadens, applications are still limited to very narrow domains. Also, the text passages processed to date are not long, complex, or literary. These systems do best with short, practical texts to be processed for applications where the information to be gleaned is consistent over time and can be clearly specified. Unfortunately, the analysis of complex noun phrases, which is essential to the expression of subjects or topics in bibliographic retrieval, is one of the most difficult areas of linguistics and one that tends to require a great deal of world knowledge.

Knowledge representation: Frames and semantic networks. Many different data structures have been used in KBSs, but frames and semantic networks (nets) are among the most common. A frame is like a record or a relation in a database, but it is more flexible. Frames usually correspond to objects such as rules, physical entities, actions, scenarios, or events. A frame may describe a class or a particular instance of a class. In other words, it may correspond to a concept, such as architectural design, or to a particular instance of that concept, such as the design of the Louvre. Individuals and classes can inherit characteristics from a parent class in a frame system, in that the system will supply the characteristics of the parent as those of the child unless it is specifically overrid-

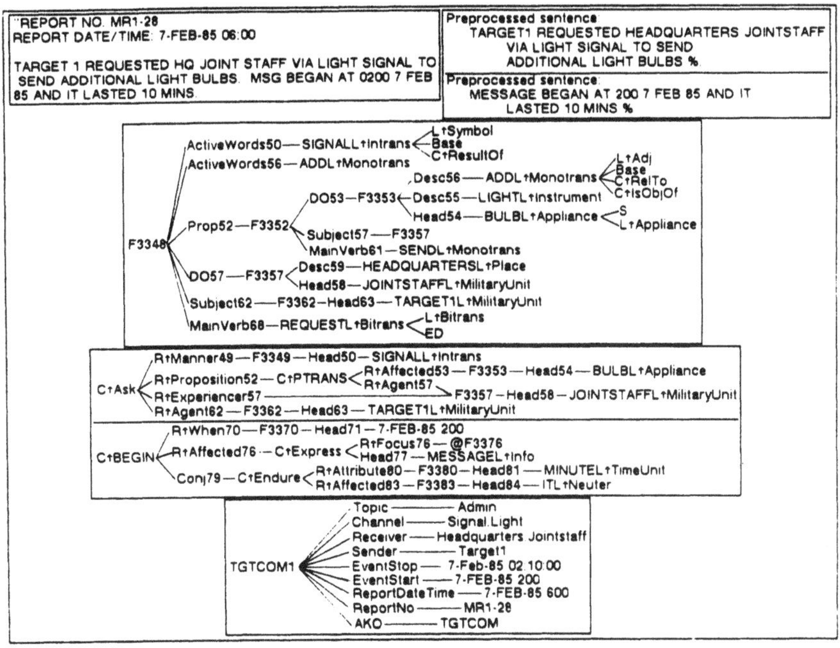

Figure 15.13. Example of PAKTUS Text Processing.

den by the knowledge engineer or the user. This feature not only provides a great saving in space, but it also increases the reasoning power of the system in the absence of information.

In addition to being very flexible in the types of data they can represent, frames also allow flexibility in attribute designation. Slots may be filled, not only by values and pointers, but also by other frames or by subroutines that are activated when the slot is accessed (demons). For example, a slot may contain a demon that specifies how to locate a valid value for that slot, as do the demons described above in the concept templates (application-specific frames) of PAKTUS. Because of their power and flexibility, frames are often a unifying data structure in KBSs.

Figure 15.14 reflects how a semantic network can be expressed in frames. The semantic network is taken from Figure 15.2, but shows relations between the concepts that are, in some cases, more specific than the BT, NT, RT designations previously used. For a much more detailed discussion of semantic networks and an excellent analysis of conceptual structures in general, see Sowa (1983).

A brief examination of the frames in Figure 15.14 will show their very close relationship to facet analysis, although facet analysis is a process of establishing patterns for entire disciplines or broad areas of knowledge, while frames usually correspond to concepts. This difference is not as profound as one might think. Frames are, to use Sowa's terminology (p. 128), actually schemata that reflect

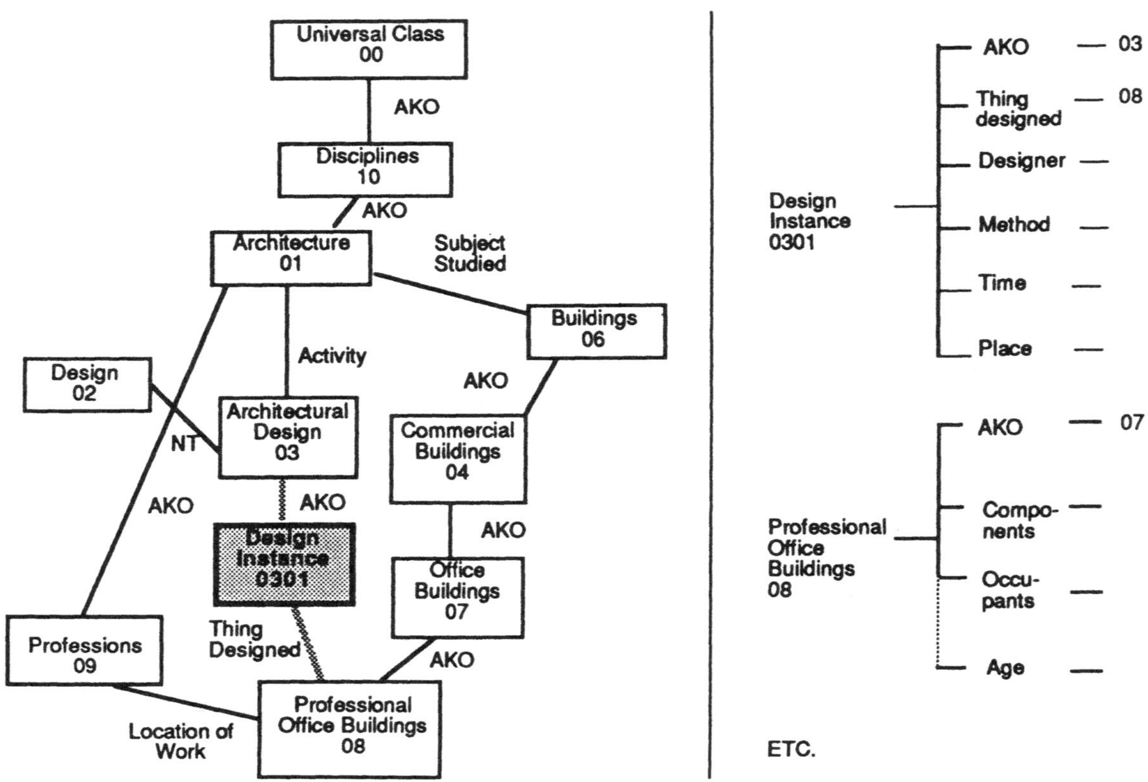

Figure 15.14. Semantic Network with Corresponding Frame Representation.

the broad definition of a concept, which includes the pattern of its relationships to other entities. A particular occurrence of such a pattern is called an instance or instantiation of it. As shown in "Design Instance 0301" in the figure, the frame really represents a subject in our terminology; that is, it is a way of representing the relationships among a number of concepts.

A frame shows pragmatic relationships, not just the semantic or definitional relationship between one concept and others. Although it includes the BT/NT (AKO) relationships of the thesaurus, it also includes the kinds of relationships that are expressed only in subject headings, class numbers, indexing strings, or other expressions created in the index language to represent subjects.

In comparing facet structures to frames, we can also see that the frame for "Design Instance 0301," for example, has a greater level of detail than the faceted classification we showed in Figure 15.7, namely in having slots for the designer and for the method of design. A library would have to have an extremely large and specialized collection in the area of architectural design before it would be interested in differentiating classes at this level of detail. However, in a system whose goal is to represent the full meaning of a phrase or sentence, such as in an NLU system, this detail must be included. Figure 15.7 also did not show facets for time and place; however, provision for these aspects is common to all indexing languages, even though it did not appear in our example. While we have pointed to some differences between facet structures and frames, they are really differences at the level of application.

Integration of KBSs. Before we leave the technical aspects of KBSs, we need to consider one final point. In order to reach their full potential usefulness, ESs need to be integrated, both with conventional systems and with each other. We have already stressed the size of library catalogs and other bibliographic databases and the investment they represent. Many other organizations have major investments in their databases, which provide the backbone of their day-to-day operations. Obviously, a useful system must be able to access and use that information. Facilities for integrating an ES with a database were not part of the commercial ES software packages initially marketed, which have supported only "stand-alone" applications where the ES itself contained all the information needed to function. However, hooks into databases are now becoming more common, as the utility of a system that cannot access existing databases is unacceptably limited.

The cost of the hardware needed to support sophisticated user interfaces and development environments is also now becoming much more manageable than the $20,000+ for the AI workstations that were once required. One can have ESs, of course, without windowing, multitasking, bit-mapped graphics, and other features of the workstation interfaces, but it is evident that these capabilities with or without ESs are a great benefit to sophisticated applications. The exploitation of these devices, even in conventional systems, will probably effect a considerable improvement in retrieval system performance. This probability is another aspect of our earlier observation that conventional computing has by no means yet been fully absorbed or exploited in libraries. Inexpensive workstations are a very important part of spreading high technology in this environment.

Realizing the full potential of KBSs also requires that they communicate and cooperate, not just with conventional computing environments, but with one another as well. We have already mentioned a form of this interaction when we discussed interfacing an ES with an NLU system on an "as needed" basis.

An online search service might build a single, general search strategy ES that could then communicate with ESs for particular databases that could be supplied by the database vendors. Tying this notion to our previous use of NLUs, the search ES might, for instance, query an NLU system to find out the relationship between townhouses and office buildings to help formulate search strategy or query logic. It might, then, query the vendor's database ES to find out if the database uses an indexing language, and determine what the preferred terms are for the two concepts.

Functions of ESs

Most of the functions for which KBSs have been used to date have equivalent uses related to classification. These include advising, tutoring, modeling, and diagnosing. Many of these activities, but particularly diagnosis, are supported by classing activities by the system. Systems that incorporate classing as a major function have been studied as a group by Clancey (1984). He is attempting to characterize different types of fundamental problems to be solved by ESs in order to allow easier comparisons among systems and more effective design. In this pursuit, he defines a class of problems that can be solved by "classification," although he deliberately uses a more restrictive definition of this term than ours. In our terminology his "classification" would be "classing," and a fairly restricted variety of classing.

Specifically, Clancey defines classification as choosing among a set of predetermined, specifiable, and enumerable solutions, a process that can be implemented in an ES in a relatively straightforward manner. To sense the limits of this definition, we turn to the observations of Pople (1982) in the medical domain, who observes:

> Problem solving procedures for making true/false judgments concerning evoked hypotheses may be of many forms. There is nothing particularly demanding about the control strategy required for managing the consideration of a succession of binary choice tasks. The program can be set up in a straightforward fashion to proceed sequentially through the list of possibilities, considering each in accordance with the specified problem solving procedure.
>
> The main difficulty with the binary choice approach is that it fails to aggregate diagnostic possibilities into decision sets; instead, each considered diagnosis is evaluated as though independent of all other alternatives. This requires absolute criteria for decision making, as the problem solver is denied access to the powerful heuristics that enable decisions to be rendered relative to a postulated decision set.
>
> These heuristics, which provide guidance to the physician concerning the need

> for additional discriminating information and permit use of efficient decision strategies such as "the process of elimination," can be used only in the context of tasks structured as differential diagnoses.

In our own application area, this analysis is equivalent to saying that terms can only be considered one at a time. The system cannot isolate a set of possible solutions and compare and select among them.

Looking at a binary choice classification procedure in some detail, however, will serve nicely for purposes of illustrating how ESs class. Clancey identifies three component processes in this simple form of classing: data abstraction, heuristic association, and refinement. Consider an ES in which there is a target database of possible solutions and a user input to be matched against one of them. This matching process can involve multiple iterations of the following steps:

1. Transforming the input data
2. Considering alternative solutions (hypotheses) in some systematic fashion
3. Using matching rules to associate the (possibly transformed) input with the features associated with the alternative solutions being considered.

These three operations correspond respectively to data abstraction, heuristic association, and hypothesis refinement, as Clancey defines them.

Data abstraction. Data abstraction is an optional step that occurs if the input information must be generalized in some way before it can be matched against the features of the categories in the solution space. It is implemented by rules in the knowledge base that (a) generalize, (b) transform quantitative data to qualitative data (qualitative abstraction), or (c) associate a description of an entity with its name (definitional abstraction). Generalization is embodied in rules like, "If *x* is a bird, then *x* can fly," or "If *x* is a monkey, *x* is an animal," while qualitative abstraction is performed by rules like, "If the bath water is greater than 120 degrees F., then the bath water is hot."

An example of a definitional abstraction is shown in the following rule:

If *x* is a domesticated animal AND *x* is kept primarily for pleasure of its owner THEN *x* is a pet.

These rules all make the data entering the system more general and, therefore, more likely to match the knowledge base features that consider classes of solutions. That is, the knowledge base cannot, obviously, have rules for every tenth of a degree of patient temperature, but it can have a data abstraction rule to transform any quantity over 101 degrees for an adult to "high" and rules associated with solution categories that have "high" fever as part of their conditions.

Heuristic association. Heuristic association bridges the gap between the transformed data and the solution space, although the final solution might not be immediately selected. In an ES this process must be specifiable, but it can jump over certain steps, such as associating symptoms with a disease rather than with the physiological processes causing the symptoms which, in turn, are caused by the disease.

Hypothesis refinement. Hypothesis refinement is accomplished through the set operations that allow movement in the hypothesis space (classification structure) during the matching process. These operations are:

- Refinement—looking for more specific cases
- Discrimination—choosing among close alternatives
- Characterizing—generalizing to expand the search to new cases.

They are familiar to anyone who has ever used a classification scheme, subject heading list, or thesaurus.

To pull these notions together, consider how an ES would function that classed journal articles using only their titles, a situation that usually involves limited and uncertain information. The data abstraction operations correspond to such procedures as breaking the title into concepts and developing synonyms or more general terms as alternatives to match against the indexing language. An example of a heuristic would be assigning a term to a document that was not in the document title with a high probability because of the presence of one or more other terms in the title that are highly associated with it. Rules of this type will be illustrated in more detail when we discuss the BIOSIS sysytem. The MEDAID system described elsewhere in this book by Humphrey is also a rich source of heuristic examples.

Similarities of KBSs and Retrieval Systems

Both librarians and knowledge engineers represent knowledge and relational information in abstract structures that are used to provide information, facilitate search, and support classing operations. Both systems are complex, but they are complex in different ways. A major contrast is that indexing languages concentrate on organizing very large numbers of possible classes (solutions), while the present generation of ESs that class have a relatively small number of solutions but use classification to represent the knowledge that allows the system to choose among these solutions.

Complexity in ESs stems in part from the range in the types of information that must be represented (rules, facts, etc.). For classing systems, in particular, it stems from the necessity of including information about how to class and all the pertinent attributes associated with the target categories. In contrast, an indexing language need only list the categories themselves with some relational information to link them and guide the human user. The rules for classing are sometimes made explicit in indexing languages, but they are far less detailed and complete than would be necessary for a machine to reproduce human performance. Rule specification is so difficult, complex, and expensive that most classing systems contain only a few dozen categories, rather than the thousands of alternatives provided by an indexing language.

As the mention of thousands of categories indicates, however, indexing languages also have complexities of a type not yet encountered in ESs. By the standards of indexing-language builders, who deal with thousands, if not hundreds of thousands of solution categories, the problem of organizing a few categories for search in an ES is trivial (assuming a binary decision model). If there are only a few dozen solution categories, then a search strategy can take each in turn as a hypothetical solution and see if it can find evidence to support that category, as many simple ESs do. In indexing languages where the category lists alone can run to more than 20 volumes of text, just moving about efficiently in the solution space is of major concern. Moreover, while retrieval systems cover narrow domains of knowledge, libraries in general, and most of the major commercial databases, such as Chemical Abstracts or BIOSIS, cover far larger domains than current knowledge-based systems of any type.

On the other hand, there is a basic commonality in the problems, which is reflected in the similarity between the relational analysis carried out by librarians building indexing languages and by knowledge engineers constructing frame-based KBSs. The knowledge structures of KBSs are well suited to describing indexing languages. Librarians may even have some contribution to make, and where better than in their own systems, to problems of organizing large or generalized knowledge bases. It is easy for anyone who has dealt with faceted classification schemes to predict problems in using templates in NLU.

For instance, our previous example about the faceted classification that always assumed that the students were the recipient of the action has an exact analog in a well known scenario-based system (Lebowitz, 1980) that "understands" newspaper articles about terrorists. In this system the victim of violence is always the terrorist's victim, so the system completely misinterpreted its input when it ran across a story in which the the terrorist was shot. Librarians do not necessarily have solutions to these problems, but they do have a good intuitive notion of what happens when a highly structured knowledge organization meets the real world and what is required to maintain complex conceptual structures over time.

KNOWLEDGE-BASED SYSTEMS FOR CLASSIFICATION IN LIBRARIES

Having looked closely at all aspects of the application area and considered the relevant technologies, we now turn to the problem of identifying applications for KBSs in the area of classification in libraries. We will begin with criteria for selecting KBS applications, given the current state of the art. We will also have something to say about the economics of KBSs and the strategies for developing new technology in libraries and gaining acceptance for it. We will consider a few applicable experimental systems to illustrate the current state of the art and conclude with some additional suggestions and comments on the prospects for the further development of KBS technology.

Criteria for Selecting Initial Applications

There are many constraints on the choice of suitable applications for KBSs, including the state of KBS technologies themselves, the economics of the applications, and the availability of expertise and data. We will begin our discussion with the most concrete problem that faces libraries, the availability of the computer and communications technologies needed to support KBS development and deployment.

The computing infrastructure. There are no hard and fast limits between what can be done with conventional systems and what can be done in AI, but some applications are certainly more easily generated with AI tools. AI workstations provide development environments that greatly facilitate the development of rapid prototypes, the use of sophisticated graphic displays, and the viewing of multiple tasks at once. They are also optimized for processing programs in LISP or PROLOG (the favored programming languages for AI), which greatly improves the speed with which AI applications written in these preferred languages can be executed. The power of the AI workstation is often entwined in our thinking with the power of AI itself.

Fortunately, these workstations are increasingly coming within reach of the average computer consumer. The library that was able to invest in a first-generation IBM PC with a hard disk drive can now, five years later, obtain for the same money a multitasking 32-bit microcomputer with a high resolution color screen and the speed and storage capacity necessary for reasonable AI performance.

The AI programming environments and shells are also decreasing steadily in price. At this writing, the best ones for ES system development still cost over $50,000, but packages with considerable capabilities are available for far less money. An additional problem for many libraries, however, is exploiting such equipment over networks where the interface may still be the lowest common denominator—a dumb terminal with no graphics capability. Looked at another way, one could say that a problem for centralized library networks (the organizations that are the most likely to be able to fund AI-based systems) is how to deliver such systems to their client libraries. In talking about very near-term applications, we have to keep this problem in mind.

Solutions are already being found (e.g., devices that lessen the dependency on telephone lines and central computers). We have already seen a rash of products that can be used locally on IBM PCs and other microcomputers that present the user with a much more sophisticated interface to a commercial database than the network can provide through its central facilities. Communications will become even less of a burden when optical disk technology takes full hold, allowing libraries to have completely stand-alone systems, at least for those databases that are used heavily.

Moreover, communications technology is also changing rapidly. The major trunk telephone lines in the United States and Europe and the local lines in major cities are rapidly being converted to fiber optic cable, which has much higher channel capacities than present phone lines. In addition, telephone communication will become digital, which will eliminate the need for modems. These two developments together will provide the channel width necessary to communicate digital imagery, graphics, and other bit-intensive data at acceptable speeds within the next five to ten years. In other words, the infrastructure that can support more sophisticated computing is falling into place.

Rules of thumb for expert/NLU systems applications. Assuming the technology is available to support an ES or natural language processing application, the next questions revolve around the suitability of the application for such an approach. ESs, for instance, have been implemented at many different levels of complexity, but the literature is fairly unanimous about some criteria for success. A primary consideration is whether the task the system is to support is one that some identifiable and available person knows how to perform well. Those who design ESs are constantly having to persuade potential clients that if they do not know how to do something, the system is not going to know how to do it either.

To take a case in point, an ES can reproduce the behavior of expert searchers, providing it can handle the semantic aspects of searching (which is doubtful at present), but it cannot improve on that performance except insofar as consistency, speed, and some additional insight through the observation of multiple experts may help. A good system might aid even good professional searchers in overcoming any inappropriate searching habits they may have acquired over the years. Nonetheless, the role of the system is to provide expert assistance to users, not to solve problems that have not yet been solved.

The first requirement, then, is a body of expertise. It need not be knowledge of a professional; it can equally well be knowledge of an experienced clerical worker, a mechanic, a hobbyist, or anyone who has a body of knowledge acquired through a substantial investment of time and effort. Additional requirements are that the expertise be accessible, that it not take too long to extract, and that the skill be sufficiently scarce or perishable.

Limitations of present generation expert/NLU systems for classification applications in libraries. Natural language processing is only starting to develop as a science, and many potential library applications are heavily dependent on its future development. For those applications involving media other than text, the situation is even worse. Our ability to get a machine to understand visual media, for example, is very limited.

Many potential ES applications in libraries will presumably suffer from a problem that the library experts themselves experience, namely difficulty in verification of performance. Experts performing such tasks as indexing and searching vary widely in their behavior, and there is considerable difficulty in assessing relative performance. This fact will certainly present difficulties in verifying the performance of an ES, just as it has presented problems in verifying the performance of conventional systems performing similar tasks. This problem has a depressing effect on library innovation generally. If one cannot prove that a change in practice produces better results, it is harder to gain acceptance for it.

There are other problems that apply primarily to automated indexing besides the natural language processing barriers. If one considers the current technology of ESs that class, the number of categories considered is usually counted in the tens or at most in the hundreds. Currently large ESs have only a few thousand rules. Even if there were only one rule per class, the number of rules required for a medium-sized indexing language would exceed present capacities. There is also a tremendous amount of labor involved in building such rules.

Classes are not fully enumerated in many indexing languages. Even the LCC uses tables of subdivisions that apply to particular sections of the scheme, while the LCSH makes extensive use of standard subdivisions. Classes must, therefore, often be synthesized, which adds to the classing problem.

Economics and Implementation Strategies

The history of indexing languages and of library automation provides many instructive insights as to the probable strategies for implementing KBSs. For instance, individual libraries, except the Library of Congress, have not been able to accept the burden of developing and maintaining major indexing languages. The major bibliographic databases with large indexing languages and sophisticated indexing are also maintained by a very large user base. Most of the large classification schemes and many large alphabetical indexing languages are, at least, partially government-supported.

Similarly, library automation did not make much headway until a means was found to gain government support, centralize the effort, and spread the cost among a large group of users. One may argue that the microcomputer has made it much more feasible for small libraries to develop their own software, and that is undoubtedly true. However, the development and maintenance of large knowledge bases is more akin to that of a large indexing language than to the development of software.

Major KBS development in this field will be done by national libraries, large commercial database developers and vendors, or cooperative networks and other consortia. Individuals and libraries may make an important contribution through the development of prototypes and the generation of ideas, but the actual implementation of a full-scale system that involves a large knowledge base is probably beyond their resources.

While innovation that has come through the national and state libraries and the consortia has succeeded in making major changes in the way libraries operate, these changes have been largely incremental. For example, the Online Computer Library Center (OCLC), the largest of the bibliographic networks, did not originally start out to automate libraries: Their immediate aim was only to make cataloging in the form of catalog cards available more cheaply and efficiently than had been possible up to that time (1968). Attempts to introduce radical technological change have not been so successful, partly because of the investment represented by existing library cataloging, whose conservative influence we have already noted.

In terms of acceptance, there are obvious benefits to incremental development and to close links with existing bibliographic databases. Fortunately, there is no reason why KBS cannot be introduced in this way. They need not create immediate, profound revolutions in library practice, but rather can be used initially to enhance particular functions in small ways.

Three Case Studies from the Current Literature

To further understand KBSs it is useful to examine some representative KBSs that fall within the scope of this chapter. Rather than attempt to survey all current KBS projects that might relate to classification in libraries, we will look at three recently published descriptions of KBS prototypes in some detail, considering:

- Their functions
- Their knowledge base
- The KBS techniques they employ
- The feasibility of implementing them as operational systems.

The three systems, CoalSORT, EP-X, and the BIOSIS automatic indexing system, are taken more or less in order of increasing sophistication from an AI perspective. However, their order also considers first searching and then indexing.

CoalSORT. CoalSORT, recently described by Monarch and Carbonell (1987), is a conceptual browser designed to serve as either a search or an indexing tool. While its designers evidently have plans to extend the system's power, at present it appears to consist primarily of a frame-based semantic network and the software needed to allow users to display portions of it and to move around in the conceptual structure. The domain is very narrow: It covers catalyst applications in coal liquefaction and contains 500 concepts that have been used to index about 100 documents. The expert knowledge in the system is embodied almost entirely in the semantic network. At present, there is no procedural knowledge in the system.

The frames for the concepts in the system contain dictionary-like definitions of the concepts, which is a bit unusual; however, they also contain the information about the relationships of the concepts to other concepts in the network, as we would expect. The examples given in the article do not seem to be very uniform as to the type of information that is included, but samples can be seen of the standard indexing AKO, nonspecified, and synonym relationships, as well as a broad range of others. These appear to include the performance parameters of catalysts (e.g., contact-efficiency), as well as attributes such as *used as, example, example of, parts, site, company, side-effect, chemical-process,* and *catalyst-usage*, to name only a few. Subcategories can inherit from their parents. One wonders, however, if the very unstructured frames that exist in the system will support reasoning very easily and how, if it became very large, it could be maintained.

The interface component of the system is a multiwindow screen with a mouse, which allows users to select concepts they wish to add to their search statement or to explore further. The windowing allows users to keep to view continuously their current query, the concepts they have already examined, and documents found to date. The user may view documents at any point in the search. With the present hardware, however, the system can show only one concept frame at a time, and the system allows the user to add only that concept to the search, rather than any of the other concepts shown in the frame. The researchers stress the use of the semantic network to improve consistency among indexers as well as between indexers and searchers in applying concepts.

Improvements needed are features that would already be found built-in or requiring only minor extension in the sophisticated commercial ES environments. These include an editor that uses inheritance and inversion to fill frames for new subcategories with the default characteristics of the parent class or automatically make the inverse links, for instance "part" and "part-of." An additional common system feature mentioned here is presenting multiple frames in a single window as an interconnected graph at various levels of detail. Other challenging aspects include extending the inference capability for use in update, user guidance, and automatic construction of diagrammatic models of the physical processes embodied in the semantic networks as part of the user interface (Figure 15.15).

EP-X. The Environmental Pollution Expert (EP-X) project has certain things in common with CoalSORT in that both are concentrating on enhancing interfaces using a knowledge-based approach. The EP-X project looks for ways to expand the power and usability of retrieval systems from a human factors viewpoint, based on a study of human intermediaries. This information is used to define enhancements to the semantic information available in an existing commercial database and to the user interface that is required to have the system perform as an intelligent search assistant.

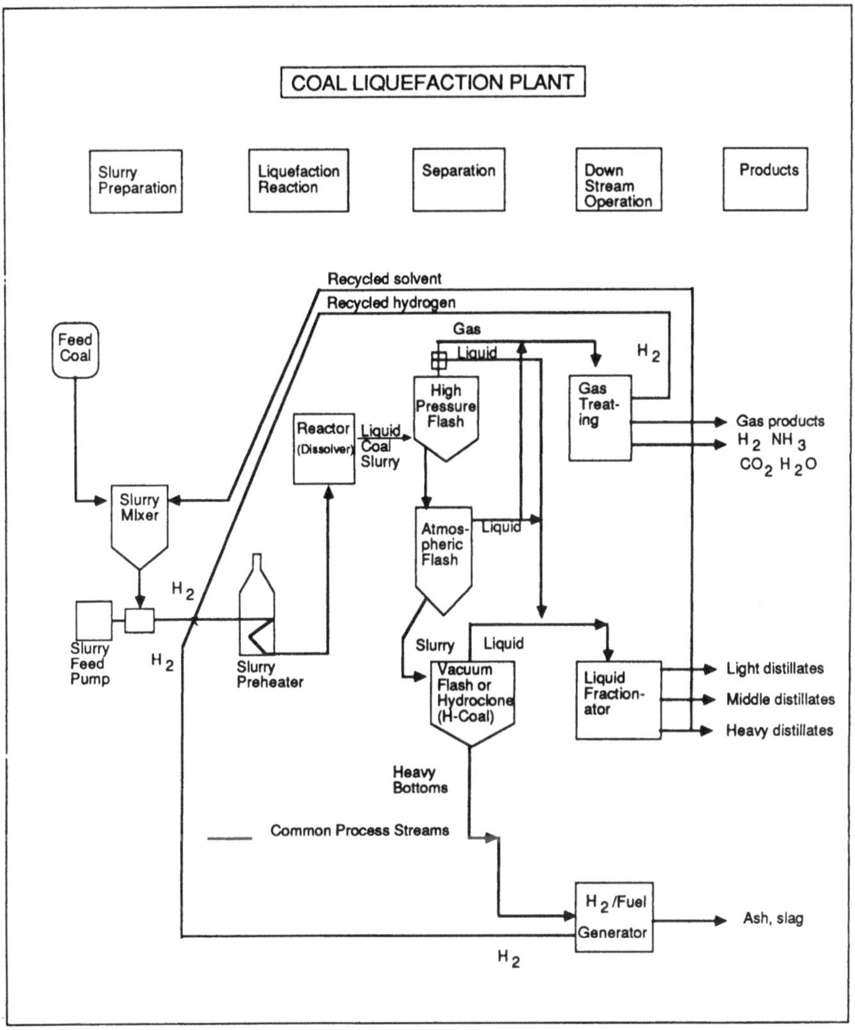

[Monarch & Carbonell, 1987, p. 49; Redrawn]

Figure 15.15. Proposed CoalSORT Diagrammatic Interface.

Whereas CoalSORT is basically a rapid prototype of a retrieval system concept, the two EP-X papers discussed here represent the output of a long-term research effort. Also, the EP-X system incorporates the knowledge of expert searchers, while CoalSORT utilizes a domain expert's model of the field as the interface, but makes no attempt to provide and/or exploit information about the manner in which the database has been constructed. The EP-X project is much more comprehensive, and the researchers provide a more sophisticated analysis of the full range of problems of searching large bibliographic systems.

The two papers reviewed from the EP-X project cover somewhat different areas. Krawzcak, Smith, and Shute (1987) report on the general design of the interface and the results of an initial user test. The paper by Smith, Shute, Chignell and Krawzcak (1987) goes into more detail about the kinds of information gathered from observing expert searchers and the structure of the EP-X knowledge base and emphasizes the role of the human factors specialist in the design of the system. The vocabulary is a subset of the Chemical Abstracts thesaurus.

The knowledge base consists of a hierarchical frame-based semantic network of concepts and a set of template types, also stored as frames, that express the patterns that we called the pragmatic relationships among concepts (e.g., the uptake of a pollutant by an organism). These patterns are referred to as contextual information or topics. The developers also introduce the notion of semantic primitives, which appears to correspond more or less to our usage of the term concept. The semantic primitives are linked into a tangled hierarchy. In other words, they form a thesaurus. The document indexing is an instantiation of one or more topic frame templates in exactly the same way that the architectural design of office buildings (Instance 0301) was an instantiation of Architectural design in Figure 15.14.

Finally, the authors identify a set a relations that hold between user search terms and the knowledge base, which they call triggers, because each relation invokes a different kind of response on the part of the system to resolve a potential ambiguity or miscommunication. We have rephrased the developers' descriptions in order to map the cases to our previous discussions of index languages.

Five of the six cases have to do with mapping concepts to the system vocabulary—the equivalent of mapping to a thesaurus. For example:

1. The input term maps (or fails to map) to a synonym or equivalent of an existing term — [US -> United States].
2. The input term maps to the same concept in different contexts in the classification scheme — [Lead as a pollutant or as part of an item whose manufacture may pollute (e.g., lead batteries)].
3. The input concept maps to multiple concepts because the input term has been decomposed into two or more terms (semantic primitives) in the vocabulary—[Desulphurization ->Sulphur and its compounds + removal/treatment].

The final case is where the role is ambiguous. Air, as a polluted medium, might be polluting another polluted medium or it might be polluted by it. In other words, the system cannot know which slot in the contextual information frame the concept should fill.

Note that the information that would have to be solicited from the user in order to complete the match correctly in each case is different. The knowledge base, with its record of term relationships, is the basis for identifying these possible sources of miscommunication and "triggering" the proper rule-based clarification mechanisms.

BIOSIS. To this point we have considered systems that were basically networks of term relations used to help the user browse in the system or to help the system make intelligent suggestions to the user to modify strategy. In this example, an automated indexing system under development for BIOSIS (Vleduts-Stokolov 1987), we will see a fuller implementation of a KBS. We will see a system that uses a knowledge base, including a significant amount of procedural knowledge, to assign documents to categories automatically. It includes not only semantic information, but also information about the indexing rules and practices of a complex indexing system. This system not only uses classification in its knowledge base, but also classes. Furthermore, we will see that it is considerably more sophisticated than the classing model described by Clancey, and it is certainly more sophisticated than some of the early ESs. It quite possibly extends the state of the art in this area of AI technology.

Like the MEDLINE project, BIOSIS is designed as an indexer aid, although the work to date has not aimed to interface the KBS to a production system. The MEDLINE system is intended for interactive support of indexers, with indexers entering some concepts and responding to system queries, while the system takes an active role in filling in other information and prompting, correcting, or advising the indexer as the process proceeds. In the BIOSIS system, the KBS is an autonomous preprocessor that produces preliminary indexing for subsequent indexer review.

The implementation of the BIOSIS system will have to include the mechanisms for indexer interaction to the extent of facilitating indexer review of the output. The efficiency of the review process has a great deal to do with whether the automatic indexing application is cost effective. It must take less time for the indexers to review the indexing than it does for them to index documents without the automated pre-indexing. In this case, the system does not do all the indexing tasks by design so the indexers have to look at the document in any case. Having some data supplied should certainly reduce the indexing time, if the system is sufficiently reliable.

The BIOSIS system uses the information in the titles of biological documents to assign as many categories as possible of those that would be assigned by human indexers. The biological sciences titles are expressive, and a very high percentage of the concepts that are present in the final BIOSIS indexing are present in the title. This feature of BIOSIS makes indexing from the title alone more effective than it would be in many other domains. Human indexers assign up to 15 Concept Headings per document from a list of 600 categories. They use a three-level weighting system, which the automatic system does not attempt to replicate. Natural language terms are matched to the 600 categories through an intermediary language of 440 Concept Primitives. The Concept Headings and the titles are expressed in the intermediary language. The Concept Primitives are arranged into hierarchies to support inferencing—not only genus/species hierarchies, but part/whole hierarchies, as well. For instance, if an article is about the heart, then many headings having to do with the cardiovascular system are also appropriate. The same is true of whole/part relationships, but often in reverse—from part to whole. That is, what is toxic to the nervous system is toxic to the whole organism. Because the title is usually very specific, the system often works up the hierarchy in this way, rather than down. Further information on the derivation of the primitives is in Vleduts-Stokolov's article.

In a manner reminiscent of Klingbiel's automatic indexing approach described above, the mapping is made from the title to the Concept Primitives by a Semantic Vocabulary (SV), which contains 15,000 words and phrases that occurred more than 10 times in the collection of article titles indexed by BIOSIS in one year and are related to at least one Concept Primitive. This cutoff point of 10 occurrences undoubtedly saves the SV from exponential growth and establishes a baseline of effort between the automatic indexing system and the indexers.

In addition to the 15,000 phrases in the SV, BIOSIS has thousands of genus/species entries in other files for organisms, drugs, and toxic chemicals that can be used by the system, but do not have to be in the SV. The actual entry vocabulary, therefore, is massive. Each SV is expressed as a string of Concept Primitives, or, for more complex concepts, as a frame whose slots are Concept Primitives or recursive pointers to other frames. As the titles are scanned, the longest phrases that match SV entries are selected. The addition of rules to the system also allows it to resolve some of the ambiguities in the input at this stage. Finally, the Concept Primitives obtained directly from the title are supplemented with those that can be inferred from the Concept Primitive hierarchy described above.

The information used in the SV translation is greater than we have indicated. We cannot go into much detail here, but it is important to mention that information about pragmatic relations (in this case statistical co-ocurrence information) is also included. A year's worth of BIOSIS indexing was analyzed to determine how often headings were used in conjunction with other headings. This information appears in the form of weights in the translation process. For instance, in an entry for "Fatty acids," the system contains rules that specify in effect that the term "Nutrition" will be assigned with an 80% probability if the context of the occurrence is food products and 50% if the context is food. A set of SV entries with an explanation of the notation used is shown in Figure 15.16.

```
Stroke Volume (26)
    CARDIOVASCULAR SYSTEM;  PHYSIOLOGY
Fatty Tissue (12)
    "Pathology"
        [5:  organ-system(s) -affected-by:  DIGESTIVE SYSTEM
         6:  chemicals-involved-in-pathological-changes:  LIPIDS
         7:  systems-involved-but-not-affected-by:  METABOLISM];
Stroke(s)  (322)
    "Pathology"
        [5:  organ-system(s)-affected-by:  BLOOD VESSELS;
        NERVOUS SYSTEM];
Head Stroke (10)
    "Pathology"
        [3:  caused-by:  EXTERNAL EFFECT; HOT TEMPERATURE];
Stroke-Prone (55)
    "Pathology"
        [3:  caused by:  GENETICS
         5:  organ-system(s)-affected-by:  BLOOD VESSELS;
         NERVOUS SYSTEM];
Fatty (76)
    "Biochemical"
        [2:  structural class:  LIPIDS];
Fatty Acid)(s) (1161)
    "Biochemical"
        {2:  structural class:  LIPIDS];
    1:  If FOOD PRODUCTS -> FOOD PROPERTY;
        NUTRITION (80%); else
    2:  If FOOD -> NUTRITION (50%);
Smoker(s), Smoking (493)
    BEHAVIOR; ADDICTION; HUMAN, BC = 86215;
    "Biochemical"
        [4:  origin-of-substances:  "Organism"
            [1:  general-taxonomic-category:  DICOTYLEDONES
             2:  biosystemic code:  BC = 26775;
             3:  beneficial-or-non-beneficial-property-of-organism:
                 TOBACCO CROPS
            4:  ECOLOGICAL-CHARACTERISIC-OF-ORGANISM:
                TERRESTRIAL];
        6:  physiological-action-of-substance:  TOXIC];
```

(a)

Each entry starts with a header consisting of one or several synonymous natural language word(w(s) or phrases(s) printed flush left. The number in parentheses following the header indicates the annual frequency of occurrence of the term(s). The frequency of occurrence of any SV header does not include occurrences of any SV entry of which the first entry is a substring. Thus the frequency of the entry "Fatty" does not include the frequency of "Stroke Volume," etc.

The header is followed by the semantic representation, consisting of a set of Concept Primitives and/or frame(s) filled in with Concept Primitives or recursively with other filled frames. Concept Primitives are printed in capital letters and separated by semicolons. A frame consists of the frame's name in quotation marks, followed in brackets by as list of frame slots involved, each with the corresponding slot number followed by a colon, the name of the slot (in lower case) followed by a colon, and the Concept Primitive(s) or filled frames that fill the slot [as in the header "Smoker(s)...].

The representation can contain expression of the form "BD = n," where n stands for a five-digit Biosystematic Code used a BIOSIS for designating 865215" means hominidae, "BC = 26775" means solanaceae.

The SV entry can contain contextual restrictions used for solving the = A then *w1* = B, else *w1* = C" is rendered in the abbreviated form "if A -> B, else C." The notation "->" can be verbalized as "then use." Any Primitive can be followed by a probabilistic estimate or weight.

(b)

[Vleduts-Sokolov, 1987, p. 273; Redrawn]

Figure 15.16. (a) Typical Entries from the Semantic Vocabulary. (b) Notations Used in the Entries

The next step, in accordance with Clancey's model is heuristic association—matching the generalized input and category descriptions with each other. The first step in the matching is to limit the search space by selecting only those categories where the Concept Primitives generated by the title through the SV are at least sufficient to assign the Concept Heading. This information is contained in a filter table.

At this point the process becomes hypothesis-driven; that is, each of the possible matching Concept Headings is considered in turn. Each one has a pattern associated with it for matching that concept against the rewrite of the title into the Concept Primitives that was achieved through the SV. This pattern includes Boolean expressions that are combinations of Concept Primitives, as well as specifications of the slots and frames in which the combinations of Primitives must have occurred in the SV or the contexts in which they must appear in the title. These patterns are searched against the title representations. The weights mentioned above are also combined and must reach a certain threshold; thus, the system does include some uncertainty factors in its calculations. This final stage can be thought of as "refinement" in Clancey's terms.

The BIOSIS system has reached the point at which it could be incorporated into a production environment, and, apparently, there are plans to do so. There is a maturity in the role, size, and scope of this system that is lacking in most other KBSs proposed for libraries. For this reason it seems especially appropriate to point out how closely bound this system is to current practice. It had its origins as a conventional automatic indexing system, but the designers have made good use of AI techniques to achieve a level of performance that would have been impossible without the rule base. It makes use of all the information that is available in a complex real world system, and it fits as a definable and limited upgrade to that system. It represents a very substantial amount of human analytical work, but it is work that builds on the system's existing knowledge structures. Moreover, most of the analysis is clearly of permanent value, and the system should not only improve productivity in an expensive operation, but should also improve the quality of the output. In other words, it meets the criteria for a practical implementation of KBSs as the state of the art.

The examples from a librarian's perspective. All three of the above examples incorporate classification in the form of semantic networks. They vary in the degree to which this semantic information is exploited in system performance. We have seen a browser, a prototype of a more comprehensive intelligent interface, and an autonomous automatic indexing system with sophistication that seems to place it at the end of the prototyping cycle. This last system was not interactive, which presents a valid example of batch use of a KBS. The other two systems, however, were user interfaces. One observation that can be made from both of them is the extreme importance of improved computing hardware in upgrading interfaces—larger screens, better graphics, better user communication devices, and, above all, the ability to give the user a more comprehensive view into the system through the very narrow window of a workstation screen.

The relational analysis embodied in the semantic networks is certainly not new to librarianship. Librarians have been building hierarchies for as long as there has been subject access to library collections. Even quite sophisticated combinations of role and hierarchical analysis date back to Ranganathan's work in the early part of this century. The one contribution of KBSs here is the frame-based software environments that make it very easy to process and exploit these structures.

The intellectual difficulty of constructing complex semantic networks is certainly a barrier to implementing KBSs. Anyone who has taught thesaurus construction knows that relational analysis is something that many people do not do naturally or easily. Furthermore, in libraries, other indexers and users have to be able to reason in somewhat the same way as the indexer doing the analysis, otherwise the enterprise will be quite hopeless. Yet, relational analysis turns out to be subjective. The more complex the structures, the worse the consistency problem within the system and between the system and its users. Moreover, the richer the structure, the more difficult it will be to alter if there is radical change in the domain being described. These things taken together have inhibited the use of faceted classification, indexing roles, and string languages.

Including sophisticated semantic information in a retrieval system is an idea that has been around for a long time, but has had mixed results. The possible contribution of KBSs in conjunction with improved computing and human factors technology may be, on the one hand, better management of classificatory information, and, on the other, better presentation of this information to users. They need to be able to manage searching, which is inherently a very complex activity, without being overwhelmed by the problem. The two interface systems have illustrated some tentative approaches to this problem, but they also illustrate how far we have to go. One cannot read the EP-X material, for instance, without being struck by how difficult it is to incorporate classification information into an interface in a way that is really useful, particularly to untrained or casual users.

On the future of indexing languages. It is clear from the CoalSORT example that indexing languages could change dramatically under the impact of KBSs. They could evolve away from being languages to being compact descriptions of narrow areas of knowledge. One could also argue that bibliographic retrieval itself could give way to question-answering systems, so there would be no indexing languages. While we think KBSs may have a role in supplying information in the future, we believe that these knowledge bases for question answering, just as present-day books in a library, will still have to be organized in some fashion. Furthermore, there will probably need to be some brief and abstract representation of this organization and a need to compare descriptions of different knowledge bases, in order to select appropriate ones for intensive search. In other words, KBSs, particularly natural language systems as they emerge, may change our interaction with information at the microlevel. However, it is actually at the macrolevel that librarians now operate, and they or "librarian systems" will probably continue to provide this kind of broad guidance for distinguishing large units of information one from the other. Something like our current knowledge organization practices will, therefore, continue in use.

Indexing languages and KBSs. At a more mundane level, the conversion of many thesauri to frame-based programming environments would make cross-reference checking and all kinds of searching using inheritance easier. It would also make it easier to attach rules to the thesaurus to improve indexing or searching and to incorporate the thesaurus as part of a knowledge-based search or indexing system. All languages, even LCC, DDC, and LCSH could greatly benefit from these tools. The graphics packages available with the more sophisticated shells would be very helpful in managing hierarchies and doing other kinds of logic checks on the system. In addition, the conceptual analyses now being embodied in some natural language systems may be useful to library classifiers. However, the results are not as yet well supported by theory, and the semantic analysis tends to be no less pragmatic than that incorporated in indexing languages.

The applications of natural language systems to classing are certainly more obvious than the applications to classifying, but a thesaurus for a domain could be created from, for instance, a PAKTUS knowledge base for that domain. Synonyms, broader and narrower terms, and specific term relations that might suggest related term entries could be determined by examining the relationships among the concepts as expressed in PAKTUS, which correspond roughly to Vleduts-Stokolov's Concept Primitives. She suggests that the Concept Primitives could be used to cluster concepts and determine hierarchical structures in the SV to, in effect, construct a thesaurus for BIOSIS searching. Moreover, all SV headings that had the same meaning as a user's search query, based on the fact that they map to the same Primitives, could be clustered on demand, providing a useful tool for natural language text searching (Vleduts-Stokolov, 1987, p. 274).

There is another obvious application of KBS to indexing languages: using a KBS to help manage the update problem. While automatic KBS-aided reindexing of library materials is certainly one possibility for the future, another would be to use the KBS to maintain several simultaneous networks corresponding to states of the system over time and provide some means of mapping and translating between them. Again, this idea is not dissimilar to Bate's Front-End System Mind. One could maintain multiple versions, for instance, of the DDC centrally, allowing libraries to utilize whatever part of the network their local policy dictated. Similarly, of course, a library could reclassify by using the net to update the classification of their collection automatically from one version of Dewey to the next.

Applications to searching. We will not go into searching applications here in any depth. It is very important to help the user with the system's indexing and classing rules. This kind of help is easier to provide than support that is highly dependent on language processing, such as natural language interfaces. Yet it can be of considerable benefit.

Using natural language preprocessing to screen the output of systems with no explicit semantic information in their indexing is another relatively feasible possibility in restricted domains. Coordinate indexing, free-text, and statistically-based systems could all benefit. It would require analyzing an information request to determine its basic structure. The titles or opening paragraphs of the retrieved texts can then be matched against the basic conceptual frame in order to find documents with concepts in the wrong roles or ones that were retrieved on the basis of the wrong meaning of a word in the query.

Applications to indexing. For applications to indexing we have two excellent and contrasting models in Vleduts-Stokolov for BIOSIS and Humphrey for MEDLINE. It is easy to see how techniques could be extended to other systems, for instance, to classing in the DDC with its myriad of rules or assigning subject headings in LCSH. In this case, the approach developed for indexers might also aid users.

Natural language processing will soon become a factor in indexing. Systems such as PAKTUS that have highly usable tools for modifying their lexicons and grammars, and for learning concepts, can be adapted to new domains quickly enough to be practically applied. One of their potential applications is certainly automatic indexing, at least of short texts. Automatic indexing of scholarly journal articles is a more difficult undertaking, but we should see progress even in that area if there is sufficient demand for it.

New technology will, of course, expand the possibilities. We have dwelt appropriately at some length on NLU, but other technologies are also important. In the KBS area, there is increased facility in planning and detecting user plans, improved modeling capabilities, cooperating KBS technologies, new insights into tutoring and other user interaction techniques, and, perhaps most importantly, machine learning. Because of the amount of human effort now required to build knowledge bases, it is generally felt that machine learning is the key to widespread KBS use. This field, coincidentally, is another AI area with very heavy dependency on classification. The steadily decreasing cost of workstations and computing power will also have a major impact in making KBS techniques affordable and in improving user interfaces.

Indeed, some analysts believe that AI will quickly lose its identity as a field. For example, at the July 1987 meeting of the American Association for Artificial Intelligence, a vice-president of Texas Instruments, a major player in AI, stated that he expects AI to be fully integrated into the mainstream of computer science by the 1990s. (W. Joe Watson, as quoted in Waldrop, 1987). The workstations, the programming environments, and the concepts will simply be part of modern computing practice. KBSs will simply become a part of the standard practice of library automation and be used wherever they are needed.

Some concluding observations. Perhaps the one fact that is most apparent from this chapter is the very close link between classification and KBSs. Classification underlies not just KBSs for classification activities, but KBSs for almost any activity. It means that indexing languages are a storehouse of semantic information than can be used to very good advantage for AI applications. It also means that many librarians have an excellent base training for constructing KBSs. Many of us should find it a very natural approach to problems.

KBSs and classification are symbiotic disciplines in libraries. Classification will play a major role in any system that reproduces current human information use; that much is obvious. It is more speculative, but we think true, that the opposite dependency also holds. Paradoxically, just as KBSs have demonstrated yet again the centrality of semantic information to human reasoning, proponents of indexing have been engaged in a major struggle to justify the use of controlled vocabularies and the expense of developing thesauri. Studies such as the Cranfield (Cleverdon, 1970), (Swanson, 1971) and Aberystwyth (Keen, 1973) experiments called into question the value of complex relational information. Lack of flexibility in highly structured environments is often cited as a possible cause of poor performance.

The findings of Blair and Maron (1985) that text searching has such poor recall should have come as no shock to any librarian, but the publication of those findings in a computer journal was a major jolt to information system implementers who were unfamiliar with the problems of bibliographic searching. It may have contributed to more skepticism about free-text searching as a complete solution to retrieval problems, but the overall perception of the high efficacy of unstructured full-text search still remains. Indeed, it is a very useful retrieval device, but it has its limitations, just as indexing languages have theirs. No one approach, at present, is superior for all problems.

The lessons of Cranfield may also afflict the AI community. For instance, the EP-X experimenters found that users failed to exploit the classification information available to them as it was initially designed into the interface, and they did not perform very well. The experimenters concluded that the system might have to take a much more active role in order to get the users to take advantage of the improved capability they felt they were providing.

At the heart of this seeming contradiction between additional information and poorer performance is the problem of complexity, as well as flexibility. Knowledge-based technology has the potential to increase flexibility in retrieval systems and shoulder some of the burden of system complexity, but only if it is carefully used. As we improve these systems, we can increase the sophistication of the knowledge bases that they produce and support.

It will not be a simple or trivial matter to exploit KBSs in libraries, particularly for user interfaces. However, libraries have a long history and much experience to draw on in the field of knowledge representation and use. If we use it systematically to upgrade our own systems, we should be able to help not only ourselves and our users, but the whole community of KBS researchers.

REFERENCES

Bates, M. (1986). Subject access in online catalogs: a design model. *Journal of the American Society for Information Science, 37,* 357–376.

Berman, S. (1971). *Prejudices and antipathies.* Metuchen, NJ: Scarecrow.

Blair, D. C., & Maron, M. E. (1985). An evaluation of retrieval effectiveness for a full-text document-retrieval system. *Communications of the ACM, 28,* 289–291.

Bookstein, A. (1986). Probability and fuzzy set applications to IR. *Annual review of information science and technology, 20,* 117–151.

Chan, L. M. (1978). *Library of Congress Subject Headings: Principles and Applications.* Littleton, CO: Libraries Unlimited.

Clancey, W. J. (1984). Classification problem solving. In *Proceedings of the National Conference on Artifical Intelligence,* pp. 49–55, August 6–10, 1984 at the University of Texas at Austin. [1984 Conference of the American Association for Artificial Intelligence. Proceedings distributed by William Kaufmann, Inc. 95 First St., Los Altos, CA 94022.]

Cleverdon, C. (1970). Progress in documentation: evaluation tests of information retrieval systems. *Journal of Documentation, 26,* 55–67.

Cochrane, P. A. (1982). Classification as a user's tool in online public catalogs. *Universal classification: Subject analysis and ordering systems: Proceedings of the 4th International Study Conference on Classification Research.* Frankfurt: Index Verlag, 260–268.

Croft, W. B., & Lewis, D. D. (1987). An approach to natural language processing for document retrieval. *Proceedings of the Annual International ACMSIGIR [Association for Computing Machinery Special Interest Group in Information Retrieval] Conference on Research & Development in Information Retrieval,* New York: ACM Press, pp. 26–32.

Das Gupta, P. (1987). Boolean interpretation of conjunctions for document retrieval. *Journal of the American Society for Information Science, 38,* 245–254.

Dewey, M. (1979). *The Dewey Decimal Classification and Relative Index* (11th abridged ed.). Albany, NY: Forest Press.

Dewey, M. (1989). *The Dewey decimal classification and relative index* (20th ed.). Albany, NY: Forest Press.

Doszkocs, T. E. (1983). CITE NLM: Natural language searching in an online catalog. *Information Technology and Libraries, 2,* 364–380.

Dyer, M. G. (1983). *In-depth understanding.* Cambridge, MA: MIT Press.

Fidel, R. (1984). Online searching styles: A case-study-based model of searching behavior. *Journal of the American Society for Information Science, 35,* 211–221.

Foskett, A. C. (1971). *The subject approach to information* (2nd ed.). London: Clive Bingley.

Immroth, J. P. (1971). *Analysis of vocabulary control in Library of Congress classification and subject headings.* Littleton, CO: Libraries Unlimited.

Janosky, B., Smith, P. J., & Hildreth, C. (1986). Online library catalog systems: An analysis of user errors. *International Journal of Man-Machine Studies, 25,* 573–592.

Keen, E. M. (1973). The Aberystwyth index language test. *Journal of Documentation, 29,* 1–35.

Klingbiel. P. (1973). Machine-aided indexing of technical literature. *Information Processing and Management, 9,* 79–84.

Klingbiel, P. (1985). Phrase structure rewrite systems in information retrieval. *Information Processing and Management, 21,* 113–126.

Krawzcak, D., Smith, P., & Shute, S. (1987). EP-X: A demonstration of semantically based search of bibliographic databases. *Proceedings of the Annual International ACMSIGIR [Association for Computing Machinery Special Interest Group in Storage and Retrieval] Conference on Research & Development in Information Retrieval,* pp. 263–271. New York: ACM Press.

Lancaster, W. (1986). *Vocabulary control for information retrieval* (2nd ed.). Arlington, VA: Information Resources Press.

Lebowitz, M. (1980). *Generalization and memory in an integrated understanding system (Research Report 186)* (AD 093 083). New Haven, CT: Dept. of Computer Science, Yale University.

Loatman, R. B. (1987). A hybrid architecture for natural language understanding. *Proceedings of the SPIE [Society of Photo-Optical Instrumentation Engineers]: Applications of Artificial Intelligence V, 786,* 416–423.

Maron, M. E. (1961). Automatic indexing: An experimental inquiry, *Journal of the Association for Computing Machinery, 8,* 404–417.

Mills, J. (1955). Chain indexing and the classified catalog. *Library Association Record, 57,* 141–148.

Monarch, I., & Carbonell, J. (1987). CoalSORT: A knowledge-based interface. *IEEE Expert, 2,* 39–53.

Oddy, R. (1977). Information retrieval through man-machine dialog. *Journal of Documentation, 33,* 1–14.

Pople, H. E., Jr. (1982). Heuristic methods for imposing structure on ill-structured problems: The structuring of medical diagnostics. In *Artificial intelligence in medicine* (pp. 119–190). Washington, DC: American Association for the Advancement of Science/Westview Press.

Ranganathan, S. R. (1963). *Colon classification* (6th rev. ed.). London: Asia Publishing House.

Ranganathan, S. R. (1967). *Prolegomena to library classification.* London: Asia Publishing House.

Rauzino, Vincent C. (1983). Natural language processors. *Computerworld, 17,* 45–52.

Richmond, P. (1981). *Introduction to PRECIS for North American usage.* Littleton, CO: Libraries Unlimited.

Salton, G., & McGill, M. J. (1983). *Introduction to modern information retrieval.* New York: McGraw-Hill.

Salton, G., Fox, E. A., & Vorhees, E. (1985). Advanced feedback methods in information retrieval. *Journal of the American Society for Information Science, 36,* 200–210.

Sears List of Subject Headings (13th ed.). (1986). New York: H. W. Wilson.

Smith, P., Shute, S., Chignell, M., & Krawczak, D. (1987). *The role of the human factors engineer in designing the interface to a knowledge-based system* (Technical Report ISSE-174). Columbus, OH: Department of Industrial and Systems Engineering, Ohio State University.

Soergel, D. (1974). *Indexing languages and thesauri: Construction and maintenance.* Los Angeles: Melville Publishing Company.

Sokal, R. R., & Sneath, P. H. A. (1963). *Numerical taxonomy.* San Francisco: W. H. Freeman.

Sowa, John F. (1983). *Conceptual structures: Information processing in mind and machine.* Reading, MA: Addison-Wesley.

Swanson, D. R. (1971). Some unexplained aspects of the Cranfield tests of indexing performance factors. *Library Quarterly, 41,* 223–228.

Travis, I. L. (1982). Faceted classification in an online environment. *Proceedings of the 4th International Study Conference on Classification Research.* Frankfurt: Index Verlag.

U.S. Library of Congress (1983). *Class T: Technology: Library of Congress classification schedules: A cumulation of additions and changes through 1981.* Detroit, MI: Gale Research.

U.S. Library of Congress (1984). *Supplement to the LC Subject Headings, January-December.* Washington, DC: US Government Printing Office.

U.S. Library of Congress. Subject Cataloging Division. (1986). *Library of Congress subject headings* (10th ed.). Washington, DC: US Government Printing Office.

U.S. National Aeronautics and Space Administration. (1982). *NASA thesaurus* (NASA SP-7051). Washington, DC: NASA Scientific and Technical Information Branch.

Vleduts-Stokolov, N. (1987). Concept recognition in an automatic text-processing system for the life sciences. *Journal of the American Society for Information Science, 38,* 269–287.

Waldrop, M. M. (1987). Artificial intelligence moves into the mainstream. *Science, 237,* 484.

Williamson, N. (1989). The Library of Congress classification in the computer age. *Classification Theory in the Computer Age.* Albany, NY: School of Information Science and Policy, University at Albany, State University of New York.

Wilson, P. (1968). *Two kinds of power: An essay in bibliographic control.* Berkeley, CA: University of California Press.

Woods, W. (1970). Transition network grammars for natural language analysis. *Communications of the ACM, 13,* 591–606.

Zadeh, L. (1965). Fuzzy sets. *Information and Control, 8,* 338–353.

16

Managing and Budgeting For Expert Systems*

E. Dale Cluff
Director of Libraries
Texas Tech University

INTRODUCTION

Expert systems. The very words conjure up numerous images. How does one manage and budget for expert systems? The thought of expert systems in libraries is very new. There just isn't enough experience or information to be able to make safe decisions about the impact they will have on the human, material, monetary, and space resources of the library. But who said all decisions made by library managers had to be safe? The profession, thankfully, has its share of pioneers who are willing to risk and innovate, fail and succeed, share and encourage.

Though expert systems, in one form or another, have been around much longer in fields such as manufacturing, space, and engineering, entry into the library and information sciences arena is recent. This recency makes managing and budgeting for them even more challenging. The job would be easier had we the advantage of the experiential base that we now have with other technologies. Nevertheless, in spite of the risk, I shall forge ahead with the assignment. I will explore what I think are some of the issues associated with managing and budgeting for expert systems.

In a discussion of expert systems, some will find the topic to be controversial. We may not all agree on all aspects of the topic. Indeed, my hope is that we would find points over which we disagree. On that note, let me share an experience that happened to me recently. I attended a professional meeting with several of my librarian friends. As part of the business, some changes to the bylaws had been recommended. During the course of the discussion, I suggested

*A portion of this chapter is from "The Role and Responsibility of the Library in Preservation and Conservation," by E. Dale Cluff, in *Conserving and Preserving Library Materials, edited by K.L. Henderson and T. Williams. Reprinted with permission from the University of Illinois Graduate School of Library and Information Science. © 1983 by The Board of Trustees of The University of Illinois.*

an amendment to the recommended amendment. As soon as I had finished giving a rationale for my point of view, one of my colleagues, sitting three or four rows behind me, stood and spoke against my motion. Discussion ceased. The question was called for. I was the only one in the group of about 45 people who boldly said "aye." All of the rest voiced a resounding "nay." Being the last item on the agenda, the meeting adjourned. My friend, who had spoken in opposition, came right up to me and said that he hoped I would not take his opposition personally. Wanting to give the appearance that it hadn't bothered me at all, I came to full stature, looked him in the eye, grinned, and said, "Hey, no problem, I've been opposed by better men than you." One nice thing about expert systems at their present state of development is there is no room for embarrassing Freudian slips. They will do and say only what they are programmed to do.

Any change in an organization causes fear, doubt, expectation, uneasiness, stress, anxiety, and any number of other emotions depending upon how far-reaching the change, the degree of involvement in the process by members of the organization, and the individual temperament of staff.

It is so important to have broad staff interest and support early in the change process that I would like to spend a few moments on this. Like most changes, if expert systems are viewed as being imposed from the top or as being the concern of only a small number in the organization, the program is in for a rocky future. Conversely, problems will appear if the program is too heavily dependent upon committee efforts. Strong support from the top is also needed for a successful change.

To strike a balance, then, between a top- and grass- roots-implemented program is the goal. This balance will insure strong support and commitment at all levels for the program. Leadership at the top is needed to train, direct, listen, design, set resource support parameters, and evaluate while staff is needed to engender enthusiasm, carry out the plans, give initial feedback, educate the library user, and make program modification suggestions. A program, especially a new one, will function much more smoothly and will have a greater chance of success if this kind of teamwork is evident.

A smoothly functioning organization might be visualized as a sphere rolling along at a comfortable pace. All parts of the organization are interacting with a single purpose. Then, someone suggests an idea which necessitates change in the organization. This change causes stress because it requires adjustments in schedules, relocation of parts of the organization, additional training, and changes in thought patterns, routines, and working partners. The change requires additional funds, people, supplies, and equipment, or a reallocation of such. The stress becomes more severe in those parts of the organization from which resources are being siphoned. As this siphoning occurs, stress increases and the organization takes on the shape of a sphere with a bulge on its surface (Figure 16.1). The bulge represents the part of the organization into which the dollar and human

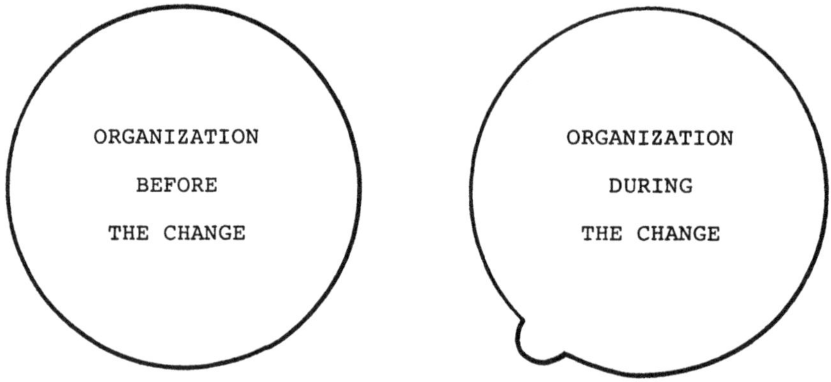

resources, including considerable human energies, are being directed. We all know how difficult it is to handle a ball containing a bulge. This is the period in the life of the organization which is most crucial. The goal is to round out the sphere and to get all parts of the organization readjusted and working smoothly again. This can be done more quickly when leadership and staff are together at the genesis of the change. When they are together, stress is minimal, resistance to the change low, commitment high, and the program successful. The organizational sphere adjusts, the bulge deflates, and it is rolling smoothly once again. An organization, like a human body, has a way of either severing or incorporating an appendage. If the appendage (bulge) is seen as unnecessary, it is rejected. Conversely, if the appendage is seen as helpful, it will be accepted and willingly incorporated. Introduction of an expert system(s), if handled well, will be accepted by most staff and become not only a valuable, but essential, part of the operation of the library.

Let's take a look now at expert systems from four somewhat different, but related points of view:

1. Applications in libraries
2. Implementation considerations
3. Cost implications
4. Impact of expert systems on library personnel

APPLICATIONS

I won't dwell heavily on the applications aspect of expert systems since others have done that quite well. However, I take the prerogative to add one or two applications from a speculative point of view.

Thinking about areas where robotics and expert systems might be applied in libraries opened the door for the following. Can you picture a robot automatically shelving books? Perhaps the "eye" of the robot is busily scanning the call numbers, which can be optically read, while the arm places the book in its proper place. Miksa (1987) reported that in 1883 Cutter predicted 100 years hence, robots would be used to pick books off of shelves. Though I have no knowledge of the use of robotics in libraries, they are certainly being used in industry. A possible environment in which robotics could play an important role in libraries is in the area of warehousing. Several large research libraries have already outgrown space and have constructed storage units, often remote from the main library collection. In the future, perhaps storage units could have robotics designed into them. Robots could retrieve and reshelve books for the user. Another related application is use in closed stacks arrangements. Again, robots could retrieve and reshelve. Compact shelving might be an environment in which robotics could be applied.

The sophistication of an expert system for a given application depends upon the specialized use of that system. The more that is required of the system, the more it will take to design it and consequently, the more it will cost. For example, a question we might ask when considering the use of expert systems for directional help is, should we design graphics into it or do we want it to give only textual responses? Graphics might be helpful if a floor plan would expedite getting the user to the service point or to a particular spot in the stacks. The important thing to remember, as we conclude this section on applications, is that an expert system works where the knowledge base can be well defined, focused, and delineated.

IMPLEMENTATION

At this point I would like to raise some implementation issues. Numerous considerations must be carefully weighed and questions asked before embarking on expert system implementation for one's library. The most important thought I could leave with you is to be cautious of the "bandwagon approach." Expert systems for expert systems' sake or robotics for robotics' sake is obviously not the way to go. However, if there is a legitimate place for this technology in your library then the appropriate approach is to follow the same line of thinking you would for any change. Expert systems are just another tool. They are not and will not be the ultimate answer to all of our service ills. Working expert systems into present library services begins with the need being identified; then it follows the normal planning process.

Numerous questions need to be asked when considering installing or implementing an expert system. A very critical question to ask is what will be the acceptance level of the library patron? Most of us have had experiences where we have made a decision (introduced a new service, changed an existing service) based on the assumption that it would please our user and found, to our chagrin, after hours of planning and dollars expended, that our patrons did not like it. How will the system you are planning to install tie in with system-wide (university, public library, corporation) plans and development? How supportive is the upper administration, governing body, and so on? It goes without saying that without our bosses' support, the system will likely fail.

Do you have people on the staff who possess the knowledge to design the appropriate architecture for the expert system? You would likely be better off working closely with a systems engineer, a knowledge engineer, computer specialist or the like. Your staff and the computer persons will likely be better able to delineate the project, set appropriate goals that will address the user needs and formalize key concepts, strategies, and so on. These people would develop the system to a point where it could be given for feedback from the potential users of the system. At this phase the question of whether the knowledge base is large enough to paramount. The rules for accessing the knowledge base are also vital; they must be precisely defined.

Other questions related to the architecture of the system include whether it will be a stand-alone system with just one copy or whether it will become part of a local area network. Would it appropriately be run on personal computers, minicomputers, or a larger system? Will it be accessible on public access catalog terminals or will there be dedicated terminals? Will there be printers associated with the system? Where will the expert system be located in the library itself? If it has to do with public service, should it be distributed throughout the entire library on different floors or centralized in one area?

Some other questions which need to be answered include: Who will load the software? This relates to the question of who on the staff will know how to work the system. Will all reference librarians be trained to care for and teach its use or will these aspects be the responsibility of the systems person? Or someone else? How will the user be trained to operate the system? Regardless of the instructions designed into the system, or the number of prompts it contains, there will be a need to have some instructions affixed to the workstation, regardless of how brief or simple.

How will the system be cataloged? Let's say you have designed an expert system to guide a patron to a reference tool. You would want to give the user the opportunity to discover the expert system as he or she is searching in the library catalog for some information on the subject(s) desired. In other words, while searching the library's catalog, the user should be able to discover the expert system. How will the expert system be listed? It really isn't a print source. How should it be classified? This example is fairly straightforward since AACR2 has rules for software on data files (MRDF) and they are listed as a format document in OCLC. Other expert systems might not be so easy. To get us thinking further about this question, let me ask those of you who represent libraries which acquired Info Trac, how many of your libraries cataloged it? Under what was it listed? This example is fairly straightforward. After all, it is a periodical index and a serial since it is regularly updated. What about resources we are acquiring on compact disc? Anyone purchase ERIC on CD? Are you going to catalog ERIC on CD-ROM?

The bottom line, when considering implementation implications, is planning. Expert system use in the library must be well thought out and well planned. You would do the same for any other tool you might be considering. I illustrate my point by relating an experience. Standing tall and proud in the 1974 addition to a major university library is, what was at the time, a modern innovation that was designed to move books automatically between circulation and the stack levels. A book elevator, or lift, was designed and installed to "save" time and labor. This several thousand dollar innovation has stood dormant, having never worked, as a reminder to be sure that the idea is workable before implementing it. An understanding of what expert systems will do for the user must be clear; then a systematic and methodical plan formulated.

COST IMPLICATIONS

Let's shift gears now and discuss the financial impact of expert systems and robotics on the library. I would like to focus briefly on "the delicate balance." Another way of stating it might be "the temperamental triad." The three main parts of a library budget are people, materials, and maintenance and operations (M&O). Figure 16.2 is a graphic illustration of this delicate balance. You plug in your own figures. The arrow is an indicator that percentages vary by library. I have used 50/10/40 for illustrative purposes only. Now, the question: For budgetary purposes, what do you call expert systems? In other words, into what category would you place dollars expended for an expert system?

Some librarians have been successful at getting the materials budget renamed "information" and having it accepted by the purchasing department (whether it be the state or local one), thereby being able to acquire more than tangible objects that go into inventories where auditors can be satisfied. In other words, they can now acquire "disposable" information. In these states, paying for subscriptions to online data base vendors out of the old "materials"—now "information"—portion of the budget is natural and accepted.

Should expert systems be charged against the people part of the budget? Or, are they more appropriately materials because their end result is information (so is help obtained from a reference librarian)? Or perhaps as we have done historically, because they are associated with computers, should they come out of the M&O or "other" portion of the budget such as equipment, phone charges, maintenance contracts, and so on?

We ask ourselves, what does it matter? Does it really matter? The answer is loud and clear. It matters! It matters because:

1. Institutional and state laws direct how we use the various parts of our budget. For example, in Texas it is easier to buy books out of equipment money than purchasing equipment with money which has been earmarked for books. In one instance we purchased equipment from the materials budget, but only after acquiring special permission. It is difficult to shift people money (salary money which has accrued to the budget because of a vacancy or someone is on leave without pay) to other parts of the budget (e.g., M&O). The opposite is very difficult. In Texas we were recently given authorization to purchase maps and AV materials with book funds without the necessity of going through a special bidding process. For years we purchased maps and sheet music on a bid basis through the Purchasing Commission rather than having them handled as books or periodicals. There are many other examples of how institutional and state regulations dictate how we are to use the money for libraries.

2. Libraries compare themselves with other libraries for budget justification and for other reasons. Though we know the downside of statistics and especially of comparison, the game goes on all the time. I had been at Texas Tech University for just a year or so when I received a letter from the president of the university. Now, I don't know how you feel when you get a letter from the person above your boss. Since that generally doesn't happen, I took the letter quite seriously. He stated that he had noted that nearly 50% of the library budget is used for personnel and he wanted to know how that compared with the seven largest state-supported university libraries in Texas. Of course, I was delighted because I knew about the "temperamental triad" and had decided some time prior to ever receiving that letter that TTU library was a lean, mean machine. I saw this as a fine opportunity to educate my superiors. Of course, we came out

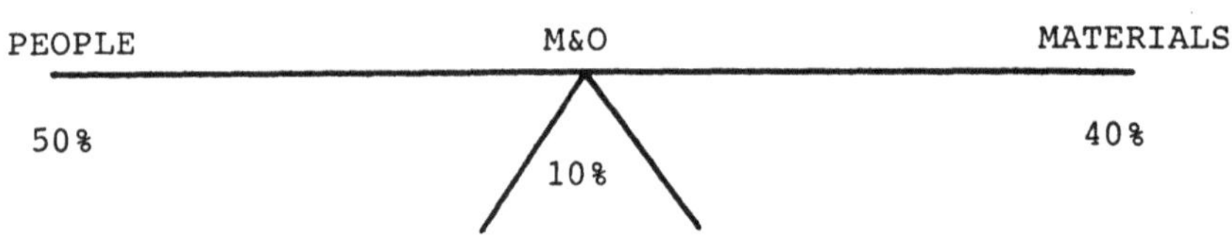

looking very good, I received a nice letter of thanks, and we went on. My point is that we do use comparative statistics. We do compare ourselves with others using fairly standard components of our budgets. It is important, when we do so, to compare apples with apples. The Texas State Library and the Texas Council of State University Librarians cooperatively produce a volume of statistics annually which I as well as many other administrators use fairly often. It includes page after page of categories by which we academic libraries in the state are compared. We must carefully, and I think cooperatively, decide what areas of the budget should be used to pay for expert systems. It will take unified efforts to convince the appropriate bodies to change appropriate laws and guidelines.

We must get away from pigeonholing library budgets. We must work toward greater flexibility in the use of the precious dollars allocated for providing this critically important service. We librarians are certainly partially to blame for the "counting" mentality we have. I particularly appreciated the comments by White (1987):

> Stop counting and reporting the things that aren't worth counting . . . I refer . . . to holdings and to rank orders that suggest that libraries have moved from one place to another. While these statistics report holding rankings, they suggest a qualitative ranking. That may have been a fun game in the 1950s and 1960s, but it is a death trap now. These statistics are not only relatively meaningless, we also know them to be grossly inaccurate. Do we know how many books we really have? Should we care? Should anyone care? . . . Start counting and reporting things that do matter. What matters is that we are able to get people things they need, and that we are able to help them identify and determine what it is they need. That, of course, is not *ownership*, it is *access* and it is *delivery*.

Now that I have hopefully made a case for a little more flexibility in the way we use our library budgets, I want to address some of the specific considerations associated with financing expert systems in libraries.

At the risk of being repititious, I do want to remind us of the issue of free versus fee. Librarians have struggled with this issue for years. Remember how we each had to determine how we would handle computer-assisted reference or database searching for our patrons? We had to decide whether we were going to require the patron to pay for all or part of the service or to subsidize all or part of the service out of our library budget. (I raise the question again. For those of you who are subsidizing part of it, out of what part of the budget does it come?) We have the same question to decide when we introduce expert systems into our library. When you begin to ask the hard questions, you will find that the subissues are little different for expert systems and computer-assisted reference.

Let's get to the bottom line. How much money is it going to cost us to implement expert systems? The answer is obvious. It depends on how expert systems fit into your library's mission and how quickly you move and how much you want. The amount could be very little or very large, depending upon the application. The types of costs are several. There will be initial costs and ongoing costs. There will be personnel costs. There will be hardware and software costs. There may be telecommunications costs.

Let's look first at labor or personnel costs. It is customary to have a knowledge engineer work with the librarian in building the knowledge base for an expert system. This is not always necessary, but if it is, unless the knowledge engineer is feeling particularly gracious, it will cost to hire one as a consultant. Of course, if the library is planning to go into expert systems in a big way, administration may decide it wise to hire a knowledge engineer as a permanent member of the staff. A similar decision was made in many libraries in the past to hire systems persons to oversee automation in the library. Other staff may need to be hired to help plan, design, and implement expert systems. Additional staff may be needed to help train people on the library staff in the use of these systems and to teach patrons how to use them if they are part of the public services of the library. At this point there is very little available from vendors.

We must be careful when selling the need for expert systems to our administrators. Perhaps the time is past when it was assumed that automation meant staff replacement or labor savings. Just as computing has not generally saved personnel costs over the past several years, expert systems won't either. We must be sure to sell the need based on improved service rather than on being able to decrease our staff costs. Indeed, just as has happened in many libraries, staff costs may increase because of the need to add staff or to hire staff with different backgrounds, many of whom can demand higher salaries.

It is probably safe to say that as expert systems become more acceptable in libraries the costs will go down just as they have in other areas of library automation. Once we get beyond the experimental and research stages of expert systems, we will find some types easy to obtain. They will become available off the shelf from library expert system vendors. It is a truism that libraries who begin to apply expert systems early on will bear a greater cost burden than the library that waits until much of the research and development is behind us. Of course, there may be disadvantages to waiting, especially if the situation and circumstances are such that your library needs to move ahead.

Most of us are aware that the initial costs of purchasing equipment, such as computers, are not necessarily the greatest cost. The ongoing cost of maintenance and replacement often are greater, especially over time. This will also be true of expert systems, which operate on computing equipment. You may already have the necessary equipment to handle some systems, thus keeping additional costs to a minimum. We are also aware that ongoing costs for certain types of software can be quite expensive. The lesson here is to be sure to factor in annual costs for any expert system. Continuing costs will center on maintaining the knowledge base and distributing new versions of the expert system. Robotics will likely cost more than expert systems. In addition to the cost of the robots may be the cost of reconfiguring the shelving—height, width, type of shelves, aisle width, and so on.

The cost of equipment and software for expert systems varies greatly. Systems requiring a specialized LISP machine environment may run between $90,000 and $120,000; A KEE (Knowledge Engineering Environment) about $50,000; ART (Automated Reasoning Tool) about $60,000. A 386 chip machine technology system will run about $8,000; Goldworks will cost about $6,000. A TI Personal Consultant EASY 2.0 runs about $400; while the TI Personal Consultant PLUS 3.0 will cost about $3,000. The GURU (Micro Data Base System, Inc.) is about $6,250. Please remember that these prices are only estimates. Educational discounts and other variables may lower these estimates.

I would hope that library managers would not dismiss expert systems out of hand because they don't think they can afford them. We must and will afford them if they will provide valuable advantages to the overall service to our publics. Our budgets will handle this technology in direct proportion to its proven need. Good managers will find ways to do a job if it is needed.

IMPACT ON PERSONNEL

Remember the resistance many library staff members had and still have to the invasion into the library scene of the "terrible" computer? The fears of being replaced by a machine have dissipated throughout library land. But that outcry of concern by many library staff in retrospect might be classified as only a slight tremor when compared to what might be described as a disastrous earthquake when staff first hear of the encroachment into their parlance of such frightful sounding words as "artificial intelligence," "expert systems," "knowledge engineers," and especially "robotics." You can imagine the high degree of insecurity felt by staff as they picture themselves being replaced in cataloging and reference by these machines and experts.

There is no basis for fear that expert systems will replace library personnel. However, White and Woodward at Drexel are trying to simulate what a reference librarian does (Riggs, 1987). What will likely happen is this technology will enable librarians to focus their energies on more challenging professional work. In reference, librarians will be released from the need to answer myriads of directional and quick reference questions. Instead of telling numerous patrons where the water fountain is and many others how to use the Readers Guide, the reference librarian will spend more time with complicated questions, instruction, collection development, and being more effective members of the planning team. Another opinion, this one held by Rao Aluri and Donald E. Riggs (1987), is "there is no guarantee that . . . the expert systems will reduce the workload of reference librarians in terms of not having to answer too many low-skill and repetitious questions."

Smith (1986) gives an eloquent justification for the introduction of expert systems in reference service. She says:

> Robot librarian might be just the thing to relieve us from overwork, burnout, boredom, and frustration. Academic reference librarians are caught up in a situation where there are too few people to do the work that needs to be done; the job keeps expanding; the reference sources proliferate; information retrieval becomes increasingly complex; and, in spite of all our efforts at bibliographic instruction, naive end users continue to parade through our turnstiles. We are committed to making our users "library literate" but how many times can you explain how to find periodicals in the library without sounding like a robot yourself?

There may be some who oppose having machines at information and reference desks. There were and still are librarians who think that it is not wise to place para- professionals at the reference desk even though data show that the majority of questions fielded at the reference or information desk are elementary and can easily be fielded by someone without a library degree. We have already proven that paraprofessionals can handle the majority of the cataloging in a given library. The need for original cataloging in most libraries is presently down to 15–20% of all cataloging. This blessing was a direct result of the computer and networking. Expert systems promise to reduce that percentage even more. Another impact of expert systems on the staff deals with the decreasing pool of qualified catalogers. Perhaps these systems will reduce the need to recruit catalogers.

Gary K. McCone (1987) reported that "the coming influx of expert systems in libraries will have a marked effect on librarians and their role in information dissemination." He notes the difference between the traditional and the future library (Table 16.1). The traditional library dispenses information, keeps materials, is passive, is generally centralized and emphasizes the physical collection, while the future library distributes knowledge, is a broker of information and knowledge, gives active assistance, is distributed and is tied in to electronic networks emphasizing access.

I think there is no question that the advent of expert systems will have a very real impact on library staff. That impact will be felt in various ways. The most critical of these, however, is psychological. It is threatening to think of a

Table 16.1. Libraries.

Traditional	Future
Information	Knowledge
Keepers	Brokers
Passive text	Active assistants
Centralized	Distributed
Physical collection	Electronic networks

machine that behaves somewhat as a human does. Self- esteem can suffer terribly if a librarian thinks that a machine is now going to store and use his or her knowledge that he or she has worked so hard and long to gain. There will likely be some reluctance on the part of the librarian to transfer his or her knowledge to the machine. Managers must educate, prepare, and involve staff carefully before expert systems are introduced into the organization.

I have addressed expert systems for libraries from the point of view of finances and management. I have raised more questions than given answers. Many questions have not been asked. Many answers still wait to be discovered. The future is exciting indeed.

REFERENCES

Aluri, R. & Riggs, D. E. (1987). Unpublished manuscript.

McCone, G. K. (1987). Expert systems or librarian ex machina. *Library Information and Technology Association Newsletter, 30*, 4.

Miksa, F. (1987, November). *Accessing information in 2011 A.D.* Paper presented at the 6th Texas Conference on Library Automation, Houston, TX.

Riggs, D. C. (1987, November). *Expert systems and robotics: What are they and what exists now?* Paper presented at the 6th Texas Conference on Library Automation, Houston, TX.

Smith, K. (1986). Robot at the reference desk? *College and Research Libraries, 47*, 486–490.

White, H. S. (1987). Trouble at the OK corral university library. *Library Journal, 112*, 154–155.

17
The Future

Donald E. Riggs
Arizona State University Tempe, AZ

At best, the current status of expert systems in libraries can be described as primitive. It is difficult to purchase an expert system from the marketplace. However, it is becoming much easier to buy expert system shells geared for library applications. And the cost for shells is becoming less as more of them are being developed for libraries.

The future for expert systems in libraries is very bright. And these knowledge-based systems are bringing the most sophisticated technology ever implemented in libraries. Advancements in technology are happening at an unbelievable rate. Every eight years computer technology has advanced in performance parameters by the order of 100 times. Five such periods of advancement may be distinguished historically. For the sake of comparison with another area, the aircraft industry has only seen one such comparable advance in its 75-year history. As new "super" microcomputers are developed, libraries will be able to introduce more comprehensive expert systems.

ACCESS

One of the primary advantages of expert systems is that they can be accessed at different locations in the library (e.g., they can provide reference assistance at locations other than just the reference desk). Transportability of expert systems from one library to another is a feature that will become more evident in the future. As the front-end subsystems for expert systems are refined, a great potential lies in the ability to access a library's expert system from one's home via a modem-equipped personal computer. Just to mention this possibility may appear to be a bit far-fetched at the current time when expert systems are just beginning to get off the ground in providing basic services. However, it is already possible to access online library catalogs from anywhere in world via telephone dial-in. Online catalogs now make it possible to perform a subject search from one's home and get a printout of journal articles (from one's home printer) on a particular topic. Accessing the various expert systems from one's home is on the near horizon and it will be another positive and productive step toward improving library and information services. And we will find that this type of accessibility will definitely increase the usage of libraries.

IMPACT ON LIBRARY STAFF

Librarians have a natural uneasiness about expert systems. They are witnessing the first experience with machines that think like humans. Loss of self-esteem through deskilling is not uncommon among them. Transfer of intellectual activity from the librarian to the machine is a psychological aspect that is inescapable. And job security is another apprehension conjured by the introduction of expert systems.

Implementing expert systems in libraries will not replace librarians. However, some library jobs will be done as well by expert systems as by staff. Library administrators should not justify their budget requests for expert systems on the premise that they will save funds and reduce the need for additional staff. Expert systems may deter the need for more staff, but they carry a cost factor that has to be included in the library's annual budget request. The primary emphasis should be placed on the improvement of service.

Expert systems are making the librarian's work much more enjoyable. For example, an intelligent machine that can handle the repetitive questions asked at the information and reference desks is a tremendous asset. More time can now be devoted to the more challenging professional work.

The future will bring a greater appreciation for the utility of expert systems in libraries. Librarians will undergo some initial psychological uneasiness due to apprehensions about these intelligent, knowledge-based systems. We can expect several research projects devoted to the impact of expert systems on the work of librarians.

PRODUCTIVITY

Advancements will surely be made in the level of intelligent problem solving offered by expert systems. Such systems are expected to reach a level of performance comparable to that of a human expert in a specialized problem area. The high-level knowledge base and associated control mechanism of expert systems are in essence a model of the expertise of the best practitioners of the library problem area in question. Productivity in various areas of the library (e.g., cataloging, instructional services, reference) will be improved by expert systems. Expert systems do not suffer boredom, burnout, or fatigue; they can work around the clock and do not quit after the normal eight-hour day. They are always systematic in their approach to problem solving and they do not become frustrated at naive users. The use of libraries continue to grow each year, but the size of library staffs remains stable. The growing number of users has, for example, made the reference librarian's life very difficult. Long lines of users waiting at the reference desk for assistance tend to cause reference librarians to react to current pressure to help each user in a quick way, and not get involved in an extended reference interview. Such pressure will also cause librarians to misunderstand questions, forget the existence of certain reference sources, give wrong answers, and do other things that reflect badly on the competence of the library. When they become more refined, expert systems will provide a dramatic improvement in productivity in reference service. Users will find future expert systems to have an effective deductive reasoning capability that will be able to ask questions, solve problems, and justify their conclusions.

Efficiency and effectiveness will both be improved by library expert systems. The librarian's time will be freed from much of the repetitive routine work, and more time will be available for creative work. And, in the long run, creativity will foster greater productivity.

ANOTHER NEW DIMENSION

The central thrust of expert systems is to mimic the functions of the human brain. The human brain distributes information across a vast network of nerve cells (neurons). Recent and future advances in neural networks will play a significant role in developing the capabilities of expert systems. Creating artificial neurons (similar to those in the human brain) that are interconnected will permit the sharing of information and performing tasks simultaneously. This two-dimensional approach works best at recognizing patterns. Instead of looking for patterns, expert systems distill the decision-making process used by human experts into rules of thumb. It is predicted that a combination of expert systems and neural networks could find the answers to those problems too complex for either to solve alone.

There is much more research required before one can truly replicate the human brain. Nevertheless, a much better understanding is being grasped on how the brain functions. Combining the principles of neural networking with library expert systems will result in a powerful "intellectual" library tool. We will probably not see this combination occurring until around the latter part of the 1990s.

Developing the computer's ability to function like the human brain is a extraordinary phenomenon. And since expert systems are moving in this direction, they are indeed going to become more recognizable and appreciated as true "experts" in libraries. The assistance realized from them will be one of the greatest things to happen in the history of library service. We are entering an era where the creativity of librarians can be finally be released.

> Machines will do the humdrum work of humanity. The computers will keep the world going, and human beings will be free at last to do things only human beings can do—to create. (Isaac Asimov)

Expert Systems Selected Bibliography

Rao Aluri
Burr-Brown Corporate Library
Tucson, AZ

Addis, T. R. (1986). *Designing knowledge-based systems*. Englewood Cliffs, NJ: Prentice-Hall.

Addis, T. R. (1982, October). Expert systems: An evolution in information retrieval. *Information Technology: Research and Development, 1*(4), 301–324.

Adiga, S. (1984, Winter). Expert Systems: An overview. *Science Software Quarterly, 1*(4), 7–11.

Alberico, R. (1987, November). Knowledge representation: The realm of the possible. *Small Computers in Libraries, 7*(10), 4–9.

Alberico, R. (1987, December). More on knowledge representation. *Small Computers in Libraries, 7*(11), 10–16.

Alberico, R. (1988, February). User-supported artificial intelligence. *Small Computers in Libraries, 8*(2), 4–9.

Alberico, R. (1988, July/August). Software for expert systems: Languages versus shells. *Small Computers in Libraries, 8*(7), 4-12.

Alberico, R., & Micco, M. (1989). *Expert systems for reference and information retrieval*. Westport, CT: Meckler.

Alexander, T. (1985, May). Special report: Part one: Artificial intelligence. *Popular Computing, 4*(7), 66–69, 142–145.

Alty, J. L. (1982). The impact of microtechnology: A case for reassuring the roles of computers in learning. *Computers and Education, 6*(1), 1–5.

Alty, J. L., & Coombs, M. J. V. (1984). *Expert systems concepts and examples*. Manchester, UK: NCC Publications.

Aluri, R. (1988, March). Expert systems for libraries. *Library Administration & Management, 2*(2), 91–94.

Aluri, R., & Riggs, D. E. (1988). Application of expert systems to libraries. In J. A. Hewitt (Ed.), *Advances in library automation and networking: A research annual* (Vol. 2, pp. 1–43). Greenwich, CT: JAI Press.

Amsterdam, J. (1985, May). Special report: Part two: Expert systems. *Popular Computing, 4*(7), 70–72, 150, 153.

Anderson, P.F. (1988, October). Expert systems, expertise, and the library and information professions. *Library & Information Science Research, 10*(4), 367-388.

Barr, A. & Feigenbaum, E A. (Eds). (1981). *The handbook of artificial intelligence*. Los Altos, CA: William Kaufmann.

Beechhold, H. F. (1985, January 28). Expert choice: It's tough to learn, but could be a valuable tool. *InfoWorld, 7*(4), 45–50.

Belkin, N. J., & Vickery, A. (1985). Question-answering and expert systems. In *Interaction in information systems: A review of research from document retrieval to knowledge-based systems* (pp. 144–187). London: British Library.

Berkeley, E. C. (1985, May). Artificial intelligence and real intelligence. *Computers and People, 34*(5), 6.

Bernold, T., & Albers, G. (1985). *Artificial intelligence: Towards a practical application*. New York: Elsevier Science Publishers.

Berry, D. C., & Broadbent, D. E. (1986, October). Expert systems and the man-machine interface. *Expert Systems, 3*(4), 228–231.

Bianchi, G., & Giorgi, M. (1986). Towards an expert system as intelligent assistant for the design of an online documentation service. In *Proceedings of the 10th International Online Information Meeting*. London, England (pp. 199–208). Oxford, England: Learned Information.

Bibel, W., & Petkoff, B. (1984). *Artificial intelligence: Methodology, systems, applications*. New York: Elsevier Science Publishing Co.

Bigger, C. J., & Coupland, J. W. (Eds). (1983). *Expert systems: A bibliography*. Piscataway, NJ: Institution of Electrical Engineers.

Binkley, R. D., & Parrott, J. R. (1987). A reference-librarian model for computer-aided library instruction. *Information services and use, 1*, 31–38.

Black, W. J. (1986). *Intelligent knowledge based systems: An introduction*. Wokingham, Berkshire, England: Von Nostrand Reinhold (UK).

Black, W. J., Hargreaves, P., & Mayes, P. B. (1985). HEADS: a cataloguing advisory system. In *Advances in intelligent retrieval: INFORMATICS 8. Proceedings of an Aslib/British Computer Society Joint Conference* (pp. 227–239). London, England: Aslib.

Blanning, R. W. (1984). Expert systems for management: Research and applications. *Journal of Information Science, 9*(4), 153–162.

Blanning, R. W. (1984, December). Management applications of expert systems. *Information and Management, 7*(6), 311–316.

Boose, J. H. (1985, November). A knowledge acquisition program for expert systems based on personal construct psychology. *International Journal of Man-Machine Studies, 23*(5), 495–525.

Boose, J. H. (1986). *Expertise transfer for expert system design*. Amsterdam/New York: Elsevier.

Borko, H. (1985, June). Artificial intelligence and expert systems research and their possible impact on information science education. *Education for Information, 3*(2), 103–114.

Borko, H. (1987). Getting started in library expert systems research. *Information Processing & Management, 23*(2), 81–87.

Bramer, M. A. (1979). A survey and critical review of expert systems. In *Expert systems in the microelectronic age*. Edinburgh, Scotland: Edinburgh University Press.

Bramer, M. A. (Ed.). (1985). *Research and development in expert systems: Proceedings of the Fourth Technical Conference of the British Computer Society Specialist Group on Expert Systems, University of Warwick, 18–20 December 1984*. Cambridge [Cambridgeshire]/New York: Cambridge University Press.

Bramer, M. A. (Ed.). (1987). *Research and development in expert systems III: Proceedings of Expert Systems '86, the Sixth Annual Technical Conference of the British Computer Society Specialist Group on Expert Systems, Brighton, 15–18 December 1986*. Cambridge [Cambridgeshire], NY: Cambridge University Press.

Bramer, M. A., & Bramer, D. (Comps.). (1984). *The fifth generation: An annotated bibliography*. Reading, MA: Addison-Wesley.

Brittain, M. (1987). Implications for LIS education of recent developments in expert systems. *Information Processing & Management, 23*(2), 139–152.

Brodie, M. L., & Lylopoulos, J. (Eds.). (1986). *On knowledge base management systems: Integrating artificial intelligence and database technologies*. New York: Springer-Verlag.

Brooke, D. L. (1983, December). *Natural language processor as a universal front end to expert systems* (AD-A138455/1). Wright-Patterson AFB, OH: Air Force Inst. of Tech.

Brookes, B. C. (Ed.). (1986). *Intelligent information systems for the information society: Proceedings of the Sixth International Research Forum in Information Science (IRFIS 6)*. Frascati, Italy. Amsterdam/New York: North-Holland.

Brooks, H. M. (1987). Expert systems and intelligent information retrieval. *Information Processing & Management, 23*(4), 367–382.

Brooks, H. M. (1986, March). Fifth generation bibliographic systems: 3. So you want to build an expert system. *MARC Users' Group Newsletter, 86*(1), 46–58.

Brooks, H. M. (1983). Information retrieval and expert systems—approaches and methods of development. In K. P. Jones, (Ed.), *Intelligent information retrieval: Informatics 7, Proceedings of a conference held by the Aslib Informatics Group and the Information Retrieval Group of the British Computer Society* (pp. 65–75). London, England: Aslib.

Brooks, H. M., Belkin, N. J., & Daniels, P. J. (1986). Research on information interaction and intelligent information provision mechanisms. *Journal of Information Science: Principles & Practices, 12*(1/2), 37–44.

Brouwer-Janse, M. D., & Pitt, R. B. (1986). Knowledge acquisition methodological issues and problem-solving profiles. In *ECAI '86 7th European Conference on Artificial Intelligence Proceedings* (Vol. 2, pp. 120–127). London, England: Conference Services.

Brownston, L. (1985). *Programming expert systems in OPS5: An introduction to rule-based programming*. Reading, MA: Addison-Wesley.

Buchanan, B. G., & Shortliffe, E. H. (Eds.). (1984). *Rule-based expert systems: The MYCIN experiments of the Stanford Heuristic Programming Project*. Reading, MA: Addison-Wesley.

Burch, B. (1986, August). AI product update: What's new with LISPs, PROLOGs, and expert systems? *Computer Language, 3*(8), 93–100.

Burton, H. D. (1985). The intelligent gateway processor: Effective computer access to distributed information resources. *Quarterly Bulletin of the International Association of Agricultural Librarians and Documentalists, 30*(3), 55–60.

Butkovich, N.J. et. al. (1989). An expert system at the reference desk: Impressions from users. *Reference Librarian, 23*, 61-74.

Butler, D. (1985, November). Experience using artificial intelligence. *Data Processing, 27*(9), 64–65.

Campbell, J. H. (1984). *Implementations of PROLOG*. Chichester, England: Ellis Horwood Ltd.

Carande, R. (1988, December). INDEXES: A micro-based expert system. *Small Computers in Libraries, 8*, 26–27.

Carne, E. B. (1984). *Artificial intelligence (Artificial intelligence and modern telecommunications)*. New York: Plenum Press.

Cavanagh, J. M. A. (1986). Intra-active retrieval systems. In M. E. Williams & T. H. Hogan (Eds.), *Proceedings of the 7th National Online Meeting* (pp. 59–65), New York, NY. Medford, NJ: Learned Information.

Cavanagh, J. M. A. (1987). The automated readers' advisor: Expert systems technology for a reference function. In M. E. Williams & T. H. Hogan (Eds.), *Proceedings of the 8th National Online Meeting* (pp. 57–65), New York, NY. Medford, NJ: Learned Information.

Cawkell, A. E. (1986, January). The human machine interface-part 4. *Communication Technology Impact, 7*(10), 9–12.

Cercone, N., & McCalla, G. (1984, September). Artificial intelligence: Underlying assumptions and basic objectives. *Journal of the American Society for Information Science, 35*(5), 280–290.

Chadwick, M., & Hannah, J. A. (1986). *Expert systems for microcomputers: An introduction to artificial intelligence*. Blue Ridge Summit, PA: TAB Books.

Chan, D., & Cochran, J. K. (1988, February). Using expert-system shells for graduate student advising. *Engineering Education, 78*, 310–312.

Chandrasekaran, B. (1986, Fall). Generic tasks in knowledge-based reasoning: High-level building blocks for expert system design. *IEEE Expert, 1*(3), 23–30.

Chang, R. (1986, July). The expert systems are coming. *Technicalities, 6*, 9–11.

Chen, Y.-S. (1989). Organizational strategies for decision support and expert systems. *Journal of Information Science, 15*(1), 27-34.

Chignell, M. H. (1986). Information retrieval: An intelligent interface perspective. *Proceedings of the IEEE international conference on systems, man, and cybernetics* (pp. 372–377). New York: IEEE.

Chignell, M. H., Loewenthal, A., & Hancock, P. A. (1985) Intelligent interface design. In *IEEE 1985 proceedings of the international conference on cybernetics and society* (pp. 620–623). New York: IEEE.

Chorafas, D. N. (c1986). *Fourth and fifth generation programming languages*. New York: McGraw-Hill.

Chorafas, D. N. (1987). *Applying expert systems in business*. New York: McGraw-Hill.

Clancy, W. (1987). *Knowledge-based tutoring: The GUIDON program*. Cambridge, MA: MIT Press.

Clare, J. (1984, March). Natural language and knowledge-based system. *Data Processing, 26*(2), 40–42.

Clark, K. L. (1982). An introduction to logic programming. In *Introductory readings in expert systems*. London, England: Gordon and Breach.

Clarke, A., & Cronin, B. (1983, October). Expert systems and library/information work. *Journal of Librarianship, 15*(4), 277–292.

Colbourn, M., & McLeod, J. (1983, Winter). Computer guided educational diagnosis: A prototype expert system. *Journal of Special Education Technology, 6*(1), 30–39.

Cooke, N. M., & McDonald, J. E. (1986, October). A formal methodology for acquiring and representing expert knowledge. *Proceedings of the IEEE, 74*(10), 1422–1430.

Coombs, M. J. (Ed.). (1984). *Developments in expert systems*. London/Orlando, FL: Academic Press.

Cooper, W. S. (1984). Bridging the gap between AI and IR (artificial intelligence and information retrieval). The British Computer Society Workshop Series. In *Research and development in information retrieval*. Cambridge, England: Cambridge University Press.

Covington, M. (1985, December). Programming in logic part 1: With PROLOG the user supplies only the facts; the computer finds the solution. *PC Tech Journal, 3*(12), 83–95.

Covington, M., & Vellino, A. (1986, November). PROLOG arrives. *PC Tech Journal, 4*(11), 52–69.

Cowart, R., & Robyns, A. (1985, August 27). Smart talk: Artificial intelligence enriches programmers' languages. *PC Week, 2*(34), 45–48+.

Craven, P., & Graven, G. (1985, August). Fifth generation librarians: The challenge of knowledge engineering. *Outlook on Research Libraries, 7*(8), 1–3.

Cronin, B. (1986, January 13). Micro-based systems pave low-cost route to commercial AI. *Computerworld, 20*(2) 54–55.

Cross, G. R. (1986, October). Legal knowledge (development of intelligent legal information processing systems). *Proceedings of the IEEE, 74*(10), 1445–1450.

Crystal, M. I., & Jakobson, G. E. (1982, September). FRED, a front end for databases. *Online, 6*(5), 27–30.

Cuadrado, C. Y., & Cuadrado, J. L. (1986, November). Handling conflicts in data: A decision support system in PROLOG. *BYTE, 11*(12), 193–202.

Curtis, A. C. (1984, October). A comparison of LISP and MUMPS as implementation languages of knowledge-based systems. *Journal of Medical Systems, 8*(5), 399–406.

d'Agapeyeff, A. (1986, March-April). What are expert systems? *Journal of Computer Assisted Learning, 2*(1), 28–36.

D'Ambrosio, B. (1985, June). Building expert systems with M.1: A knowledge-engineering tool for the IBM PC. *BYTE, 10*(6), 371–375.

D'Ambrosio, B. (1985, January). Expert systems—myth or reality? *BYTE, 10*(1), 275–282.

D'Ambrosio, B. (1985, April). Insight—a knowledge system: An expert system with limited potential. *BYTE, 10*(4), 345–347.

D'Angelo, A. (1985). A mechanism for representing and using metaknowledge in rule-based systems. In *Approximate reasoning in expert systems*. New York: Elsevier Science Publishing Co.

Dahlberg, I. (1985). Expert systems and classification. *International Classification, 12*(1), 1.

Davidson, C. H., Davidson, P. L., & Ruberg, K. (1988, June). Expert Systems and the use of information in building design and construction. *Journal of Documentation, 44*, 91–118.

Davies, R. (1983, January). Documents, information, or knowledge? Choices for librarians. *Journal of Librarianship, 15*(1), 47–65.

Davies, R. (1986, March). Fifth generation bibliographic systems: 2. The computer: A tool, machine, or partner? *MARC Users' Group Newsletter*, *86*(1), 36–45.

Davies, R. (Ed.). (1986). *Intelligent information systems: Progress and prospects*. New York: Halsted Press.

Davies, R. (1987). Outlines of the emerging paradigm in cataloguing. *Information Processing & Management*, *23*(2), 89–98.

Davies, R., and James, B. (1984, October). Towards an expert system for cataloguing: Some experiments based on AACR2. *Program*, *18*(4), 283–297.

Davis, R. (1984). Amplifying expertise with expert systems. In P. H. Winston & K. A. Prendergast (Eds.), *The AI business: The commercial uses of artificial intelligence* (pp. 17–40). Cambridge, MA: MIT Press.

Davis, R., & Lenat, D. (1982). *Knowledge-based systems in artificial intelligence*. New York: McGraw-Hill.

de Vries, P. H. et al. (1985, April). An overview of medical expert systems. *Methods of Information in Medicine*, *24*(2), 57–64.

Dean, B. L. (1986, July). Artificial intelligence techniques: Applications for courseware development. *Educational Technology*, *26*(7), 7–15.

Dean, G., & Whitlock, Q. (1984). Developments relevant to CBT (computer based training). In *A handbook of computer-based training*. New York: Nichols Publishing Co.

Defude, B. (1984). Knowledge based systems versus thesaurus: An architecture problem about expert systems design. In *Research and development in information retrieval*. Cambridge, England: Cambridge University Press.

Dembo, K. (1984, March). Application of artificial intelligence in sales. *Data Processing*, *26*(2), 31–33.

DeSalvo, D. A., & Liebowitz, J. (1986). The application of an expert system for information retrieval at the National Archives. *Telematics and Informatics*, *3*(1), 25–38.

Deschaelets, G. (1986). The intelligent interface concept in online searching. *Canadian Journal of Information Science*, *11*(2), 13–34.

Desmond, J. (1986, October). AI develops a deeper, louder voice in commercial markets. *Software News*, *6*(10), 66–75.

Desmond, J. (1987, July). 'Blue Propellers' bringing AI to MIS. *Software News*, *7*(8), 32–42.

Doszkocs, T. E. (1986, July). Natural language processing in information retrieval. *Journal of the American Society for Information Science*, *37*(4), 191–196.

Drechsler, F., & Bateson, J. (1986). *Management, information, and expert systems*. Distr. by Biblio Distribution Ctr., Totowa, NJ. Irish Academic Press.

Dreyfus, H., & Dreyfus, S. (1986, January). Why computers may never think like people. *Technology Review*, *89*(1), 42–61.

Dreyfus, H. L., Dreyfus, S. E., & Attanasiou, T. (1986). *Mind over machine: The power of human intuition and expertise in the era of the computer*. Oxford, UK: B. Blackwell.

Dubois, E. (1986, October). A knowledge representation language for requirements engineering. *Proceedings of the IEEE*, *74*(10), 1431–1444.

Dubois, J. E., & Sobel, Y. (1985, August). DARC system for documentation and artificial intelligence in chemistry. *Journal of Chemical Information and Computer Sciences*, *25*(3), 326–333.

Duda, R., & Gaschnig, J. (1981, September). Knowledge-based expert systems come of age. *BYTE*, *6*(9), 238–281.

Duda, R., & Shortliffe, E. H. (1983, April 15). Expert systems research. *Science*, *220*(4594), 261–268.

Eastman, C.M. (1988). An approach to the evaluation of catalog selection systems. *Information Processing and Management*, *24*(1), 23-30.

Edmonds, E. (1987). Expert systems and document handling. *Information Processing & Management*, *23*(2), 77–80.

Eibl, G. (1985). Current work on expert systems and natural language processing at SIEMENS. In *Artificial intelligence: Towards a practical application*. New York: Elsevier Science Publishers.

Eliot, L. B. (1986, Summer). Analogical problem-solving and expert systems. *IEEE Expert*, *1*(2), 17–28.

Emrich, M. L. (1985, August). *Expert systems bibliography: 1981-1984* (DE850-18160). Oak Ridge, TN: Oak Ridge National Laboratory.

Epstein, S. (1983, January). Challenges expert systems, problem solving, and learning! *Sigart Newsletter* (83), 16–17.

Ercegovac, Z. (1984). Knowledge-based expert systems: A profile and implications. In M. E. Williams & T. H. Hogan (Eds.), *Proceedings of the 5th national online meeting* (pp. 39–46), New York, NY. Medford, NJ: Learned Information.

Ercegovac, Z. (1986). Artificial intelligence and cataloging reasoning: Promises and pitfalls. In M. E. Williams & T. H. Hogan (Eds.), *Proceedings of the 7th national online meeting* (pp. 109–117), New York, NY. Medford, NJ: Learned Information.

Evers, K., Holand C., & Bachert, R. F. (1986). SADT: An effective tool for knowledge acquisition. In *Human factors in organizational design and management—II. Proceedings of the second symposium* (pp. 153–156). Vancouver, B.C., Canada. Amsterdam, Netherlands: North-Holland.

Feigenbaum, E. A. (1980, September). *Knowledge engineering: The applied side of artificial intelligence* (AD–A092 574/3). Springfield, VA: NTIS.

Feigenbaum, E. A., & McCorduck, P. (1984). *The fifth generation: Artificial intelligence and Japan's computer challenge to the world* (Rev. and updated ed.). New York: New American Library.

Fenly, C., & Harris, H. (1988). *Expert systems: Concepts and applications*. Washington, DC: Cataloging Distribution Service, Library of Congress.

Ferrara, J. M. et al. (1985, April). Expert systems authoring tools for the microcomputer: Two examples. *Educational Technology*, *25*(4), 39–41.

Fersko-Weiss, H. (1985, October). The intelligent computer. *Personal Computing*, *9*(10), 62–69.

Fersko-Weiss, H. (1985, November). Expert systems: Decision-making power. *Personal Computing*, *9*(11), 97–105.

Fersko-Weiss, H. (1986, December). AI update: 1986 hits and misses. *Personal Computing*, *10*(12), 99–107.

Fichtelman, M. (1985, June). The expert mechanic: Expert systems needn't be esoteric or waste resources. *BYTE*, *10*(6), 205–216.

Fidel, R. (1986, January). Toward expert systems for the selection of search keys. *Journal of the American Society for Information Science*, *37*(1), 37–44.

Fieschi, M., & Joubert, M. (1986, January). Some reflections on the evaluation of expert systems in medicine. *Methods of Information in Medicine*, *25*(1), 15–21.

Finin, T. W. (1986, October). Interactive classification: A technique for acquiring and maintaining knowledge-bases. *Proceedings of the IEEE*, *74*(10), 1414–1421.

Ford, F. N. (1985, January). Decision support systems and expert systems: A comparison. *Information and Management*, *8*(1), 21–26.

Forsyth, R. (Ed.). (1984). *Expert systems: Principles and case studies*. London/New York: Chapman and Hall; New York: Methuen.

Forsyth, R. (1984, May). Machine learning systems. *Aslib Proceedings*, *36*(5), 219–227.

Forsyth, R., & Rada, R. (1986). *Machine learning: Applications in expert systems and information retrieval*. Chichester: E. Horwood; New York: Halstead Press.

Fox, C.J., Frakes, W., & Gandel, P. (1988, December). Foundational issues in knowledge-based information systems. *Canadian Journal of Information Science*, *13*(3/4), 90-102.

Fox, J. (Ed.). (1984). *Expert systems*. Maidenhead, Berkshire, England: Pergamon Infotech.

Fox, J., Greaves, M. F., Myers, C. D., & Pegram, S. (1985, April). Knowledge acquisition for expert systems: Experience in leukaemia diagnosis. *Methods of Information in Medicine*, *24*(2), 65–72.

Fox, M. S., & McDermott, J. (1986, February). *Role of data-bases in knowledge-based systems*. (AD-A 166 365). Pittsburgh, PA: Carnegie-Mellon University.

Frel, H. P., & Jauslin, J. F. (1983, January). Graphical presentation of information and services: A user-oriented interface. *Information Technology: Research and Development*, *2*(1), 23–42.

Frenzel, L. E. (1987). *Crash course in artificial intelligence and expert systems* (1st ed.). Indianapolis: H. W. Sams.

Frost, R. A. (1986). *Introduction to knowledge-base systems*. New York: Macmillan; London: Collier Macmillan.

Gauch, S., & Smith, J.B. (1989). An expert system for searching in full-text. *Information Processing and Management*, *25*(3), 253-263.

Georgeff, M. P., & Lansky, A. L. (1986, October). Procedural knowledge (artificial intelligence). *Proceedings of the IEEE*, *74*(10), 1383–1398.

Georgescu, I. (1984). The hypernets method for representing knowledge. In *Artificial intelligence: Methodology, systems, applications*. New York, NY: Elsevier Science Publishing Co.

Gevarter, W. B. (1984). *Artificial intelligence: An overview*. Sacramento, CA: Business/Technology Books.

Gevarter, W. B. (1984). *Artificial intelligence, expert systems, computer vision, and natural language processing*. Park Ridge, NJ: Noyes Publications.

Gevarter, W. B. (1983, August). Expert systems: Limited but powerful. *IEEE Spectrum*, *20*, 39–46.

Gibb, F. (Ed.). (1986). *Expert systems in libraries: Proceedings of a conference of the Library Association Information Technology Group and the Library and Information Research Group, November 1985*. London: Taylor Graham.

Gibb, F., & Cronin, B. (1985, December). Prototype identification using a knowledge-base management system (short communication). *Education for Information, 3*(4), 307–312.

Gibb, F., & Sharif, C. (1988, January). CATALYST: An expert assistant for cataloguing. *Program, 22*, 62–71.

Giboney, V. (1986, August). Conventional programming and expert systems. *Computer Language, 3*(8), 53–60.

Gold, J. (1986, January 14). Do-it-yourself expert systems. *Computer Decisions, 18*(2), 76–81.

Goldberg, R. N., & Weiss, S. M. (1982). An experimental transformation of a large expert knowledge-base. *Journal of Medical Systems, 6*(1), 41–52.

Goldenberg, J. (1985, September). Experts on call. *PC World, 3*(9), 192–201.

Goldsmith, G., & Williams, P. W. (1986). *Online searching made simple: A microcomputer interface for inexperienced users* (Library and Information Research Report 41). London: British Library.

Golumbic, M. C. et al. (1986, May). A knowledge-based expert system for student advising. *IEEE Transactions on Education, E-29*(2), 120–124.

Gondran, M., & Gosling, J. (trans.). (1986). *Introduction to expert systems*. London; New York: McGraw-Hill.

Grimson, W. E. L., & Patil, R. S. (1988). *AI in the 1980s and beyond*. Cambridge, MA: MIT Press.

Guenthner, F. et al. (1986, January). A theory for the representation of knowledge (expert systems). *IBM Journal of Research and Development, 30*(1), 39–55.

Gupta, M. M. et al. (1985). *Approximate reasoning in expert systems*. New York, NY: Elsevier Science Publishing Co.

Ham, M. (1984, January). Playing by the rules. *PC World, 2*(1), 34–41.

Harmon, P. et al. (1987). *Expert systems: Tools and applications*. New York: Wiley.

Harmon, P., & King, D. (1985). *Expert systems: Artificial intelligence in business*. New York: Wiley.

Harris, L. R. (1984). Natural language front ends. In P. H. Winston & K. A. Prendergast (Eds.), *The AI business: The commercial uses of artificial intelligence* (pp. 149–161). Cambridge, MA: MIT Press.

Hart, A. (1986). *Knowledge acquisition for expert systems* (1st American ed.). New York: McGraw-Hill.

Harter, S. P., & Peters, A. R. (1985, October). Heuristics for online information retrieval: A typology and preliminary listing. *Online Review, 9*(5), 407–424.

Hawkins, D. T. (1987, September). Artificial intelligence (AI) and expert systems for information professionals—Basic AI terminology. *Online, 11*(5), 91–98.

Hawkins, D. T. (1988, January). Applications of artificial intelligence (AI) and expert systems for online searching. *Online, 12*(1), 31–43.

Hayes-Roth, F. (1984, September). The knowledge-based expert system: A tutorial. *Computer, 17*(9), 11–28.

Hayes-Roth, F. (1984, October). Knowledge-based expert systems. *Computer, 17*(10), 263–273.

Hayes-Roth, F., Waterman, D. A., & Lenat, D. B. (Eds.). (1983). *Building expert systems*. Reading, MA: Addison-Wesley.

Heine, M. H. (1982, October). A simple, intelligent front end for information retrieval systems using Boolean logic. *Information Technology: Research and Development, 1*(4), 247–260.

Henderson, D., Martin, P., Mayer, L., & Monaster, P. (1989, Winter). Rules and tools in library schools [Expert systems in the teaching of introductory reference courses]. *Journal of Education for Library and Informaiton Science, 29*(3), 226-227.

Herther, N. (1985, June). New technology for library microcomputer artificial intelligence. *Small Computers in Libraries, 5*(6), 12–15.

Hickman, F. (1986). Knowledge acquisition: The key to success for commercial expert systems. In *KBS 86: Knowledge-based systems: Proceedings of the international conference* (pp. 205–214). London: Online.

Hill, T. (1987, July 28). Expert-systems shells may be the key to artificial intelligence. *PC Week, 4*(30), 47–54.

Hillman, D. J. (1985, February). Artificial intelligence (human factors). *Human Factors, 27*(1), 21–32.

Hipgrave, R. (1985, December). Developments in information technology and their significance for education and training library and information work. *New Zealand Libraries, 44*(12), 229–231.

Hjerppe, R. (1983). What artificial intelligence can, could and can't do for libraries and information services. In *Proceedings of the 7th international online information meeting* (pp. 7–25), London, England. Oxford, England: Learned Information.

Hjerppe, R., & Olander, B. (1989, January). Cataloging and expert systems: AACR2 as a knowledge base. *Journal of the American Society for Information Science, 40*(1), 27-44.

Hjerppe, R., Olander, B., & Manklund, K. (1985). *Project ESSCAPE: Expert systems for simple choice of access points for entries: Applications of artificial intelligence in cataloging*. (ED 262 796). Linkoping, Sweden: LIBLAB.

Hopkin, V. D. (1984). Comment: Some human factors implications of expert systems. *Behaviour and Information Technology, 3*(1), 79–83.

Hopkinson, A. (1983, December). New technology and exchange formats online databases. *Journal of Information Science Principles & Practices, 7*(4/5), 139–147.

Humphrey, S. M. (1987, March). *The indexing aid project: Knowledge-based indexing of the medical literature* (PB87–175790/AS). Bethesda, MD: National Library of Medicine.

Humphrey, S.M. (1989). MedIndEx system: Medical indexing expert system. *Information Processing and Management, 25*(1), 73-88.

Humphrey, S. M., & Miller, N. E. (1986). The NLM Indexing Project. *Proceedings of the 49th ASIS annual meeting* (pp. 106–112), Chicago, IL. Medford, NJ: Learned Information.

Humphrey, S. M., & Miller, N. E. (1987). Knowledge-based indexing of the medical literature: The indexing aid project. *Journal of the American Society for Information Science, 38*(3), 184–196.

Hunt, V. D. (1986). *Artificial intelligence and expert systems sourcebook*. New York: Chapman & Hall.

Hurt, J. M. (1988, August-September). Artificial intelligence: A challenge for information Science education *Bulletin of the American Society for Information Science, 14*, 21.

IEEE Computer Society and American Association for Artificial Intelligence. (1984). *The First Conference on Artificial Intelligence Applications: Sheraton, Denver Tech Center, December 5–7, 1984*. Silver Spring, MD: IEEE Computer Society Press.

IEEE Computer Society. (1984). *Proceedings: IEEE Workshop on Principles of Knowledge-Based Systems, December 3–4, 1984, Denver, Colorado; sponsored by IEEE Computer Society*. Silver Spring, MD: IEEE Computer Society.

IEEE Computer Society. (1985). *The Second Conference on Artificial Intelligence Applications: The Engineering of Knowledge-based Systems, Foutainbleau Hilton, Miami Beach, Florida, December 11–13, 1985*. Washington, DC: IEEE Computer Society Press.

Ingwersen, P. (1984, October). A cognitive view of three selected online search facilities. *Online Review*, *8*(5), 465–492.

International Federation of Library Associations, the Hague (Netherlands). (1985, August). *Papers presented at the International Federation of Library Associations (IFLA) General Conference (51st)*. Chicago, IL: ERIC (ED 262796).

Jackson, P. (1986). *Introduction to expert systems*. Wokingham, England; Reading, MA: Addison–Wesley Pub. Co.

Janus, S. (1987, October 20). Creating an expert system demands thorough planning, narrow focus. *PC Week*, *4*(42), 156–157.

Jeng, L.-H. (1986, Winter). An expert system for determining title proper in descriptive cataloging: A conceptual model. *Cataloging and Classification Quarterly*, *7*(2), 55–70.

Jenkins, R. A. (1986). *Supercomputers of today and tomorrow. The parallel processing revolution*. Blue Ridge Summit, PA: TAB Books.

Johnson, D. S. (1987, July). Artificial intelligence—Secret weapon in the battle to improve productivity. *Administrative Management*, *48*(7), 35–39.

Jones, K. P. (1984, May). The effects of expert and allied systems on information handling: Some scenarios. *Aslib Proceedings*, *36*(5), 213–217.

Jones, M. (1984, Fall). Expert systems: Their potential roles within special education. *Peabody Journal of Education*, *62*(1), 52–66.

Jones, R. (1986, April). Commercial expert systems. *Data Processing*, *28*(3), 115–119.

Jones, R. (1986, January). European expert systems project for systems developers. *Data Processing*, *28*(1), 15–17.

Karna, K. N. (Ed.). (1985). *Expert systems in government symposium*, McLean, Va. Washington, DC: IEEE Computer Society Press.

Karna, K. N. et al. (Eds.). (1986). *Expert systems in government symposium, October 22–24, 1986, Tysons Westpark Hotel, McLean, Virginia*. Washington, DC: IEEE Computer Society Press.

Kearsley, G. (1985, November). The CBT advisor: An expert system program for making decisions about CBT. *Performance and Instruction*, *24*(9), 15–17.

Kehoe, C. A. (1985, December). Interfaces and expert systems for online retrieval. *Online Review*, *9*(6), 489–505.

Keller, R. (1987). *Expert system technology: Development and application*. Englewood Cliffs, NJ: Yourdon Press.

Kelly, P. (1986, April). Expert systems using shells. *Data Processing*, *28*(3), 139–141.

Keravnou, E. T., & Johnson, L. (1986). *Competent expert systems: A case study in fault diagnosis* (1st American ed.). New York: McGraw-Hill.

Kerschberg, L. (Ed.). (1986). *Expert database systems: Proceedings from the first international workshop*. Menlo Park, CA: Benjamin/Cummings Pub. Co.

Kidd, A. (1985, May). Human factors in expert systems. *Data Processing*, *27*(4), 15–17.

Kidd, A. (1987). *Knowledge acquisition for expert systems: A practical handbook*. New York/London: Plenum Press.

Kinnell, S. K., & Chignell, M. H. (1987). Who's the expert?: Conceptual representation of knowledge for end user searching. In M. E. Williams & T. H. Hogan (Eds.), *Proceedings of the 8th national online meeting* (pp 237–243), New York, NY. Medford, NJ: Learned Information.

Kinnucan, P. (1984, January). Computers that think like experts. *High Technology*, *4*(1), 30–37+.

Klahr, P., & Waterman, D. A. (1986). *Expert systems: Techniques, tools, and applications*. Reading, MA: Addison-Wesley.

Kleshev, A. S. (1984). Problem-oriented representations for development of knowledge-base for expert systems. In *Artificial intelligence and information-control systems of robots*. New York: Elsevier Science Publishing Co.

Kochen, M. (1985). Information about how to retrieve information: Its relation to the information retrieved. In *Empirical foundations of information and software science*. New York: Plenum Press.

Kohout, L., & Bandler, W. (Eds.). (1986). *Knowledge representation in medicine and clinical behavioural science*. Cambridge, MA: Abacus Press.

Kolokouris, A. T. (1986, November). Machine learning: One approach to teaching computers to learn is with a language, such as Marvin's, that grows. *BYTE*, *11*(12), 225–231.

Konopasek, M., & Jayaraman, S. (1984, May). Expert systems for personal computers: The TK!Solver approach. *BYTE*, *9*(5), 137–154.

Kostrewski, B. (1986). Biomedical information: Education and decision support systems. *Journal of Information Science Principles and Practice*, *12*(1–2), 63–69.

Kowalik, J. S. (Ed.). (1986). *Knowledge-based problem solving*. Englewood Cliffs, NJ: Prentice-Hall.

Kraft, A. (1984). XCON: An expert configuration system. In P. H. Winston & K. A. Prendergast (Eds.). *The AI business: The commercial uses of artificial intelligence* (pp. 41–49). Cambridge, MA: MIT Press.

Krawczak, D. A. et al. (1985). EP-X: A knowledge-based system to aid in searches of the environmental pollution literature. In *Second conference on artificial intelligence applications: The engineering of knowledge–based systems* (pp. 552–557). Miami Beach, FL, Washington, DC: IEEE Computer Society Press.

Kriz, J. (Ed.). (1987). *Knowledge-based expert systems in industry*. Chichester: Ellis Horwood; New York: Halstead Press.

Krulee, G.K., & Vrenios, A. (1989, January/February). An expert system model of a reference librarian. *Library Software Review*, *8*, 13-15.

Kulikowski, C. A. (1983, June). Expert medical consultation systems. *Journal of Medical Systems*, *7*(3), 229–234.

Kulikowski, C. A., & Ostroff, J. H. (1985). Constructing an EXPERT knowledge-base for thyroid consultation using generalized artificial intelligence techniques. In *Computer-assisted medical decision making*. New York: Springer Verlag.

Lampert, A. (1985, January 15). Expert systems get down to business. *Computer Decisions*, *17*(1), 138–144.

Lane, C. D. (1986, July). Graphical access to medical expert systems II: Design of an interface for physicians. *Methods of Information in Medicine*, *25*(3), 143–150.

Langley, P., & Carbonell, J. G. (1984, September). Approaches to machine learning. *Journal of the American Society for Information Science*, *35*(5), 306–316.

Larson, J. A. (1986, June). A visual approach to browsing in a database environment. *Computer*, *19*(6), 62–71.

Lawlor, J. (1984, January 15). *Artificial intelligence and expert systems*. Los Alamitos, CA: Southwest Regional Laboratory for Educational Research and Development.

Lawrence, S. (1984). *Artificial intelligence: The search for perfect machine*. Hasbrouck Heights, NJ: Hayden Book Co.

Lee, G. J. (1985, November-December). AI: Applications and implications for the library. *Library Software Review*, *4*(6), 370–373.

Lee, R. M. (1985, January). On information system semantics: Expert vs decision support systems. *Social Science Information Studies*, *5*(1), 3–10.

Lee, N. S. (1986, Summer). Programming with P-Shell. *IEEE Expert*, *1*(2), 50–63.

Lehner, P. E., Adelman, L., Hall, R. B., & Zirk, D. (1985, October 14). *Human factors in rule-based systems*. (AD-A 165-309). McLean, VA: PAR Technology Corp.

Leigh, W., & Paz, N. (1988, March). Conventional and knowledge-based information retrieval with Prolog. *Information Technology and Libraries*, *7*, 67–72.

Leith, P. (1983, February). Hierarchically structured production rules. *Computer Journal*, *26*(1), 1–5.

Lenat, D. B. (1984, September). Computer software for intelligent systems. *Scientific American*, *251*(3), 204–213.

Letendre, A. (1985). *Expert systems*. Ottawa: Govt. of Canada, Regional Industrial Expansion.

Levine, R. I. et al. (1986). *A comprehensive guide to AI and expert systems*. New York: McGraw-Hill.

Liebowitz, J. (1986, April). Useful approach for evaluating expert systems. *Expert Systems (GB)*, *3*(2), 86–96.

Machovec, G. S. (1984, December). Expert systems in libraries. *Online Libraries and Microcomputers*, *2*(12), 1–4.

Manuel, T. (1986, August 7). What's holding back expert systems? *Electronics*, *59*(28), 59–65.

Marcus, C. (1986). *PROLOG programming: Applications for database systems, expert systems, and natural language systems*. Reading, MA: Addison-Wesley.

Marcus, R. S. (1983, November). An experimental comparison of the effectiveness of computers and humans as search intermediaries. *Journal of the American Society for Information Science*, *34*(6), 381–404.

Marcus, R. S. (1985). Development and testing of expert systems for retrieval assistance. *ASIS '85. Proceedings of the 48th ASIS annual meeting* (pp. 289–292). Las Vegas, NV. White Plains, NY: Knowledge Industry Publications.

Marcus, R. S. (1986). Design questions in the development of expert systems for retrieval assistance. In *ASIS '86: Proceedings of the ASIS annual meeting* (pp. 185–189). Medford, NJ: Learned Information.

Marklund, K. (1985, June). Dimensional flowcharting to improve library performance. *Microprocessors and Microprogramming*, *2*(2), 113–128.

Martins, G. R. (1984, November 1). The overselling of expert systems. *Datamation*, *30*(18), 76–80.

Mason, R. M. (1985, April 15). Artificial intelligence: Promise, myth, and reality. *Library Journal, 110*(7), 56–57.

Mason, R. M. (1986, March). Office automation and information technology trends: Their impact on libraries and information center management. *Microcomputers for Information Management, 3*(1), 1–14.

Mayoh, B. H. (1984). Unified theory of knowledge representation. In *Artificial intelligence: Methodology, systems, applications*. New York: Elsevier Science Publishing Co.

McCartney, J. (1982, March). Expert systems: Expertise captured in a system. *Data Processing, 24*(3), 26–27.

McDonald, D. R. (1986). Expert systems: One view of the future. In *SCIL 1986. Software/computer conference and exposition for information managers and librarians conference proceedings* (pp. 125–128), Atlanta, GA. Westport, CT: Meckler Publishing.

McGrath, D. (1984, September). Artificial intelligence: A tutorial for educators. *Electronic Learning, 4*(1), 39–43.

McMullen, B. E., & McMullen, J. F. (1985, April). Specialized software: The problem-solving program you need is probably out there somewhere—here's how to find it. *Popular Computing, 4*(6), 75–80.

Meador, R., & Wittig, G. R. (1988, June). Expert systems for automatic cataloguing based on AACR2: A survey of research. *Information Technology and Libraries, 1*(2), 166–171.

Meadows, C. T., Hewett, T. T., & Aversa, E. S. (1982, September). A computer intermediary for interactive database searching: 1. Design. *Journal of the American Society for Information Science, 33*(5), 325–332.

Meadows, C. T., Hewett, T. T., & Aversa, E. S. (1982, November). A computer intermediary for interactive database searching: 2. Evaluation. *Journal of the American Society for Information Science, 33*(6), 357–364.

Melin, N. (1985, December). Artificial intelligence: Coming soon to a library near you. *Information Today, 2*(11), 15, 27.

Menvel, T., & Evanczuk, S. (1983, November 3). Commercial products begin to emerge from decades of research. *Electronics, 56*(22), 127–131.

Merry, M. (Ed.). (1986). *Expert systems '85: Proceedings of the fifth technical conference of the British computer society, specialist group on expert systems, University of Warwick, 17-19 December 1985*. Cambridge; New York: Cambridge University Press.

Metzler, D. P. et al. (1985). An expert system approach to natural language processing. *Proceedings of the 48th ASIS annual meeting* (pp. 301–307), Las Vegas, NV. White Plains, NY: Knowledge Industry Publications.

Metzler, S. (1986, March-April). Knowledge processing and conventional data processing: The differences. *Computers and People, 35*(3), 21–27.

Micco, H. M., & Smith I. (1987, January/February). Expert systems in libraries: Do they have a place? *Library Software Review, 6*, 25–28.

Micco, H. M., Smith, I., Hsiao, S., & Intaravitak, S. (1987, March/April). Knowledge representation: Subject analysis. *Library Software Review, 6*, 82–87.

Micco, H. M., & Smith, I. M. (1986). Designing an expert system for the reference function subject access to information. In J. M. Hurd (Ed.), *Proceedings of the 49th ASIS annual meeting* (pp. 204–210), Chicago, IL. Medford, NJ: Learned Information.

Michaelsen, R. H., Michie, D., & Boulanger, A. (1985, April). The technology of expert systems: Transplanting expert knowledge to machines. *BYTE*, *10*(4), 303–312.

Michaelsen, R. H., & Michie, D. (1986, July). Prudent expert systems applications can provide a competitive weapon. *Data Management*, *24*(7), 30–34.

Michie, D. (1984, September). Automating the synthesis of expert knowledge. *Aslib Proceedings*, *36*(9), 337–343.

Michie, D. (Ed.). (1982). *Introductory readings in expert systems*. New York: Gordon and Breach.

Miller, P. L. (1986). *Expert critiquing systems: Practice-based medical consultation by computer*. New York: Springer-Verlag.

Milopoulos, J., Shibahara, T., & Tsotsos, J. K. (1983, October). Building knowledge-based systems: The PSN experience. *Computer*, *16*(10), 83–89.

Mingers, J. (1986, November). Expert systems-experiments with rule induction. *Journal of Operations Research Society*, *37*(11), 1031–1037.

Minsky, M. (1975). A framework for representing knowledge. In P. Winston (Ed.), *The psychology of computer vision* (pp. 211–280). New York: McGraw-Hill.

Morris, A., & O'Neill, M. (1988). Information professionals - Roles in the design and development of expert systems? *Information Processing and Management, 24*(2), 173-181.

Moser, J., & Christoph, R. (1987). Management expert systems (M.E.S.): A framework for development and implementation. *Information Processing and Management*, *23*(1), 17–23.

Moskiwitz, L. (1986, November). Rule-based programming. *BYTE*, *11*(12), 217–224.

Mukhopadhyay, U. (1986, May). An intelligent system for document retrieval in distributed office environments. *Journal of American Society for Information Science*, *37*(3), 123–135.

Nagy, T. et al. (1985). *Building your first expert system*. Culver City, CA: Ashton-Tate.

National Technical Information Service. (1985, May). *Artificial intelligence, 1984-April 1985 (Citations from the NTIS Database)*. (PB85–859619). Springfield, VA: NTIS.

National Technical Information Service. (1986, June). *Artificial intelligence: Market aspects, 1983-June 1986 (Citations from the Computer Database)*. (PB86–870334). Springfield, VA: NTIS.

National Technical Information Service. (1983, April). *Expert computer systems, 1977-April, 1983 (Citations from the international information service for the physics and engineering communities database)*. (PB83–862946). Springfield, VA: NTIS.

National Technical Information Service. (1986, February). *Expert systems applications, 1970-February 1986 (Citations from the engineering database)*. (PB86–857539). Springfield, VA: NTIS.

National Technical Information Service. (1984, April). *Knowledge representation and knowledge programming for artificial intelligence, 1975-March 1984 (Citations from the international information service for the physics and engineering communities database)*. (PB84–863547). Springfield, VA: NTIS.

National Technical Information Service. (1986, March). *PROLOG programming language, 1974-March 1986. (Citations from the INSPEC: Information services for the physics and engineering communities database)*. (PB86–859154/GAR). Springfield, VA: NTIS.

Nedobity, W. (1985). Terminology and artificial intelligence. *International Classification, 12*(1), 17–19.

Nesary, M. (1986, June 17). Integrated software and an expert twist. *Computer Decisions, 18*(13), 36, 40.

Nowak, E. J., & Szablowski, B. F. (1984). Expert systems in scientific information exchange. *Journal of Information, 8*, 103–111.

O'Shea, T., & Eisenstadt, M. (Eds.). (1984). *Artificial intelligence: Tools, techniques, and applications*. New York: Harper & Row.

Obermeier, K. K. (1985). Expert Stystems. In A. Kent (Ed.), *Encyclopedia of library and information science* (Vol. 38, pp. 158–176). New York: Marcel Dekker.

Obermeier, K. K. (1984). Natural language front-ends for expert systems. In M. E. Williams & T. H. Hogan (Eds.), *National online meeting: Proceedings* (pp. 265–272). New York, NY. Medford, NJ: Learned Information.

Obermeier, K. K., & Cooper, L. E. (1984). Information network facility organizing system (INFOS): An expert system for information retrieval. In B. Flood (Ed.), *Challenges to an information society: Proceedings of the 47th ASIS annual meeting* (pp. 95–98), Philadelphia, PA. White Plains, NY: Knowledge Industry Publications, Inc.

O'Neill, M. (1989, April). Expert systems. *Aslib Proceedings, 41*(4), 163-168.

Paice, C. (1986, October). Expert systems for information retrieval? *Aslib Proceedings, 38*(10), 343–353.

Parker, R., & Mokhoff, N. (1983, Fall). An expert for every office. *Computer Design, 22*(12), 37–46.

Parker, T. (1986, August). Artificial intelligence in the public domain. *Computer Language, 3*(8), 71–74.

Parrott, J. R. (1986, September). Expert systems for reference work. *Microcomputers for Information Management, 3*(3), 155–171.

Parrott, J.R. (1988). REFSAM: A bimodal knowledge-based reference training and consultation system. *Reference Services Review, 16*(1/2), 61-68.

Parry, J. D., & Ferrara, J. M. (1984). *The potential of computer-based expert systems for special educators in rural settings*. Logan, UT: Utah State University.

Parry, J. D., & Ferrara, J. M. (1985, Fall). Computer based expert systems. *Small School Forum, 7*(1), 11–13.

Pfau, D. R., & Zack, B. A. (1986, February 19). Understanding expert system shells. *Computerworld, 20*(7A), 23–24.

Pollitt, A. S. (1984, May). A 'front-end' system: An expert system as an online search intermediary. *Aslib Proceedings, 36*(5), 229–234.

Pollitt, A. S. (1986). A rule-based system as an intermediary for searching cancer therapy literature on MEDLINE. In R. Davies (Ed.), *Intelligent information systems: Progress and prospects* (pp. 82–126). Chichester, England: Ellis Horwood.

Pollitt, A. S. (1987). CANSEARCH: An expert systems approach to document retrieval. *Information Processing and Management, 23*(2), 119–138.

Pountain, D. (1985, October). Computers as consultants. *BYTE, 10*(10), 367–376.

Pournelle, J. (1984, November). Artificial experts: The computer as diagnostician has definite limits. *Popular Computing, 4*(1), 59–62.

Prangnell, R. D. (1987, April). MARKUP: An expert assistant for marking up bibliographic data. *Program, 21*, 174–182.

Proceedings WESTEX-87: Western conference on expert systems, Anaheim, CA. (1987). Washington, DC: IEEE Computer Society Press.

Purcell, K. (1985, October). Legal expert systems: A "law practice on disk" raises ethical questions about all expert systems. *Popular Computing, 4*(12), 30, 35.

Quinlan, J. R. (1982). Fundamentals of the knowledge engineering problem. In *Introductory readings in expert systems*. London, England: Gordon and Breach.

Rada, R., Backus, J., Gaimpa, T., Gibbs, C., & Goel, S. (1987, September). Computerized guides to journal selection. *Information Technology and Libraries, 6*, 173–184.

Raghavan, V.V., & Sharma, R.S. (1986). A framework and a prototype for intelligent organisation of information. *Canadian Journal of Information Science, 11*(3/4), 88-101.

Rauch-Hindin, W. (1985, September). AI tools bridge technology gap. *Systems and Software, 4*(9), 89–92, 94–96.

Raulefs, P. (1985). Knowledge processing expert systems. In T. Bernold & G. Albers (Eds.), *Artificial intelligence: Towards a practical application*. New York: Elsevier Science Publishers.

Rees, B. (1985). Artificial intelligence in a large-scale enterprise: The experience of Digital Equipment Corporation. In T. Bernold & G. Albers (Eds.), *Artificial intelligence: Towards a practical application*. New York: Elsevier Science Publishers.

Reiss, G. (1986). Knowledge acquisition and the Oleophillic advisor. In *Proceedings WESTEX-86. IEEE western conference on knowledge-based engineering and expert systems* pp. 102–104. New York: IEEE.

Richardson, J. (1988, August-September). Expert systems for reference service. *Bulletin of the American Society for Information Science, 14*, 19–20.

Richardson, J. (1989, March). Toward an expert system for reference service: A research agenda for the 1990s. *College & Research Libraries, 50*(2), 231–248.

Riggs, D.E. (1988). Productivity increases in public services: Are expert systems the answer? *Journal of Library Administration, 9*(4), 89-99.

Roberts, S. K. (1983, September). Computers simulate human experts. *Mini-micro Systems, 16*(10), 207–208 +.

Rodgers, K. (Comp.). (1986, January). *Artificial intelligence (LC science tracer bullet)*. Washington, DC: Library of Congress.

Rosenberg, S. (1981). Expert systems and the design of powerful user interfaces. In *The information community: Proceedings of the 44th ASIS annual meeting, vol. 18, Washington, DC, October 25-30, 1981* (pp. 285–287). White Plains, NY: Knowledge Industry Publications.

Roth, G. L., & McEwing, R. A. (1986, Fall). Artificial intelligence and vocational education: An impending confluence. *Educational Horizons, 65*(1), 45–47.

Rothfeder, J. (1986, January 14). Is there intelligent life in the PC? *PC Magazine, 5*(1), 139–148.

Roysdon, C., & White, H.D. (Eds.). (1989). *Expert systems in reference services*. New York: Haworth Press.

Ruby, D. (1986, March 4). Smart systems on the PC: A crop of new products lets PC users program their own expert systems. *PC Week, 3*(9), 91–94.

Ruszkowski, J. (1986, April). ELSA. A method for medical knowledge acquisition and processing to aid medical reasoning. *Methods of Information in Medicine, 25*(2), 79–86.

Ruyle, K. E. (1986, October). Artificial intelligence: A developing technology: Part one of a series. *Industrial Education, 75*(7), 18–20.

Ruyle, K. E. (1986, November). How artificial intelligence impacts industrial education. *Industrial Education, 75*(8), 42+.

Ryan, S. A. (1984). A computer-based nursing consultant: The COMMES system. *Journal of Clinical Computing, 12*(6), 193–202.

Ryan, S. A. (1985, April). An expert system for nursing practice: Clinical decision support. *Journal of Medical Systems, 9*(1/2), 29–42.

Sachitanandy, N. N. (1985, May). Towards machines that think (artificial intelligence). *Computers and People, 34*(5), 21–27.

Sanchez, E., & Zadeh, L. A. (Eds.). (1987). *Approximate reasoning in intelligent systems, decision and control*. Oxford; New York: Pergamon Press.

Sawyer, B., & Foster, D. L. (1986a). *Programming expert systems in Modula-2*. New York: Wiley.

Sawyer, B., & Foster, D. L. (1986b). *Programming expert systems in PASCAL*. New York: Wiley.

Schank, R. (1984). Intelligent advisory systems. In P. H. Winston & K. A. Prendergast (Eds.), *The AI business: The commercial uses of artificial intelligence* (pp. 133–148). Cambridge, MA: MIT Press.

Schell, G. P., & Smith, P. C. (1985). The application of decision support systems to public information systems. *ASIS '85: Proceedings of the 48th ASIS annual meeting* (pp. 284–288), Las Vegas, NV. White Plains, NY: Knowledge Industry Publications.

Schlein, S. (1985, December). Expert systems in the real world: A users' report. *PC Products, 2*(12), 74–75.

Schutzer, D. (1986). *Artificial intelligence: An applications-oriented approach*. New York: Van Nostrand Reinhold.

Schwarz, H. (1986). Expert systems and the future of cataloguing: A possible approach. *LIBER Bulletin, 26*, 23–50.

Selected expert-systems development environments. (1986, April 28). *Information Week*, (63), 41.

Seligman, M. (1983, October). The fifth generation. *PC World, 1*(7), 282–287.

Sell, P. S. (1985). *Expert systems: A practical introduction*. New York: Wiley.

Sharif, C. A. Y. (1988). *Developing an expert system for classification of books using micro-based expert system shells* (British Library Research Report 32). London: British Library Research and Development Department.

Shen, S.N.T. (1987, September/October). An evaluation of expert shell EXPERT-EASE. *Library Software Review, 6*, 303-311.

Shoval, P. (1985). Principles, procedures, and rules in an expert system for information retrieval. *Information Processing and Management, 21*(6), 475–487.

Siegel, P. (1986). *Expert systems: A non-programmer's guide to development and applications*. Blue Ridge Summit, PA: TAB Books.

Silverman, B. G. (Ed.). (1987). *Expert systems for business*. Reading, MA: Addison-Wesley.

Simmons, R. F. (1987). A text knowledge base from the AI handbook. *Information Processing & Management, 23*, 321–339.

Simons, G. L. (1986). *Expert systems and micros*. New York: Wiley.

Skuce, D. et al. (1985). A rule-oriented methodology for constructing a knowledge-base from natural language documents. In *Expert systems in government symposium* (pp. 378–385). Washington, DC: IEEE Computer Society Press.

Smith, K. F. (1986, September). Robot at the reference desk? *College and Research Libraries*, *47*(5), 486–490.

Smith, L. C. (1980). Implications of artificial intelligence for end user use of online systems. *Online Review*, *4*(4), 383–391.

Smith, L. C. (1985, Spring). A guide to information sources in artificial intelligence. *Science and Technology Libraries*, *5*(3), 79–100.

Smith, L. C. (1986). Knowledge-based systems, artificial intelligence and human factors. P. Ingwersen (Ed.), *Information technology and information use: Towards a unified view of information and information technology* (pp. 98–110). London: Taylor Graham.

Smith, L. C. (1987). Artificial intelligence and information retrieval. *Annual Review of Information Science and Technology*, *22*, 41–77.

Smith, L.C. (1988, August/September). Artificial intelligence. *Bulletin of American Society for Information Science*. *14*(6), 12-22.

Smith, P. J., & Chignell, M. (1984). Development of an expert system to aid in searches of the chemical abstracts. In B. Flood (Ed.), *Challenges to an information society. Proceedings of the 47th ASIS annual meeting* (pp. 99–102), Philadelphia, PA. White Plains, NY: Knowledge Industry Publications, Inc.

Smith, P. J. et al. (1984). Development of a knowledge-based bibliographic information retrieval system. *Proceedings of the 1984 conference on systems, man, and cybernatics* (pp. 222–225), Halifax, Nova Scotia. New York: IEEE.

Sorensen, K. (1986, April 21). Expert systems emerging as real tools. *InfoWorld*, *8*(16), 33–38.

Sowa, J. F. (1984). Knowledge engineering. In *Conceptual structures: Information processing in mind and machine* (pp. 277–338). Reading, MA: Addison-Wesley.

Sowell, S.L. (1989, Winter). Expanding horizons in collection development with expert systems: Development and testing of a demonstration prototype. *Special Libraries*, *80*(1), 45-50.

Sowizral, H. A. (1985). Expert systems. In M. E. Williams (Ed.), *Annual review of information science and technology* (Vol. 20, pp. 179–199). White Plains, NY: Knowledge Industry Publications.

Sparck–Jones, K. (1983). *Report on a visit to the U.S. 27.1.83-4.2.83* (BLRD Report 5762). London: British Library, Research and Development Department.

Sparck-Jones, K. (1984, May). Proposals for R&D in intelligent knowledge-based systems (IKBS). *Journal of Information Science*, *8*, 139–147.

Sparck-Jones, K. (1988). Intelligent interfaces for information retrieval systems: Architecture problems in the construction of expert systems for document retrieval. In P.A. Yates-Mercer (Ed.), *Future trends in information science and technology* (pp. 47-73). Los Angeles: Taylor Graham.

Staples, B. (1983, August). Computer intelligence: Unlimited and untapped. *Creative Computing*, *9*(8), 164–66.

Starfield, A. M. (1983, November). Mastering engineering concepts by building an expert system. *Engineering Education*, *74*(2), 104–107.

Steels, L., & Campbell, J. A. (Eds.). (1985). *Progress in artificial intelligence*. Chichester, West Sussex: Ellis Harwood.

Stevens, L. (1985a). *Artificial intelligence (history and applications)*. Hasbrouck Heights, NJ: Hayden Book Co.

Stevens, L. (1985b). *Expert systems (artificial intelligence)*. Hasbrouck Heights, NJ: Hayden Book Co.

Stokes, G. E. (1985). Knowledge based software in support of CAI (computer aided instruction). In *Computers in education: Proceedings of the IFIP TC 3 4th world conference*, Norfolk, VA. Amsterdam, Netherlands: Elsevier Science Publishers.

Storrs, G. (1985, May). Expert knowledge. *Personal Computer World*, *8*(5), 204–206.

Strehlo, K. (1986, June). The PC prescription. *Personal Computer World*, *4*(6), 369–378.

Sumner, F. H. (1983, January). The future of information technology: A personal view. *Aslib Proceedings*, *35*(1), 1–13.

Swartout, W. R. (1985). Explaining and justifying expert consulting programs. In *Computer-assisted medical decision making*. New York: Springer Verlag.

Tello, E. R. (1986, August). Guru: A complete, integrated software package that includes an expert-system shell. *BYTE*, *11*(8), 281–285.

Thompson, B. A., & Thompson, W. A. (1985, April). Inside an expert system: From index cards to PASCAL program. *BYTE*, *10*(4), 315–330.

Thompson D. (1988, April). AI—Tailormade for librarians. *Canadian Library Journal*, *45*, 73–75.

Thompson, R. H., & Croft, W. B. (1985). An expert system for document retrieval. In K. N. Karna (Ed.), *Expert systems in government symposium* (pp. 448–456). Washington, DC: IEEE Computer Society Press.

Thorkildsen, R. J. et al. (1986). Artificial intelligence: Applications in education. *Educational Research Quarterly*, *10*(1), 2–9.

Todeschini, C., & Farrell, M.P. (1989, January). An expert system for quality control in bibliographic databases. *Journal of the American Society for Information Science*, *40*(1), 1-11.

Tou, J. T. (1985, June). Knowledge engineering revisited. *International Journal of Computer and Information Sciences*, *14*(3), 123–133.

Townsend, C., & Feucht, D. (1986). *Designing and programming personal expert systems*. Blue Ridge Summit, PA: TAB Books.

Travis, I.L. (1989). Knowledge-based systems in information work: A view of the future. *Reference Librarian*, *23*, 41-60.

Tsotsos, J. K. (1985, September-October). Expert systems overview: Where does the phrase fit? *CIPS Review (Canadian Information Processing Society)*, *9*(5), 12–14.

Tucker, M. (1986, March). Expert systems blaze trails to AI success. *Mini-micro Systems*, *19*(4), 69–78.

Turban, E. (1985, December). Expert systems—a management perspective. *International Journal on Policy and Information*, *9*(2), 33–50.

Vaghi, S. (1986, April). Come out of your shell. *Personal Computer World*, *9*(4), 182–188.

Van Horn, M. (1987, January). RuleMaster: An expert-system software package for MS-DOS machines. *BYTE*, *12*(1), 341–342.

Van Horn, M. (1986). *Understanding expert systems*. Toronto/New York: Bantam Books.

Vedder, R. G., Fortin, M. G., Lemmerman, S. A., & Johnson, R. N. (1989, March). Five PC-based expert systems for business reference: An evalution. *Information Technology and Libraries*, *8*(1), 42–54.

Vermeir, D., Laenens, E., & Dierick, J. (1988). Applying AI techniques for patent information retrieval. *World Patent Information*, *10*, 26–36.

Vickery, A. (1984, August). An intelligent interface for online interaction. *Journal of Information Science: Principles and Practices*, *9*(1), 7–18.

Vickery, A., & Brooks, H. M. (1987, June). Expert systems and their applications in LIS. *Online Review*, *11*(3), 149–165.

Vickery, A., & Brooks, H. M. (1987). PLEXUS—The expert system for referral. *Information Processing and Management*, *23*(2), 99–117.

Vickery, A., Brooks, H., Robinson, B., & Vickery, B. C. (1987, March). A reference and referral system using expert system techniques. *Journal of Documentation*, *43*(1), 1–23.

Vickery, A., Brooks, H. M., & Vickery, B. C. (1986a). An expert system for referral: The PLEXUS project. In R. Davies (Ed.), *Intelligent information systems: Progress and prospects* (pp. 154–183). Chichester, England: Ellis Horwood.

Vickery, A., Brooks, H. M., & Vickery, B. C. (1986b). Developing an expert system for referral. In *Proceedings: Second international expert systems conference*. Medford, NJ: Learned Information.

Vickery, B. C. (1986, September). Knowledge representation: A brief review. *Journal of Documentation*, *42*(3), 145–159.

Waldron, V. R. (1986, June). Interviewing for knowledge. *IEEE Transactions on Professional Communication*, *PC-29*(2), 31–4.

Walker, A., & McCord, M. (1987). *Knowledge systems and PROLOG: A logical approach to expert systems and natural language processing*. Reading, MA: Addison-Wesley Pub. Co.

Walker, G., & Janes, J. W. (1984). Expert systems as search intermediaries. In B. Flood (Ed.), *Challenges to an information society: Proceedings of the 47th ASIS annual meeting* (pp. 103–105), Philadelphia, PA. White Plains, NY: Knowledge Industry Publications.

Walker, T. C., & Miller, R. K. (1986). *Expert systems*. Madison, GA: SEAI Technical Publications.

Warner, A.J. (1989, April/May). Artificial intelligence and the user interface. *Bulletin of the American Society for Information Science*, *15*(4), 17-19.

Waterman, D. A. (1986). *A guide to expert systems*. Reading, MA: Addison-Wesley.

Waterman, D. A., & Hayes-Roth, F. (1982). *An investigation of tools for building expert systems: Prepared for the National Science Foundation*. Santa Monica, CA: Rand.

Waters, S. T. (1986, September). ANSWERMAN, the expert information specialist: An expert system for retrieval of information from library reference books. *Information Technology and Libraries*, *5*(3), 204–212.

Watstein, S., & Kesselman, M. (1986, September). In pursuit of artificial intelligence. *Library Hi Tech News*, *30*, 1+.

Watters, C.R. (1986). Expert bibliographic retrieval? *Canadian Journal of Information Science, 11*(3/4), 80-87.

Webster, R. (1985, October 15). A new insight into expert systems. *PC Magazine, 4*(21), 191–194.

Webster, R., & Byers, T. J. (1985, March). Expert systems on microcomputers: New products make it possible to experiment with artificial intelligence on a micro. *Computers & Electronics, 23*(3), 69–72.

Weiner, J. (1985, January). Logic programming and PROLOG. *Computers & Electronics, 23*(1), 68–71.

Weiss, S. M., & Kulikowski, C. A. (1984). *A practical guide to designing expert systems*. Totowa, NJ: Rowman & Allanheld.

Williams, M. E., & Hogan, T. H. (1984). *National online meeting 1984 proceedings*. Medford, NJ: Learned Information.

Williams, P. W. (1985). The design of an expert system for access to information. *Proceedings of the ninth international online information meeting* (pp. 23–29). Oxford: Learned Information.

Williamson, D. (1986, Winter). Information retrieval research at the National Library of Medicine. *SIGIR Forum, 19*(1–4), 15–20.

Williamson, M. (1985). *Artificial intelligence for microcomputers: The guide for business decision makers*. New York: Brady Communications Co.

Williamson, M. (1985, October 15). Knowledge-based expert systems—Part 3. *PC Week, 2*(41), 53–54.

Williamson, M. (1985, July 9). Knowledge-based systems: Turn your computer into an intelligent colleague. *PC Week, 2*(27), 47–52.

Williamson, M. (1986, July 14). Expert systems shells: Design tools help MIS answer management's call. *Computerworld, 2*(28), 51–60.

Williamson, M. (1987). *Using expert systems in business*. Englewood Cliffs, NJ: Brady Communications.

Williamson, M., & Schlein, S. (1985, December). Made-to-order mentors. *PC Products, 2*(12), 32–76.

Winn, V. A. (1982, December). Information research and development at the open university: Current activities and interests. *Library and Information Research News, 5*(20), 11–16.

Winston, P. H. (1984). *Artificial intelligence* (2nd ed.). Reading, MA: Addison-Wesley.

Winston, P. H., & Prendergast, K. A. (Eds.). (1984). *The AI business: The commercial uses of artificial intelligence*. Cambridge, MA: MIT Press.

Wolfgram, D. D. et al. (1987). *Expert system for the technical professional*. New York: Wiley.

Yaghmai, N. S., & Maxin, J. A. (1984, September). Expert systems: A tutorial. *Journal of the American Society for Information Science, 35*(5), 197–305.

Yazdani, M., & Narayanan, A. (Eds.). (1984). *Artificial intelligence: Human effects*. Chichester: Ellis Horwood.

Zarri, G. P. (1985). Interactive information retrieval: An artificial intelligence approach to deal with biographical data. In *Advances in intelligent retrieval: INFORMATICS 8. Proceedings of an Aslib/British Computer Society joint conference* (pp. 101–119), Oxford, England.

Author Index

Subject Index

www.ingramcontent.com/pod-product-compliance
Lightning Source LLC
LaVergne TN
LVHW011910200926
848484LV00002B/586